P9-DGR-188

Twenty-First Century Economics

HB
3730
.T93
1999

Twenty-First Century Economics

Perspectives of Socioeconomics
for a Changing World

Edited by

William E. Halal and Kenneth B. Taylor

St. Martin's Press
New York

KALAMAZOO VALLEY
COMMUNITY COLLEGE
LIBRARY

APR 1 9 2000

TWENTY-FIRST CENTURY ECONOMICS
Copyright © William E. Halal and Kenneth B. Taylor, 1999. All rights reserved.
Printed in the United States of America. No part of this book may be used or
reproduced in any manner whatsoever without written permission except in the
case of brief quotations embodied in critical articles or reviews. For information,
address St. Martin's Press, 175 Fifth Avenue, New York, N.Y. 10010.

ISBN 0-312-16199-9 (cloth)
ISBN 0-312-21900-8 (paper)

Library of Congress Cataloging-in-Publication Data

21st century economics : perspectives of socioeconomics for a changing
world / edited by William E. Halal and Kenneth B. Taylor.
     p.   cm.
Includes bibliographical references (p.) and index.
ISBN 0-312-16199-9 (cloth) ISBN 0-312-21900-8 (paper)
1. Economic forecasting.   2. Twenty-first century—Forecasts.
3. Social prediction.   I. Halal, William E.   II. Taylor, Kenneth
B., 1950– .   III. Title: Twenty-first century economics
HB3730.A142   1998
330.9'001'12—dc21   98–12393
                                                                  CIP

First published: March 1999
10 9 8 7 6 5 4 3 2 1

Contents

List of Tables

List of Figures

Acknowledgments

The editors owe debts of gratitude to many people whose support was essential to producing this book. We are grateful for the skilled help of our editor, Michael Flamini, and the other professionals at St. Martin's Press who do all the crucial behind-the-scenes work that authors always depend on. The Society for the Advancement of SocioEconomics, founded by Amitai Etzioni, provided an intellectual home where we first formulated plans for this work. We are deeply grateful to Hossein Askari for helping us contact Robert Solow to write the Foreword. Our assistants, Mary Ann DiMola, Carolann Weidmayer, and Kathy Brown performed their usual heroic efforts in creating the index, graphics, and other tasks. Our most important acknowledgments are reserved for the 18 scholars who contributed chapters. This book is really theirs in a collective sense.

Foreword

Robert M. Solow, Nobel Laureate in Economics,
Massachusetts Institute of Technology

Probably the most often quoted line I ever wrote is this: "You can see the computer revolution everywhere except in the productivity statistics." It was true when I wrote it, fairly casually, a decade ago, and the funny thing is that it is still true. The period since the introduction and explosion of information technology (IT) has been a time of slow growth of productivity at the national level. Whatever the computer has done for us, it has not made us sensationally better at producing marketable goods and services. My own belief is that this paradox cannot be explained away just by the difficulty of measuring the real quality-adjusted output of modern service industries, although the difficulty is no doubt there.

The need to resolve the paradox—if that is what it is—has given rise to a small cottage industry. Some of the explanations that have been suggested must have some truth to them. I already have mentioned the appeal to mismeasurement (not merely mismeasurement, but downward bias). Another candidate is the possibility that industry is still fumbling and learning about the use of information technology, and the best is yet to come. Who knows? There are other explanations. More data and further analysis will no doubt eventually tell us more about what has been going on. The mild suggestion I want to make here—with this book in mind—is that industrial productivity may not be the right central issue. Computer technology plays a part in production, obviously. But perhaps the really important and interesting consequences of the computer revolution are not about the technology of production after all but elsewhere in the economy and the society.

A causal look through the chapter headings in this book does not reveal any concentration on the nitty-gritty of production. Instead, what these authors find interesting are IT-induced changes in the way firms, industries, economies, and governments are organized, and how they relate to one another within and between the categories I have just mentioned. One can easily see how the computer and its IT offshoots have permitted or required dramatic changes in the way organizations are structured and the way they function. That is certainly enough to change the lives of people who are involved in those organizations—that is, just about all of us. But nothing much is implied about real output per hour worked, when "output" has its ordinary meaning. This would be a quite different way of resolving the computer paradox: If you look in the wrong place, you are not likely to find anything.

That is not the end of the matter, however, unless you take a very restricted view of the scope of economic reasoning. To take the most straightforward example, modern information technology surely changes the significance of sheer distance in economic life. This shift is all the stronger in conjunction with the shift from goods to services. In what a friend of mine calls "the weightless economy," the distances between colleagues, between suppliers and users, between front office and back office, all matter much less than they used to. Without further analysis, that is just a gee-whiz statement. But the analysis is going on, as chapters in this book attest.

If I can pursue this point a bit further, the downgrading of distance can be expected to have effects not merely on the location of economic (and other) activity but on the economics of agglomeration, or clustering of firms and their employees. Some forces making for agglomeration may be weakened by IT: for example, it is possible, although not certain, that the need for face-to-face contact among buyers and sellers, or among creators and purveyors of ideas, can be replaced by screen-to-screen contact. On the other hand, if vertical agglomeration is becoming less important, because it is information and not objects that needs to travel up the chain, it may be that locations with comparative advantage in back-office work, or software production, or prose-writing will attract larger collections of enterprises engaged in those activities, even if they have different upstream connections. I have heard that Malaga in Spain is becoming a large center of employment for just that sort of reason.

Another important and closely related piece of economics that may need redoing in light of information technology is the nature of returns to scale. Armchair reflection will not get very far; there are obvious ways in which the computer could impart a bias toward decreasing or increasing returns to scale, and the answer need not be the same in every branch of economic activity. This is an important issue for the economics of monopoly and competition, and therefore for the making of economic policy.

It is obvious from the contents of this book that IT raises questions about the functioning of social and political institutions that stretch beyond the boundaries of economics as that discipline is practiced today. If those questions can be answered, some of the implications for institutional change will have further consequences for the economy and therefore for economics. There may well be surprises. As the productivity paradox teaches us, the economic significance of a technological innovation is not always closely correlated with the shock value of the innovation itself. But that is just another reason for the analysis to go forward on all intellectual fronts.

Introduction: The Transition to a Global Information Economy

William E. Halal and Kenneth B. Taylor

A s the twenty-first century approaches, it is becoming increasingly clear that economic life will be different on the other side of the millennium. Communism has collapsed, new corporate structures are emerging constantly, government is being "reinvented," entirely new industries are being born, and the world is unifying into a global market governed by the imperatives of knowledge.

This book, *Twenty-First Century Economics,* is designed to assist scholars, students, and policymakers in better understanding today's avalanche of economic change. The editors have assembled a group of leading scholars to provide authoritative analyses of the powerful forces now shaping economic systems and to estimate where these trends are leading.

Our guiding premise is that this upheaval emanates primarily from a historic transition between two epochs. Today's information revolution is creating new systems of political economy, just as the industrial revolution produced the old systems that are now being transformed. For the first time in history, economic affairs are being organized about the pursuit of knowledge. After a long struggle to develop agriculture, industry, and services, now mastery over the use of knowledge promises huge advances in human betterment, and it also presents equally huge challenges.

To grasp the truly revolutionary nature of this transition, consider a few broad facts that sum up the power being unleashed by advances in computer technology. During the past few decades, our ability to handle information has multiplied by roughly a factor of 1 million, and we are likely to witness another millionfold increase over the next few decades.[1] This new found power to manage knowledge is reorganizing economic structures, permitting huge increases in productivity, eliminating unneeded routine labor, creating more direct distribution channels, spurring customization of high-quality goods and services, opening up vast new markets, and facilitating global operations of almost any business.

The information revolution also exerts a huge multiplier effect because this increased ability to acquire knowledge accelerates scientific progress. That is largely why we are witnessing historic breakthroughs in all fields. For example, biogenetics may soon gain control over life processes, just as physical science now confers the power to create hydrogen bombs and explore space.

In short, a more sophisticated, technological foundation for economies is being built that transcends our former constraints. This emergence of powerful, worldwide information networks can be thought of metaphorically as the growth of a "central nervous system" for the planet that facilitates the functioning of modern knowledge societies.

Although the prospect of a knowledge economy has great potential and may be intellectually exciting, it presents a variety of equally unprecedented challenges that are also covered in the following chapters. Demands for environmental sustainability will require an unusual degree of innovation in technological systems and economic practices. A far more complex, diverse social order is emerging that must be managed with more sophisticated systems of political economy. And economic stratification, intense competition, and lessened public support will require new institutions for maintaining civil order.

Demographic changes will pose a particularly difficult series of challenges within leading nations. Between now and 2030, over 70 percent of the increase in world population will occur in less-developed countries. Emigration from these parts of the world is accelerating, a trend likely to continue during the first half of the coming century.[2] The vast majority of those seeking to immigrate into member countries of the Organization for Economic Cooperation and Development (OECD) are both poor and unskilled. This migration is occurring at a time when many OECD corporations are moving production abroad to take advantage of low-wage workforces. These trends are challenging the governments of OECD counties to creatively deal with the sociopolitical tensions and economic disruptions caused by unprecedented movements of population and production.

In addition, the population of OECD countries is growing older. This trend could cause other potential problems, given the social welfare institutions created during the post–World War II era, the increased voting power of the older cohort, and the high public deficit and debt levels in these countries. The results could be rising interest rates, diminishing investment, and slower economic growth. Financial markets already are punishing profligate government spending by pushing up the interest rates on the national debt of those nations that are the most fiscally irresponsible.[3]

The best available forecasts suggest that this process of transition should be fairly well completed in a decade or two, carrying current economic systems to some higher but more difficult ground that none as yet truly understands. The purpose of this book can be best viewed as a scholarly project intended to clear up as much of this uncertainty as possible.

The book is organized into three parts. First, we explore the forces that are driving economic change, then we sketch out the microeconomic effects on corporate structure and behavior, and finally we examine the new systems of political economy that are emerging.

Part I: Forces Shaping the Economic Order

The electrifying use of information technology, a world-wide transition to free markets, an awakening hunger for modernization, and other powerful forces of globalization are producing one of the most dramatic trends of our time—the unification of a diverse world into a coherent whole. As capital, information, technology, and people begin to move across borders, this unifying process is now integrating Western and Eastern Europe into a single economic community, dropping economic barriers among nations in the Americas, and producing a dynamic Pacific Basin. In time, these same forces may drive economic blocs together to produce open trade among most nations, huge new developing markets, and some form of global governance.

These trends raise crucial questions about the nature of economic life in the future.[4] What parallels can be drawn from the industrial revolution to chart the outlines of the knowledge revolution? In what ways should the new global order be an extension of previous economic and political patterns, and in what ways may it differ? What is the significance of this profound watershed in history?

Five chapters by leading scholars present diverse academic perspectives ranging from economics, to geography, to sociology, each focusing on how a particular set of forces is producing a distinctively different dimension of economic change.

Dimensions of Change

Observers are justifiably confused because we are experiencing now a multi-dimensional transformation that leads in different, often contradictory directions. In the opening chapter Ernest Sternberg delineates the current transformation and defines the multiple economic possibilities of the twenty-first century. He finds that capitalism is a dynamic, evolutionary process that has come to drive not only economic change but increasingly the social, political, cultural, and personal dimensions of society. Sternberg calls for a new interpretive economics that will enable us to act upon multiple economic challenges and opportunities.

The New Geoeconomic Reality

The technological revolution born of innovative microcircuitry has lowered transaction costs to levels where anything can be made anywhere and then sold anywhere in the world. In chapter 2 Peter Dicken acknowledges this revolutionary impact of communications technologies, but goes on to explain how other forces and constraints have ascended to shape the structure of the evolving global economy. Dicken argues that the power of national governments, transnational corporations, and technology make geographical distance and location fundamental to understanding the emergent twenty-first-century global economy.

Mastering the Knowledge Revolution

While the information revolution is well known, it is not generally understood that this amounts to a true revolution. A world designed primarily to manage information and knowledge introduces unheard-of possibilities that seem destined to transform the economic order. In chapter 3 William E. Halal draws on a wide range of evidence and opinion to sketch out the principles of knowledge-based economies, focusing on the changing role of the global corporation. Halal concludes that the unique imperatives of knowledge are driving three major trends that amount to revolutions in their own right among business and other institutions: shifts from control to freedom, from conflict to community, and from materialism to knowledge and spirit. He further suggests that these forces are likely to produce a "reversal" in economic thought roughly around 2000 to 2005.

Regions and Globalization

In chapter 4, Allen J. Scott examines how geographical proximity confers strategic advantage through the presence of positive externalities and reduced transactions costs. Scott contends that world capitalism is going through a phase of intensified regionalization, which is reallocating economic power away from the sovereign state and toward the international and regional levels.

Voluntary Simplicity

Amitai Etzioni has pioneered in studying the delicate balance all social systems must maintain between economic forces and social behavior. In chapter 5 Etzioni turns his attention to the distinctive trend toward voluntary simplicity. Manifest in many ways and to various degrees, modern voluntary simplicity arises in reaction to increased competitiveness in the workplace, rampant consumerism, and breakdown in traditional values and mores. Etzioni examines this fascinating trend and then explores the socioeconomic implications of voluntary simplicity spreading to communities and society.

Part II: Emerging Models of the Firm

Because the firm forms the basis of microeconomic activity, part II surveys new perspectives emerging in the management of business and other economic institutions. Information technology, global competition, environmental demands, and the rise of a more educated breed of employees and consumers have rendered the traditional corporate hierarchy obsolete. Corporations are reengineering old business bureaucracies into far more efficient systems for delivering goods and services, decentralizing operations to semiautonomous units, and redefining relations with their various stakeholders. These changes are producing an unusual blend of intense *competition and cooperation,* as seen in a frenzy of collaborative alliances, even among fierce corporate competitors.

Chapters in this section draw on the work of economics and management scholars to sketch out the new corporate forms that are emerging. Systemic changes in microeconomic behavior are particularly significant because they may in turn produce systemic changes in macroeconomic behavior, so we also explore the likely consequences for economic systems.

Structure and Behavior of Knowledge Enterprises

Sten A. Thore has studied the impact of information technology (IT) within capitalist economic systems. Chapter 6 opens this section by outlining the explosion in economic diversity born of high technology. Thore argues that the complexity of emergent technologies is sweeping away the old economic order and creating a new one, the shape of which is only now beginning to take discernable form. The evidence indicates that IT is accelerating the rate of change in market economies, creating "hypergrowth" conditions that demand skillful product-cycle management. Powerful disequilibrium pervades IT industries, rendering traditional, analytical models useless in understanding observed processes or outcomes. Thore predicts that U.S. knowledge-based corporations will retain their global competitive advantage well into the twenty-first century.

Organizational Networks and Cellular Units

One of the most visible changes in business is the move from hierarchies to networks. Where the mechanistic nature of the industrial age produced the need for firm control over routine tasks, the complex tasks of the information age demand collaborative alliances among shifting economic partners. The result is that networks are becoming the distinctive structural form of the future, whether in information systems or organization systems. In chapter 7 Raymond Miles, Charles C. Snow, John A. Matthews, and Grant Miles draw on extensive studies of dynamic corporations that have perfected this structure. They describe a new form of "cellular" network organization as well as the strengths and weaknesses of various forms and suggest how further development of organizational networks will carry institutions into the twenty-first century.

The Internal Market Economy

While all contributors agree that modern organizations must be designed as fluid, organic networks, there is less clarity on how this system should work economically. How can managers know where and when economic value is created or destroyed in a network? Who has the authority for governing its various parts? How are responsibility and accountability ensured? Some scholars, most notably Russell L. Ackoff, have proposed a market model of organization that provides an economic foundation to answer such questions. In chapter 8 Ackoff outlines the rationale for this view and presents a variety of examples illustrating that market organizations offer the accountability, entrepreneurial freedom, and dynamic responsiveness that are characteristic of all markets.

The Coming Ecological Transformation

The rise of large middle classes in Asia, South America, and possibly Africa will increase the number of people living at industrial levels of consumption from 1 billion currently to about 10 billion over the next three to five decades. Thus a tenfold increase in the level of industrialization is likely, producing a commensurate strain on ecological systems.[5] Paul Ekins is one of the world's foremost economists focusing on this huge challenge. In chapter 9 he defines the emerging principles of "green economics" and sketches out the ecologically safe practices that progressive corporations and governments are developing.

A Case Study of Lufthansa

Chapter 10 presents the successful experience of the German airline corporation Lufthansa in applying these concepts. Mark Lehrer draws upon his research of European flag carriers to examine Lufthansa's managerial response to deregulation, market turbulence, and technological change. Starting in 1995 Lufthansa instituted an internal market system, breaking several of its divisions into legally separate units. While recognizing that internal markets were not a panacea, management believed their presence would foster entrepreneurship and accountability at all levels of the new corporate structure. The exciting corporate turnaround that followed is a fascinating example which other multinational firms may seek to emulate.

Part III: Between Laissez-Faire and Industrial Policy

At the macroeconomic level, a variety of perspectives are being experimented with to map that large, poorly charted domain lying between the two extremes of laissez-faire capitalism and state-controlled socialism.

Although most people today share the view that socialism is dead and capitalism reigns triumphant, great confusion lies below the surface of this common belief. Many economists argue that it is *markets* rather than *capitalism* that are spreading around the globe, and the two are not always the same since market systems differ greatly.[6]

This distinction is becoming crucial as powerful forces alter economic systems in unexpected ways. In the East, the struggles of Russia, Eastern Europe, and Asia to adopt Western-style capitalism is running into severe obstacles and causing great suffering because there appears to be a basic incompatibility with the strong communitarian cultures of these nations. The main question facing policymakers, then, is what type of market system would be best suited to the unique cultures and traditions of eastern nations?

To make matters more confusing still, the West could face its own crisis at a time when capitalism is supposedly triumphant. Europe and the United

States are deregulating markets and withdrawing former social welfare benefits to rejuvenate enterprise, but the rise of brutally competitive markets and the loss of public support may provoke severe political disorder.[7]

The chapters in this section sketch out new models of economic policy being developed in nations around the world, including the latest thought on postcommunist economies, the fate of social democracy and the welfare state, industrial policy, and new forms of economic policy. A final chapter by the editors attempts to synthesize the themes and conclusions of previous chapters into a coherent whole.

Guidance from Great Economists

We begin this exploration of macroeconomic systems in the twenty-first century with a discussion of alternative paradigms. In chapter 11 James Angresano, a comparative economic systems specialist, uses the rich concepts of Gunnar Myrdal, Joseph Schumpeter, and Friedrich Hayek to remind us that many of the solutions to seemingly intractable economic dilemmas can be found in the pathbreaking insights pioneered many years ago. Using the wisdom of these three great economists leads to a more realistic understanding of economic phenomena that can become the basis for a new, interdisciplinary paradigm.

The Future of Post-Communist Economies

Robert J. McIntyre has for many years studied the dilemma facing postcommunist nations as they struggle with the formidable transition to free markets. In chapter 12 he outlines the deeply rooted obstacles facing these nations as well as the forces and policies of change. Critical of Western-style neoclassical initiatives in these transitional countries, McIntyre rejects the no-third-way assumption. He argues that current policies lead to a path that no country has followed successfully. He also cites recent public opinion suggesting that a new type of social compromise is emerging that may lead to economic institutions distinctly different from European capitalism.

Restructuring of the Japanese System

Although not as striking as the collapse of communism, the collapse of the Japanese "bubble economy" nonetheless has caused a major reversal from the recent heights in which Japan was considered invincible. Many think the entire Japanese system must be restructured. Koji Taira is a leading authority on the Japanese economy. In chapter 13 he outlines the economic logic of the Japanese system, international impressions of Japan, the changes under way, and the dilemmas change poses to the traditional Japanese business firm and culture. Taira states that the dynamic tension between those who wish to reconstruct the past and those who envision a new twenty-first century Japan will be resolved soon by the imperatives of national and international trends.

Scandinavian Economies

Sweden, Denmark, Norway, and Finland had thrived for decades under their unique economic combination of free markets and democratic controls, but this system also is being reconsidered. Victor Pestoff, an economist at the new Baltic Sea University, has studied the Scandinavian system for many years. In chapter 14 he describes the crisis of the welfare state in Sweden. He argues that despite the need for change, the main underpinnings of Sweden's "civil democracy" remain intact. His exhaustive analysis suggests that the social enterprise model provides a powerful framework for empowering workers. It will remain the keystone of any systemic change in Sweden's future and can provide an alternative to the welfare state throughout Europe.

Economic Stratification and Human Welfare

The advance of free markets is unleashing such intense global competition that wages and benefits are being driven down in advanced economies, and continual economic restructuring is forcing rounds of layoffs, even among managers and professionals. This same competitive pressure also is forcing governments around the world to dismantle many of their welfare programs, leaving people with a smaller safety net to cushion life against economic hardship. Mark A. Lutz is a leading economist in the field of "human economy," which strives to reorient orthodox economic thought toward the more meaningful goal of serving human needs and dignity. In chapter 15 Lutz seeks to provide the rationale for such a critical reconception of economics and how it may help resolve the difficult issues facing all of us as we enter the twenty-first century.

Universal Capitalism

The liberal societies of the Western world have harbored an internal contradiction in that political democracy and economic freedom often relate in uneasy tension. Democracy is based on "one person, one vote" and social policy reflecting the dictum of "equality and justice for all." Capitalism allocates "economic votes" unequally and supports economic institutions that foster inequality. Among the many novel solutions proposed to resolve this dilemma, the universal stock ownership plan is perhaps the most ambitious. In chapter 16 Kenneth B. Taylor describes the tradition of universal capitalism in the United States and the history of this plan. He concludes with reflections on current trends and the potential for addressing the contradiction between capitalism and democracy in the future.

The Civil Society

Many scholars are mindful of a variety of forces that could move economies away from raw, survival-of-the-fittest capitalism toward a system that promotes the broader social welfare. Severyn T. Bruyn has studied extensively the social foundations that undergird all economic systems and recently has worked with the United Nations to develop concepts for forming civil economic communities spanning regions and the entire world. Chapter 17 describes his insights on the concept of community-based economic institutions. He describes this logic of the "third sector" from an international perspective, providing copious examples. Bruyn concludes that the elements of "stakeholder capitalism" are converging in such a way to as to support the evolution of civil economies in the coming century.

A Synthesis of Progressive Economic Thought

Our conclusion synthesizes all previous chapters into a coherent sketch of the economic systems that are likely to evolve at the beginning of the twenty-first century. In addition, we also explore the prospect for new economic paradigms combining the free markets that have created enviable wealth in capitalist nations such as the United States as well as the economic collaboration that has created equally enviable quality of life in social democracies in Europe and Asia. While numerous challenges exist, evidence suggests that the knowledge revolution is driving nations in both of these directions, leading to the possible design of vibrant economies that are more productive precisely because they encourage socially harmonious free enterprise.

Notes

1. William Halal, "A Forecast of the Information Revolution," *Technological Forecasting & Social Change* 44, no. 1 (August 1993): 69–86.

2. Hal Kane, "What's Driving Migration?" *World Watch* (January/February 1995).
3. "Caught in the Debt Trap," *The Economist,* April 1, 1995, 59–60.
4. Lester Thurow, *The Future of Capitalism* (New York: William Morrow & Co., 1996).
5. Megan Ryan and Christopher Flavin, "Facing China's Limits," in Lester Brown, ed., *State of the World* (New York: W. W. Norton, 1995), 113–131.
6. Robert Ozaki, *Human Capitalism* (Tokyo: Kodansha, 1991).
7. Peter Drucker, *Post-Capitalist Society* (New York: Harper Collins, 1993).

PART I

Forces Shaping the New Economic Order

CHAPTER 1

Transformations: The Forces of Capitalist Change

Ernest Sternberg, State University of New York at Buffalo

A Time of Profuse Change

It appears that we can bid farewell to twentieth-century industrial capitalism. Assembly-line production, labor-management confrontation, hierarchical business bureaucracy, rigid public-private demarcations, and ideological cold war are becoming merely fond memories. If so, what are we moving on to?

Perhaps we are entering a postindustrial age that relies on information, analysis, and rational decision making. Or we are entering a postmodern age in which our lives are suffused by the hyperreality of commercial images. Then again, we might already be living in a new era of global interdependence that wipes away national boundaries. Or maybe we are at the edge of a new mercantilist age when governments and businesses in every country are collaborating to reassert national economic power. Perhaps we are entering an age when global corporations dominate local economies. Or we are crossing an industrial divide into a time when local groupings of entrepreneurial firms are acquiring ever greater economic importance. Undoubtedly we are in a time when social movements are forcing government and business to respond to progressive issues of gender, sexual orientation, ethnicity, and environment. Or perhaps ours is an age when new fundamentalisms are reorienting us toward lasting verities.

Indeed, momentous transitions are upon us. But are the transitions to postindustrialism, postfordism, postmodernity, or postnationalism? It seems that the old industrial era has barely expired before several new ones have been declared, posthaste. Concepts of capitalist change have vied with each other to reveal our one, true, and imminent economic condition.

Sadly, however, a new age is barely announced before it is debunked, typically as a myth. Volumes of speculation on the information age are spurned as "the myth of the postindustrial economy" and "mythinformation."[1] Notions of a transition from mass production to new economic regimes characterized by flexible and entrepreneurial firms are not even a decade old when they are derided as a "mythical geography."[2] An assortment of new eras and sudden myths rub uncomfortably against each other.

Surely, there is much hype and exaggeration in many of the visions and countervisions. But if we draw out the best and most serious arguments, we would, I believe, find in these notions of radical change hard kernels of plausibility. This chapter takes us on an excursion through eight concepts of capitalist transformation.[3] Passing through them in rapid succession, we can observe what seems to me a striking feature: Each of them seems plausible, even though in combination they question and contradict each other.

How can we make sense of these contending forces of economic change? Conventional economic ideas about technologies, changing tastes, and capitalist crises cannot adequately account for the simultaneity of these radical transformations. I propose that Karl Polanyi's view of capitalism as a society dominated by a rampaging—if often valuable—market mechanism can provide us with a powerful explanation. As the excesses of nineteenth-century laissez-faire led to the development of modern, state-regulated, bureaucratic industrial capitalism, so industrial capitalism has unleashed forces that are leading to its transformation.

The new ages are true *transformations*—as Polanyi might have understood the term. Transformation does not consist solely of incremental changes in individual preferences, nor only of structured social adjustments (although it can contain both incremental and structural features). Rather, capitalist transformation has the outstanding feature that it changes human agents: The individuals, organizations, and institutions that take part in it.

We live in the midst of profuse change. Capitalism has become a dynamic, evolving economic civilization driving our cultures, our capacities for economic well-being, our relationship to the environment, and our personal identities in divergent directions. As we make our way into twenty-first-century capitalism, we will need a new interpretive economics that allows us to better discern and act upon multiple capitalist possibilities.

New Capitalist Ages—An Inventory

The Information Age

Among our series of capitalist transformations, postindustrialism already has become venerable and has inspired a large body of commentary. By now its proponents mostly accept that the period after industrialism can be concisely and specifically understood as the information age.[4]

By contrast with the former industrial economy, which enlarged personal incomes and built national might with machinery, natural resources, and material goods, the new information economy generates wealth and power through the exercise of knowledge. The dominant industries are those that collect, analyze, and transmit information. Ever larger proportions of the labor force work in information occupations—white-collar office work, science and engineering, consulting, and research. Even those businesses that still produce goods are now ever more dependent on their ability to handle information.[5]

The rise of this new world sometimes is attributed to the increasing productivity of the manufacturing industries that dominated the preceding era. Now they can efficiently produce more goods at lower unit cost, so that in the advanced capitalist economies, where incomes increased over much of the latter twentieth century, consumers now prefer to spend larger proportions of their incomes on education, advice, information, and entertainment.

By this reasoning, the information era comes into being because of an incremental change in economic preferences. However, most commentators on the information age attribute its rise to new technologies. Computing, telecommunications, electronic mass media, and new technologies of imaging and photonics—these collectively referred to as "information technology"—accelerate our drive into the information age. Some associate the "information age" so closely with these technologies that they use the term interchangeably with "computer age" and "information technology age."[6]

But we also can make a reasonable argument for the rise of the new age without making technology its driving cause. Indeed, the strongest argument for the ascendance of the postindustrial age manage to steer clear from enthusiasm for microelectronics and advanced communications.[7] It attributes the rise of the new age to the changing needs of twentieth-century industrial capitalism. According to this argument, the origins of the information economy lie in the complexities inherent in old industrial society. Industrial innovations, the bureaucratic and corporate organization of society, the information imperatives of organized warfare on a world scale, new demands for education and social services—in short, ever greater complexity—increased the need for rapid access to information. The industrial world itself, therefore, had in it the seeds of the birth of the information age.[8]

The rise of the new information age has the profound consequence that a new mode of understanding becomes prominent in economic and political decisions. Data are collected, economic and social trends are measured, and decisions are made through technical-analytical reasoning. Spurning the ideological power politics of the past, businesses and governments of the information age make their choices through technocratic calculation.[9] A new elite attains wealth and power with advanced credentials acquired through university education. A cool new culture of science, analytical reasoning, and office efficiency gains worldwide ascendance. Human reasoning comes to be understood as a form of information processing, in which individuals can be conceived as nodes in cybernetic systems. Human communications comes to be defined as data transmission, well enough channeled through optical or electronic fibers. Entertainment, talk, commerce, and work can just as well occur on-line. Politics takes place through plebescitary feedback systems.

Broad-band telecommunications systems, high-speed microprocessing, fiber optics, and miscellaneous other remarkable technologies certainly expand our capacities for processing information. As this capacity increases, businesses, governments, and individuals demand more information services, thereby reinforcing the development of the new technologies. The economic pressures to develop these technologies, and the desire to use them, come about simultaneously in the context of a massive transformation of advanced capitalism. The outcome is a new economic age dominated by information and analysis.

The Economy of Images

The tumultuous intellectual embrace of postmodernity has filled library shelves with speculations about another new capitalist age. But this new age of images appears as a bizarre obverse of the information economy.

In the economy of images, we have lost metaphysical bearings and exhausted intellectual and esthetic traditions. In the previous era, the modern world, the arts thought of themselves as operating in an independent and isolated sphere, from which they could reflect on the apparent rationality and purposefulness of industrial life. But, by now, these modes of detached artistic expression have been explored and exhausted. The distinction between artistic production and the products of the commercial world—between art and artifact—has collapsed.

Those who write about the postmodern age are much more likely to examine consequences for literature, visual art, or criticism than for the economy. Commentators on the information economy can, therefore, be forgiven if they have not recognized that postmodernity has implications that run counter to those of postindustrialism.[10]

In our time, the electronic and mechanical capacity to reproduce art and present images has led to the proliferation of imaginative artifice. The firmly founded reality of modern industrialism has given way to a hyperreality of rampant, disjointed significations.[11]

The operation of an automobile now becomes a mode of self-liberation. Garments cease to be tailored bolts of cloth and become vehicles to ruggedness, motherhood, respectability, and other identities. When eating still functioned as an analog of industrial production, foods took the form of a stock assortment of gastronomic inputs, but in the frozen-food counter and fast-food restaurant they become accessories to carefully designed ambiance.

Real estate development and suburban architecture now create residential and shopping environments with elaborate thematic structure (fishing village, ethnic festival, wilderness hideaway). Tourist destinations—postmodern products of ever-greater economic importance—are designed to represent exotic cultural experiences, although often with negligible ethnographic veracity, even when sited on location. And ketchup loses its meaning as an American tomato condiment to become an object of sensuous nostalgia. Such images become so pervasive that they are no longer merely gimmicks for drawing consumers to a product. They are now the very medium through which we experience our own desires.

This new economy of images appears to have arisen when industrial production could easily satisfy elementary wants for material goods and practical services. Purveyors of commercial products now realize that they can better sell not homely objects but seductive images through which the consumers could simulate the exercise of their passions—images to which specific goods or services are more or less incidental. The very business of producing significations now becomes the dominant element of advanced capitalism.

Technologies of television, video, and motion pictures facilitate and reinforce this economic transformation. But as we saw in our visit to the information economy, technology does not independently bring about the new world but recursively participates in it.

Unlike the information economy, the economy of images has little regard for information processing, computing, and technical analysis. The adventurousness of cigarettes has, after all, very little to do with information. And the overwhelming excess of images becomes, if anything, an obstacle to coherent thinking. In this economy, technical-analytical specialists hold no sway. Engineers and operators of the electronic media are needed, but merely as functionaries. The skills that dominate the economy are those of expressive performance, visual arts, graphic design, public relations, product and package design, virtual reality, and video production.

In the most advanced economy of images, that of the United States, the industries that prosper are those that produce theme parks, advertisements, shopping malls, retail environments, and motion pictures. The country's true economic power now resides in industries that shape evocative representations. And these productions are now coterminous with and indistinguishable from American culture. As American motion pictures, consumer products, and fast-food establishments disperse around the world, their continually reinvented representations are emerging as a global culture.

The new worldwide economy of images encompasses much more than advertisers and media empires. Even business firms that make ordinary goods, such as automobiles, expend as much on designing the product's image as on its mechanical properties. Postmodern firms attain wealth—as postmodern politicians attain prestige—if their presentations (the images enwrapping the products they sell) are so designed as to elicit the viewer's desires and fears. The dominant core of the economy is now engaged not in commodity production nor in the processing of information, but in the shaping of significations.

The Age of Global Interdependence

Among notions of dramatic economic change, the one that is probably most influential is the idea that industries and regions now operate in a global economy. This globalization is sometimes presented as a matter of degree, as only an incremental change in capitalism. But globalization also can be seen as a pervasive capitalist transformation affecting every aspect of economic life.[12]

We observe this internationalization as every country must increasingly concern itself with international trade, finance, investment, currency exchange, commodities prices, and debt balances. Its business enterprises must respond to price changes, product introductions, industrial process innovations, and marketing campaigns arising around the world.

To say so is, of course, commonplace by now. What is more revealing is that, even when the enterprise makes products that do not currently compete on world markets, it finds that the arrangements for making and selling the product have, nevertheless, become internationalized. Domestic research to develop the product responds to related research being conducted around the world. Investment funds arrive through global financial markets. An international insurance syndicate provides protection against risk. Consultants of various nationalities provide advice on accounting, management, or quality assurance. Patents, trademarks, licenses, and other intellectual property are secured in several countries. Materials have multinational origins. Components undergo processing in several countries. And even at the domestic production site, the product finally is assembled by a multinational and multiethnic labor force. To produce a complex product, even one meant for the domestic market, the firm must interweave multiple webs of international relationships.

These relationships come to be regulated and routinized through multinational agreements. Currencies are coordinated, trade and tariff agreements are signed, free ports and processing zones are declared, border regions acquire a multinational character, and continental trade blocs emerge—as forerunners to freer world trade. The demise of the Soviet bloc heralds a new, interdependent world market in which the poorer nations at last have the chance to raise their standards of living.

In this new world, the business firms, cities, and regions that prosper are those adapt to the global economy. The key skills consist of foreign language competence, cross-cultural awareness, knowledge of foreign markets, and understanding of international trading rules. International awareness becomes an essential condition for economic advancement.

Global interdependence also brings a litany of scourges: cross-border and oceanic pollution, global climate change, and destruction of the ozone layer as well as globe-trotting influenzas and pandemics. At the same time, the very expansion of global relationships generates the multinational agreements, intergovernmental bodies, and transnational organizations through which the world eventually can stabilize markets and control their side effects.

This new interdependence has arisen out of the untenable early-twentieth-century system of national economies that operated through autarkic capitalist institutions, trade barriers, recurrent world depression, world war, and cold war. With the United States the victor in World War II, it could become the hegemonic world economic actor, imposing Anglo-American economic liberalism on recalcitrant Asians and Europeans. Technologies of communications, computing, and transportation were at work once again, reducing the costs of trade, travel, and cooperation across borders. Within a few decades America's disproportionate economic influence declined, and European and Asian producers took their place alongside North American firms in complex relationships of competition and cooperation.

This new global economy now not only furthers prosperity but enlivens the arts. International borrowings proliferate in music, performing arts, and sciences. Dress, recreation, medicine, broadcasting, and athletics are all enriched through international contact. A full-fledged age of global interdependence is upon us.

The New Mercantilism

The spread of information and image-making services in an internationalized economy has a paradoxical consequence. Contrary to the expectations associated with postindustrialism, it increases the domestic economic importance of advanced manufacturing. As against the tendency toward global interdependence, it strengthens the determination of nations to build their domestic technological fortunes.

Visionaries of a "new mercantilism" (a term more likely to be used by critics than proponents) contend that we are entering an economic condition in which advanced technologies and sophisticated manufacturing are becoming strategic resources for national prosperity.[13] The new mercantilists admit that a higher proportion of each economy now is devoted to services and information. Since these are not traded or transported across borders as easily as goods are, the manufacturing industries become, curiously enough, *more* important in international economic relations.[14] The mercantilists also admit that business services, government, health care, broadcast entertainment, and information processing employ more people than before. But these services use advanced technologies developed in the manufacturing sector, the part of the economy that invests heavily in research and engineering.

Since information sectors depend on manufacturing for their technologies, the decline of one nation's manufacturing bodes ill for the survival of its advanced information industries as well. Contrary to some expectations, advanced capitalist states now confront the increased strategic importance of technologically advanced manufacturing.[15]

Now more than ever before, nations must build their capabilities in advanced technology. They must forge ahead of other nations in the production of semiconductors, computers, and peripherals; fiber optics, optoelectronic switching, cellular phones, and satellites; advanced imaging, graphic design devices, and high-definition television; and new aerospace and high-speed transit technologies. They must build the engineering capability to integrate such equipment and software in complex systems for computing, communications, imaging, and transportation.

Nations do certainly (as we shall observe in the next capitalist age) host multinational corporations that operate at sites dispersed around the world. But the most successful international German and Japanese firms retain national allegiances. Where they set up foreign plants, they do so to overcome trade barriers, hire low-cost labor, or gain access to technology. Despite their multinational demeanor, these firms keep their headquarters and core technological capabilities in the home country.

In a world of self-interested nation-states, such a response is inevitable. The realities of national survival and the coercive capabilities of government mean that reasons of state take precedence over the diffuse logic of global interdependence.[16] So, capitalist nations now purposefully cultivate their strategic industries and technologies. In the previous economic era they may have done so through straightforward government directives or by nationalizing business enterprise. But the Cold War and its state of perpetual mobilization gave to Western nations experience in conducting more complex contractual relationship between military and commercial sectors.

Drawing on these lessons, capitalist nations build their strategic industries through a complicated range of interfirm, industry-university, government-industry, and military-civilian consortia. Even in the ostensive market liberalism of the United States, these military-industrial relationships (as well as Japanese consultative industrial policy) are becoming the model for a new collaborative capitalism.[17]

This embrace of industrial policy is what leads some to describe this new economy as "mercantilist." The word refers to the seventeenth-and eighteenth-century European monarchies' practice of manipulating trade barriers with the goal of accumulating treasure and thereby building national wealth. Technologically advanced production capability now serves as the equivalent of treasure. Government and industry in each country jointly embrace industrial policy to build the technological exchequer.

In this economy service jobs, including those in information handling and entertainment, do exceed the number of technical jobs. But for that very reason, the nation's endowment of engineers, technicians, and laboratories is all the more crucial. The nations of the world are building new mercantilist arrangements to generate new technology, manage trade, and conduct advanced manufacturing more intensively.

The New Age of Corporate Control

Toyota, Exxon, Matsushita, Walt Disney, Hoechst, Pepsico, Phillips, their counterparts, and their entourage of corporate-service firms now dominate the world's economic life. They exercise two forms of corporate control that have now become pervasive. First, they intensify control over labor through technologies of automation and information handling. And second, they extend control over globally dispersed administrative subunits. Corporate activity has achieved an administrative intensity and global presence that make it more insidious than ever before.

The twentieth century has, of course, long been recognized as the time when giant oligopolistic hierarchies have come to control the bulk of each capitalist economy. But the recent expansion of corporate control is so systemic and pervasive that it reflects, in effect, a transformation of advanced capitalism. The advantages to scale that arise from high-volume production; abilities to use automated systems to adapt production to varied tasks; the possibilities for coordination opened up by advanced computing and communications technologies; and the technologies and political agreements that facilitate international movement—all these have worked together (or have been brought together through corporate influence) to extend corporate control.

The spread of corporate power is related intimately to the rise of global finance. No longer controlled by identifiable individuals or families, the largest corporations are owned by countless investors who own portfolios of stocks and bonds and exert minimal influence over individual holdings. The largest shareholders are themselves corporations: pension funds, insurance companies, banks, and mutual funds.

Corporate officers and financial managers operate as a worldwide interlocking elite. They may disagree and compete over individual investments, but they share a mutual interest in approved operating procedure, proper business climate, and acceptable relationships with governments, interest groups, and labor.[18] Although they manage worldwide operations, they maintain proximity to each other by locating headquarters operations in selected global cities, particularly New York, Frankfurt, Tokyo, and London.[19]

Despite their ostensible support for open economic competition, multinationals use elaborate strategies to retain their preeminent economic positions. They cultivate control over bundles of patents, intellectual property, and engineering expertise. They tightly control logos, trademarks, reputations, and semblances of quality to secure formidable advantages in world markets. They engage in aggressive pricing, acquisitions, and takeovers when dangerous competitors have been identified. Most of all, they benefit from their participation in the global corporate elite and its networks of mutual obligation. Contrary to the free-market romance, those who are outsiders—who are inexperienced, come from nations with few links to this elite, and are unendowed with access to financing—have a minuscule chance of acquiring corporate power.

This age of corporate domination also operates through more intensive control over labor. Able to relocate productive operations across regions and nations, corporate supervisors can better suppress labor organization. New communications technologies allow managers to restrict labor organization further by dispersing workers to computer terminals at remote sites, while maintaining central supervision. With access to technologies of electronic tracking, now they can minutely supervise rates of work in new sweatshops composed of data-input workers. And the ranks of artisans and skilled workers are diminished as various forms of computer-integrated automation turn workers into mere machine tenders.[20] The middle class declines and a new class division emerges between those who deal with routine data input and those who participate in the managerial elite.

Having nearly incontrovertible power cutting across political boundaries, corporate control now shapes the economic destinies of nations and regions. Operating plants close down to open again in offshore locations where workers are more docile, labor costs are low, regulatory protections are lax, government is amenable, and tax exactions are minimal. Even without closing down a production unit, threats to reassign workloads among plants can enforce labor discipline adequately.

In the shadow of the multinationals, national governmental attempts at industrial policy—at a new mercantilism—are doomed to flounder. What seems like the rise of an information age is in large part a by-product of the corporate imperative to control and command complex enterprises. And their global reach has as its most salient effect not global interdependence but global domination of local economies.

Corporate control on this scale also serves to shape consumer desires. The ascendance of a hyperreality of images is the very practical outcome of premeditated corporate marketing. Having cowed governments, multinationals can use advertising to induce tastes for trivial or harmful goods such as soft drinks, cigarettes, liquor, or infant formula in countries where the poor have little discretionary income.

A new world political economy has taken shape, wherein a new global class controls a multinational investment and production apparatus. Its members live in selected world cities, attend selected universities, speak a few elite languages (with English as the lingua franca), travel through the same airports, wear the same corporate attire, and stay at standardized hotels. They are not necessarily scheming in unison, but in effect they are emerging as a global elite, spreading the uniform culture of corporate supervision throughout the world.

The Age of Flexible Specialization

These turbulent times have not been good for the corporate bureaucracies that dominated twentieth-century capitalism. Their economic endurance rested on long production runs of identical items, the division of the production process into simple and routine tasks, rigid job categories, the separation of the white-collar staff from the blue-collar line, and union-management confrontation. They relied for their functioning on administrative formulas associated with Frederick Winslow Taylor, the classic proponent of routinized efficiency in the workplace, and with Henry Ford, the captain of the assembly line.

We are now entering a posttaylorist or postfordist era in which their wisdom no longer prevails.[21] This is a time of the disintegration of vertically integrated corporate power and the ascendance of smaller, more entrepreneurial, more specialized, and more adaptable capitalist firms, firms that are reliant on an ever more versatile workforce.

Capitalism has crossed this industrial threshold because markets for mass-produced items have now been saturated. Consumers in the prosperous economies are less and less interested in off-the-rack clothes, mass-market processed foods, identical homes, and standardized automobiles. Business firms serving these consumers can no longer survive by producing long runs of identical items but must respond, rather, to highly variegated and rapidly shifting tastes.

At the same time, foreign competitors, bristling with new products and processes, break into entrenched domestic markets by targeting specialized market niches. The ascendance of destabilizing new technologies, from biotechnology and advanced ceramics to ever newer generations of computing equipment, further puts pressure on private firms to adapt rapidly. In this volatile environment, bureaucratically organized industrial corporations are at a disadvantage.

More and more firms now survive only if they plan on short production runs, invest in equipment that can perform more varied tasks, and introduce new products more rapidly. Companies can facilitate such change by relying more on computer technology to keep track of operations and by involving engineers and designers more closely in production. To produce higher-quality products in greater variety, and for shorter runs, the enterprises introduce innovative forms of workplace organization that do not rely on hierarchical supervision.

Small, entrepreneurial firms are the ones best positioned to make this transition. They are small enough to respond to specialized tastes and nimble enough to adapt rapidly to change. When a large number of such firms are located in the same geographical region, they can rely on each other for information and specialized services that giant industrial corporations once tried to maintain under one organizational umbrella. The very technologies that make the economic environment so unstable—the technologies of computing and communications—help interrelate these companies with each other and their customers, further increasing their capacities for quick response.

The firms often find that they survive best when they agglomerate in new industrial regions, such as Silicon Valley or the Third Italy. There they can engage in a variety of flexible relationships with each other: They gain access to inside information, make use of (and help develop) a regional pool of properly trained labor, and engage in a varied buying, selling, and contracting relationships. Despite the apparent globalization of the economy, capitalist production is becoming ever more dependent on interfirm relations made possible by geographical proximity.

Larger corporate organizations persist, but they have to change their modes of doing business. In the current insecure environment, they divest themselves of subsidiaries far removed from traditional capabilities. They strengthen their hold over core technologies and build up interrelated clusters of product lines. They turn away from the elaborate, centrally administered research wings, information-systems bureaus, and headquarters operations that once sought to coordinate multiple subunits. Instead, they seek flexibility through relationships with myriad corporate allies, strategic partners, suppliers, and subcontractors.

The mass-production employee of the former industrial age is now obsolescent; his routine skills are the very ones that can be automated. Quite contrary to the expectation that automation and computerization would degrade workers' skills and make them machine tenders, the new environment has put a premium on human versatility. When it comes to introducing new products, adapting to new fashions, changing production procedures, and absorbing new technologies, robots have nowhere near the necessary adaptability. Business firms can no longer rely either on rigidly supervised unskilled workers or on automation. Instead, they hire more educated and capable workers and encourage greater worker involvement in production decisions.

The new capitalist transition brings with it, therefore, the rise of new and dynamic capitalist regions, a new economic dependence on human versatility, and a new international culture of entrepreneurship.

The Age of New Movements

In the capitalist changes we have observed so far, business firms, governments, and their administrators are the primary historical actors. They are the ones who carry out capitalist change. But such transformation weighs on individuals—on citizens, consumers, family members, and workers—as an overpowering force that determines their personal destinies.

By the new century, citizens of the advanced capitalist world have acquired the awareness by which they can respond to unbridled economic change. They have gained this ability in part through the education that capitalist prosperity itself has brought about. And technologies of information, broadcasting, and communications have been at work once again, giving citizens ever more knowledge of rights, prerogatives, and risks. The outcome is the rise of new movements to direct economic affairs toward social benefit.

The new movements arise, however, also for a more profound reason. The very capitalist changes we have discussed have transformed the allegiances of the individual. In the old industrial era, citizens devoted their primary allegiance (other than to family) to class, nationality, military unit, and workplace. By contrast, the new individual acquires a range of identities, concerns, and devotions: to gender, natural environment, sexual preference, and assorted public issues. He or she participates in social movements that seek to assert the rights of minorities, reduce human risks, ensure economic security, and resist the despoliation of human surroundings.

In the late 1960s radical youth movements were briefly seen as a new vanguard for social activism.[22] A decade later movements of community power and local control gained ascendancy. In response to the decline of manufacturing industries and to the corporate power to shift business locations at will, movements arose here and there to protest plant closing, demand worker involvement in corporate decisions, and strive for industrial democracy. Scattered movements in advanced capitalist nations also sought to use localized organizations, mobilized community groups, and the scant power of local governments to exert local influence over local economies. But by the end of the century, social movements gain the most influence when their issues have relevance across many localities.[23]

Burgeoning movements now operate across regions and nations to sustain the natural environment, ensure the safety of consumer products, pressure for health-care protections, protect rights of the disabled, and raise public awareness of an increasingly large repertoire of threats—risky food additives, hazardous waste dumping, excessive population growth, explicit musical lyrics, and unwise sexual practices.

The movements now have the ability to make capitalist development attend to such values. Indeed, the movements have such thoroughgoing and widespread effects that the logics of politics and markets have been transformed. The outcome is a new capitalism, a social economy pervaded by a range of humane concerns. This new economy differs starkly from the welfare state of the former industrial era: It does not focus primarily on economic redistribution or the bureaucratically mandated provision of entitlements. The new social movements demand that their representatives gain ongoing consultative and decision-making influence over governmental and business decisions.

Whether on toxic pollution, minority access to work, or consumer safety, the movements obtain access to information, gain the ability to monitor performance, make their views and knowledge known in varied forums (corporate boards, mass media, legislatures, consultative bodies), engage in open dialog with those holding contrary perspectives, and often succeed in participating in critical decisions.

Despite their diversity, the social movements share a common thread: the open, participatory ethic. They seek the power to participate in decisions affecting vital human concerns. The social movements can, thereby, shape a business firm's record in employment safety, product reliability, and release of toxins, not to mention relations with persons of varied ethnicities, sexual orientations, genders, and conditions of infirmity.

As their demands suffuse business life, the movements are having profound effects on the operations of the economy. Each business firm, government bureau, and university now operates in an ethically far more complex environment than ever before. It attends to the likely responses to its actions by a range of internal and external constituencies and stakeholders.

This moral guidance of business decisions presages a truly social economy: a capitalism in which guardians of a variety of human concerns become integral participants in business life. As against an information economy dominated by analytical reasoning, this new social economy operates through open negotiations, debate, and dialog. Although in the economy of images consumers have their lives defined by the fantasies transmitted through the media, in this social economy citizens become forceful participants in setting the directions of their businesses and govern-ment. In this new capitalism, economic events no longer occur through the heedless exercise of corporate power nor through the automatic operations of a global market mechanisms. Rather, they emerge through diffuse social oversight, broad participation, negotiations, and reasoned argument.

The Age of New Fundamentals

The global spread of turbulent change looms as profound threat to personal identity. Clans, ethnicities, religions, and sects throughout the world are, therefore, refurbishing antique cultures, rediscovering original values, re-claiming eternal truth, and acquiring the power to fight for verity. The very transformations just described add to the urgency of this task. The informa-tion age and its technocratic policies are pervading human life with an ag-nostic ethic of analysis. International commerce marches through home and community as a dizzying parade of new enticements. Multinational corpo-rate bureaucracies, global financial markets, government-business mercan-tilist alliances, and slick high-technology entrepreneurs have overwhelming power to corrupt governments, destabilize economies, desecrate precious values, and wreak havoc with honored custom.

The fundamentalism that arises as a response should not be confused with traditionalism. Traditional community fought and lost its conflict with in-dustrial society in the nineteenth century.[24] The traditional practices that re-mained made their peace with the industrial world and found marginal roles within it. Traditionalists and orthodox religionists of all stripes became con-tent to relegate religion—as art also was relegated in the modern world—to an isolated sphere of personal contemplation. By the mid-twentieth century, colonial and postcolonial governments worked out a modus vivendi and served as a buffer between the modern elite and the traditional masses. As this accommodation is breaking down, orthodox religionists are becoming dis-credited by their docility. At the same time, industrial life is in disarray, over-taken by a number of ineluctable transformations.

The rise of fundamentalisms is accelerating not because of the spread of modern, secular, technological industrialism but because of its dissolution.

In this environment, fundamentalists mine their inalienable reserves of history, relic, origin, scripture, and legend for gems of reliable belief. Properly prepared and mounted, they become treasured beliefs protected by eternal patent. As compared to the ever-new, ever-disconcerting, ever-manipulated images through which media shape our self-conceptions, fundamentalism recreates that eternal conceptual foundation on which we can rely.[25]

The fundamentalists draw selectively on their cultural endowment, and thereby reconstruct it in forms that are not always recognizable to traditionalists.[26] They identify topics of passionate commitment (modest attire, inoffensive art, fetal life) that barely concerned their forbears. The new fundamentalists are not averse to technology. They embrace computer networks, cable television, and satellite communications. At the university, even if the humanities and social sciences are suppressed, engineering and natural science are preserved.

Nor are the fundamentalists anticapitalistic. This era's prototypical fundamentalist state, the Islamic Republic of Iran, retains much private enterprise, private property, and private trade. The bazaar, the market, and the merchant are valued resources for the upkeep of the faith. As in the Protestant origins of capitalism, in this new capitalist age as well, commerce, savings, and investment can be vehicles for piety—as long as the enterprise adheres to fundamental precepts and the movement shares in the financial rewards.

In this new age, businesses observe codes of propriety with respect to demeanor, attire, gender, and calendar. They cultivate links with the faithful, foster worship in the workplace, and pay tithes. Economic life is transformed by the devotion to eternal verities.

Every part of the world sees the rise of movements that assert new fundamentals. In postcommunist states, the coalescence of zealous belief is hardly even slowed by the need to replenish the clergy. For revivalist *Haredi* Jews, Revolutionary Guards, Hindu activists, and Moral Majorities possibly the greatest political impediment is that they do not readily make alliances with each other. There is, therefore, a basic difference between the new fundamentalists and the new social movements. The social movements embrace dialog, participation, negotiations, and political give-and-take. Fundamentalists may be willing to engage in tactical accommodation but hold to beliefs that ultimately cannot be compromised. Both may be concerned about ethnic identity, but the social movements introduce issues of ethnicity to the firm as a matter of civil rights, while the fundamentalisms do so in order to assert ethnic control. While the new age of social movements reshapes capitalism through pluralist participation, the new world of fundamentalisms transforms it through purposeful and intransigent commitment.

The Forces of Transformation

For half a century now, notions of radical change have proliferated, spreading as rapidly as, it seems, faith in progress waned. Not only postindustrialism, postmodernity, and the rest, but the atomic age, computer age, space age, gene age, and other new eras made their appearance.[27] News of their coming has been widely broadcast, and they are by now only passably momentous. Dramatic changes are not what they used to be. Perhaps the cravings for revolutionary new ages are signs of our times, just millenarian hopes in rationalist guise. Possibly, the very profusion of new ages demonstrates our loss of direction, enticing us with our final dramatic hopes before we lose faith in the new.

Then again, the logical flaw in such a nihilistic rejection seems all too apparent. To declare this a time when new ages have expired is a hopeless self-contradiction, since of course it is a declaration of a new age. And if we take one new age seriously, the others also can make a claim for our attention. Indeed, capitalism is brimming with the forces of change. Each of the "new ages" illuminates our current or imminent possibilities. Our challenge is to make sense of their multiplicity.

One way we could do so is by choosing one vision of change, pronouncing it correct, and rejecting the rest. Indeed, just this kind of intellectual temper often characterizes the discourse on contemporary change, in part because its participants feel they are engaged in forecasting and feel duty-bound to pick the correct future. And the information age, globalization, postmodernity, and so on each has its enthusiasts, who take their favorite capitalist force as a personal mission. To bet on the correct new age is to pin down the future and demonstrate oneself a seer. The best payoff comes from choosing the right future, not from highlighting the present possibilities.

Instead of choosing the correct future, we can try another strategy: Conflate multiple changes into one enormous historical tendency. The writings on contemporary change often do try to do so, as, for example, does the social-science literature that goes under the rubric "industrial restructuring."[28] However, by collapsing a number of contemporary tendencies (and rejecting a number of others), the idea of industrial restructuring homogenizes our conceptions of the present, undermining our ability to discern multiple possibilities.

To grasp fully the meanings of our inventory of new ages, we should forgo these more usual ways of making sense of radical change. I suggest, therefore, that we acknowledge the possibility of multiple, simultaneous transformations. In taking on this intellectual attitude, we are not staking out a position about the future. It may well be that all or most of the visions of a new age will turn out merely to be late-modern myths. It also may turn out that one new age or a particular combination of two or three will dominate the future. But we cannot yet tell. The present is indeed pregnant with our futures and—as far as we can tell—has not yet delivered. Our task is to inquire into this capitalist gestation.

If all the new ages, singly or in combination, are concurrently plausible, then there must be some force that is taking us in several divergent directions. What force underlies divergent capitalist changes?

Technologies, Tastes, or Crises?

The academic discipline conventionally given to considering the economic domain, orthodox economics, draws its conclusions about dramatic change from its underlying assumption: that market mechanisms allow self-seeking individuals to resolve new needs and pressures efficiently. The economists seek explanations for change in events external, or exogenous, to the market system: in changing technology or changing tastes.

Let us take the first tack, technology. New technologies are indeed implicated in the forces of capitalist change. The information age, as well as the age of new social movements, the new mercantilism as well as the new fundamentalism, all occur in part because of technological change. One particular cluster of technologies, the new "information technologies"—consisting of computing, telecommunications, and broadcasting—plays a particularly central role. Could each of the new ages be the result of technology?

The explanation is plausible as long as we treat each new age—each transformation—in isolation. But it becomes implausible in the face of multiple transformations. The same set of technologies could not possibly cause both global corporate coordination and local business flexibility, or both global interdependence and nationalist mercantilism. When divergent new ages are juxtaposed, they illustrate the impossibility of technological determinism. Technology is certainly bound up in the rise of the new ages, but the forces generating each envisioned age give motive and direction to technological change as much as they are driven by it. I conclude that none of the proposed new eras results merely from technological invention.

Taking the other tack, conventional economists may suggest that these supposed new ages result simply from changing individual tastes. According to this orthodox viewpoint, the economic visions described here may be worth some passing comment but are hardly of great consequence, since the very fact that adjustment is occurring suggests that markets, which efficiently guide the acts of individual consumers and producers, are responding to changing tastes, which affect demand for information, product variety, environmental protection, or fundamental values. Yet to say so only extends the problem back further. How do we explain changing tastes? Not being well equipped to answer the question, economists are again likely to search for exogenous causes, such as "social" and "cultural" factors thought to lie outside the economic realm. Yet our investigation of capitalist transformations suggests that the new ages do not arise from extraeconomic events but from tendencies inherent to capitalism.

By turning away from technology and tastes as prime movers of capitalist change, we remove the main suspects in what would be a fruitless search for a exogenous perpetrators. To find the sources of transformation, we should turn our attention back to tendencies inherent to contemporary capitalism.

The economists schooled in the traditions of Marxist thought do hold views of the economy that seek to grasp historical dynamism, so they fare much better in comprehending dramatic changes—when these are considered only one at a time. Hence, we find neo-Marxist postindustrialism, "regulation school" postfordism, critiques of the commodification of the sign (of the economy of images), and critiques of the globalization of capital. But these neo-Marxist depictions of change also do not stand up in the face of multiple new ages. Neo-Marxists would have to object to ideas of open, simultaneous, unresolved transformations. After all, in Marxist thought, a new capitalist age has to be posed as the working out of capitalist contradictions in some identifiable direction. But in our inventory of new ages, we can as well conclude that capitalism's fate is not inscribed in history; we face, instead, a number of simultaneous changes whose directions are yet unresolved.

Neo-Marxist notions of capitalist change often treat "capital" as if it were a disembodied force undergoing periodic crises and morphological adjustments. Capital has such effects because capitalist production concentrates power in a class. Whether collusively or not, members of the class respond to these strains through machinations that variously harm, exploit, or co-opt those lacking political-economic power. The inequitable consequences of this power disparity set off new capitalist strains. These sequences of crises and structural adjustments arise, then, from the fundamental fact of unequal control and contrary interests inherent to capitalist production.

Our inventory of new ages, by contrast, suggests not structural crisis but turbulent change. Markets and marketlike processes at the core of capitalist society exert pressures on human agents (individuals, organizations, and institutions), who respond through cultural, industrial, and technological strategies. Those holding power through wealth or office certainly have disproportionate influence over this response, but they are themselves pulled along by the forces of transformation. We have no foolproof understanding of class interests, since interests are themselves being transformed.

Our inquiry into the new ages therefore suggests a line of reasoning that economists of both conventional and radical persuasions are likely to avoid: the idea that the very operations and development of the capitalist system changes the human beings that participate in it. To accept that logic would suggest that we cannot adequately understand radical change as the outcome of structurally opposed interests, since the nature of interests is changing. And, by the same logic, individual acts of exchange are more than utilitarian behaviors. Their effects exceed the costs and benefits that the exchangers can calculate rationally. The capitalist economy may have the puzzling consequence of changing the human beings, cultures, and organizations through which it operates.

An Economics of the Future

During the height of World War II, the iconoclastic economist Karl Polanyi argued that the depression and world war marked the end of nineteenth-century capitalism, an economic world in which rampant laissez-faire had come to dominate Western society. In the newly transformed capitalism that had taken its place, society had found ways to protect itself from the market's excesses.[29] Government regulation, public policy, and unionization sought to protect the public, the environment, and the worker; macroeconomic policy and trade policy intended to protect the economy itself; and— a subject Polanyi did not address—trusts and holding companies arose to protect business enterprises from the vagaries of continuous competition.

Polanyi could observe such changes because of the way he conceived of capitalism: He saw it as a society dominated by the relentless force of an autonomous market mechanism. Capitalist society changes as a result of the inherently destabilizing effects that this mechanism exerts on individuals, organizations, and culture. Government-regulated, bureaucratically organized industrial capitalism—for which the twentieth century will be remembered—arose, therefore, as a response to the uncertainties and destructive side effects of laissez-faire market systems. By the mid-twentieth century, under American hegemony of the noncommunist world, this system attained a tenuous stability.

Polanyi did not live to realize that this mid-twentieth-century industrial capitalism contained the driving forces that would transform it once again. I suggest that we look at our inventory of new ages in that light. Even though the new ages make for quite a bewildering assortment, they all reflect the logical consequences of a rampant economic force at the core of twentieth-century industrial society. This logic works itself out differently in each of the new ages.

First, as the complexity of industrial society increased needs for information, businesses and governments reorganized to provide (and take advantage of) ever more rapid flows of information. In the face of masses of information, they increasingly turned to analysis as the definitive form of decision making. Their acts came to be woven into systems of information collection, distribution, processing, and display. Soon individuals and organizations came to act, and even to perceive themselves, as information processors.

Second, during industrial society, businesses came to realize that they have the most to gain by shaping consumers' desires. The purposeful and manipulative shaping of significations became so pervasive that even the shapers came to believe them. Advertisements, public relations, Hollywood storylines, and media personalities gained the power to so thoroughly define the world that we now understand our own lives through the mediated realities of commercial images.

Third, in the wake of an industrial capitalism that expanded international commerce, we were exposed to a multitude of transnational and global contacts. Organizations and individuals lost their parochial visions, becoming diverse, multicultural participants in a world economy.

Fourth, the increasing internationalization of commerce that characterized the industrial world also brought upon us a new mercantilism. Organizations lost the traditional bearings of government checks-and-balances and private competition. They increasingly turned to new hybrid partnership arrangements meant to reassert national wealth through advanced technology.

Fifth, as a result of the growing sophistication of managerial hierarchies first established in the old industrial society, we became ever more enmeshed in the operations of giant corporate enterprises. These global bureaucracies attained transnational mobility, came to dominate national and local governments, and turned workers into machine tenders and data-entry clerks.

Sixth, old industrial society accelerated economic uncertainty to the extent that the industrial era's own fordist organizations crumbled. Nimble entrepreneurs set up a new generation of flexibly specialized firms that hired educated and versatile workers who could respond rapidly to economic shifts.

Seventh, the same twentieth-century industrial society has helped us expand our identities beyond class, nationality, and workplace to new allegiances. These gave rise to a range of social movements that would penetrate business and government with social agendas.

Eighth, the changes in industrial society posed ever greater threats to clans, ethnicities, and religions, giving rise to an age in which we rediscovered our adherence to fundamental precepts.

The new capitalist ages come into being, therefore, not simply through new technologies, nor simply as incremental trends, nor only as structural changes occurring beyond the grasp of human actors. Rather, they are truly the effects of *transformations*. Capitalist transformation may contain technological, incremental, and structural characteristics, but it also has the additional, defining feature that it changes the actors (individuals, organizations, institutions) that participate in it.[30]

As a result of the uncontrolled forces unleashed when market became the central force in society, nineteenth-century laissez-faire capitalism was transformed into twentieth-century industrial society. The government-regulated, oligopolistic, bureaucratic welfare state of modern capitalism itself contained the forces that are transforming capitalism once again.It is through the simultaneous and interacting effects of these transformations that twenty-first-century capitalism is taking shape. It is an evolving, tumultuous economic civilization, bursting with inspiring and frightening possibilities.

At beginning of the twenty-first century, we are still in the midst of several transformations and do not yet know which one, or which combination of them, will dominate the future. The notions of transformation diverge from each other because they reflect the divergent possibilities of our time. We should not try to obscure these divergent possibilities with a homogenous picture of change. We should, rather, seek to discern and reveal the multiple tendencies that are reshaping the world.

Our modes of thinking about the economy are, however, still under the spell of the nineteenth-and twentieth-century societies in which concepts of capitalism were shaped. We must now develop a new, interpretive economic discipline that can provide insight into the changes overtaking our world. It is this economics of the future that will allow us to better discern the outcomes of multiple transformations and better prepare us to act on them.

Notes

This chapter came to be written only because the author had the fortune to have as colleagues Arthur Hui-Min Chen, Sam Cole, Bruno B. Freschi, Ibrahim Jammal, and Magda Cordell McHale, who led him to appreciate the intellectual dilemmas posed by contemporary change. His thanks to them, as well as to John Friedman and Susan Christopher for their illuminating comments.

1. See Stephen S. Cohen and John Zysman, *Manufacturing Matters: The Myth of the Post-Industrial Economy* (New York: Basic Books, 1987); and Langdon Winner, *The Whale and the Reactor: The Search for Limits in an Age of High Technology* (Chicago: University of Chicago Press, 1986), especially the essay "Mythinformation," 98–120.

2. See A. Amin and K. Robins, "The Re-Emergence of Regional Economies? The Mythical Geography of Flexible Accumulation," *Environment and Planning: Society and Space* 8 (1990): 7–34; and Richard A. Walker, "Regulation, Flexible Specialization and the Forces of Production in Capitalist Development," Revised paper presented at the Cardiff Symposium on Regulation, Innovation and Spatial Development, University of Wales, September 13–15, 1989.

3. Some of the visions of new capitalist ages are closely associated with an author or two, although the disputes among the visionaries are contentious enough, and each has enough of a following that each vision has turned into something of a school. In presenting these schools in so short a space, I stylize and simplify them, so that we lose the authors' subtleties and nuances. I do this in order to sharpen the contrasts and tensions and to heighten the sense that the visions suggest divergent capitalist directions.

4. Classic works on the postindustrial economy include Daniel Bell's *The Coming of Post-Industrial Society: A Venture in Social Forecasting* (New York: Basic Books, 1976) and John McHale's *The Changing Information Environment* (London: Paul Elek, 1976). Note Bell's acceptance of the concept of information economy in "Communications Technology—For Better or Worse," *Harvard Business Review* 57, no. 3 (1979): 20–42. Recent literature on the information economy, with plenty of references to the rest of this voluminous scholarship, includes Tom Forester, ed., *Computers in the Human Context: Information Technology, Productivity, and People* (Oxford: Basil Blackwell, 1989), and Kevin Robins, ed., *Understanding Information: Business, Technology and Geography* (London: Belhaven, 1992). For a thorough bibliography through the mid-1980s, see Miriam Whitaker and Ian Miles, *Bibliography of Information Technology: An Annotated Critical Bibliography of English Language Sources Since 1980* (Aldershot, U.K.: Edward Elgar, 1989).

5. An important attempt to measure the growth of the U.S. information economy appears in Marc Uri Porat, *The Information Economy: Definition and Measurement* (Washington, D.C.: Office of Telecommunications, U.S. Department of Commerce, 1977).

6. This is true in many of the chapters included in Forester, ed., *Computers in the Human Context*.

7. Daniel Bell's argument in *The Coming of Post-Industrial Society* suggests a broad historical sweep extending beyond merely technological causation. Ian Miles and colleagues specifically try to divorce concepts of the information economy from technological determinism. See Ian Miles, Howard Rush, John Bessant, et al., *IT Horizons* (Aldershot, U.K.: Edward Elgar, 1988), and Ian Miles and

Kevin Roberts, "Making Sense of Information," in Kevin Robins, ed., *Understanding Information*. Therefore, Langdon Winner (in "Mythinformation" in *The Whale and the Reactor*) was overstating his case in fully associating concepts of information society with enthusiasm for new technologies.

8. Unfortunately, the literature on the information economy has not dwelt on this point. One author who attributes the rise of the information economy to "complexity" in industrialism is Melvin Kranzberg in "The Information Age," in Forester, ed., *Computers in Human Context*, 19–32, especially 21–24.

9. Much of Bell's *Coming of the Post-Industrial Society* stresses the rise of rational calculation as a dominant force in that new society. A similar depiction of contemporary capitalism as being characterized by technocratic decision making also appears in Jurgen Habermas's early essays, particularly "The Scientization of Politics and Public Opinion," in *Toward a Rational Society* (Boston: Beacon Press, 1970, trans. J. J. Shapiro). For a discussion of technocratic vs. other conceptions of present-day political economy, see Ernest Sternberg, "Incremental Versus Methodological Policymaking in the Liberal State," *Administration and Society* 21, no. 1 (May 1989): 54–77.

10. For example, Fred Block asserts the choice between the labels "postindustrial" and "postmodern" is arbitrary. See his *Postindustrial Possibilities* (Berkeley: University of California Press, 1990), 4, n. 7.

11. I am broadly and freely taking from several sources, but I am particularly influenced by the work of Jean Baudrillard, especially *The Mirror of Production* (St. Louis: Telos Press, 1975, trans. Mark Poster) and *Simulations* (New York: Semiotext(e), 1983, trans. Paul Foss, Paul Patton, and Philip Beitchman). I am also influenced here by Arthur Kroker and David Cook, *The Postmodern Scene* (Montreal: New World Perspectives, 1986). For a neo-Marxist treatment of the same phenomena, see W. F. Haug, *Critique of Commodity Esthetics* (Cambridge: Polity Press, 1986). There is also a more conventional literature observing the growing role of images and advertising in American capitalism. See, for example, Stuart Ewen, *All-Consuming Images: The Politics of Style in Contemporary Culture* (New York: Basic Books, 1988).

12. Reflections on global interdependence have moved far beyond a specialized literature and now suffuse political and economic discussions. Early reflections on transnationalism appeared in Robert O. Keohane and Joseph S. Nye, Jr., eds., *Transnational Relations and World Politics* (Cambridge, Mass.: Harvard University Press, 1971). A recent summary statement with extensive references to further literature is John Accordino, *The United States in the Global Economy: Challenges and Policy Choices* (Chicago: American Library Association, 1992). A sophisticated assessment on the politics of interdependence among states vs. the politics haunted by possibilities of armed conflict appears in Robert O. Keohane and Joseph S. Nye, Jr., "Power and Interdependence Revisited," *International Organization* 41, no. 4 (Autumn 1987): 725–753. A set of articles reflecting the naive enthusiasm in much contemporary discussion

can be found in William E. Brock and Robert D. Hormats, eds., *The Global Economy: America's Role in the Decade Ahead* (New York: W. W. Norton, 1990).

13. Generally such points are made by those who see more intensive international technological competition and growing state involvement in the economies of capitalist states. Therefore, such arguments are found in the literature roughly on the subject of "industrial policy." For a guide to the industrial policy literature, see Ernest Sternberg, *Photonic Technology and Industrial Policy: U.S. Responses to Technological Change* (Albany, New York: State University of New York Press, 1992), chap. 4. For arguments on the continuing or growing importance of manufacturing trade, see Cohen and Zysman, *Manufacturing Matters.* Similar points on the revival of the political importance of trade are made by Richard Rosencrance in *The Rise of The Trading State* (New York: Basic Books, 1986). For a rather different argument in response to the postindustrialism thesis, see Jonathan Gershuny, *After Industrial Society?* (Atlantic Highlands, New Jersey: Humanities Press, 1978), which contends that we are entering a time when services are ever more being replaced by devices that perform services for us (as washing machines replace laundry services).

14. See Block, *Postindustrial Possibilities,* p. 19.

15. See Cohen and Zysman, *Manufacturing Matters.*

16. Political scientists would refer to this argument as "realism."

17. See Sternberg, *Photonic Technology and Industrial Policy,* chaps. 5–8.

18. To maintain continuity with previous conceptions of change, here I am purposefully avoiding a common approach to globally mobile capital that treats "capital" as a disembodied force undergoing periodic crises and morphological adjustments. Many of the observations about worldwide corporate and financial power can be made through a more institutional analysis, which I am suggesting here.

19. The literature on the worldwide interlocking elite is reviewed in John Friedmann, "Where We Stand: A Decade of World City Research," Paper presented at the Conference of World Cities in a World-System, Sterling, Va., April 1–3, 1993. See, for example, articles in Richard B. Knight and Gary Gappert, ed., *Cities in a Global Society* (Newbury Park, Calif: Sage Publications, 1989).

20. A well-known representative of the corporate domination literature is H. Braverman's *Labor and Monopoly Capital* (New York: Monthly Review Press, 1974). Harley Shaiken extended this argument in *Work Transformed: Automation and Labor in the Computer Age* (New York: Holt, Rinehart and Winston, 1985). For an example of growing technological control of the workforce, see Congress of the United States, Office of Technology Assessment, *The Electronic Supervisor: New Technology, New Tensions* (Washington, D.C.: U.S. Government Printing Office, September 1987).

21. An influential work on the breakup of mass markets is Michael Piore and Charles Sabel, *The Second Industrial Divide* (New York: Basic Books, 1984). On implications for human resource development, see Lauren Benton et al.,

Employee Training and U.S. Competitiveness: Lessons for the 1990s (Boulder, Colo.: Westview Press, 1991). A book that looks at practical implications for economic policy is Paul Hirst and Jonathan Zeitlin, eds., *Reversing Industrial Decline? Industrial Structure and Policy in Britain and Her Competitors* (Oxford: Berg Publishers, 1989). A critical review of this literature appears in Amin and Goddard, "The Re-emergence of Regional Economies?"

22. Such themes appear in Jurgen Habermas's early work, as in *Toward a Rational Society,* chaps. 2 and 3.

23. For an extensive review of the recent literature on social movements, consult Arturo Escobar's "Culture, Practice and Politics: Anthropology and the Study of Social Movements," *Critique of Anthropology* 12, no. 4 (1992): 395–432.

24. The conflict between community and industrial society, see Ferdinand Tonnies, *Community and Society* (East Lansing: Michigan State University Press, 1957), especially the translator's introductory sections, which compare Tonnies's concepts with those of other social thinkers.

25. For a similar contrast, see Benjamin R. Barber, "Jihad vs. McWorld," *The Atlantic* 269 (March 1992): 53–55 ff.

26. A series of volumes that makes this distinction between traditionalism and fundamentalism begins with Martin E. Marty and R. Scott Appleby, *Fundamentalisms Observed* (Chicago: University of Chicago Press, 1991). This series is emerging as by far the best source of comparative fundamentalisms.

27. For an entertaining list of revolutionary new ages announced since World War II, see James R. Beniger, *The Control Revolution: Technological and Economic Origins of the Information Society* (Cambridge, Mass.: Harvard University Press, 1986).

28. Examples of work on the theme of industrial restructuring include Ash Amin and John Goddard, eds., *Technological Change, Industrial Restructuring, and Regional Development* (London: Allen and Unwin, 1986), and Susan S. Fainstein et al., *Restructuring the City: The Political Economy of Urban Redevelopment* (New York: Longman, 1983).

29. Karl Polanyi, *The Great Transformation* (Boston: Beacon Press, 1957, originally published 1944).

30. That, too, is what I take to be the most subtle message in Polanyi's *Great Transformation.* See Ernest Sternberg, "Justifying Public Intervention without Market Externalities: Karl Polanyi's Theory of Planning in Capitalism," *Public Administration Review* 53, no. 2 (March/April 1993): 100–109.

CHAPTER 2

Globalization: An Economic-Geographical Perspective

Peter Dicken, University of Manchester, England

Introduction

Much of the academic and popular literature, whether explicitly or implicitly, adopts the position that globalization processes are leading inexorably towards a homogenized world in which geographical differentiation is being/will be obliterated.[1] Phrases such as "the death of distance" or "the end of geography"[2] resonate within these globalization discourses. According to this view, dramatic technological developments have made capital—and the firms controlling it—"hypermobile," freed from the "tyranny of distance" and no longer tied to "place." In other words, it implies that economic activity is becoming "deterritorialized." The sociologist Manuel Castells argues that the forces of globalization, especially those driven by the new information technologies, are replacing this "space of places" with a "space of flows."[3] Anything can be located anywhere and, if that does not work out, can be moved somewhere else with ease. Seductive as such ideas might be, a moment's thought will show just how misleading they are. Although transport and communications technologies have indeed been revolutionized, both geographical distance and, especially, *place* remain fundamental.

The objective of this chapter, therefore, is to challenge the end-of-geography position. Just as Fukuyama's heralding of "the end of history" already has proved to be unsubstantiated,[4] so, too, to talk of the end of geography is to misinterpret the complex manner in which geography (in terms of space and place) infuses *all* social processes and institutions. The chapter is organized into two major parts. First, I outline the major contours of the new geoeconomic map and then set out some of the fundamental bases of my argument that geography matters to an understanding of globalization processes. Second, I explore what I regard as being the three most significant, tightly interconnected forces that are shaping and reshaping the geoeconomy: transnational corporations, states, and technology. In discussing these three forces I will focus specifically on their geographical dimensions.

The Contours of the New Geoeconomic Map

The conventional unit of analysis in studies of the world economy is the nation-state. Virtually all the statistical data on production, trade, investment, and the like are aggregated into national "boxes." However, such a level of aggregation is less and less useful, given the nature of the changes occurring in the organization of economic activity. This is not to imply that the national level is unimportant. On the contrary, one of the major themes of this chapter is that nation-states continue to be key players in the contemporary global economy. In any case, we have to rely heavily on national-level data to explore the changing maps of production, trade, and investment. But national boundaries no longer "contain" production processes to the extent, and in the ways, they once did. Such processes slice through national boundaries and transcend them in a bewildering array of relationships that operate at different geographical and organizational scales. We need to be able to get both below and above the national scale to understand what is going on.

Over time, new global divisions of labor—new patterns of geographical specialization—emerge and interdigitate with older forms to create highly complex patterns of economic activity at different geographical scales. For much of the period following the industrial revolution of the eighteenth and nineteenth centuries, the global structure was essentially that of a core, a semiperiphery, and a periphery. These components were connected together through trade flows that themselves were articulated by the core economies. Manufacturing was overwhelmingly a core activity.

This relatively simple pattern (although it was never, of course, quite as simple as this description suggests) no longer applies. During the past few decades, trade and investment flows have become far more complex. The straightforward exchange between core and peripheral areas, based on a broad division of labor, is being transformed into a highly complex, multipolar, multiscalar structure; a "mosaic of unevenness in a continuous state of flux" in the words of M. Storper and R. Walker.[5] This involves the fragmentation of many production processes and their geographical relocation on a global scale in ways which slice through national boundaries. New centers of industrial production—newly industrializing economies (NIEs)—have emerged, most notably, although not exclusively, in East Asia. Both old and new industries, both manufacturing and services, are involved in this resorting of the global jigsaw puzzle. The geographical center of gravity of the global production system undoubtedly has shifted from its long-established position "in" the North Atlantic (focused on northwest Europe and the eastern seaboard of the United States) toward the Pacific Basin (focused on Japan and the East Asian NIEs).

Arguably, we now inhabit a world economy that has crystallized around the three poles of the *global triad,* North America, Europe, and East Asia.[6] During the past 10 to 15 years, the degree of economic concentration in the triad has increased very substantially. In 1980, 76 percent of total world manufacturing output and 71 percent of merchandise trade was located there. By the mid-1990s the triad's share of both measures had increased by around 10 percentage points: To 87 percent of world output and 80 percent of world trade. These trends imply that the global triad is, in effect, "sucking in" more and more of the world's productive activity, trade and direct investment. The triad sits astride the global economy like a modern three legged Colossus. It constitutes the world's "megamarkets." Whether it is more than a statistical artifact, however, is subject to debate. Two of the three poles, Europe and North America, are both more formally organized politically into regional trading blocs (the European Union and the North American Free Trade Agreement, respectively). The third and most dynamic of the three triad regions, East Asia, has no formal political organization, although various possibilities are being proposed. But if the triad does represent a functional reality, actual or potential, with internally oriented production and trade systems it poses major problems for those parts of the world—notably the least developed countries—which are not integrated into the system.[7]

The global triad is one view of the contours of the contemporary geoeconomic map. Insofar as both business decision makers and politicians believe in its existence, it will continue to have a major influence on patterns of economic activity. But, of course, as individuals we do not think of ourselves, first and foremost, as living in one or other parts of the global triad. We live in specific localized communities—cities, towns, villages. A fundamental fact of all economic life is that all economic activity is ultimately *localized in specific places.*

Not only does every economic activity have to be located somewhere, but also—and more significantly, there is a very strong propensity for economic activities to form *localized geographical clusters* or *agglomerations*. In fact, the geographical concentration of economic activities, at a local or subnational scale, is the norm, not the exception. Recently the pervasiveness and the significance of geographical clustering has recently been recognized—and has come to occupy a central position, in the writings of some leading economists and management theorists, notably Paul Krugman, Michael Porter, and Kenichi Ohmae.[8] However, economic geographers and location theorists have been pointing to the pervasiveness of this phenomenon of geographical concentration for decades.[9] One of the leading contributors to the geographical literature, Allen Scott, explores the regionalization of the global economy in some depth in chapter 4 in this volume. Here we need only make some basic observations.

The reasons for the origins of specific geographical clusters are highly contingent and often shrouded in the mists of history. As Gunnar Myrdal pointed out many years ago, "Within broad limits the power of attraction today of a center has its origin mainly in the historical accident that something once started there, and not in a number of other places where it could equally well or better have started, and that the start met with success."[10] Whatever the specific reason for the initiation of a localized economic cluster, its subsequent growth and development tends to be based on two sets of agglomerative forces: *traded and untraded interdependencies.*

Traded Interdependencies

Geographical proximity between firms performing different, but linked, functions in the production chain may reduce the transaction costs involved and make possible a higher intensity of interfirm transactions between neighboring firms. In fact, it does not always follow that firms located close to each other actually are linked together through such transactions. Firms may be geographically proximate but functionally unrelated. They will, however, benefit from the second category of agglomerative forces.

Untraded Interdependencies

These are the less-tangible benefits derived from geographical clustering, both economic—such as the development of an appropriate pool of labor—and sociocultural. Amin and Thrift emphasize this sociocultural basis of agglomeration, arguing that it facilitates three particular processes: (1)

face-to-face contact; (2) social and cultural interaction—"to act as places of sociability, of gathering information, establishing coalitions, monitoring and maintaining trust, and developing rules of behavior"; and (3) enhancement of knowledge and innovation—"centers are needed to develop, test, and track innovations, to provide a critical mass of knowledgeable people and structures, and socio-institutional networks, in order to identify new gaps in the market, new uses for and definitions of technology, and rapid responses to changes in demand patterns."[11] More broadly, large-scale urban agglomerations make possible the supply of a whole range of other facilities that would not be possible under geographically dispersed circumstances.

In a whole variety of ways, therefore, once established, a localized economic cluster or agglomeration will tend to grow through a process of cumulative, self-reinforcing development. The cumulative nature of these processes of localized economic development emphasizes the significance of historical trajectory. It has become common to use terminology from evolutionary economics to describe the process as being *path-dependent*.[12] Thus a region's (or a nation's) economy becomes "locked in" to a pattern that is strongly influenced by its particular history. This locking in may be either a source of continued strength or, if it embodies too much organizational rigidity, a source of weakness. However, even for "successful" regions, such path dependency does not imply the absolute inevitability of continued success. The important point is that *place* matters; that *territorialization* remains a significant component in the organization of economic activity.

The geoeconomy, therefore, can be pictured as a geographically uneven, highly complex and dynamic web of production chains, economic spaces, and places connected together through threads of flows. But the spatial *scale* at which these processes operate is, itself, variable. So, too, is the meaning that different scales have for different actors within the global economic system. The tendency is to collapse the scale dimension to just two: the global and the local. Much has been written about the global-local tension at the interface between the two. Firms, states, local communities, it is argued, are each faced with the problem of resolving that tension. However, the processes of globalization are not simply unidirectional, from the global to the local. All globalization processes are deeply embedded, produced, and reproduced in particular contexts. As Nigel Thrift argues, the global is not some deus ex machina. Rather, the "local and the global intermesh, running into one another in all manner of ways."[13] However, it is a mistake to focus only on the two extremes of the scale—the global and the local—at which economic activities occur. It is more realistic to think in terms of interrelated scales of activity and of analysis: For example, the local, the national, the regional (i.e., supranational), and the global. These have meaning both as activity spaces in that economic and political actors operate and also as analytical categories that more accurately capture some of the complexity of the real world.

We also need to bear in mind that these scales are not independent entities. Individual industries (production/commodity chains) can be regarded as vertically organized structures that operate across increasingly extensive geographical scales. Cutting across these vertical structures are the territorially defined political-economic systems that, again, are manifested at different geographical scales. It is at the points of intersection of these dimensions in "real" geographical space where specific outcomes occur, where the problems of existing within a globalizing economy—whether as a business firm, a government, a local community, or an individual—have to be resolved.

Globally, we are moving from a situation of *shallow integration,* manifested largely through arm's-length trade in goods and services and international movements of portfolio capital, to one of *deep integration,* which involves not merely trade but also production organized primarily by transnational corporations (TNCs). However, although there are undoubtedly globaliz*ing* forces at work, we do not have a fully global*ized* world economy. Globalization should be regarded as a complex of interrelated processes rather than an end-state. Such tendencies are highly uneven in time and space. In taking such a process-oriented approach, it is important to distinguish between processes of internationalization and processes of globalization. Too often, these terms are used interchangeably.

Whereas internationalization involves the simple extension of economic activities across national boundaries, globalization is a qualitatively different process, involving the functional integration of internationally, dispersed activities. Both processes—internationalization and globalization—coexist. In some cases, what we are seeing is no more than the continuation of long-established international dispersion of economic activities. In others, however, we undoubtedly are seeing an increasing dispersion and integration of activities across national boundaries. We are witnessing the emergence of a new geoeconomy that is qualitatively different from the past but in which both processes of internationalization and globalization and of shallow and deep integration continue to coexist. However, they do so in ways that are highly uneven in space, in time, and across economic sectors.

The Primary Forces Shaping the Geoeconomic Map

Unraveling the complexity of the contemporary geoeconomy is a difficult task. It is tempting to seek a single causal mechanism, such as technological change or the transnational corporation, and, as is so often done, to downplay the role of the state in our allegedly "borderless" world. The approach adopted here is to argue that these three forces are tightly interconnected and that, together, they help to clarify at least the broad contours of the contemporary geoeconomic map. What we observe as the outcome of so-called globalization processes is primarily the result of a dynamic interaction between TNCs and states set within a context of a volatile technological environment. There are, of course, critical differences among these three forces. Both TNCs and states are institutions, with all the structural features of such agencies. But they are very different kinds of institutions with different goals and objectives and different stakeholders. They exist in a dynamic relationship with each other. As D. M. Gordon observes, "it is perhaps most useful. . . . to view the relationship between [trans]nationals and governments as both cooperative and competing, both supportive and conflictual. They operate in a fully dialectical relationship, locked into unified but contradictory roles and positions, neither the one nor the other partner clearly or completely able to dominate."[14]

Technology is also socially and institutionally embedded, but it does not, of itself, possess agency. It is created and adopted (or not) *by* human agency: individuals, organizations, societies. In a capitalist market economy, choices and uses of technologies are influenced primarily by the drive for profit, capital accumulation and investment, increased market share, and so on. In this section I deliberately focus on the geographical dimensions of the three forces. I begin with technology not because it plays the deterministic role in shaping the global geoeconomy but because it is a fundamental facilitator or enabler of economic-geographical change. I focus on two aspects of the geography of technological change: first, the tendency for technological activity to be highly localized geographically; second, the transformation of time-space relationships.

Technological Change Is Intrinsically Geographical

Technological change is "the prime motor of capitalism," "the fundamental force in shaping the patterns of transformation of the economy,"[15] "the chronic disturber of comparative advantage."[16] However, while being justifiably seduced by the broad sweep of technological change, by periodic shifts in technoeconomic paradigms,[17] and by the timespace shrinkage qualities of technological changes in transportation and communications, we need to bear in mind that all technologies originate in specific geographical locations and that their subsequent diffusion has a strong geographical dimension. This is true even of such apparently "spaceless" phenomena as the Internet.

The large-scale shifts in technoeconomic paradigm that have occurred periodically throughout history and that have had such a transformative effect on society have all had very distinctive geographies. Technological leadership in one Kondratiev wave, for example, is not necessarily maintained in succeeding waves. The technological leaders of the first Kondratiev (K1) were Britain, France, and Belgium. In K2 these were joined by Germany and the United States. K3 saw technological leadership firmly established in Germany and the United States, although the other lead countries were still prominent and had been joined by Switzerland and the Netherlands. By K4 Japan, Sweden, and the other industrialized countries were in the leadership group. Most recently, K5 has seen a more prominent role in technological leadership played by Japan and, more unexpectedly, by the emergence of two of the East Asian NIEs, Taiwan and South Korea, to prominent technological positions in specific areas. But there is a further dimension to the geography of technological leadership. "Just as on the international stage, so within each of the leading national economies: The locus of the leading-edge innovative industries has switched from region to region, from city to city. From the birth of New IT [information technologies] in the second Kondratiev and on through the third, Berlin and the Boston–New York Corridor were the main global centers of innovation; during the fourth, they were supplemented or supplanted by new urban centers such as Southern California, Silicon Valley, the Western Crescent around London, the Stuttgart-Munich Corridor, and the Tokaido Megalopolis."[18]

Such geographically concentrated technological activity does not occur by accident. As J. S. Metcalfe and N. Dilisio assert, "conditions of knowledge accumulation are highly localized."[19] Innovation—the heart of technological change—is fundamentally a learning process. Such learning—by "doing," by "using," by observing from and sharing with others—depends on the accumulation and development of relevant knowledge of very wide variety. Of course, the development of highly sophisticated communications systems facilitates the diffusion of knowledge at unprecedented speed and over unprecedented distances. The fact remains, however, that knowledge is produced in specific places and often used and enhanced most intensively in those same places. A key concept, therefore, is that of the *innovative milieu* that forms the specific sociotechnological context within which innovative activity is embedded. It consists of a mixture of both tangible and intangible elements: the economic, social, and political institutions themselves, the knowledge and know-how that evolves over time in a specific context (the "something-in-the-air" notion identified many decades ago by Alfred Marshall), and the "*conventions,* which are taken-for-granted rules and routines between the partners in different kinds of relations defined by uncertainty."[20]

The scale of such milieux may vary from the national down to the local. Distinctive national innovation systems exist, as R. R. Nelson has demonstrated.[21] But at the heart of such national systems we invariably find geographically localized innovative milieux. Consequently: Geography plays a fundamental role in the process of innovation and learning, since innovations are in most cases less the product of individual firms than of the assembled resources, knowledge and other inputs and capabilities that are localized in specific places. The clustering of inputs such as industrial and university R & D [research and development], agglomerations of manufacturing firms in related industries, and networks of business-service providers may create scale economies, facilitate knowledge-sharing and cross-fertilization of ideas and promote face-to-face interactions of the sort that enhance effective technology transfer. . . . Two main features help explain the advantage of spatial agglomeration in this context: the involvement of inputs of knowledge and information which are essentially "person embodied," and a high degree of uncertainty surrounding outputs. Both require intense and frequent personal communications and rapid decision-making, which are arguably enhanced by geographic proximity between the parties taking part in the exchange. Indeed, in the present era of rapid global dissemination of codified knowledge, we may even argue that tacit, and spatially more "sticky" forms of knowledge are becoming more important as a basis for sustaining competitive advantage."[22]

Local innovative milieux, therefore, consist essentially of a nexus of untraded interdependencies set within a temporal context of path-dependent processes of technological change.[23] I outlined the major elements of these processes in general terms earlier. The point of emphasizing the "untraded" nature of the interdependencies within such milieux is to distinguish the "cement" that binds this kind of localized agglomeration from that which may be associated with the minimization of transaction costs (e.g., of materials and components transfers) through geographical proximity. M. Storper uses the term "technology district" to differentiate geographical clusters based on "product based technological learning" from those based on other types of industrial district.[24] Such technological agglomerations form one of the most significant features of the contemporary global economy, as Scott demonstrates in chapter 4 of this book.

It is, of course, the transformation of time-space relationships through technological developments in transportation and communications systems that have received most attention in the globalization literature. There can be no doubt that, in time-space terms, the world has shrunk. But such shrink-age, and all the connotations and interpretations associated with it, is far more complex than usually recognized. Although the world has become more com-pressed in relative terms, this phenomenon is highly uneven geographically. Technological developments in transportation and communications affect places (and people) in a highly differentiated way. What the geographer Don-ald Janelle called "time-space convergence" affects some places far more than others. While the world's leading national economies and the world's major cities are being pulled closer together, others—less-industrialized countries or smaller towns and rural areas—are, in effect, being left behind. In reality, the time-space surface is highly plastic. Some parts shrink while other parts be-come, in effect, extended. By no means are benefits from technological inno-vations in transportation observed everywhere.

A similar unevenness applies in the sphere of electronic communications, although perhaps in rather less obvious ways. While in a general sense com-munications costs are becoming increasingly insensitive to distance, there re-main immense geographical (and social) variations in access to such technologies. The electronic highways of the information age do not, in fact, have universal interconnectedness. In general, the places that benefit most from innovations in the communications media are the "important" places. New investments in communications technology are market-related; they go to where the returns are likely to be high. The cumulative effect is to rein-force both certain communications routes at the global scale and to enhance the significance of the nodes (cities/countries) on those routes. For example, although developing countries contain around 75 percent of the world's population they have only around 12 percent of the world's telephone lines." A new geography of rich and poor is emerging with the poor now those de-prived of access to. . . . communications technology."[25] Within this geo-graphically uneven communications surface there is also a social dimension. Not everybody—whether business firms or private individuals—has equal access. Despite the general decline in communications costs driven by tech-nological change, the costs of usage are far from trivial.

"Contested Territory": The State in the Contemporary Geoeconomy

Just as it is all too easy to perceive the "end of geography" as the inevitable outcome of technological change, so, too, it is all too easy to accept that the "end of the state" is nigh. K. Ohmae's scenario of a "borderless world" is just the latest in a line of claims of this kind.[26] While recognizing that the posi-tion of the nation-state certainly is being redefined, I reject the view that it is no longer a major player in the global economic system. I agree with R. Wade's position that "reports of the death of the national economy are greatly exaggerated."[27] While some of the state's capabilities are, indeed, being reduced, and while there may well be a process of "hollowing out" of the national state, the process is not a simple one of uniform decline on all fronts.[28] The nation-state remains a most significant force in shaping the world economy, for, although national boundaries may be far more permeable than in the past, as a territorial unit it continues to be the container of distinctive "cultures" and institutional practices (as captured, for example, in R. D. Whitley's concept of the business system[29]). The fact that nation-states act as containers of distinctive "cultures" means that "ways of doing things"—including how states attempt to regulate economic activities within and across their jurisdictions—tend to vary across national boundaries. Of course, such containers are not watertight; cultural leakage is common and is being accelerated by technological developments in the communications media. Nevertheless, there is a good deal of compelling evidence to support the notion of the persistence of national distinctiveness—although not necessarily uniqueness—in structures and practices that help to shape local, national, and international patterns of economic activity.

All states, therefore, continue to perform a key role in the ways in which their economies operate, although they differ substantially in the specific measures they employ and in the precise ways in which such measures are combined. Although a high level of contingency may well be involved (no two states behave in exactly the same way even in the face of identical circumstances), certain regularities in basic policy stance may be identified. These regularities reflect the kinds of cultural, social, and political structures, institutions, and practices in which they are embedded. For example, the precise policy mix adopted by a state will be influenced by such variables as: the nation's political and cultural complexion and the strength of institutions and interest groups; the size of the national economy, especially that of the domestic market; the nation's resource endowment, both physical and human and its capacity to alter that endowment; the nation's relative position in the world economy, including its level of economic development and degree of industrialization.[30]

Within the literature on the political economy of economic development it has become common to distinguish between two broad ideal-types: The market-rational (regulatory) state, on one hand, and the plan-rational (developmental) state on the other.[31] This distinction has proven to be an extremely useful, if crude, framework within which to understand, in particular, some of the major economic policy differences of individual states, especially the differences between the older industrialized economies of Europe and North America and the newly industrializing countries of East Asia. However, such a dichotomization tends to create an impression of homogeneity within the developmental state group that is patently not there.

Although they are grouped together frequently, the world's NIEs are a highly heterogeneous collection of countries. They vary enormously in size (both geographically and in terms of population), in their natural resource endowments, and in their cultural, social, and political complexions. But they all do tend to have one feature in common: the central role of the national state in their economic development. Despite many popular misconceptions, none of today's (or yesterday's) NIEs is a free-wheeling market economy; the state plays a highly interventionist role in every case. However, even allowing for this central characteristic, M. Douglass warns, with some force, that it is highly misleading to group the Asian NIEs into an "undifferentiated model of the 'developmental state.' A closer examination reveals significant differences among them in terms of the state's relations to capital, labour, and the external economy."[32]

The nation-state continues to be highly significant in the world economy. Its territorial "container" role, molded by its individual history, means that a considerable degree of geographical distinctiveness and diversity remains. Despite increasing openness, national boundaries still represent significant discontinuities on the earth's surface. Only in very few cases is one not aware of moving from one country to another. Even within the European Union, where internal border checks are being dismantled rapidly, this remains the case. However, this example also points to another key development: the increasing tendency for nation-states to enter into regional economic groupings based, at least initially, on trade agreements.

There is no doubt that the number of regional trading arrangements has grown dramatically. Between 1948 and 1994, 109 such agreements (many of them bilateral) were notified to the General Agreement on Tariffs and Trade (GATT). There was an especially marked upsurge during the late 1980s and 1990s: Between 1990 and 1994, no fewer than 33 regional trading agreements were so notified. Again, however, it must be recognized that all such regional groupings cannot be treated as homogeneous phenomena. Most are no more than simple free trade agreements. Only a very small number involve higher degrees of integration, and only one, the European Union, can be regarded as having a really high degree of political integration. There are enormous differences, therefore, in the degree of political-economic integration among the three poles of the global triad. Indeed, in the Asia-Pacific region, there is no formal institution comparable to either the European Union (EU) or the North American Free Trade Agreement (NAFTA). Indeed, the Asia-Pacific Economic Cooperation Forum (APEC) is committed to an open, multilateral trading system rather than an inward-looking one. "APEC was promoted by several nations who are deeply committed to the multilateral trading system and concerned about the possibilities of a world divided into blocks that would discriminate against outsiders. Thus, while APEC is itself a regional arrangement, it has the paradoxical mission of combating (preferential) regionalism."[33] Again, therefore, the picture is one of geographical diversity within the state system rather than of uniformity.

Transnational Corporations Are Not "Placeless"

More than any other single institution, it is the transnational corporation that has come to be regarded as the primary shaper of the contemporary global economy. The rise of the TNC—especially of the massive global corporation—is seen to pose the major threat to nation-state autonomy. Not only has there been a massive growth of foreign direct investment (FDI), but the sources and destinations of that investment have become increasingly diverse. But FDI is only one measure of TNC activity. Because the FDI data are based on ownership of assets they do not capture the increasingly intricate ways in which firms engage in international operations through collaborative ventures and through coordinating and controlling production chain transactions. Hence, a much broader definition of the TNC must be adopted than that normally used in the conventional literature. A transnational corporation should be defined as a firm that either owns operations in more than one country or that has the power to coordinate and control such operations even if it does not own them.

The TNC sculpts the coordination and configuration of production chains and, therefore, much of the changing geography of the global economy through decisions to invest or not to invest in particular geographical locations. The resulting flows of materials, components, and finished products as well as technological and organizational expertise between geographically dispersed operations also molds the process. Although the relative importance of TNCs varies considerably—from industry to industry, from country to country and between different parts of the same country—there are now few parts of the world in which TNC influence, whether direct or indirect, is not important. In some cases, indeed, TNC influence on an area's economic fortunes can be overwhelming.

A major ingredient of the "globalization" scenario is the idea that many TNCs are global corporations whose ways of doing things are converging toward a single globally integrated model. The pressures of operating in a globally competitive environment, it is argued, are creating a uniformity of strategy and structure among TNCs. By implication, all TNCs are moving inexorably along the same path. In so doing TNCs lose all identification with or allegiance to particular countries or communities. They become, in effect, placeless. Both Robert Reich and Kenichi Ohmae claim that TNCs have become, or are becoming, "denationalized." In Ohmae's exhortation to managers: "Before national identity, before local affiliation, before German ego or Italian ego or Japanese ego—before any of this comes the commitment to a single, unified global mission. . . . Country of origin does not matter. Location of headquarters does not matter. The products for which you are responsible and the company you serve have become denationalized."[34]

I believe that this scenario of placeless global corporations needs to be challenged. It is yet another example of the end-of-geography thesis that does not stand up to empirical verification. Not only are there very few, if any, truly global corporations, but TNCs also remain strongly affected by specific national and local environments. In particular, the TNC's home environment remains fundamentally important to how it operates, notwithstanding the geographical extensiveness of its activities. All TNCs have an identifiable home base, which ensures that every TNC is essentially embedded within its domestic environment. Of course, the more geographically extensive a TNC's operations, the more likely it will be to take on some characteristics of its host environments. But even where there is substantial local adaptation and local embeddedness, the influence of the firm's geographical origins remains very strong.

If the global corporation hypothesis is valid, then we would expect to find that at least the majority of the world's largest TNCs would have most of their assets and employment outside their home country. In fact, careful scrutiny of data from the United Nations Conference on Trade and Development (UNCTAD) reveals no clear evidence to support the view that even the 100 largest TNCs are global in terms of these indicators.[35] There is little evidence of TNCs having the share of their activities outside their home countries which might be expected if they are global firms.[36] Similarly, Y-S. Hu's analysis of company data led him to conclude that "the TNC . . . is a national corporation with international operations (i.e., foreign subsidiaries)."[37]

Thus, despite many decades of international operations, TNCs remain distinctively connected with their home base. Ford is still essentially an American company, ICI a British company, and Siemens a German company. As J. Stopford and S. Strange observe: However great the global reach of their operations, the national firm does, psychologically and sociologically, "belong" to its home base. In the last resort, its directors will always heed the wishes and commands of the government which has issued their passports and those of their families. A recent study of the boards of directors of the top 1000 US firms, for example, shows that only 12 per cent included a non-American—rather fewer, in fact, than in 1982 when there were 17 percent . . . The Japanese firm with even one token foreign director would be hard to find. Even in Europe, with the exception of binational firms like Unilever, you do not find the top management reflecting by their nationality the geographical distribution of its operations."[38]

This is not to argue that TNCs necessarily retain a loyalty to the states in which they originate. The nature of the embeddedness process is far more complex than that. The basic point is that TNCs are produced through an intricate process of embedding in which the cognitive, cultural, social, political, and economic characteristics of the national home base play a dominant part. TNCs, therefore, are "bearers" of such characteristics, which then interact with the place-specific characteristics of the countries in which they operate to produce a set of distinctive outcomes. But the home-base characteristics invariably remain dominant. This is not to claim that TNCs from a particular national origin are identical. Obviously this is not the case; within any national situation there will be distinctive corporate cultures, arising from the firm's own specific corporate history, that predispose it to behave strategically in particular ways. Take the case of the automobile industry. As U.S. companies, Ford and General Motors are quite distinctive from Toyota, Volkswagen, Fiat, or Renault. But they are also different from each other. Similarly, Toyota and Nissan are distinctive, but not identical, Japanese automobile firms; the same point can be made about the French auto producers, and so on. However, there are generally greater similarities than differences between firms from the same national base. As pointed out in the previous section, nation-states act as containers of distinctive assemblages of institutions and practices. Such business systems (to use R. D. Whitley's terminology) influence and are influenced by the firms that develop within them. Such containers help to produce particular kinds of firms.

Recent detailed empirical research by L. Pauly and S. Reich provides strong evidence to support the view that nationally based differences between TNCs tend to persist contrary to the notion of a convergence toward a standard global model of firm structure and behavior. These authors examine United States, Japanese, and German TNCs in terms of several criteria: corporate governance and financing, research and development, foreign investment, and intrafirm trade practices.

The experiences of the firms analyzed by Pauly and Reich provide strong arguments to counter the convergence hypothesis. Their evidence "shows little blurring or convergence at the cores of firms based in Germany, Japan, or the United States. . . . Durable national institutions and distinctive ideological traditions still seem to shape and channel crucial corporate decisions. . . . there remain systematic and important national differences in the operations of [TNCs]—in their internal governance and long-term financing, in their R & D activities, and in their intertwined investment and trading strategies. . . . the domestic structures within which a firm initially develops leave a permanent imprint on its strategic behavior."[39]

Some aspect of the TNCs-are-not-placeless argument is that the conditions in which firms develop in their home countries continue to exert a very strong influence on their subsequent behavior when operating elsewhere. The other aspect that geography matters concerns the extent to which firms operating in different countries take on some of the characteristics of their host environments. Although the influence of the home-base is highly significant, it is not totally deterministic of how firms operate abroad. For a whole variety of reasons—political, cultural, social—foreign firms invariably have to adapt some of their domestic practices to local conditions.[40] It is virtually impossible to transfer the whole package of firm advantages and practices to a different national environment. What results, therefore, is a varying mix of home-country and host-country influences. But although local adaptation almost invariably occurs, Pauly and Reich are probably correct in observing that although TNCs operate from different home bases they "appear to adapt themselves at the margins but not much at the core."[41]

There are, of course, many other aspects of TNC activity and behavior that are intrinsically geographical but cannot be addressed here. For example, by definition, TNCs constantly must make strategic decisions, and build and modify organizational structures in the light of the strategic tension between global integration and local responsiveness.[42] They create complex internal and external networks which, themselves, have distinctive geographies. Such networks are being restructured continuously in light of both internal and external forces for change. The creation and development of regional economic blocs is a particularly important stimulus for organizational-geographical change as firms reposition themselves and reconfigure their production chains to serve broad regional, rather than individual national, markets. These, and other, aspects of TNC activities are discussed in detail in the work of P. Dicken.[43]

Conclusion

In effect, the global economy is made up of a variety of complex intraorganizational and interorganizational networks—the internal networks of TNCs, the networks of strategic alliances, of subcontracting relationships, and of other, newer organizational forms. These intersect with geographical networks structured particularly around linked agglomerations or clusters of activities. Hence, these localized clusters are embedded in various ways into different forms of corporate networks that, themselves vary greatly in their geographical extent. Some TNCs are globally extensive; others have a more restricted geographical span. Either way, however, firms in specific places—and, therefore, the places themselves—are increasingly connected into international and global networks. The precise role played by firms in these networks will have very significant implications for the communities in which they are based. At the same time, the very character—the history, culture, institutional structures—of particular places itself exerts a considerable influence on the processes and networks we have been discussing. Specifically, place and spatial relationships within and between territorial complexes of economic activity are, in themselves, an intrinsic part of the production system as a whole. Organizational and geographical processes constitute a mutually interactive dynamic.

Technological change plays a major role in this dynamic, through its influence on both the mobility of tangible and intangible goods and services, people, and information and on the changing nature of the production process itself. But the role of technological change is not deterministic. The role of the state also remains central to these processes. TNCs may operate across borders, but their operations have to be grounded in specific national territories. Although they may be able to negotiate favorable operating conditions, they cannot totally escape either the fundamental institutional and regulatory practices contained within state boundaries or the particular social and cultural conditions that characterize the particular local community where they locate. The specific assemblage of characteristics of individual nations and of local communities not only influence how globalizing processes are experienced but also influence the nature of those processes themselves. We must never forget that all global processes originate in specific places. Thus the end of geography is an illusion.

Notes

This chapter was completed while I was Visiting Professor in the Department of Geography at the National University of Singapore. I wish to thank the

University and, especially, Associate Professor Teo Siew Eng, Head of Geography, and her colleagues for their support and hospitality. The chapter draws extensively on the third edition of my book, *Global Shift*.

1. For a counterview, see: P. Hirst and G. Thompson, "The Problem of 'Globalization': International Economic Relations, National Economic Management and the Formation of Trading Blocs," *Economy and Society* 24 (1992): 408–442; and P. Hirst and G. Thompson, *Globalization in Question* (Cambridge: Polity Press, 1996). P. Dicken, J. A. Peck, and A. Tickell explore various aspects of the globalization debates in "Unpacking the Global," in R. Lee and J. Wills, eds., *Geographies of Economies* (London: Edward Arnold, 1997).

2. This term was used as part of the title of a book on the global financial system; see Richard O'Brien, *Global Financial Integration: The End of Geography* (London: Royal Institute of International Affairs, 1992).

3. Manuel Castells's arguments were developed initially in his book *The Informational City* (Oxford: Blackwell, 1989) and have been elaborated more recently in his *The Rise of the Network Society*, vol. 1 (Oxford: Blackford, 1996).

4. Of course, Fukuyama was not writing literally of the end of history but rather of what he saw as the victory of liberal democracy, "the end point of mankind's ideological evolution."

5. See M. Storper and R. Walker, "The Spatial Division of Labour: Labour and the location of Industries," in L. Sawers and W. K. Tabb, eds., *Sunbelt/Snowbelt: Urban Development and Regional Restructuring* (New York: Oxford University Press, 1984), chapter 2.

6. See K. Ohmae, *Triad Power: The Coming Shape of Global Competition* (New York: Free Press, 1985).

7. A useful discussion of this problem can be found in chapter 11 of B. Stallings, ed., *Global Change, Regional Response: The New International Context of Development* (Cambridge: Cambridge University Press, 1995).

8. See, for example, the following works by P. Krugman: *Geography and Trade* (Leuven: Leuven University Press, 1991); *Development, Geography and Economic Theory* (Cambridge, Mass.: MIT Press, 1995); and *Pop Internationalism* (Cambridge, Mass.: MIT Press, 1996). See also K. Ohmae, *The End of the Nation State: The Rise of Regional Economies* (New York: Free Press, 1995); and M. E. Porter, *The Competitive Advantage of Nations* (London: Macmillan, 1990).

9. See chapters 5 and 6 of P. Dicken and P. E. Lloyd, *Location in Space: Theoretical Perspectives in Economic Geography*, 3d ed. (New York: Harper & Row, 1990), where the authors review the traditional economic-geographical and location-theoretic approaches to spatial concentration. The newer generation of economic geographical literature is represented in, for example: A. Amin and K. Robins, "The Re-Emergence of Regional Economies? The Mythical Geography of Flexible Accumulation," *Environment and Planning, D: Society and Space* 8 (1990): 7–34; A. Malmberg, "Industrial Geography: Agglomera-

tion and Local Milieu," *Progress in Human Geography* 20 (1996): 386–397; A. Malmberg, O. Solvell, and I. Zander, "Spatial Clustering, Local Accumulation of Knowledge and Firm Competitiveness," *Geografiska Annaler* 76B (1996): 85–97; A. J. Scott, *New Industrial Spaces: Flexible Production Organization and Regional Development in North American and Western Europe* (London: Pion, 1988); A. J. Scott, "The Geographic Foundations of Industrial Performance," *Competition & Change* 1 (1995): 51–66; M. Storper, "The Resurgence of Regional Economies, Ten Years Later: The Region as a Nexus of Untraded Interdependencies," *European Urban and Regional Studies* 2 (1995): 191–221; M. Storper, *The Regional World: Territorial Development in a Global Economy* (New York: Guilford Press, 1997); and M. Storper and R. Walker, *The Capitalist Imperative: Territory, Technology, and Industrial Growth* (Oxford: Blackwell, 1989).

10. G. Myrdal, *Rich Lands and Poor* (New York: Harper & Row, 1958), p. 26.

11. A. Amin and N. Thrift, "Living in the Global," in A. Amin and N. Thrift, eds., *Globalization, Institutions and Regional Development in Europe* (Oxford: Oxford University Press, 1994), 13.

12. See, for example: G. M. Hodgson, *Economics and Evolution: Bringing Life Back into Economics* (Cambridge: Polity Press, 1993); and J. de la Mothe and G. Paquet, eds., *Evolutionary Economics and the New International Political Economy* (London: Pinter, 1996).

13. N. J. Thrift, "Doing Regional Geography in a Global System: The New International Financial System, The City of London and the South East of England, 1984–1987," in R. J. Johnston, J. Hauer, and G. A. Hoekveld, eds., *Regional Geography: Current Developments and Future Prospects* (London: Routledge), 180–207.

14. D. M. Gordon, "The Global Economy: New Edifice or Crumbling Foundations?" *New Left Review* 168 (1988): 24–64, quoted on 61.

15. C. Freeman and C. Perez, "Structural Crises of Adjustment, Business Cycles and Investment Behaviour," in G. Dosi, C. Freeman, R. Nelson, G. Silverberg, and L. Soete, eds., *Technical Change and Economic Theory* (London: Pinter, 1988), chap. 3.

16. F. Chesnais, "Science, Technology and Competitiveness," *Science Technology Industry Review* 1 (1986): 85–129.

17. Christopher Freeman and his colleagues have written extensively on this issue. See, for example, Freeman and Perez, "Structural Crises of Adjustment."

18. P. Hall and P. Preston, *The Carrier Wave: New Information Technology and the Geography of Innovation, 1846–2003* (London: Unwin Hyman, 1988), 6, emphasis added.

19. J. S. Metcalfe and N. Diliso, "Innovation, Capabilities and Knowledge: The Epistemic Connection," in Mothe and Paquet, eds., *Evolutionary Economics,* chap. 3, quoted on 58.

20. Storper, "Resurgence of Regional Economies," 208.

21. R. R. Nelson, ed., *National Innovation Systems: A Comparative Study* (New York: Oxford University Press, 1993).

22. A. Malmberg and P. Maskell, "Towards an Explanation of Regional Specialization and Industry Agglomeration," *European Planning Studies* 5 (1997): 25–41, quoted on 28–29.

23. Storper, "Resurgence of Regional Economies."

24. M. Storper, "The Limits to Globalization: Technology Districts and International Trade," *Economic Geography* 68 (1992): 60–93. A similar idea, although expressed in a rather different way, is captured in the concept of the *technopole*. M. Castells and P. Hall, *Technopoles of the World: The Making of 21st Century Industrial Complexes* (London: Routledge, 1994).

25. M. Batty and R. Barr, "The Electronic Frontier: Exploring and Mapping Cyberspace," *Futures* 26 (1994): 699–712, quoted on 711.

26. K. Ohmae, *The Borderless World: Power and Strategy in the Interlinked Economy* (New York: Free Press, 1990). See also C. P. Kindleberger, *American Business Abroad* (New Haven, Conn.: Yale University Press, 1969).

27. R. Wade, "Globalization and Its Limits: Reports of the Death of the National Economy Are Greatly Exaggerated," in S. Berger and R. Dore, eds., *National Diversity and Global Capitalism* (Ithaca, N.Y.: Cornell University Press, 1996), chap. 2.

28. See Dicken, Peck, and Tickell, "Unpacking the Global," for a discussion of this issue. The concept of the "hollowing out" of the state is discussed by B. Jessop, "Post-Fordism and the State," in A. Amin, ed., *Post-Fordism: A Reader* (Oxford: Blackwell, 1994), chap. 8.

29. R. D. Whitley, *Business Systems in East Asia: Firms, Markets and Societies* (London: Sage, 1992).

30. For a full discussion of state economic policies and detailed examples from different contexts, see D. Dicken, *Global Shift: Transforming the World Economy,* 3d ed. (New York: Guilford Press, 1998).

31. In fact, Henderson and Appelbaum put forward a fourfold typology. See J. Henderson and R. P. Appelbaum, "Situating the State in the East Asian Development Process," in R. P. Appelbaum and J. Henderson, eds., *States and Development in the Asian Pacific Rim* (London: Sage, 1992), chap. 1.

32. M. Douglass, "The 'Developmental State' and the Newly Industrialized Economies of Asia," *Environment and Planning, A* 26 (1994): 543–566, quoted on 543.

33. R. Z. Lawrence, *Regionalism, Multilateralism, and Deeper Integration* (Washington, D.C.: The Brookings Institution, 1996), 87–88.

34. Ohmae, *The Borderless World,* 94.

35. UNCTAD, *World Investment Report 1996: Investment, Trade and International Policy Arrangements* (New York: United Nations, 1996).

36. Using slightly different data, W. Ruigrok and R. Van Tulder reach similar conclusions in *The Logic of International Restructuring* (London: Routledge, 1995).

37. Y.-S. Hu, "Global Firms Are National Firms with International Operations," *California Management Review* 34 (1992): 107–126.
38. J. M. Stopford and S. Strange, *Rival States, Rival Firms: Competition for World Market Shares* (Cambridge: Cambridge University Press, 1991), 233.
39. L. W. Pauly and S. Reich, "National Structures and Multinational Corporate Behavior: Enduring Differences in the Age of Globalization," *International Organization* 51 (1997): 1–30, quoted on 1, 4.
40. T. Abo provides a detailed empirical analysis of the experience of Japanese foreign manufacturing transplants in his edited work *Hybrid Factory: The Japanese Production System in the United States* (New York: Oxford University Press, 1994).
41. Pauly and Reich, "National Structures and Multinational Corporate Behavior," 25.
42. See Y. Doz, *Strategic Management in Multinational Companies* (Oxford: Pergamon, 1986); and S. Pralahad and Y. Doz, *The Multinational Mission* (New York: Free Press, 1987).
43. Dicken, *Global Shift*.

CHAPTER 3

The Infinite Resource: Mastering the Boundless Power of Knowledge

William E. Halal, George Washington University

Introduction

Just a few years ago, most people would have laughed at the idea that business should focus on creating *knowledge*. Yet knowledge has come to dominate management attention recently as the information revolution rewires the corporation. The development of entrepreneurial organizations, collaborative alliances, and intelligent information systems comprise a watershed in economics: the discovery of powerful new principles for managing the boundless power of knowledge that drives creative enterprise. It is now clear that knowledge is the most strategic asset in enterprise, the source of all creativity, innovation, value, and social progress— the *infinite resource*.

Rewiring the Corporation

Big corporations have been dismantling their hierarchies, and myriad entrepreneurs have been starting new ventures everywhere. Now we celebrate entrepreneurial firms like ABB, composed of 5,000 self-managed units interacting freely within an "internal market." Even the U.S. government is trying to become entrepreneurial. The significance? Executives are freeing up the skills and creativity of countless ordinary people to release the knowledge lying dormant at the bottom of economies.

We also witnessed a remarkable rush of collaboration as the benefits of alliances were discovered by all organizations—large and small, partners and competitors, private and public, domestic and foreign. Having fanned an information explosion by releasing the raw energy of free enterprise, alliances harness it into productive exchanges as firms pool their technologies, marketing know-how and core competencies. In system terms, cooperation amplifies the flow of knowledge through this global network, with mounting gains in its velocity and value.

And now a third force is emerging with still more power. Just within 1997, the information revolution has accelerated a burst of activity in *organizational learning, intelligent organizations, intellectual assets,* and other exciting new concepts focusing directly on the creation and management of knowledge. All companies now boast of having an intranet managed by a CIO (chief knowledge officer) or director of corporate learning. In effect, chief executive officers (CEOs) are tracking successful management to its ultimate source—the brain of the corporation and its central nervous system connecting diverse people and numerous units into a coordinated, creative whole.

Limited Only by Intelligence, Skill, and Imagination

The possibilities are truly unimaginable, especially because we do not yet really understand the mysterious, boundless quality of this unique form of power. Knowledge inhabits a more ethereal realm with principles we are only now coming to grasp and purposes we can only imagine. Unlike other resources we are accustomed to, information is a fluid that constantly alters as it moves, increasing as it interacts and overflowing boundaries. Ray Smith, CEO of Bell Atlantic, describes this as the principle of "loaves and fishes": "Unlike raw materials, knowledge can't be used up. The more you dispense, the more you generate."[1]

Previous economic revolutions exploited a new technology, but with severe limits. The agrarian revolution spawned civilization by providing secure food supplies—but people still lived in primitive conditions and fought over limited resources. The industrial revolution harnessed machines to provide material goods—under the threats of nuclear war and environmental destruction.

The information revolution is fundamentally different because it taps a resource that is almost limitless and especially powerful. Unlike physical resources—land, labor, and capital—knowledge constantly is being created, and the supply is inexhaustible, so it resolves the age-old clash over limited means. I think it is accurate to say that—for the first time—we have access to a resource that is boundless.

The potential is so great because information technology (IT) offers a more powerful way of understanding an infinitely complex world. Science is revealing an unfathomable depth of intricate life throughout the universe, from the microscopic domain of minute organisms, to the outer reaches of space, and to the inner world of human consciousness. As physicist Freeman Dyson put it, the complexity of life stretches "Infinite in All Directions."[2]

Moreover, the information revolution is our first serious attempt to make knowledge the main task of entire societies. The world at 1997 employed almost 1 billion personal computers (PCs), each more powerful than the mainframes that formerly occupied entire rooms, cost millions of dollars, and required teams to operate. And the really big changes are yet to come. Andy Grove, CEO of Intel, claims that "computer power will soon be practically free and practically infinite."[3]

Information is the infinite resource, therefore, because it represents a boundless supply of boundless power to manage a world of boundless potential. The meteoric rise of millions of entrepreneurs such as Bill Gates and entire economies such as South Korea illustrates that we have broken the bonds once holding humankind captive to a material world. All of the normal obstacles remain, but the only serious limits lie in our intelligence, skill, and imagination. And because such prospects are almost certain to exceed our boldest estimates, we are likely to be surprised by an impending tidal wave of change that will dazzle our imaginations and test our abilities.

The New Principles of Progress

But economics traditionally has been called "the dismal science." It was based on *limited* resources, which *decrease* when shared, to produce a world of *scarcity.* That is why information is revolutionary—it challenges what we learned in the past.

This chapter brings together economic trends, data from my international survey of progressive management practices, and the views of prominent leaders to examine the revolutionary new principles for managing knowledge. Here's a quick overview of these confusing but exciting economic heresies that we will soon examine more fully:

1. Principle 1. Complexity Is Managed Through Freedom. Success is no longer achieved by planning and control but through entrepreneurial freedom among people at the bottom.
2. Principle 2. Cooperation Is Economically Efficient. Economic strength does not come from power and firmness but out of the cooperative flow of information within a corporate community.
3. Principle 3. Knowledge Is Guided by the Spirit. Abundance is not the result of material riches but of understanding the subtle workings of an infinitely complex world.

The Coming Economic Passage

Grasping the enormity of these ideas will challenge corporate managers, government officials, and scholars for years. But the relentless growth of IT should continue to drive change. Nicholas Negroponte, director of MIT's Media Lab, considers IT "A force of nature that cannot be stopped, the ultimate triumph of decentralization, globalization, and empowerment."[4]

Later I will sum up my forecasts suggesting that major advances in IT will enter the mainstream sometime during the next few years. At the end of this chapter, we will examine how the forces unleashed by this onslaught of technology are likely to drive three revolutions corresponding with the imperatives of these three principles: revolutions from control to freedom, from conflict to community, and from materialism to spirit.

As these changes reach a critical mass of people and organizations, we are likely to experience a "reversal" in economic thought roughly during the years 2000 to 2005; it should be experienced as "passing through the eye of a needle."

Economic life should be different on the other side of this passage. When the dust settles in a decade or so, business, government, and other institutions are likely to become decentralized clusters of internal enterprise units operating from the bottom up to self-manage complexity, thereby driving innovation continuously throughout society. They also will be integrated symbiotically with their various stakeholders, forming tightly knit but shifting communities of diverse economic actors. And the entire system will focus sharply on leveraging knowledge to guide strategies that serve social as well as financial goals.

It may help to think of this as a somewhat refined amalgam of three prominent corporate models that form a new theory of the firm able to master the difficult times ahead—the dynamic enterprise of MCI, combined with the collaborative working relations of Saturn, all guided by the intelligence of Microsoft.

What Replaces the Hierarchy?

It's rather obvious now that the hierarchical organization that dominated history is passing rapidly, if not already dead. The collapse of communism is but the most visible failure of hierarchy everywhere, including the decline of old corporate bureaucracies and anti-big-government sentiment.

But management today is adrift as it struggles through conflicting ideas and difficult issues—even as the level of turbulence, diversity, and change is poised to explode when the knowledge revolution reaches full force in a few years.

Management Is Swamped in Confusion

Although we have learned to improve quality, reengineer processes, form teams, and build networks, often we are swamped in confusion over today's constantly shifting maze of diverse management concepts—the flavor-of-the-month syndrome.

It is estimated that 31,000 gurus are advising companies on wildly different approaches to management, including "The Wisdom of Wolves," "Leadership Secrets of Attila the Hun," and even Indian tribal ceremonies. The flood of new management ideas is so great that scholars find no agreement on a management paradigm, and some are hard at work forming a "theory of fads."[5]

The problem becomes apparent when we try to pin down the operating principles for such popular ideas as organizational networks. Who holds the authority for major decisions in such systems? How will we know if the nodes in a network create value or destroy it? How is performance evaluated? Accountability ensured? Rewards and resources allocated? And so on.

If the answer is that top management handles these issues, what is really different? Isn't this merely a more flexible version of the hierarchy with most of the same disadvantages? After all, the old industrial age hulks of GM and IBM were awash in powerful alliances with clever partners even as they floundered in bureaucracy. If the answer is that people are free to do what they think is best, what prevents anarchy—achieving consensus among thousands of employees? Sheer good will?

Despite all the brave talk of "empowering people" to "network" in "learning organizations," the fact is that most companies remain largely controlled from the top—even though we now understand that the bulk of knowledge exists at lower ranks. It is refreshing to see other prominent scholars finally acknowledge this problem. Years ago I wrote: "The chief executive is usually the chief bottleneck." In 1996 Gary Hamel wrote in the *Harvard Business Review:* "The bottleneck is at the top."[6]

Lack of Solutions to Chronic Problems

These conflicts are also responsible for our lack of good answers to chronic problems caused by today's restructuring, which has become notorious for entrenched resistance, meager economic gains, overburdened staffs, badly served clients, and alienated people. Restructuring is certainly needed, but current approaches focus on layoffs and cost-cutting imposed on workers who have little to gain from these measures—at the very time that managers also know they must empower people, encourage collaboration, and cultivate knowledge.

A similar contradiction is destroying the legitimacy of corporate leaders. While executive pay has reached celebrity levels, employee pay has been flat for two decades, and one-third of the work force is struggling with marginal, low-paid jobs. When Robert Allen fired 40,000 workers while pocketing $3 million, AT&T suffered such damage to its reputation that the company plunged to the bottom of *Fortune* magazine's annual ranking of most admired companies. *Business Week* noted: "Making 200 times the average paycheck . . . doesn't generate respect."[7]

The prevailing view is nicely seen in the comic strip "Dilbert." Cartoonist Scott Adams has turned the absurdities of today's management into a humorous statement, making the strip a national icon representing smart young employees struggling against confused, self-serving managers. Adams may exaggerate a bit, but Dilbert captures the public's low opinion of management today.

The Big Changes Are Yet to Come

Most important, prevailing concepts are not likely to withstand the massive changes looming ahead.

The spreading of IT has unleashed hypercompetition to create a frontier of new products, markets, and services that nobody really understands yet. Entire industries such as banking, media, and education are entering some poorly grasped and widely feared upheaval. Electronic education is making today's classrooms obsolete, for instance, and so across the land academics are baffled over how to redefine what they should do, where this is going, and what it means. The liberating power of information systems also is unleashing a reservoir of employee resentment to undermine old power structures. One CEO held an electronic meeting over the company's intranet only to see executives attacked so viciously that he had to pull the plug.

Can organizations cope with this tidal wave of revolutionary change without motivated workers and inspiring leadership? How will we understand what is needed without seeing the full scope of this historic transition? One of the biggest obstacles is that managers generally do not understand how to create a different breed of bottom-up, entrepreneurial organizations, and they have a hard time believing that people would behave responsibly without direct control. To make matters worse, this topic is taboo for discussion because it involves the sensitive issue of power, adding to the confusion that thrives in management today.

This dilemma will resist solution as long as we continue to think about management within a hierarchical, profit-centered framework. Major corporations comprise economic systems that are as large and complex as national economies, yet commonly they are controlled from the top down: defining strategic initiatives, moving resources and people around, setting financial targets, and monitoring department budgets. How does this differ from the central planning that failed under communism? Why would control be bad for a national economy but good for a *corporate* economy? Can any fixed structure be useful in a world of constant change?

The Principles of Enterprise, Cooperation, and Knowledge

The following sections more fully explain the "principles of progress" now emerging to define the "New Management" needed for an information age, or what scholars call a "theory of the firm" for a knowledge-based economy.[8]

Defining the Internal Enterprise System

One of the least understood aspects of the New Management is the way autonomous business units, cross-functional teams, intrapreneurship, internal customers, and other entrepreneurial features are being used to energize organizations. If we hope to avoid the top-down disadvantages of hierarchy, a different type of organization is needed based on principles of *enterprise*. The significance of this concept is profound because it logically leads to forming complete internal market economies.

Many progressive firms have developed various versions of this basic idea, as I've explained more fully elsewhere.[9] Instead of hierarchical terms—departments, divisions, and so on—units are defined as "internal enterprises" or what the Pinchots call an "intraprise." Like all enterprises, the key to success is clearly agreed-upon standards of accountability, the widest possible entrepreneurial freedom, and the support of corporate systems and leaders. Forced by the necessity to cope with a complex new era, a variety of leading organizations have moved toward this concept, as shown in table 3.1.

Rather than a fixed structure, this is a *process* or a self-organizing *metastructure* that evolves constantly to offer all the advantages of *markets:* accountability for results, entrepreneurial freedom, incentives for achievement, rapid response time, customer focus, creativity, and the like. Charles Handy calls it a "contractual organization."[10] Because of its flexibility, the internal market concept provides an economic foundation that also facilitates other practices, such as networks, alliances, and virtual relationships.

It is important to note that there are no perfect organizational designs—internal markets incur the same disorder, risk, and turmoil of external markets. The idea is not useful in military operations, space launches, and other situations requiring close coordination of thousands of people and intricate plans, nor in routine operations facing a relatively simple, stable environment. Thus managers have to trade off the costs and gains of hierarchy vs. enterprise to find the mix that best suits the organization.

But if we hope to create dynamic organizations able to master a tenfold increase in complexity that looms ahead as far as the eye can see, it will be necessary to extend free enterprise beyond anything that now exists. Today's flexible hierarchies will not be adequate for the revolutionary technologies, sophisticated products, demanding customers, bright young employees, diverse markets, and hypercompetition now appearing around the globe. Stephen Goldsmith, mayor of Indianapolis, provided a keen summary of this view: "As we search for more effective ways to organize life in the Information Age, one of the first things we should do is to break up large, unresponsive, monopolistic governments. . . . I have learned that nothing improves government more than the introduction of competition."[11]

Within this context, most organizations look as primitive as the old Soviet economy. Consider IBM, a focal point of Corporate America. Lou Gerstner seems to have saved Big Blue from the financial abyss, but the value of its individual divisions totaled $115 billion in 1996 while the parent company's stock was valued at $65 billion. This $50 billion difference represents wealth that has been lost by IBM's corporate management. Managers claim the software division alone wastes $200 million each year getting headquarters approval of its 10,000 software projects.[12]

Rather than really using IBM's vast wealth of knowledge and creative people to pioneer the IT frontier, Gerstner's main contribution seems to

Table 3.1 Exemplars of Internal Enterprise

Dynamic Corporations: Many dynamic corporations have adopted various aspects of internal enterprise, including MCI, Xerox, Johnson & Johnson, Hewlett-Packard, Motorola, Alcoa, Clark Equipment, and Mobil Oil. General Motors withstood a labor strike to give its auto divisions the power of internal customers able to choose outside suppliers over GM units.

Internal Labor Markets: Intel, 3Com, Raychem, and an increasing number of other companies post all job openings to allow the best person to find each position. Knowledge workers are organized into self-managed teams that are paid for their performance and free to choose their leaders, coworkers, hours, methods, and all other aspects of their work.

Outsourcing and Insourcing: A powerful trend driving the shift from hierarchy to enterprise is outsourcing functions to external suppliers and insourcing to internal enterprises. This trend reached the point where Volkswagen's new "world-beater" plant in Rio de Janeiro has 80 percent of its production work done by employees of VW suppliers—an example of outsourcing within companies.

Entrepreneurial Government: Governments around the world are transforming their old bureaucracies into entrepreneurial systems. The United States, for instance, recently formed "performance-based systems" that hold agencies accountable for results and grant them wide freedom to operate free of the federal bureaucracy. Agencies such as the Department of Defense, General Services Administration, and the Government Printing Office are privatizing formerly monopolistic functions to encourage a healthy dose of internal competition.

Competing Public Utilities: Competition among utilities will soon make the battles among AT&T, MCI, and Sprint seem mild; the Baby Bells are entering the fray, and a free-market energy system is evolving in which users select among competing power suppliers.

School Choice: K–12 schools are on the verge of an entrepreneurial revolution as parental choice, voucher system, and charter schools replace the old bureaucracies with principles of enterprise.

Abroad: Japanese firms are doing business outside of their *kieretsu* families and moving to merit pay; Matsushita turned its research labs, product groups, and sales offices into self-supporting units that do business with one another. ABB's 4,500 independent profit centers have become a model of internal markets. Siemens and Lufthansa are among the German firms that have adopted the concept recently, and Semco has done the same in Brazil.

Source: Adapted from William E. Halal et al., *Internal Markets* (New York: John Wiley & Sons, 1986).

consist of imposing discipline: firing half the workforce, slashing costs and debt, and refocusing marketing efforts on IBM's old corporate customers. Here's how IBM managers describe their new boss: "His blunt style sent tremors through the organization"; "If you expect to be stroked, forget it"; "He is terribly concerned about stature, particularly his own."[13]

Hierarchical control may still may pass for leadership in such situations, but—like painting over rotted timbers—it merely masks the underlying weakness and invites catastrophe. How long can an aging Big Blue withstand the relentless advances of countless other computer makers? Competitors such as Dell Computer are applying their low-cost, on-line strategy to large machines, and even China is becoming a player.[14]

The solution is a fundamentally different approach to management that harnesses the creative talents of average people. As Fortune 500 dinosaurs downsized by 3 million employees during the past decade, smaller firms and new ventures upsized by creating 21 million new jobs.[15]

Total quality management (TQM), reengineering, and other popular practices are useful, but the main need is to shift the locus of power from top to bottom, to think of management in terms of enterprise rather than hierarchical control. I know this sounds revolutionary, but this *is* a revolution—the information revolution–one that is at least as dramatic as the industrial revolution. Just as the idea that communism might yield to markets seemed preposterous only a few years ago, a similar restructuring seems to be coming in large corporations—a "corporate perestroika."

One sign of this impending change can be seen in the devolution of power, responsibility, and rewards to operating levels. Performance-based pay for self-managed teams and business units has been growing steadily and is now beginning seriously to alter the relationship with corporate management. Here's how the trend is seen by the Hay Group, America's largest consulting firm in compensation: "Companies are putting more and more compensation on the variable side, as opposed to fixed salary, and they're weighing it more heavily to performance."[16] It takes only a little imagination to extend these trends to the point where the logic of enterprise rules rather than the logic of hierarchy. If we could recognize that economic value is created fundamentally by operating units, the way ahead becomes clear. Corporate executives should relinquish direct control by creating internal enterprises of all units down to the level of work teams.

It does not mean that CEOs give up power. They design these structures and provide leadership to unify units into a cooperative, strategically guided system. This pivotal change would also resolve today's nagging issues of downsizing, reengineering, and quality by placing the responsibility for such issues on self-managed teams that are accountable for the use of resources to serve clients profitably. In this capacity, CEOs may be more influential because they would be leading a system in which everyone shares the responsibility for success.

Forming a Cooperative Corporate Community

Principle 2 extends our understanding of strategic alliances with suppliers and business partners to include collaborative relations with employees, customers, and government. James Moore put it this way: "Competition as we've known it is dead."[17] The logical conclusion is tightly knit "corporate communities" that join the interests of all stakeholders into a productive whole.

But what about the traditional "tough" approach to business? Why would centuries of economic conflict change? It would do so because the information revolution is overthrowing this old system as surely as the industrial revolution overthrew the medieval economic system.

Just as the assembly line shifted the critical factor of production from labor to capital, the computer is shifting the critical factor of production from capital to *knowledge.* Knowledge differs because the marginal cost of duplicating it is trivial and its value increases when shared, making cooperation advantageous to all parties. This new economic reality is leading to the realization that cooperation is now efficient because it creates value. As the examples in table 3.2 illustrate, various collaborative alliances are thriving because they offer a competitive advantage.

The information age may reward cooperation, but the downside is that cooperation restricts autonomy, and so dynamic companies avoiding permanent ties by forming alliances with alternative partners. Any relationship is likely to change with shifts in technology, markets, and clients, and firms want to maintain the option of switching to other partners. So the principle of cooperation must be tempered by the equally important principle of dynamic enterprise.

This leads to an interesting paradox that pulls organizations in opposing directions: Complexity demands entrepreneurial freedom, but there is an equal need to unify this diversity into a coherent, productive whole. Managers must build trusting partnerships that form a community of common values and purpose—while acknowledging that this is a fluid, dynamic grouping of changing members. A different business culture is evolving that recognizes the need for change and even celebrates it as a natural part of life—rather like the way students enter college and then leave with fond

Table 3.2 Exemplars of Corporate Community

Research Consortia: About 250 research consortia and 1,600 business-government research aggreements have been formed in the United States. The auto industry alone has 12 consortia in which all three major carmakers work together on developing everything from new fuels to electric cars.

Supplier and Distributor Alliances: Companies such as Nike, Dell, Chrysler, Caterpillar, and Novell have improved operations by forming close relationships with suppliers and distributors.

Employee Collaboration: Raychem, Intel, Motorola, and other firms consider collaborative employee relations a key corporate strategy. They provide training, employee freedom, and attractive rewards to reduce costs, improve sales, and generate knowledge.

Relationship Marketing: Progressive firms form a trusting relationship with clients that focuses on delivering value and engaging customers in the company. A good example is the company picnic Saturn held for 30,000 Saturn owners.

Partnerships with Competitors: While GM, Ford, and Chrysler compete against Toyota, Renault, and Fiat, they also jointly design, make, and sell cars with these same adversaries. A similar blend of cooperation and competition marks relations between IBM and Apple, Nucor and USX, and Texas Instruments and Hitachi. America Online is a partner with Netscape, Sun, Microsoft, AT&T, Sprint, and MCI as well as its direct competitors Prodigy and CompuServe.

Economic Coalitions/Ecosystems: Companies such as Microsoft and Netscape organize economic coalitions, or ecosystems, uniting suppliers, manufacturers, distributors, and others in a cluster of cooperating firms centered around a major product.

Business-Government Partnerships: American cities such as Baltimore, San Antonio, and Indianapolis and 40 states are forming partnerships with business, labor, and civic groups. The U.S. government is lending Aeroflot $1 billion in return for the Russians dropping trade barriers to the sale of aircraft.

Corporate Community: Some companies have united all of these alliances into complete "corporate communities." GM Saturn, The Body Shop, and IKEA develop trusting relationships with clients, share power with workers, cooperate with suppliers and dealers, and form partnerships with government—while also making superior profits for their investors.

Source: Adapted from William E. Halal, *The New Management* (San Francisco: Berrett-Koehler, 1996).

memories of their alma mater. Ron Oklewisz, CEO of Telepad, suggests that managers should not think of "marrying" partners but simply "dating" or "going steady."

The problem is that cooperation and community run counter to the ideology of capitalism. Americans in particular are dedicated to the idea that corporations are "owned" by shareholders and so their goal should be to maximize profits.

Business must be profitable, but this view often places managers in the difficult position of opposing the interests of their employees, customers, and others whose support is essential. Employee pay and training, for instance, are then viewed as simply costs to be avoided. Against this point of view stand such companies as Marriott and Motorola that have formed employee partnerships, enjoying returns of several hundred percent on their investments in training.[18]

Let's look more closely at the issue of downsizing, an icon symbolizing this crisis of capitalism. The famous case of Al Dunlap is particularly revealing.[19] As CEO of Scott Paper, Dunlap did succeed in restructuring the firm so effectively that the company's stock rose 225 percent. That is an impressive achievement, for which he was rightly rewarded. But it is impressive mainly in terms of the capitalist ideology noted earlier. From the emerging view of corporate community, it looks very different.

Employees. The CEO received $100 million for two years of work, and other executives profited on the order of $10 million to 20 million each. Yet 12,000 people lost their jobs, which so traumatized some that they suffered strokes and other serious illnesses. Later another 8,000 were fired when the firm was sold. What could reasonably be expected about morale, stress, and productivity?

Customers. Sales fell because customers wondered about product quality and the company's ethics. Here's what one woman said: "Dunlap appears to be the embodiment of capitalism run amok—without heart, soul, or conscience. Whenever possible, I will use only the products of Scott's competitors."

Suppliers. Dunlap scrapped the annual meeting with suppliers intended to improve working relations, raise quality, and lower prices. Despite the fact that almost all well-managed firms today are developing exactly this type of collaborative relationship with their suppliers, his logic was simply "This is nonsense."

Little wonder that the Scott case aroused such passions from fellow CEOs, scholars, journalists, and ordinary people. Peter Capelli of The Wharton School had this explanation: "Dunlap didn't create value. He redistributed income from the employees and the community to shareholders."[20]

The irony is that there seems to be little redeeming value to such mindless pursuit of wealth. Earning millions does not make people happier, nor does it meet the need for social connection and meaning that we all struggle with ultimately. After his victory, Dunlap admitted feeling blue: "It was an empty feeling. There was a hollowness there, like part of me was gone." I suggest the solution lies in appreciating the crucial changes now being introduced by the information revolution. Corporate community is not social responsibility in the sense of "doing good." It is a competitive advantage.

But our actions and beliefs have not yet caught up with this new reality. If working with employees, suppliers, customers, and even competitors is beneficial, it follows that the mission of business somehow must encompass all these interests instead of simply making profit for shareholders. Dan Mehan, AT&T's vice president for international business, summed it up this way in a personal conversation: "After the quality programs, reengineering, and other innovations are implemented, the final questions that count are: Will our customers continue to patronize us because they receive value? Will our employees want to do their jobs well? Will the community accept us as good citizens?"

Modern enterprise should become a quasi-democratic institution that serves a changing community of stakeholders. As the many fine companies noted in this book demonstrate, not only are both financial and social interests perfectly compatible, they enhance one another.

My surveys show that the majority of managers now understand they must cooperate with their stakeholders and strive to serve their interests because trusting relationships are key to economic success. This is confirmed by other prominent evidence, such as *Fortune's* annual list of America's Most Admired Companies, which rates firms on scales that include employee benefits, customer service, and public goodwill.[21]

Leveraging Knowledge with an Intelligent Infrastructure

The importance of knowledge is highlighted by the fact that the value of various knowledge assets rose from 38 percent of corporate assets in 1982 to 62 percent in 1992. Human capital alone, the value producing power of employee know-how, is estimated to account for 70 percent of all wealth in modern economies. Adding in intellectual property (patents, etc.), brand names, and other forms of knowledge brings the total to more than 80 percent of corporate assets. The problem is that managers think that only about 20 percent of this strategic asset is used.[22]

To be more effective, an "intelligent infrastructure" is needed to support the entrepreneurial community. But this infrastructure requires more than the organizational learning of individuals or teams; it is the learning of an entire corporate *system* to produce organizational intelligence (OI), a higher equivalent of human intelligence.

It is now possible to combine high-performing information networks and dynamic organization structures to produce an unusual capacity to amass raw information from diverse sources, store it in common databases, distill the data into valuable knowledge, and allow units to retrieve it from any part of the network. The principles of enterprise and cooperation would provide the management system, and a distributed network of PCs operating on an intranet would provide the information system.

Please note that an intelligent infrastructure must include more than powerful information systems. Equally indispensable is the human half of the organization—all those entrepreneurial and cooperative activities that take place when small groups of people meet to solve problems, trade ideas, and help one another. These messy human interactions comprise "tacit knowledge" as opposed to the well-structured "explicit" or "formal knowledge" stored in information systems. Tacit knowledge is indispensable because this is the way people actually think, whether the human interactions involve employees doing their work, customers making purchases, or managers solving organizational problems.

A good intelligent infrastructure, therefore, consists of a corporate-wide information system and a web of close working relationships connecting entrepreneurial units to common pools of shared knowledge. The result is a "central nervous system" that "leverages" ordinary learning to powerful new levels to form an intelligent organization. If we carry this line of thought further, each individual becomes a node in this network, which then forms a "corporate brain" possessing powers of mass intelligence. Table 3.3 offers some examples.

Beyond the Technical

Beyond these technical issues, the domain of knowledge is especially daunting because it makes no sense without also embracing some worthy purpose. If modern business is to be viable, it has to do more than be productive, adaptable to change, collaborative, and knowledge seeking. It also must

Table 3.3   Exemplars of Knowledge Systems

McGraw-Hill's Information Turbine: McGraw-Hill created a corporate-wide information network, performance incentives, and training programs to unify all units into an "intellectual community," similar to a university or research lab. The central element was a knowledge base that pooled the information gathered by units, which they then could draw on to serve their clients better—aptly called an "information turbine" because it converted raw data into a stream of knowledge that "powered" the organization.

Hewlett-Packard's Knowledge Systems: HP has developed a "Computer Systems Marketing Organization" to share product information, market data, and strategic ideas. A "Corporate Information Systems" unit is putting all management procedures and personnel practices onto a Web site and Lotus Notes. A system called "Knowledge Links" supports product divisions with purchasing services, engineering data, market intelligence, and best practices. All this is unified by a "World Innovation Network" that allows employees to probe each other's experiences on what works.

Merrill Lynch's Data Base: The world's largest security broker helps its 18,000 account managers operating in 500 offices serve their millions of clients with a computer network that stores the firm's knowledge base about securities, financial forecasts, and the like.

IBM's IS Services: IBM's Chief Information Officer uses a corporate intranet to provide units with evaluations of suppliers and to match corporate buyers with sellers. All IBM purchasing is being conducted over the net, saving $1 billion per year.

Andersen Consulting's Practice Pool: Andersen uses a global network called "Knowledge Xchange" to pool the experiences and best practices of its worldwide consulting practice. The CIO said, "Our clients should get the best knowledge in the firm, not just the best in their consultant."

Sources: Adapted from Thomas Davenport, "Some Principles of Knowledge Management," *Strategy & Business* (Winter 1996): 34–41; James Quinn et al., anaging Professional Intellect," *Harvard Business Review* (March-April 1996): 71–83; "Jack Welch's Cyber-Czar," *Business Week,* August 5, 1996, 82–83.

comprise a civilized economic system that represents a better way of life. In short, it has to serve some worthy social purpose: producing valuable products and services, offering people meaningful lives, protecting the environment, and fostering a compatible global order. If it fails this test, resistance from government, labor unions, and other interests is certain.

A good example is the tobacco industry. Nicotine now imposes annual health care costs of $100 billion in addition to the 400,000 lives it cuts short every year in the United States—far more than all illegal drugs combined. But tobacco companies have resisted attempts to curtail the health risks, and now they are going global. A study by the Harvard School of Public Health found that smoking is the single biggest cause of disability and early death: "The tobacco epidemic is a global emergency."[23] In economic terms, this industry destroys hundreds of billions of dollars worth of social value to make money for its investors. Is this a worthy pursuit for grown men and women?

Although I like the idea of social purpose, I do not argue it on moral grounds but because knowledge requires it. It is ironic that having more data often leaves us *more confused* out of the sheer limitlessness of it all. This paradox makes information meaningless without being guided by values, vision, and purpose. That's why we see a rising interest in these qualities among organizations, even including spirituality.

A focus on purpose is badly needed to quell the constant flood of problems flowing directly out of business's myopic focus on money. For instance, the health care industry recently outraged the nation by cutting costs rather heartlessly to improve profits. Predictably, Congress and most states are outlawing gag clauses that prohibit physicians in health maintenance organizations (HMOs) from telling patients about costly treatments, are preventing HMOs from forcing new mothers out of the hospital one day after delivery, and are imposing other such regulations.

How did a great profession once dedicated to serving humanity get into such a mess? The answer seems rather easy: In an attempt to run today's notion of a good business, HMOs lost sight of their main purpose. We must all control costs, obviously, and investors must be rewarded to risk capital. But the final goal of business has to serve society somehow. If HMOs could look past the bottom line, they would find vast opportunities for serving unmet health needs.

Rather than simply treating illness, progressive health care systems *prevent* illness by helping people adopt healthy lifestyles, avoid harmful habits such as smoking, prevent accidents, and adopt other wellness measures. One HMO's staff visits patients to help improve their living habits because doing so is far cheaper than paying for expensive operations later, thus costs are reduced while health care is improved. Jon Glaudemans, general manager of Aetna's Healthcare operations, agrees: "To achieve future costs savings, we must succeed in keeping patients healthy."[24]

Almost every other industry and profession lends itself to a similar transformation, and many notable companies have demonstrated the power of adopting some worthy purpose. Anita Roddick of Body Shop fame transformed the cosmetics industry by serving the burgeoning need of people around the world for safe, inexpensive ways to care for their bodies while protecting nature. Skip Lefauve invented a human-centered enterprise by designing the Saturn company in self-managed teams of workers producing top-quality, inexpensive cars that are sold free of sales pressure.

If we could seriously reexamine the myriad problems that abound today, we would see that they offer equally numerous opportunities for successful business. These problems can be reinterpreted insightfully as a vast frontier for a new type of enterprise, one that creates value out of working with its constituencies to serve everyone's needs better.

The Coming Economic Reversal

Let me play devil's advocate here by raising the doubts that dwell on the minds of most people. Why should managers struggle to adopt these draconian measures? If we just let the marketplace do its work, companies will remain competitive without all these dramatic and uncertain changes. CEOs will never relinquish their power, nor should they if we hope to maintain an orderly world. It's naive to think that we should just transform organizations into some chaotic type of enterprise system, cooperate with everyone in sight, and use knowledge to improve the social welfare.

The Old Rules No Longer Apply

The prospect of major change always evokes these objections. Who would have believed that communism would just collapse? That the U.S. government would "reinvent" itself? That the most powerful corporations would enter decline and be forced to restructure, reengineer, and reform?

The message I want to stress is that the world is entering such an uncharted new frontier, an epoch so fundamentally different that the old rules no longer apply. The conventional wisdom of the past must be replaced by concepts that conform with the new realities of infinite knowledge: Success is be best achieved through entrepreneurial freedom; strength comes through cooperative community; and abundance flows out of a subtle frontier of boundless understanding, meaning, and spirit.

These are not simply theories, they are descriptions of leading practices that represent the primary source of economic power today. And there will be little margin for error. A sharp look at a few major trends quickly reveals that a massive upheaval looms ahead. Andy Grove of Intel put it best: "The Internet is like a tidal wave, and we are in kayaks."[25]

The Coming Tenfold Leap in Growth

Has it been only a few years since the Internet became the de facto communications network for a new global order? The Internet has been accepted by roughly 50 million people and 500,000 companies around the world, and intranets and extranets have become the standard for organizational communications. By 2000, the Internet is projected to reach 250 million people—still only a few percent of its potential as the world's primary communication service.

The same exponential growth is expected for telephones, television, wireless, and other communication technologies. Satellites now beam TV coverage to 1.2 billion people on every continent and will soon reach most of the other 4 billion. Wireless service for voice, fax, data, and video is growing 50 percent per year and by 2000 should reach most people in industrialized nations and many in developing nations.

Even more revolutionary technologies lie right around the corner. Dell Computer has figured out how to sell $1 million worth of PCs over the Internet per day. Several ventures are under way to launch hundreds of satellites that will provide an "internet in the sky" for anyone around the world. Webcasting, Java applets, intelligent agents, virtual communities, the video PC, and other paradigm-breaking innovations are sure to follow.

These trends paint a bold but realistic scenario about A.D. 2000 to 2005, when all social and economic activities may be conducted electronically. The typical home or office likely will be connected into a worldwide system where people can shop, work, bank, play, learn, and even worship over interactive multimedia networks. The richness of this system should combine the intelligence of a computer, the communications of the telephone, and the vivid reality of television. Rather than hunching over a keyboard, we may use voice commands to write documents, make phone calls, hold video conferences, and watch movies and TV images—all projected on wall monitors with life-size images.

As these advanced technologies move capital, knowledge, technology, and even labor swiftly around the world seeking their highest returns, a brushfire of competition is roaring over governments, corporations, and individuals to drive change in these general directions.

To top it off, this raging process of globalization is likely to increase economic growth tenfold. Apart from the satiated West, most of the world is starved for the same material comforts now enjoyed by a few prosperous nations. Moreover, there are five times more people in undeveloped nations than in developed nations, a figure that is almost certain to double as countries industrialize. Thus the stark reality is that all of today's major crises are likely to increase by roughly a factor of ten over the long term.

Specifically, the level of industrial production, international competition, change and innovation, demand for scarce resources, environmental degradation, and cultural diversity will all grow roughly tenfold. The industrialization of China alone should at least double these crises, and India will double them again.

In short, the world faces an unprecedented challenge of creating a new system of political economy that can manage this leap in growth on a planet already suffering from congestion, conflict, scarcity, environmental stress, and complexity. To believe that an extension of our current system will somehow muddle through is wishful thinking.

The great scientist, science fiction author, and futurist Arthur C. Clarke studied obstacles to change: the countless experts who always seem to claim that "man would never fly" and all the many other great advances of history were impossible. Clarke found that the evidence to forecast these historic turning points was always available and the revolutionary impact was well understood. The problem was a failure of imagination and nerve: the inability of smart people to fathom the strong likelihood that the world soon will behave very differently, and their lack of courage to acknowledge what they suspected. [26]

Most managers are failing to lead because they suffer from Clarke's failure of imagination and nerve. Much of what passes for informed debate today is simply out of touch with the huge challenge that looms dead ahead. It could be thought of a "crisis of maturity." People in all nations must learn to manage the inevitable transition to a technological world of unfathomable complexity and change; there is no alternative.

Moving through the Passage

If these arguments are valid, economies are passing through a complex set of three revolutions that is quietly gathering momentum. Exploding complexity is relentlessly decentralizing institutional controls, the benefits of collaboration are attracting diverse parties into pockets of corporate community, and knowledge invariably leads to a search for meaning and purpose. The increasing role women play at work, different attitudes of the young, and a general shift in values also should exert strong movement in this general direction.

Something like this is certainly needed. As free markets restructure the global economy, all this creative destruction is tearing the comfortable safety nets of the welfare state, leaving people without the support of a civil society. The disparity of incomes between the top and bottom classes in the United States has returned to the levels reached prior to the Great Crash and depression, exceeding that of all other industrialized nations. Overall, indices of social well-being have fallen to new lows.[27]

At a 1996 meeting of the World Economic Forum in Switzerland, William Bennett and Rosabeth Moss Kanter cautioned that the loss of public support is causing a "backlash against capitalism." Even George Soros—perhaps the most famous capitalist of our time—issued a warning in an article titled "The Capitalist Threat." The 1997 elections of socialist leaders in France and the Labour Party in Britain highlight the problem, and they also show that there is more than one way to organize the global economy."[28]

Europeans, Japanese, and people of almost all other nations know they must encourage free markets to gain economic growth. "We are falling further behind in the race to stay competitive in a global economy," said a German politician. But they also accept the fact that they cannot abandon their citizens to the randomness of markets. A German business executive said: "We understand that poverty and other social ills are morally unacceptable and economically harmful." Norio Ohga, CEO of Sony, agrees: "We simply cannot fire people. It would only worsen the economy, and we really can't afford that."[29]

The only way I can imagine this conflict being resolved is by *moving through the passage*—by using the potential of this approaching economic reversal. The key is to see that free enterprise is not necessarily "capitalism." As I've stated earlier, enterprise is no longer powered primarily by capital—it is powered by knowledge.

Accepting this pivotal fact then opens the path to a new system of political economy appropriate for a knowledge-based global order—the model I have outlined, in which small self-managed enterprises form pockets of corporate community, all guided by knowledge to serve worthy purposes. Britain's Prime Minister Tony Blair proposed this same synthesis of the right and left: "Free markets and social welfare are not incompatible."[30]

One crucial, symbolic action would signify this institutional revolution, help us grasp it and live up to it. Americans should stop calling their economic system "capitalism." I know Americans prize free markets, but capitalism is only one type of market system dedicated to the pursuit of capital, profit, and the other material factors that worked in the industrial past.

Americans who want to draw on the energy of the future should define the economic system in terms of the resources of the future—the infinite power of enterprise, community, and knowledge. I suggest that a more accurate, fitting name would be democratic enterprise.

Events are almost certain to surprise us, and I wonder if we appreciate the difficulties ahead. Industrial age values and systems may yield to their information age equivalent, but there is still no free lunch. The price for these gains is that organizational life is likely to resemble that great icon of information technology, the Internet—dynamic and bursting with interconnected energy, but wild, untamed, and slightly out of control.

At some point soon, however, a critical mass will grasp the logic of this emerging world, bringing about historic reversal from power to freedom, conflict to community, and materialism to spirit. My surveys show that most managers sense this shift is coming, and they think it will happen sometime between 2000 and 2005.[31] What had heretofore been considered hopelessly idealistic may then become a hard, practical reality.

The mysterious, unusually difficult, and bigger-than-life quality of the coming passage reminds me of that Bible quotation that we all know intimately but have a hard time living up to: "It is easier for a camel to pass through the eye of a needle than for a rich man to enter the kingdom of heaven." Something of this sort lies dead ahead. During the next few years we are all going to be sorely tried in a crucible of crisis to transform ourselves and our institutions. It should feel like passing through the biblical eye of a needle.

Notes

1. Quoted in William E. Halal (ed.), *The Infinite Resource* (San Fransisco: Jossey-Bass, 1998).
2. Freeman Dyson, *Infinite in All Directions* (New York: Harper & Row, 1989).
3. Grove is quoted in "A Conversation with the Lords of Wintel," *Fortune,* July 8, 1996.
4. Nicholas Negroponte, *Being Digital* (New York: Alfred A. Knopf, 1995).
5. John Micklewait and Adrian Woolridge, *The Witch Doctors: Making Sense of the Management Gurus* (New York: Times Books, 1996). Jeffrey Pfeffer, "Barriers to the Advance of Organizational Science," *Academy of Management Review* 18, no. 4 (October 1993): 599–621.
6. My comment appeared in William E. Halal, *The New Capitalism* (New York: Wiley, 1986), 128. Hamel is quoted from Gary Hamel, "Strategy as Revolution," *Harvard Business Review* (July-August 1996): 69–82.
7 "Executive Pay," *Business Week,* April 21, 1997.

8. William E. Halal, *The New Management* (San Francisco: Berrett-Koehler, 1996).
9. William E. Halal et al., *Internal Markets: Bringing the Power of Free Enterprise Inside Your Organization* (New York: Wiley, 1993).
10. Charles Handy, *Understanding Organizations* (New York: Oxford University Press, 1993).
11. Halal, *Infinite Resource.*
12. "Defending Big Blue," *Newsweek,* September 30, 1996, 50.
13. Betsy Morris, "Big Blue," *Fortune,* April 14, 1997.
14. "Going Toe to Toe with Big Blue," *Business Week,* April 14, 1997.
15. Peter Lynch, "The Upsizing of America," *Wall Street Journal,* September 20, 1996.
16. Peter Behr and David Segal, "Finding New Ways to Carve Up the Rewards," *Washington Post,* August 16, 1996.
17. James Moore, *The Death of Competition* (New York: HarperCollins, 1996).
18. Bruce Pasternack et al., "People Power and the New Economy," *Strategy & Business* 7 (Second Quarter 1997).
19. "The Shredder," *Business Week,* January 15, 1996, 56–61.
20. "Backlash," *Across the Board,* July/August 1996, 24–29.
21. Halal, *New Management,* 77. Frederick Reichheld, *The Loyalty Effect* (Cambridge, Mass.; Harvard Business School, 1996).
22. Thomas Stewart, "Trying to Grasp the Intangible," *Fortune,* October 2, 1996, 157–161; Polly LaBarre, "The Rush to Knowledge," *Industry Week,* February 19, 1996.
23. Joseph Califano, "The Tobacco Talks," *Washington Post,* June 3, 1997.
24. Quoted in David Hilzenrath, "What's Left to Squeeze?" *Washington Post,* July 6, 1997, H1.
25. Grove is quoted in "A Conversation."
26. Arthur C. Clarke, *Profiles of the Future* (New York: Holt, Rinehart, and Winston, 1984).
27. *1996 Index of Social Health* (Tarrytown, NY: Fordham Graduate Center, 1996).
28. Karen Pennar, "A Helping Hand," *Business Week,* March 24, 1997, "A Continent at the Breaking Point," *Business Week,* February 24, 1997.
29. Quoted in William Drozdiak, "German Economy Lags," *Washington Post,* May 7, 1997 Quoted in Brenyon Schendler, "Japan: Is It Changing?" *Fortune,* June 13, 1994.
30. Quoted in Paula Dwyer, "Tony Blair's Labour Party" *Business Week,* April 31, 1998, 25.
31. Halal, *The New Management.*

CHAPTER 4

Regional Motors of the Global Economy

Allen J. Scott, University of California, Los Angeles

The Geopolitics of Production and Competition

In this chapter I attempt to take stock of some critical trends in the economic and political geography of global capitalism at the end of the twentieth century and to offer a few speculations about their likely trajectory over the early decades of the next century. Specifically, my objective is to sketch out the basic locational anatomy of the contemporary global system of production and competition relative to the profound international political restructuring that also has been going on in recent times. The analysis is focused on the spatial dynamics of those dense, localized production complexes that form the world's great urbanized regions and that seem more and more to constitute the motors of the entire global capitalist system. This laconic initial formula, as I will explain, opens up an extraordinarily diverse and puzzling series of questions.

To be sure, much has already been written on the twin issues of globalization and regional development. On one side, claims frequently have been advanced about the decay of the classical territorially based sovereign state and the internationalization of economic activity in an increasingly borderless world.[1] On the other side, a large literature has accumulated on the theme of the reintensification of regionalized economic growth in contemporary capitalism and on the crucial role of regions as sources of competitive economic advantage.[2] Much, too, has been written on the interplay between these two spatial levels of economic activity (the global and the local) and on the new geopolitics of production and competition that has begun to crystallize around their interconnections.[3] This chapter is a modest effort to build on these bodies of work by reexamining some theoretical ideas about regional development processes in general and investigating their implications for a world in which political barriers to economic transactions are rapidly receding. In this manner I hope to restate yet more forcefully the view that a fundamental geographical reorganization of capitalism is currently under way involving the coalescence of a group of national economies into a globalized system and its simultaneous spatial disaggregation into a network of regional production complexes.

The chapter is in part a series of analytical and empirical observations about these matters; in part it is also a set of futurological asides about a number of dominant trends that seem to be unfolding. Its point of departure resides in the idea that the expansionary thrust of capitalism over historical time has brought it to a point of development that far exceeds the spatial and institutional bounds of the traditional sovereign state. We are steadily moving from a phase of internationalism (which pertains to a set of sovereign states and their interactions) to a phase of globalism (which refers to a single world economic system). This shift is leading, in the vocabulary of the Regulationist School, to the search for new modes of social regulation at the world scale.[4] At the same time, the widening of markets implied by the same global trend is ushering in an era of heightened competition and of ever more finely grained social divisions of labor whose net effect is to reinforce the dominant locational structure of the system as a set of far-flung regional economies. This, in turn, calls for new approaches to social regulation at the local level. As these events unfold, the economic geography of the modern world is steadily being reconstituted as a loose congeries of regional production complexes joined together in dense transactional webs, and complemented by large disjoint blocks of territory that seem simply to have been left behind by the onward march of economic progress.

The Rise of Global Capitalism

A Brief Record of Trends and Events

From its very historical beginnings, capitalism has had important international dimensions. It endemically has had a tendency to push outward beyond the frontiers of the sovereign state in the search for new sources of raw materials, new markets, new investment opportunities, and so on. However, generally, in the past, this tendency has been subservient to national interests, with the major capitalist states pulling back into protectionism and autarchy when internationalization seemed to threaten them (as happened most obviously with the collapse of world trade between the two world wars). In short, hitherto capitalism has always been embodied within *national* economies, with the central apparatus of the state playing a major role in shaping its evolutionary course.[5] The vigorous development of large-scale fordist industry in the early decades of the twentieth century reinforced the connection between capitalism and the sovereign state, and all of the economically advanced countries sought, wherever possible, to promote their own self-sufficiency in major mass production sectors, such as steel, chemicals, cars, domestic appliances, packaged foods, and so on. The connection was sealed by the peculiar national versions of Keynesian and welfare-statist policy that emerged after World War II in response to certain systemic failures of the fordist model of industrial and social development.

Even so, the mutual advantages to be obtained from intercountry trade and other forms of economic exchange led to concerted political efforts over the postwar years to put in place the bases of an orderly international system. The critical initiatory event of this new economic dispensation was the Bretton Woods Conference of 1944, where arrangements for a prospective international currency system were worked out. The conference also established two major financial institutions, the International Monetary Fund and the World Bank, to carry out its mandates. In 1947 the General Agreement on Tariffs and Trade (GATT) was established to regulate trade between the main capitalist countries, with Japan joining in 1955. Under the hegemonic leadership of the United States, these and a succession of analogous arrangements became the foundation for rapid expansion of international economic exchange over the postwar years, just as they also served as bulwarks of the world anticommunist coalition.

Under the aegis of this pax Americana, the Western European and Japanese economies developed apace in the 1950s and 1960s, and the groundwork for a durable and growing international capitalist system was firmly established, notwithstanding the severe instabilities that began to make their appearance in the 1970s. By the early part of that decade the economic hegemony of the United States plainly was starting to wane, as symbolized most dramatically by President Richard Nixon's decision in 1971 to remove the U.S. dollar from the gold standard. Within two years of this event, the currencies of all the major capitalist countries were floating (leading to vastly augmented speculative surges of foreign exchange transactions around the world). The resulting climate of fiscal insecurity was then exacerbated by the oil shocks of the mid- and late 1970s. This was a time, too, when the great national fordist production systems that had flourished in North America and Western Europe over the long postwar boom were displaying signs of severe crisis, itself a symptom and a cause of an accelerating pace of internationalization. On one hand, the crisis of fordism was in part an outcome of rising imports into North America and Western Europe of mass-produced goods from Japan and the emerging newly industrialized countries; on the other hand, the same crisis induced a frantic search for lower costs of production by American and European fordist enterprise, provoking in turn a massive shift of branch plants to overseas locations. The consequence of these trends was the breakup and dispersal of much of the apparatus of fordist production and eventually the wholesale abandonment of the Keynesian, welfare-statist policies that had provided its institutional backbone.

The Current Conjuncture

In the new more open, more competitive, and markedly less interventionist economic and political realities that were beginning to materialize in the wake of the collapse of fordism in the late 1970s and early 1980s, the globalization of capitalist production systems continued its rapid, if erratic, forward advance. Many new and resurgent flexible production sectors were starting to move into leading-edge positions as foci of growth in the advanced economies, and their products were now entering world trade in large volumes alongside more traditional items of international commerce such as commodities, heavy industrial materials, and mass-produced goods. Almost all of these sectors are in one way or another caught up within extensive international commodity chains,[6] but typically they also are anchored locationally within densely agglomerated production complexes.

Such sectors constitute much of the dynamic core of modern capitalism. They are prominently although by no means exclusively accounted for by a triad of broad economic segments, namely, (1) high-technology manufacturing with its enormously diverse range of outputs; (2) an assortment of sectors engaged in the fabrication of design-intensive consumer goods ranging from high-fashion footwear, to luxury cars, to entertainment products selling in market niches throughout the world; and (3) business and financial services, which have grown with particular rapidity over the last couple of decades and which are one of the cornerstones of today's international economy. Concurrently, investments in foreign branch plants have grown apace and have been one of the major forces behind the outward extension of capitalism. It is useful to note for subsequent purposes that in contrast with the more dependent branch plants of the older centralized multinational corporations of high fordism, foreign direct investment nowadays is more apt to assume the guise of production units that are relatively independent in their command structure and functional organization.[7]

All of this development in the interstices between the world's national economies has been facilitated by continual lowering of tariff barriers and other institutional impediments to trade as well as by the dramatic improvements in transportation and communications technologies that have occurred in recent decades. With the advent of large-scale container transport by land and sea, the proliferation of inexpensive international air connections, and the advent of worldwide electronic communications systems of all sorts, the costs of transacting between different countries are falling progressively, while the velocity of circulation of goods and information has been increasing exponentially. As a result, national economic systems have, gradually but inexorably, invaded one another's territory and have become intertwined together in extended divisions of labor.

These trends can be documented in great statistical detail. World trade has grown more or less continuously over the postwar period, and it continues to expand at an accelerating rate (see figure 4.1). In 1970 total world merchandise exports represented 4.1 percent of world domestic product; in 1993 the corresponding figure—a fourfold increase—was 16.0 percent. The actual volume of world merchandise exports in 1993 was valued at $3.6 trillion, of which just over 70 percent came from the countries of the Organization for economic Cooperation and Development (OECD). World exports of commercial services account for about a further $1 trillion.[8] There is, however, great variation from country to country in the level of dependence on foreign trade. The data presented in figure 4.2 indicate that for OECD countries, the ratio of foreign trade to gross domestic product (GDP) tends to decline in value as GDP increases. For example, Luxembourg, with a GDP of $12.5 billion in 1993, had exports that were equal to 85.7 percent of GDP and imports that were equal to 79.6 percent; the United States had a GDP of $6.26 trillion, but its exports were only 10.3 percent of this amount and its imports 11.6 percent. So while the dependence of all national economies on foreign trade continues to rise, the smaller economies are relatively more open than the larger ones. An obvious and important corollary of this remark is that if we were to break national economies down into smaller regional units, their interdependence

Figure 4.1 OECD Countries: Growth of Exports Relative to the Growth of Gross Domestic Product, 1960 = 1

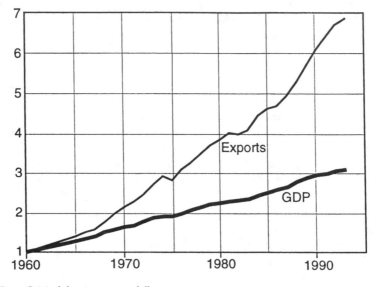

Note: Original data in constant dollars.
Source: OECD (1993a).

undoubtedly would be very high indeed (even allowing for the fact that political barriers to interregional trade rarely exist within any one country). Still more dramatic than the expansion of world trade in recent decades has been the explosive growth of international capital markets and financial operations.[9] Worldwide foreign direct investment outflows amounted to $150.0 billion in 1992, with actual direct foreign investment stocks being valued at upward of ten times this amount.[10] Indeed, much foreign trade actually consists of movements of inputs and outputs between units of production scattered over different countries but all belonging to the same firm. Over one-third of U.S. trade is now intrafirm trade.[11] At the same time, international currency transactions have been spiraling upward. In 1993 the foreign assets of deposit banks worldwide amounted to $7.0 trillion,[12] and enormous amounts of liquid capital now circulate the globe in a fraction of a second. Average daily foreign exchange transactions in 1992 reportedly amounted to $900 billion, which is actually 12 times more than the GDP of the OECD countries.[13]

Figure 4.2 (a) Foreign Trade as a Percentage of Gross Domestic Product (Where Foreign Trade is Measured as 1/2 [exports + imports], against (b) Gross Domestic Product for OECD Countries, 1993

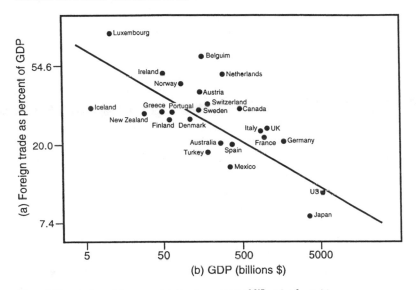

Note: The equation of the regression line is $y = 90.5x^{-0.217}$ with $R^2 = 0.46$.
Source: OECD National Accounts, 1993.

Regulatory Imperatives in Global Capitalism

One consequence of the palpable erosion of the economic boundaries between sovereign states that has been going on is that the power of individual states to control their internal economic destiny is waning.[14] Even the United States, the former world hegemon, is subject to severe stresses of internal restructuring as a result of external pressures. Yet no equivalent shift of political authority to the international level has occurred to confront the regulatory challenges raised by the globalization of capitalist economic relations.

That said, the efforts made over the post–World War II era to establish supranational mechanisms of economic coordination go some of the way to dealing with the most critical of these challenges, and many new initiatives are in progress. We now seem to be shifting into a transitional political phase on the way to a more effective global regime.[15] Here I am referring particularly to the emergence of multinational economic alliances such as the European

Union, the North American Free Trade Agreement (NAFTA), the Association of Southeast Asian Nations (ASEAN), the Asia-Pacific Economic Cooperation Conference (APEC), MERCOSUR (the Spanish acronym for the southern common market), and others, in which groups of countries essentially give up elements of their economic sovereignty in exchange for wider access to resources and markets under strong contractual and institutional guarantees of cooperation. Also, the General Agreement on Tariffs and Trade (GATT) recently has been reorganized as the World Trade Organization (WTO) and given additional authority to pursue its free-trade agendas. One further symptom of this drift is the expansion of international organizations of all varieties that has occurred of late. A total of 1,422 such organizations was recorded in 1960; by 1994 the number had grown to 36,486 of which 5,401 were intergovernmental and 31,085 were nongovernmental.[16] These developments will unquestionably be accentuated by the new climate of military détente in the contemporary world.

We are on the road, in short, toward a vastly more integrated international system or to what Kenichi Ohmae has referred to in more dramatic terms as a borderless world,[17] although we still remain far from its theoretical final point of destination. As we move in this direction, the territorially based sovereign state is giving way to the "trading state" whose economic well-being depends to greater and greater degree on its successful pursuit of export-oriented production within an international division of labor.[18] Export orientation (as opposed to import-substitution) is a strategy by means of which several underdeveloped parts of the world have managed to attain the status of newly industrializing countries (NICs),[19] and in some cases have then moved forward into full-blown capitalist development. This is not a maneuver that can be invoked at will, unfortunately, and the widening gulf between the developing world and the left-behinds constitutes one of the most perplexing and stubborn policy problems of the modern global system.

Regional Renaissance

As national economic sovereignty wanes in an increasingly borderless world, there will be some disposition on the part of the trading state (in theory at least, and abstracting away from the complicating effects of culture and nationalism) to decompose into an association of regions. This proposition alludes not so much to regions in the rudimentary sense of arbitrary geographic units on a smaller scale than the sovereign state but rather to definite localized complexes of economic and social activity inscribed durably on the landscape. Regions of this type are also crucial elements of the traditional sovereign state, although in this case they are invariably subordinate to national economic trends and policies. Under conditions of intensifying globalization, with diminishing economic mediation by central governments, their subjection to external competitive pressures will be magnified, their market reach vastly more extended, and, as a consequence, their internal structure and dynamics greatly modified. These remarks presume, of course, that a tight relationship exists between the globalization of capitalism and the character of economic development at the regional level. The nature of this relationship is by no means entirely self-evident, and in this section I shall attempt to clarify some of its inner logic.[20]

At the outset, any organized economic system always will embody various types of positive external economies, that is, increasing returns effects or productivity boosting relationships that are internal to the economy as a whole but external to the individual unit of production. In modern capitalism these externalities are essential components of competitive advantage. Three kinds of externalities are of particular significance:

1. Specialization and complementarity are major sources of external effects in the sense that the more producers can rely on efficient outside (i.e., vertically disintegrated) sources of supply for particular kinds of inputs, the better off in general they will be. In this manner they will be able not only to use cheaper inputs in flexible doses over time, but also to acquire—without damaging delays—critical inputs that they need only at infrequent and unpredictable moments.

2. The greater the ease with which producers can tap into an external supply of suitably trained, habituated, and disciplined labor at reasonable cost, the more effectively and cheaply are they able to carry out the tasks of production and the more rapidly and smoothly can they fill any vacancies that may crop up.

3. Producers interact with one another on many fronts and at many different levels, ranging from discussions about sales and purchases to working with one another in, say, business associations or joint venture activities. These interactions commonly function as vehicles for certain kinds of learning and innovation effects—untraded interdependencies—just as they also often are the basis for the formation of distinctive industrial/commercial cultures that help to underpin local economic order.[21] In a world where human capital is a critical ingredient in production, these effects are of major importance.

To these three types of external economies we may arguably add a fourth in the form of quasi-political institutional arrangements that enhance inter-firm trust and collaboration and that provide effective governance relations for groups of interrelated producers (e.g., in the case of just-in-time input-output organizations). It is possible to enumerate yet other types of externalities, but this brief inventory will suffice for present purposes. These externalities are a vital source of efficiency gains, innovation, and growth in modern capitalism, and their effectiveness usually intensifies as their scale and scope increase. Note, however, that they are always very unevenly developed and distributed across any given economy. They are prevalent within some industries (e.g., electronics or clothing), but sparse in others (e.g., steel production or petroleum refining); and whereas, say, electronics or clothing producers tend to generate strong intrasectoral external economies, their reciprocal spillover effects may be weak or even negative.

One of the striking features of external economies as just enumerated is that they all involve spatial-cum-transactional relations. They all involve forms of *access to and contact with* other units of activity, which means that the ability of firms to tap into them is dependent either on transaction costs being low over distance (if other units are widely spread out across space) or on units being close together (if spatial transactions costs are high). In practice, of course, spatial transactions costs also will vary depending on what precisely is being dispensed. Irregular, small-scale, and personalized types of transactions tend to be high per unit cost; standardized, bulk transactions tend to be low per unit cost. Depending on the nature and quantity of the external economies that prevail at any given time, and on the mix of high- and low-cost transactions that underlie them, we are likely to find widely varying levels of agglomeration and dispersal in the locational structure of the economy.

Figure 4.3 is an attempt to systematize these ideas. It displays a series of hypothetical locational outcomes for three different intensities of external economies (as identified earlier), low (labeled A), medium, (B), and high (C). For each of these cases, the figure traces out the relations between the (1) spatial costs of transacting (the horizontal axis), (2) a simple aggregate measure of physical interaction over space (the vertical axis), and (3) generalized locational response (represented by different grades of shading). The horizontal axis is meant to represent average values over what in practice always will be a wide range of costs, given the variety of transactions that exist in any given economy. We now examine the complex geographical patterns that come into being as the relationships between external economies and transactions costs change. No doubt we also would expect many parallel

Figure 4.3 **Schematized Locational Outcomes of the Interplay between Spatial Transaction Costs and External Economies**

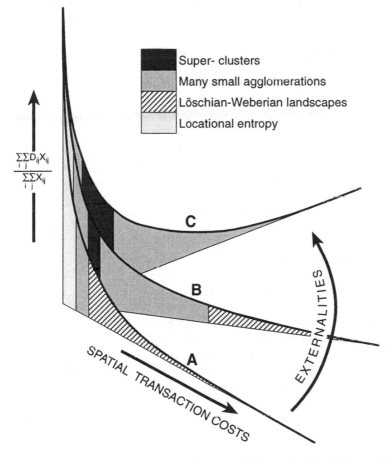

Note: The vertical axis represents average levels of spatial interaction where X_{ij} is a quantity of flow between any two places, $_i$ and $_j$ and D_{ij} is the geographic distance between the same two places.

qualitative transformations to occur in the structure of economic activity, but for present purposes, we focus only on the dimensions identified.

The main inferential outcomes from this exercise can be described in terms of four different locational scenarios.

1. When spatial transactions costs are high and the external economies to be derived from the presence of other firms are relatively low, producers simply will seek out their least-cost locations with respect to their basic inputs and/or markets. The result will tend generally to be a set of Löschian-Weberian landscapes. Producers have little to gain from large-scale agglomeration while they have much to gain from proximity to a few selected suppliers and buyers, and therefore they will simply adjust their locations to conform to the underlying geographic distribution of resources and population.[22]

2. Where externalities are abundant, the locational strategies of producers will readjust accordingly, although the nature of the readjustment will depend very much on levels of spatial transactions costs.[23] Let us consider two contrasting cases. On one hand, suppose that transactions costs are uniformly high. This circumstance will encourage firms to agglomerate together, but it also will diminish the spatial range over which producers in any given agglomeration can tap into outside resources or sell to outside markets. Consequently, the growth of the agglomeration will rapidly encounter exogenously given limits. Traditional craft communities may be advanced as one example of this phenomenon. On the other hand, if transactions costs are uniformly low, some producers will be able to consume externalities at a distance. The impulse to externality-driven agglomeration will therefore be weakened (even though the spatial reach of any given agglomeration may be wide), and at least part of the production system will disperse to locations where other kinds of cost advantages are available. The net result in both of these instances will tend to be a locational landscape characterized by many small, specialized agglomerations.

3. In circumstances where spatial transactions costs are low and rapidly approaching zero, a state of locational entropy will prevail once the place-specific sunk costs of earlier spatial patterns have lost all present value. This will occur, moreover, even where external economies are of a high order, since then there would be no spatial limits on access to them. The ultimate case where transactions costs are equated to zero would be akin to a world in which magic carpets are available, for any individual could transfer or gain access to any product or service or information in any amount over any distance instantaneously and without cost. Obviously we are very far indeed from globalization in this sense.

4. Most pertinent for the purposes of this study is the situation that is intermediate between the two cases described in point 2. In this situation,

spatial transactions costs are assumed to vary across a spectrum from high to low but to be of moderate or intermediate intensity on average. Under these conditions we can expect producers to agglomerate together in order to maximize their access to externalities and above all to varieties of externalities that are associated with irregular, small-scale, and highly personalized types of interaction. By contrast, many of the more standardized kinds of transactions linking producers to the rest of the world will be national and global in extent. Further, the extended market reach of producers will enable the social division of labor in any given agglomeration to deepen (thus creating yet more externalities), thereby stimulating additional rounds of growth.

This fourth scenario may be likened to the case of regional motors derived from and simultaneously driving a globalizing economy. As political barriers to economic interaction continue to fade, such motors may be expected to become—at least for a time—a primary element of the world system. I submit that we are poised at the early stages of the rise of a world capitalist economy characterized by just such a system of regional motors. One main reason for this claim is that contemporary forms of economic production and organization are rife with externality effects having their roots in the augmenting levels of flexibility, uncertainty, product destandardization, and competitiveness that are the hallmarks of contemporary capitalist enterprise. Through a variety of complex mediations, these conditions have encouraged vertical disintegration of production systems, flexibility of labor markets, wider opportunities for learning and innovation at the interface between market participants, and the valorization of institutions that promote trust and collaboration within selected sectors.[24] Accordingly they have also brought about a resurgence of increasing returns effects at the level of the economic system as a whole, effects that are especially evident in the three major sectoral ensembles mentioned earlier; high-technology industry, design-intensive consumer goods for niche markets, and business and financial services. Another reason for the claim is that while spatial transactions costs have fallen dramatically across a wide front in recent decades, allowing many firms ready access to global markets, there still remain important kinds of transactions that are extremely sensitive to the effects of distance. External economies tend to be well developed in the interaction networks constituted by just such transactions as these, and in order to secure them, producers agglomerate together in geographic space.

Under these conditions, superclusters of producers come into being in the shape of dense agglomerations (typically forming large metropolitan areas or world cities) tied functionally together in a global division of labor. The productive performance of these superclusters is further augmented by the economies of scale that accrue when physical infrastructures and other public services are provided to ensure their effective operation. As several analysts have pointed out recently, it is in these kinds of geographic entities that *competitive* advantage in the modern world is forged as a social and political process, in contrast with the Ricardian *comparative* advantages that are lodged in pregiven natural endowments.[25] One of the critical tricks in achieving sustained economic growth and development today is to build regional economic systems like these capable of forging a durable place for themselves within a worldwide structure of trade, investment, and competition. However, even successful regions are not immune from being locked in to dysfunctional developmental pathways, as exemplified by the occasional collapse of once-prosperous growth centers at various moments in the history of capitalism.

The Geography of Global Capitalism

Since the 1950s there have been numerous attempts to go beyond the original theory of comparative advantage as a means of understanding the geography of development and trade. Two early and noteworthy efforts in this direction were made by A. Hirschman and G. Myrdal, who claimed that processes of "polarization" and "trickle down" were at work in North America and Western Europe resulting in the formation of a small number of highly developed economic regions surrounded by swaths of relatively underdeveloped territory.[26] Hirschman and Myrdal designated the former areas as the "core" of the sovereign state and the latter as the "periphery," terms that have remained a leitmotif traceable through almost all subsequent treatments of the question of regional development, including this one. A later and more radical group of theorists reexamined the core-periphery idea, extending it to the entire world, and arguing for it in terms of a logic of uneven development and unequal exchange underpinned by neo-imperialist relations between developed and underdeveloped countries.[27] I. Wallerstein reworked many of these ideas in his account of the long historical sweep of capitalist development and the formation of the world system.[28] A yet further cycle of investigations of world capitalism based on the core-periphery idea was set in motion by F. Fröbel, H. Heinrichs, and O. Kreye, who suggested that the more economically advanced countries were becoming specialized in high-wage, white-collar work while the less-advanced countries were turning into repositories of low-wage, blue-collar labor.[29] Fröbel and coauthors argued that the principal agents of this so-called new international division of labor were the multinational corporations with their ever-extending global assembly lines.

Each of these approaches captures something of the macrogeographic logic and dynamics of the modern world. In various ways, comparative advantage, polarization and trickle down, uneven development, and the new international division of labor represent processes and phenomena that continue to leave their mark on worldwide spatial patterns of development. In light of the recent spate of published work on global-local economic relations as well as what I have just written, however, some reevaluation of these approaches also seems to be in order. I now offer a schematic resynthesis situated more or less directly in the line of the analytic tradition just described. My point of departure is the notion that in the next phase of capitalist economic and political development, we probably are going to see (and are seeing) an intensification of the amalgamation of national capitalisms into one world-wide economic structure, along with the concomitant materialization of superclusters of economic activity forming the basic motors of the whole system.

Figure 4.4 presents a rough but comprehensive glimpse of the basic geographic elements of this approaching world. Two principal points need to be made.

First, the developed areas of the world are represented in the figure as a patchwork of polarized regional economic motors, each consisting of a central metropolitan area and a surrounding hinterland occupied by ancillary communities, prosperous agricultural zones, local service centers, and the like. As indicated by the figure, some of these metropolitan-hinterland systems may coalesce with one another, as in the actual cases of Boston-New York-Philadelphia, Los Angeles-San Diego-Tijuana, Milan-Turin-Genoa, Tokyo-Nagoya-Osaka, and so on. Each metropolitan nucleus is the site of dense networks of specialized but complementary forms of economic activity together with large and multifaceted local labor markets, and each is a locus of powerful agglomeration economies and increasing returns effects. Each also is involved in intricate structures of global interaction. Accordingly, and in line with the earlier discussion, these motors tend not only to be big but also to be growing bigger constantly.

Second, large residual expanses of the modern world lie at the extensive economic frontiers of capitalism (former colonies, ex-socialist states, isolated regions,etc.). For the most part, these are underdeveloped areas that have been unable to build the economic organizations that might push them toward the forms of growth-center development described here. Even

Figure 4.4   Schematic Representation of the Contemporary Geography of Global Capitalism

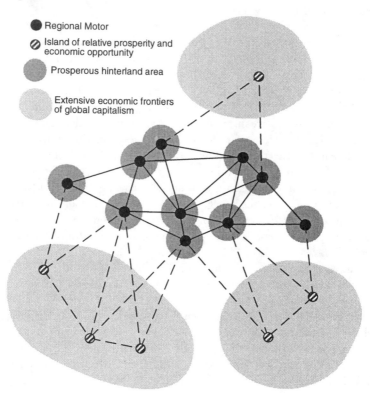

so, occasionally these areas are punctuated by islands of relative prosperity and economic opportunity,[30] and some may well be on a trajectory that takes them to much higher levels of (agglomerated) development. In the 1960s and 1970s such places as Hong Kong, Singapore, Taiwan, the Seoul region, and central Mexico were all positioned at different stages along this trajectory. Today a number of Third World metropolitan areas, such as Bangkok, Kuala Lumpur, and São Paulo–Rio de Janeiro, are following on the heels of these pioneers, while parts of Nigeria, the Ivory Coast, India, Indonesia, and possibly Vietnam seem to be poised at the initiatory phase. The burning but unresolved policy questions are how to ignite this developmental process in areas that hitherto have resisted it while at the same time averting the worst kinds of social breakdown that come with rapid industrialization and urbanization.

As world economic integration comes closer, we thus may expect that production activities will become yet more concentrated in metropolitan areas and their immediately surrounding hinterlands. Even over the last few decades, the phenomenon of the giant metropolitan area has become commonplace. To illustrate the point, Tokyo, São Paulo, New York, Mexico City, Shanghai, Bombay, Los Angeles, Buenos Aires, Seoul, and Rio de Janeiro (in descending order of size) all had populations exceeding 10 million in 1990, while an additional 25 urban agglomerations exceeded the 5 million mark.[31]

The data laid out in table 4.1 provide further elaboration of the same idea. The table shows that, in 1990, the 40 metropolitan areas in the United States with more than 1 million people contained 53.5 percent of the country's population. Those areas in the largest size category (New York, Los Angeles, Chicago) alone accounted for 17.0 percent of total population. In addition, these 40 metropolitan areas generated a little under half of national value added in manufacturing in 1972 and a little over half in 1987 (the latest year for which comprehensive data are available). This translates into an overall rate of growth of value added (after discounting inflation) of 30.6 percent between 1972 and 1987, well over the national average of 21.2 percent. However, metropolitan areas in the largest size category performed significantly more poorly than this, and in regard to manufacturing employment they actually declined by 6.2 percent over the same period. If we divide the 40 metropolitan areas into a northeastern group and a sunbelt group, we find that between 1972 and 1987, manufacturing value added grew at 8.6 percent in the former part of the country and at 81.5 percent in the latter, a rather clear echo (at least in part) of the changing fortunes of fordist and postfordist forms of industry in the United States over the recent past. In the domain of service provision, the large metropolitan areas of the United States have forged ahead with particular vigor. Between 1972 and 1992 service receipts (as defined in table 4.1) grew by 174.0 percent in the top 40 metropolitan areas, as compared with 132.7 percent in the country as a whole. In New York, Los Angeles, and Chicago, the rate of growth of service receipts was as high as 1,535.9 percent over the same period, dramatic testimony to the changing economic vocation of these cities in the new global economy.

We may expect that the world's major production regions will continue not only to grow but also to become more subtly differentiated from one another as political frontiers decay and as a more thoroughly global division of labor makes its appearance. The point is underlined by the work of P. Krugman and

Table 4.1   Manufacturing and Service Activity in U.S. Metropolitan Areas with Populations of More than 1 Million

Population Size Category (10⁶)	Number of Metropolitan Areas	Total Population 1990	Manufacturing Value Added 1972 (10^9 1987 $)	Manufacturing Value Added 1987 (10^9 1987 $)	% Change in Manufacturing Value Added 1972–1987	Service Industry[a] Receipts 1972 (10^9 1992 $)	Service Industry[a] Receipts 1992 (10^9 1992 $)	% Change in Service Industry Receipts 1972–1992
8+	3	42.3	173.8	190.7	9.7	108.8	237.2	118.0
4–8	6	33.6	104.1	164.7	58.1	55.6	189.6	241.0
2–4	12	32.0	91.8	128.8	40.3	42.9	143.8	235.2
1–2	19	25.2	98.1	127.0	29.4	33.0	88.1	167.0
All 40 areas	40	133.1	467.8	611.1	30.6	240.4	658.7	174.0
U.S. total	–	248.7	962.3	1,166.6	21.2	379.3	883.0	132.7

[a]The service industry is defined here (in terms of the 1987 Standard Industrial Classification) as SICs 70 (hotels and other lodging places), 72 (personal services), 73 (business services), 75 (auto repair, services, and parking), 76 (miscellaneous repair services), 78 (motion pictures), 79 (amusement and recreation services), 81 (legal services), 87 (engineering and management services).

Sources: U.S. Department of Commerce, Bureau of the Census: (a) *Statistical Abstract of the United States*, (b) *Census of Manufactures*, 1972 and 1987, (c) *Census of Service Industries*, 1972 and 1992.

A. J. Venables, who have demonstrated that major manufacturing regions in the United States are much more specialized than individual European countries (to which they are roughly equivalent in size).[32] But as internal tariff barriers in the European Union fall, thus widening the extent of markets, European countries/regions are now evidently moving toward much greater levels of specialization. Successful city-states like Hong Kong and Singapore provide ample evidence, moreover, that regional economic specialization (together with export-oriented development) can with the right combination of opportunity and good policy judgment be a formula for extremely rapid growth in the modern global economy.[33]

The somewhat surprising deduction that comes to the fore is that the globalization of capitalism seems to be leading not to a homogenization of geographic space but to heightened forms of differentiation from region to region. Some regions, such as New York, London, and Tokyo, are developing as massive foci of business and financial services.[34] Others, such as the American Midwest, the Third Italy, or Taiwan (each in its different way), retain a primary focus on manufacturing. Even when regions ostensibly are involved in similar lines of production, we tend to find detailed variations from one to the other. Many of the world's leading industrial agglomerations today are engaged in the electronics sector, for example, but they often differ markedly in terms of the specific electronic products they make (consumer goods, communications systems, computers, components, instruments, etc.).

I must add the important observation that the regional motors of the global economy also function as primary centers of culture and fashion generation in the modern world.[35] Many of them encompass large cultural-products industrial complexes in sectors such as filmmaking, television programming, music recording, publishing, fashion clothing production, jewelry manufacture, and so on, whose outputs are sold all over the world. They are gathering points for designers, writers, actors, artists, musicians, and other creative workers, just as they are also places where can be found abundant resources of collective cultural consumption such as museums, concert halls, libraries, art galleries, convention centers, and arts festivals. As a result they exude a definite atmosphere of cultural engagement and experimentation that coincidentally helps to keep their more commercial cultural activities and cultural-products industries at the cutting edge. Today Los Angeles, New York, London, Paris, and Tokyo vie with one another for influence in these spheres, and they are the progenitors of a cosmopolitan capitalist culture (high and low) as much as they are also critical bastions of global economic power.

KVCC KALAMAZOO VALLEY COMMUNITY COLLEGE LIBRARY

In spite of these important assets, many of these places are rife with social problems and predicaments. Above all, as globalization runs its course subjecting all areas to the same intense competitive pressures, a marked socioeconomic bifurcation seems to be in progress in many major metropolitan regions.[36] This tendency is most evident in the propensity for the economies of leading agglomerations to beget low-wage, low-skill jobs employing large numbers of people in a variety of sweatshop manufacturing sectors and low-grade service activities alongside high-wage, high-skill (professional, managerial, technical, creative, etc.) employment segments. Intertwined with this tendency is the attraction of these agglomerations to immigrants from peripheral, Third World regions (as illustrated by the migration of Central Americans to Los Angeles, Puerto Ricans and Haitians to New York, North and West Africans to Paris, and Filipino and Mainland Chinese workers to Hong Kong). The overall polarization that ensues breeds mounting tensions (often with ethnic and racial overtones), an endemic susceptibility to social explosions, and a persistent subversion of the latent function of the large metropolis as a gregarious community of communities.

Issues of Governance and Policy in a Global Mosaic of Regions

What I have tried to convey is a sense of the continuing transformation of world economic geography into a mosaic of interdependent regional production systems. This trend has been accompanied by a certain dampening of the system-coordinating capabilities of the sovereign state and a concomitant (but unequal) drift of political functions up to the international level, where piecemeal contractual and institutional regimes strive to ensure some degree of economic order, and down to the local level, where municipal and regional governments all over the world are struggling to formulate viable economic strategies in the context of competitive currents from which national governments are increasingly unable to shelter them. With the ending of the Cold War, these currents surely will continue to make themselves felt, although any major eruptions of international insecurity unquestionably would turn the tide backward again. Even so, the sovereign state remains a major factor in the contemporary political world, and any claims about its imminent demise must be viewed with caution. Those, like Ohmae, who foresee its virtual dissolution before the ascendance of globalized economic relations fail in particular to take into account the social and cultural pressures that continue to make the nation a potent political entity in the contemporary world.[37]

The International Level

With this proviso in mind, problems of global economic steering and strategic choice are nonetheless sure to become more urgent and complex with the passage of time. There is every reason to suppose that the international governance arrangements that already have been set in place will continue to multiply, although whether they will persist as an ad hoc regime of organizations and agreements (their present form) or evolve into something more like a sovereign body remains an open question at this stage.

The tasks of international economic coordination are obviously enormous, covering as they do such matters as currency exchange rates, trade relations, modes of foreign direct investment, airline and shipping activities, intellectual property rights, environmental spillovers, and so on. A considerable amount of international regulatory effort already is devoted to these and similar kinds of problems. For our purposes, an issue of particular moment is the political tasks that will become ever more pressing as—or if—the problems of the mosaic of regional economies just described begin on a massive scale to override purely national frameworks of control. If indeed something like a global system of city-states is in the incipient phases of formation, important implications for the global mode of social regulation arise. No matter whether this prospective future involves weak or strong forms of regional governance, there is undoubtedly going to be a growing demand for effective management of the entire system as regions relate to and compete with one another more or less directly all over the world. The demand is likely to be intensified by the predictable political self-assertion that major regions will engage in as they find themselves increasingly responsible for their own economic fortunes and as interregional rivalries mount accordingly. The intrinsically problematical nature of this state of affairs can be exemplified by the following six points.

1. In the future, we may expect to see an acceleration of economic development races between various regions, and all the more so as strong increasing returns effects give those regions that start early and move fast a sharp competitive edge. In pursuit of first-mover advantages, local governments may well begin in aggregate to overinvest in particular development strategies. In this process considerable waste of resources is apt to occur unless enforceable multiregion agreements about economic agendas and priorities can be constructed.

2. Even today many regional governments in different parts of the world engage in predatory poaching forays in an effort to attract critical

resources away from other regions. But when these resources have significant positive externalities for the region that is under threat, major impairment of overall industrial performance may ensue.

3. A growing political self-consciousness about economic issues is likely to induce many regions to enter into bilateral and multilateral coalitions and alliances with one another. This trend is already observable in the European Union.[38] Joint activities of this sort can be extremely beneficial to the participants but also can be detrimental to regions that are excluded. Some wider mediation of this process may well become necessary.

4. Multinational corporations are among the most important private beneficiaries of the global regional mosaic. They are also a major factor in linking different agglomerations together. Their operations almost always are programmed to take advantage of varying production conditions over space by appropriate adjustments of investment and employment levels at different locations. Their concomitant ability to play regions off against one another is an issue that still evades effective regulation.

5. Interregional migration, above all migration from poor to wealthy regions, will pose major political dilemmas for local governments, particularly where national supervision of migratory streams is becoming less effective (cf. the current debate in California about illegal immigration). How, we may ask, are sending and receiving regions to develop and enforce protocols that will eliminate the worst abuses of this process?

6. There are important questions about collective responsibility for regions that begin to fail economically, for failure in these circumstances is not so much a sum of unrelated individual failures as it is a structured collapse within a globally interdependent system.

In relation to the latter point, and perhaps most perplexing of all in this looming new world order, is the gulf that almost certainly will continue to separate developed and underdeveloped regions. This remark raises difficult questions about how to handle the political tensions that lie at this critical interface and about the appropriate forms of redistribution and aid that effective remedial treatment of the development gap will call for.

The Regional Level

The regional economic systems that I have discussed represent congeries of producers and workers held in place by powerful agglomeration economies.

As such, each of them is a collectivity in the strict sense that the whole is always considerably greater than the sum of the parts. Theorists like W. B. Arthur and P. A. David have pointed out that complex systems like these are subject to path-dependent trajectories of development.[39] Thus running parallel to the need for mechanisms of interregional coordination is the imperative of intraregional governance in order to safeguard the collective benefits of the whole as well as to steer development so that it locks into better rather than worse outcomes over time. In addition, since the competitive advantages of large agglomerations generally are enhanced when mechanisms for collaboration and cooperation are in place (thus promoting technology sharing, skills acquisition, learning, etc.), significant returns are likely to be earned from the creation of appropriate institutions of collective order at the regional level. I offer the conjecture that in the new global competition, regions will find it difficult to maintain high rates of growth and high incomes without dealing decisively with these issues of local social regulation.

The latter proposition is thrown into relief by the lacunae and breakdowns observable in many regional economic systems today: for example, in the frequent inadequacy of agglomeration-specific forms of technological research, in the deficiencies of labor training for local needs, in the emergence of low-trust business environments and forms of interfirm competition that undermine possibilities of collaboration or useful exchanges of information, and in the market failures and free-rider problems that beset all business agglomerations (in matters ranging from the provision of basic infrastrucure to the maintenance of a reputation for high-quality products). In view of such problems, various hesitant and sometimes failed experiments in the construction of regional collective order are proceeding even now throughout the capitalist world. They are manifest everywhere in the multiplication of public initiatives to promote regional economic development, often in combination with approaches that conceivably could be described as regional strategic trade policies. The clearest and most successful instances of this phenomenon are to be found in the city-states or region-states of Hong Kong and Singapore, but other less dramatic examples can be observed in parts of Europe and North America. Specific cases are: the German länder with their elaborate private-public consultative and decision-making machinery[40]; the regions of the Third Italy with their highly developed institutional infrastructures promoting technological innovation, labor training, market research, export activity, information-sharing, and so on[41]; and, embryonically, the 17 autonomous communities of Spain or the 22 elected regional councils of France. Numerous important experiments also have been in progress in such U.S. states as California, Massachusetts, Michigan, and Pennsylvania, where far-reaching economic development programs have been established to encourage the growth of local business networks and the formation of virtuous circles of agglomeration effects.[42]

Few of these illustrative cases can be considered to represent anything much more than rather primitive harbingers of a framework of political action whose main lineaments remain to be constructed. They are, however, concrete initiatives upon which more elaborate instruments of collective action and regional identity formation might conceivably be constructed as the winds of global competition blow more strongly (and, in addition, as administrative and fiscal decentralization works its course in the advanced capitalist societies[43]). From this perspective, the revival of regional politics envisioned here needs to be distinguished from the atavistic regionalism evident in parts of the former Soviet Union and Eastern Europe, which in large degree seems simply to be an expression of long-repressed ethnic and cultural grievances.

The phenomenon of economic and political devolution to the regions also raises questions about citizenship and communal association.[44] Under any circumstances, individuals and firms have definite vested interests in their local milieu, although they do not always have the incentive or the opportunity to give full voice to them. The construction of more inclusive and representative regional political forums is not only an opportunity to mobilize voice as such (and to discourage its dysfunctional counterpart, exit) but also a potential means of reinforcing competitive advantage by enhancing a sense of local community and rationalizing the political and informational bases of collective strategic choice. In view of this, it is tempting to suggest that the notion of citizenship in the emerging global order eventually may evolve away from an emphasis on national birthright and toward an emphasis on the principle of regional affiliation. I must stress here that these remarks should be interpreted as normative speculations, not as theoretical predictions of things to come. In fact, one of the hazards of the model of world economic development identified in these pages is that its genetic code, so to speak, is also the carrier of a potentially much less benign future than the one to which I have alluded. We can apprehend something of this other future in the rising levels of polarization, the simmering tensions, and the social marginalization and disorder that are already painfully obvious as the intertwined effects of globalization and neoconservative laissez-faire policies encounter one another in large American cities today.

City-States of the Twenty-First Century

Contrary to the claims of some analysts about an impending state of affairs in which "the logic and dynamics of territorial development are increasingly placeless,"[45] or in which the "end of geography"[46] is in sight, we seem rather to be entering a phase of capitalist development in which the regional concentration of production is becoming more pronounced as a mode of spatial economic organization. This trend is occurring because, on one hand, the spatial reach of regionalized production systems is nowadays effectively worldwide, while on the other hand the pull of performance-boosting externalities creates an insistent demand for proximity within important segments of the economy. In principle, we may conceive of a time when even many of these externalities can be consumed over any distance, in which case we would expect the economic geography of the world to begin to approach the state of entropy described earlier, at least once all sunk costs in prior locations have become valueless.

The current state of the world is manifestly nowhere near this notional situation. For the present, all signs point toward the continued assertion of region-based forms of economic development and political identity in the context of accelerating globalization. As we enter the twenty-first century, individual national capitalisms are to all intents and purposes beginning to merge into a single world system (which is not equivalent to a proclamation of the final withering away of the national state or the erasure of national social and cultural differences). To an increasing degree, the locational bedrock of this system coincides with a series of interdependent agglomerations of capital and labor spread out in an archipelago across the globe. These agglomerations are starting to assume some of the character of a de facto confederation of city-states. I predict that, in the future, we shall see them constructing forums of political expression that vigorously promote their individual economic needs and identities while they also and of necessity seek out new modalities of collaboration with one another in pursuit of common interests. I offer these ideas as theoretical inferences from observations about the current spatial and temporal dynamic of capitalism. Plainly, many of them will stand in need of correction as further analysis proceeds and as actual events unfold. As I conceive it, this dynamic has both progressive and regressive potentialities, and its final shape will depend no doubt in high degree on what dominant types of political mobilization come to the fore in future decades. Accordingly, these ideas also are set forth as a point of reference for debates about appropriate political practices in the continuing struggle for material prosperity and democratic social conditions for all.

Notes

I wish to thank John Agnew, Neil Brenner, Richard Rosecrance, and Michael Webber for helpful comments on an earlier draft of this chapter.

1. R. O. Keohane, *After Hegemony: Cooperation and Discord in the World Political Economy* (Princeton, N.J.: Princeton University Press, 1984); R. O. Keohane, *International Institutions and State Power* (Boulder, Colo.: Westview Press, 1989); K. Ohmae, *The Borderless World* (New York: HarperCollins, 1990); K. Ohmae, *The End of the Nation State* (New York: The Free Press, 1995); and R. Rosecrance, *The Rise of the Trading State* (New York: Basic Books, 1986).

2. P. Hirst and J. Zeitlin, eds., *Reversing Industrial Decline? Industrial Structure and Policy in Britain and Her Competitors* (Oxford: Berg, 1989); M. E. Porter, *The Competitive Advantage of Nations* (New York: Free Press, 1990); A. Saxenian, *Regional Advantage: Culture and Competition in Silicon Valley and Route 128* (Cambridge, Mass.: Harvard University Press, 1994); A. J. Scott, *Metropolis: From the Division of Labor to Urban Form* (Berkeley: University of California Press, 1988); A. J. Scott, *Technopolis: High-Technology Industry and Regional Development in Southern California* (Berkeley: University of California Press, 1993).

3. A. Amin and N. J. Thrift, "Neo-Marshallian Nodes in Global Networks," *International Journal of Urban and Regional Research* 16 (1992): 571–587; M. Storper, "The Limits to Globalization: Technology Districts and International Trade," *Economic Geography* 68 (1992): 60–93; M. Storper and A. J. Scott, "The Wealth of Regions: Market Forces and Policy Imperatives in Local and Global Context," *Futures* 27 (1995): 505–526.

4. R. Boyer, *La Théorie de la Régulation: Une Analyse Critique* (Paris: Editions La Découverte, 1986); A. Lipietz, "New Tendencies in the International Division of Labor: Regimes of Accumulation and Modes of Social Regulation," in A. J. Scott and M. Storper, eds., *Production, Work, Territory: The Geographical Anatomy of Industrial Capitalism* (London: Allen and Unwin, 1986), 16–40.

5. Not surprisingly, then, and in contrast to certain tendencies in contemporary regulationist theory, ideas about the political order of capitalism typically have been articulated as theories of the national state.

6. G. Gereffi and M. Korzeniewicz, eds., *Commodity Chains and Global Capitalism* (Westport, Conn.: Greenwood Press, 1994).

7. M. Hart, *What's Next: Canada, the Global Economy, and the New Trade Policy* (Ottawa: Carleton University, Centre for Trade Policy and Law, 1994).

8. General Agreement on Tariffs and Trade, *International Trade Statistics* (Geneva: GATT, 1993).

9. N. Thrift and A. Leyshon, "A Phantom State? The De-traditionalization of Money, the International Financial System, and International Financial Centres," *Political Geography* 13 (1994): 299–327; M. W. Zachar, "The Decaying Pillars of the Westphalian Temple: Implications for International Order and

Governance," in J. N. Rosenau and E. O. Czempiel, eds., *Governance without Government: Order and Change in World Politics* (Cambridge: Cambridge University Press, 1992), 58–101.

10. United Nations Conference on Trade and Development, *World Investment Report* (New York: UNCTAD, 1993).

11. Organization for Economic Cooperation and Development, *Intra-Firm Trade* (Paris: OECD, 1993).

12. International Monetary Fund, *International Financial Statistics Yearbook* (Washington, D.C.: IMF, 1993).

13. W. Lever, "Economic Globalisation and Urban Dynamics, II," in F. Moulaert and A. J. Scott, eds., *Cities and Enterprises on the Eve of the Twenty-First Century* (London: Pinter, 1996).

14. B. Badie, *La Fin des Territoires, Essai sur le Désordre International et sur l'Utilité Sociale du Respect* (Paris: Fayard, 1995); R. Jessop, "The Future of the National State: Erosion or Reorganisation? General Reflections on the West European Case," ms., Department of Sociology, University of Lancaster, UK, 1995.

15. J. Agnew and S. Corbridge, *Mastering Space: Hegemony, Territory, and International Political Economy* (London: Routledge, 1995).

16. Union of International Associations, *Yearbook of International Associations* (Munich: K. G. Saur, 1995).

17. Ohmae, *Borderless World.*

18. Rosecrance, *Rise of the Trading State.*

19. S. Strange, *States and Markets* (London: Pinter, 1988).

20. For more extended background material on this matter: A. J. Scott, "Industrial Organization and Location: Division of Labor, the Firm, and Spatial Process," *Economic Geography* 62 (1986): 215–231, and M. Storper and R. Walker, *The Capitalist Imperative: Territory, Technology, and Industrial Growth* (Oxford: Blackwell, 1989).

21. J. Patchell, "From Production Systems to Learning Systems: Lessons from Japan," *Environment and Planning A* 25 (1993):797–815; R. Salais and M. Storper, *Les Mondes de Production: Enquête sur l'Identité Economique de la France* (Paris: Editions de l'Ecole Des Hautes Etudes en Sciences Sociales, 1993).

22. Of course, under the (empirically meaningless) assumptions that geographic space is a tabula rasa and all economic activities are perfectly mobile, *any* positive level of spatial transactions costs, with or without externalities, will result in the convergence of the global economy around a single central point.

23. P. Krugman and A. J. Venables, *Globalization and the Inequality of Nations* (Cambridge, Mass.: National Bureau of Economic Research, Working Paper No. 5098, 1995).

24. See A. J. Scott, *New Industrial Spaces: Flexible Production Organization and Regional Development in North America and Western Europe* (London: Pion, 1988).

25. P. Krugman, *Geography and Trade* (Leuven: Leuven University Press, 1991); A. J. Scott, "The Geographic Foundations of Industrial Performance," *Competition and Change* 1 (1995): 51–66.

26. A. Hirschman, *The Strategy of Economic Development* (New Haven, Conn.: Yale University Press, 1958); G. Myrdal, *Rich Lands and Poor* (New York: Harper & Row, 1957).

27. S. Amin, *Le Développement Inégal* (Paris: Les Editions de Minuit, 1973); A. Emmanuel, *Unequal Exchange: A Study of the Imperialism of Trade* (New York: Monthly Review Press, 1972); A. G. Frank, Dependent Accumulation and Underdevelopment (New York: Monthly Review Press, 1979); D. Harvey, *The Limits to Capital* (Oxford: Blackwell, 1982).

28. I. Wallerstein, *Historical Capitalism* (London: Verso, 1983); I. Wallerstein, *The Modern World System III: The Second Era of Great Expansion of the Capitalist World Economy, 1730–1840s* (San Diego: Academic Press, 1989).

29. F. Fröbel, J. Heinrichs, and O. Kreye, *The New International Division of Labour* (Cambridge: Cambridge University Press, 1980).

30. Agnew and Corbridge, *Mastering Space.*

31. United Nations, *World Urbanization Prospects: The 1992 Revision* (New York: United Nations, Division of Economic and Social Information and Policy Analysis, 1993).

32. Krugman, *Geography and Trade;* A. J. Venables, "Economic Integration and the Location of Firms," *American Economic Review, Papers and Proceedings* 85 (1995): 296–300.

33. M. Castells, L. Goh, and R. Y-W. Kwok, *The Shek Kip Mei Syndrome: Economic Development and Public Housing in Hong Kong and Singapore* (London: Pion, 1990); R. Wade, *Governing the Market: Economic Theory and the Role of Government in East Asian Industrialization* (Princeton, N.J.: Princeton University Press, 1990).

34. S. Sassen, *The Global City: New York, London, Tokyo* (Princeton, N.J.: Princeton University Press, 1991); N. Thrift, "On the Social and Cultural Determinants of International Financial Centres: The Case of the City of London," in S. Corbridge, R. Martin, and N. Thrift, eds., *Money, Power, and Space* (Oxford: Blackwell, 1994): 327–355.

35. A. J. Scott, "The Craft, Fashion, and Cultural Products Industries of Los Angeles: Competitive Dynamics and Policy Dilemmas in a Multisectoral Image-Producing Complex," *Annals of the Association of American Geographers* 86 (1996).

36. Sassen, *Global City.*

37. Ohmae, *End of the Nation State.*

38. P. Cooke, "Globalization of Economic Organization and the Emergence of Regional Interstate Partnerships," in C. H. Williams, ed., *The Political Geography of the New World Order* (London: Belhaven, 1993), 46–58.

39. W. B. Arthur, "Silicon Valley Locational Clusters: When do Increasing Returns Imply Monopoly?" *Mathematical Social Sciences* 19 (1990): 235–251; P. A.

David, "Clio and the Economics of QWERTY," *American Economic Review* 75 (1985): 332–337.

40. P. Cooke and K. Morgan, *Industry, Training and Technology Transfer: The Baden-Württemberg System in Perspective* (Cardiff, Wales: Regional Industrial Research, 1990); G. Herrigel, "Large Firms, Small Firms, and the Governance of Flexible Specialization: The Case of Baden-Württemberg and Socialized Risk," in B. Kogut, ed., *Country Competitiveness: Technology and the Organizing of Work* (New York: Oxford University Press, 1993), 15–35.

41. P. Bianchi, "Levels of Policy and the Nature of Post-Fordist Competition," in M. Storper and A. J. Scott, eds., *Pathways to Industrialization and Regional Development* (London: Routledge, 1992), 303–315.

42. A. M. Isserman, "State Economic Development Policy and Practice in the United States: A Survey Article," *International Regional Science Review* 16 (1994): 49–100; D. Osborne, *Laboratories of Democracy* (Boston: Harvard Business School Press, 1990); C. F. Sabel, "Studied Trust: Building New Forms of Cooperation in a Volatile Economy," *Human Relations* 46 (1990): 1133–1170; J. Slifko and D. L. Rigby, "Industrial Policy in Southern California: The Production of Markets, Technologies, and Institutional Support for Electric Vehicles," *Environment and Planning A* 27 (1995): 933–954.

43. D. Woods, "The Crisis of Center-Periphery Integration in Italy and the Rise of Regional Populism: the Lombard League," *Comparative Politics* 27 (1995): 187–203.

44. A. Amin and N. J. Thrift, "Institutional Issues for the European Regions: From Markets and Plans to Socioeconomics and Powers of Association," *Economy and Society* 24 (1995): 41–66.

45. M. Castells and J. Henderson, "Techno-Economic Restructuring, Socio-Political Processes and Spatial Transformation: A Global Perspective," in J. Henderson and M. Castells, eds., *Global Restructuring and Territorial Development* (London: Sage, 1987): 1–17, quoted on 7.

46. R. O'Brien, *Global Financial Integration: The End of Geography* (London: Pinter, 1992).

CHAPTER 5

Voluntary Simplicity:
A New Social Movement?

Amitai Etzioni, George Washington University

Characterization of Voluntary Simplicity

The idea that achieving ever-higher levels of consumption of products and services is a vacuous goal has been with us from the onset of industrialization. These ideas often have taken the form of comparing the attractive life of the much poorer, preindustrial artisan to that of the more endowed industrial assembly-line worker. Many alternative approaches to life within a capitalist system have been proposed since the advent of capitalism, some more successful than others. One such approach, referred to by its adherents as voluntary simplicity, has been steadily gaining in popularity. This chapter examines this living strategy with regard to its sociological significance as a possible counterbalance to mainstream capitalist society.

Since the 1960s, criticism of consumerism has been common among the followers of counterculture movements, voiced largely in reaction to the postwar boom in consumer spending. These counterculture adherents sought a lifestyle that consumed and produced little, at least in terms of marketable objects, and sought to derive satisfaction, meaning, and a sense of purpose from contemplation, communion with nature, bonding, mood-altering substances, sex, and inexpensive products.[1] Over the years, many members of Western societies embraced an attenuated version of the values and mores of the counterculture. In fact, one survey suggests that North

American attitudes to materialism are changing. For example, "83 percent of those surveyed believe that the United States consumes too much, and 88 percent believe that protecting the environment will require 'major changes in the way we live.'"[2]

Some scholars postulate that a shift in values in relation to the material aspects of life emerges as societies move from a modern to a postmodern era. Under this paradigm,

> [m]odernized nations become postmodern as diminishing returns from economic growth, bureaucratization, and state intervention and unprecedented levels of affluence and welfare state security give rise to new constellations of values: postmaterialist emphases on the quality of life, self-expression, participation, and continued declines in traditional social norms.[3]

This change is effected through "intergenerational value replacement" in which individuals born into the high levels of material security of developed democratic capitalism emphasize (nonmaterial) subjective well-being: socialization during formative years produces deeply ingrained postmaterialist value orientations.[4]

In a survey conducted by researchers Ronald Inglehart and Paul Abramson, the percentage of respondents with clear postmaterialist values doubled from 9 percent in 1972 to 18 percent in 1991, while those with clear materialist values dropped by more than half, from 35 percent to 16 percent. (Those with mixed commitments moved more slowly, from 55 percent to 65 percent.)[5] Trends were similar for most Western European countries.[6]

Personal consumption, however, continued to grow, most dramatically during the 1980s. Consumer debt rose from approximately $350 billion in 1980 to $1,231 trillion in 1997,[7] and personal consumption expenditures jumped from $3,009.7 to $4,471.1 trillion (real dollars) between 1980 and 1994.[8] Meanwhile, the personal savings rate of Americans fell from 7.9 percent in 1980 to 4.2 percent in 1990 and has remained near this level ever since.[9] As one commentator notes, during the 1980s

> Laissez-faire economic policies and newly internationalized stock and bond markets created an easy-money euphoria among the well to do, which translated into a "get it while you can" binge in the middle echelons of the consumer society. . . . not since the Roaring Twenties had conspicuous consumption been so lauded. Over the decade, personal debt matched national debt in soaring to new heights, as consumers filled their houses and garages with third cars, motor boats, home entertainment centers, and whirlpool baths.[10]

Still, the search for alternatives to a consumerist-oriented lifestyle has survived such periods of intensive conspicuous consumption and continues to attract people, such as those involved in the voluntary simplicity approach. Voluntary simplicity refers to the decision to limit expenditures on consumer goods and services and to cultivate nonmaterialistic sources of satisfaction and meaning, out of free will rather than out of coercion by poverty, government austerity programs, or imprisonment. It has been described by one of its main proponents, author Duane Elgin, as "a manner of living that is outwardly more simple and inwardly more rich. . . . a deliberate choice to live with less in the belief that more of life will be returned to us in the process."[11]

As I already have suggested, criticism of consumerism and the quest for alternatives is as old as capitalism itself. However, the issue is increasingly relevant to our lives. The collapse of noncapitalist economic systems has led many to assume that capitalism is the superior system and therefore to refrain from critically examining its goals, even though capitalism does harbor serious defects. Recent developments in former communist countries as they grapple with the free market raise numerous concerns. Many in the East and West find that capitalism does not address spiritual concerns—the quest for transcendental connections and meanings—they believe are important to all.[12] Furthermore, as many societies with rapidly rising populations now seek affluence as their primary domestic goal, they face environmental, psychological, and other issues raised by consumerism on a scale not previously considered. For instance, the undesirable side effects of intensive consumerism that used to be of concern chiefly to highly industrialized societies now are faced by hundreds of millions of people in Asian countries and in other places where rapid economic development has occurred recently. Finally, the transition from consumption based on the satisfaction of perceived basic needs (secure shelter, food, clothing) to consumerism (the preoccupation with gaining ever higher levels of consumption, including a considerable measure of conspicuous consumption of status goods) seems to be more pronounced as societies become wealthier. Hence, a reexamination of this aspect of mature capitalism is particularly timely. Indeed, the current environment of increasing and expansive affluence might be particularly hospitable to moderate forms of voluntary simplicity.

This examination proceeds first by providing a description of voluntary simplicity, exploring its different manifestations and its relationship to competitiveness as the need and urge to gain higher levels of income is curbed. It then considers whether higher income, and the greater consumption it enables, produces higher contentment. This is a crucial issue because it makes a world of difference to the sustainability of voluntary simplicity if it is perceived as generating deprivations and hence requires strong motivational forces in order to spread and persevere, or if consumerism is found to be an obsessive and possibly addictive habit, in which case voluntary simplicity would be liberating and much more self-propelling and sustaining. An application of eminent psychologist Abraham Maslow's theory of human needs is particularly relevant here in answering the question and in determining the future of voluntary simplicity as a major cultural factor. This theory is further reinforced by examining the "consumption" of a subcategory of goods whose supply and demand are not governed by the condition of scarcity in the postmodern era. The chapter closes with a discussion of the societal consequences of voluntary simplicity.

One rather moderate form of voluntary simplicity is practiced by economically well-off people who voluntarily give up some consumer goods they could readily afford but basically maintain their consumption-oriented lifestyle. For example, they "dress down" in one way or another, or drive old cars.

These trends are reflected in the stylistic return during the 1990s to classic, "simple" design and natural looks, which, while they may appear simpler, often are just as costly, as Pilar Viladas writes: "In architecture and design today, less is more again. Houses, rooms and furnishings are less ornate, less complicated and less ostentatious than they were 10 years ago. Rather than putting their money on display, people seem to be investing in a quieter brand of luxury, based on comfort and quality."[13]

While this tendancy, referred to as downshifting, is moderate in scope, and perhaps because it is moderate, it is not limited to the very wealthy. Some professionals and other members of the middle class are replacing elaborate dinner parties with simple meals, pot-luck dinners, take-out food, or social events built around desserts only. Some lawyers are reported to have cut back on the billing-hours race that drives many of their colleagues to work late hours and on weekends to gain increased income and a higher year-end bonus and to incur the favor of the firms for which they work.[14] Some businesses have encouraged limited degrees of voluntary simplicity. For instance, many workplaces have established "casual dress" Fridays. In some workplaces, especially on the West coast, employees may dress down any workday.

It has been estimated that "by 2000, about 15 percent of Americans will have scaled back their lives in one way or another."[15] The most common recent changes have included reducing work hours, switching to lower-paying jobs, and quitting work to stay at home,[16] changes that may, but do not necessarily correlate with downshifting. In fact, as one 1996 poll found, "48 percent of Americans [had] done at least one of the following [between 1991 and 1996]: cut back their hours at work, declined or didn't seek a promotion, lowered their expectations for what they need out of life, reduced their commitments or moved to a community with a less hectic way of life."[17] Another survey reports that "one in three adults say they would accept a smaller paycheck in exchange for having a simpler lifestyle."[18]

In addition, there are people who have given up high-paying, high-stress jobs to live on less—often much less—income. In one case, a couple quit their jobs as high-paid executives in the telecommunications industry and now live on their savings, expending about $25,000 per year and using their time writing and performing volunteer work.[19]

Ideas associated with voluntary simplicity are widely held, although not necessarily reflected in actual behavior. In 1989 a majority of working Americans rated "a happy family life" as a much more important indicator of success than "earning a lot of money"—by a notably wide margin of 62 percent to 10 percent.[20]

In addition, numerous women and some men prefer part-time jobs or jobs that allow them to work at home, even if better-paying full-time jobs are open to them, because they are willing to reconcile themselves with earning a lower income in order to dedicate more time to their children and be at home when their children are there.[21] People who switch to new careers that are more personally meaningful but less lucrative also fall into this category. For instance, a 1997 source reports that "a growing wave of engineers, military officers, lawyers, and business people . . . are switching careers and becoming teachers."[22] Such career changers have significantly redefined their attitudes toward work. They ask themselves, as psychologist Barry Schwartz has put it, a crucial question: "Why have so many of us allowed ourselves to be put in a position where we spend half our waking lives doing what we don't want to do in a place we don't want to be?"[23]

People who voluntarily and significantly curtail their income tend to be stronger simplifiers than those who only moderate their lifestyle, because a significant reduction of income often leads to a much more encompassing "simplification" of lifestyle than selective downshifting. While it is possible for an affluent person to cease working altogether and still lead an affluent lifestyle, and for someone who does not reduce his or her income to cut spending drastically, it is expected that those who significantly curtail their income will simplify more than those who only moderate their consumption. Once people reduce their income, unless they have large savings, a new inheritance, or some other such non-work-related income, they must adjust their consumption.

People who adjust their lifestyles only or mainly because of economic pressures (having lost their main or second job, or for any other reason) do *not* qualify as voluntary simplifiers on the grounds that their shift is not voluntary. It can be argued that some poor people freely choose not to earn more and keep their consumption level meager. Many advocates of voluntary simplicity, however, take great pains to distinguish this way of life from one of poverty, stressing that while poverty is the life of the powerless, voluntary simplicity is empowering. As Elgin states, "Poverty is involuntary whereas simplicity is consciously chosen. Poverty is repressive; simplicity is liberating. Poverty generates a sense of helplessness, passivity, and despair; simplicity fosters personal empowerment, creativity, and a sense of ever present opportunity."[24]

The discussion here, however, focuses on people who had an affluent lifestyle and chose to give it up, for reasons that will become evident toward the end of the discussion.

Finally, holistic simplifiers adjust their whole life patterns according to the ethos of voluntary simplicity. Often many move from affluent suburbs or gentrified parts of major cities to smaller towns, the countryside, farms, and less affluent or less urbanized parts of the country—the Pacific Northwest is especially popular—with the explicit goal of leading a "simpler" life, although proponents of the voluntary simplicity philosophy are quick to point out that it is a viable living strategy in any environment. A small, loosely connected social movement, sometimes called the "simple living movement," has developed—complete with its own how-to books, multiple-step programs, and newsletters, although many have embarked on a life of voluntary simplicity independently, and some reports suggest that many who "experiment with simplicity of living said they did not view themselves as part of a social movement."[25]

The true simplifiers differ from the downshifters and even strong simplifiers not only in the scope of change in their conduct but also in that it is motivated by a coherently articulated philosophy. Elgin's 1981 book *Voluntary Simplicity*, which draws on the traditions of the Quakers, the Puritans, transcendentalists such as Ralph Waldo Emerson and Henry David Thoreau, and various world religions to provide a philosophical basis for living a simple life continues to be a major source of inspiration among voluntary simplicity's proponents.[26] Indeed, many note that the simplicity movement as a whole is much in debt to many of the world's major religions and philosophical traditions. As social historian David Shi has noted,

> The great spiritual teachers of the East—Zarathustra, Buddha, Lao-tse, and Confucius—all stressed that material self-control was essential to the good

life. . . . By far, however, the most important historical influence on American simplicity has been the combined heritage of Greco-Roman culture and Judeo-Christian ethics. Most Greek and Roman philosophers were emphatic in their praise of simple living, as were the Hebrew prophets and Jesus.[27]

These simplicity-oriented philosophies often are explicitly anticonsumerist. Elgin, for example, calls for "dramatic changes in the overall levels and patterns of consumption in developed nations," adding that "this will require dramatic changes in the consumerist messages we give ourselves through the mass media."[28] In 1997 the Public Broadcasting Corporation broadcast a special called *Affluenza*. Voluntary simplicity was said to provide a treatment for an "epidemic" whose symptoms are "shopping fever, a rash of personal debt, chronic stress, overwork and exhaustion of natural resources." It promised a follow-up on "better living for less." The Center for a New American Dream publishes a quarterly report on the same issues simply called *Enough!* The message that reducing wasteful consumerist practices is essential has been voiced on an international level as well, as witnessed by statements such as the following issued at the United Nations' 1992 Rio Conference on the Environment: "To achieve sustainable development and a higher quality of life for all people, states should reduce and eliminate unsustainable patterns of production and consumption."[29]

While one can readily profile the various kinds of simplifiers, there are no reliable measurements that enable us to establish the number of each of the three kinds of simplifiers or to determine whether their ranks are growing. One recent publication, though, estimates that nearly one out of four adult Americans, for a total of 44 million, is a "Cultural Creative," who ranks voluntary simplicity high among his or her values.[30]

Social Implications of Voluntary Simplicity

The question of whether voluntary simplicity can greatly expand its reach depends to a significant extent on the question of whether voluntary simplicity constitutes a sacrifice that people must be constantly motivated to make or is in itself a major source of satisfaction, and hence self-motivating.

Consumerism is justified largely in terms of the notion that the more goods and services a person uses, the more satisfied a person will be. Early economists thought that people had a fixed set of needs, and they worried what would motivate people to work and save once their income allowed them to satisfy those needs. Subsequently, however, it was widely agreed that people's needs can be enhanced artificially through advertising and social pressures, and hence they are said to have if not unlimited, at least very expandable consumer needs.

In contrast, critics argue that the cult of consumer goods (of objects) stands between people and contentment, and prevents people from experiencing authentic expressions of affection and appreciation by others. Western popular culture is replete with narratives about fathers (in earlier days), and recently of mothers as well, who slaved to bring home consumer goods—but, far from being appreciated by their children and spouses, found often only late in life, that their families would have preferred if the breadwinners had spent more time with them and showed them affection and appreciation (or expressed their feelings directly, through attention and attendance, hugs and pats on the back, rather than mediate that expression by working hard and long to buy things). Playwright Arthur Miller's *Death of a Salesman* is a telling example of this genre. Miller's work remains relevant today, as evidenced by the popular response to Neil Simon's *Proposals,* a remake of his story.

Social science findings (which admittedly may have many well-known limitations and do not all correlate on this topic) in *toto* seem to support the notion that income does not significantly affect contentment, with the important exception of the poor. For instance, Frank M. Andrews and Stephen B. Withey found that the level of one's socioeconomic status had meager effects on one's "sense of well-being" and no significant effect on "satisfaction with life-as-a-whole."[31] And Jonathan Freedman discovered that levels of reported happiness did not vary greatly among the members of different economic classes, with the exception of the very poor, who tended to be less happy than others.[32]

Researchers David G. Myers and Ed Diener find that among the poor in poor countries—those who cannot afford life's necessities—satisfaction with income "is a moderate predictor" of subjective well-being.[33] They also report, though, that "once people are able to afford life's necessities, increasing levels of affluence matter surprisingly little."[34] Diener and R. J. Larsen found "a mere +.12 correlation between income and happiness" and uncovered no long-term effect of increases or decreases in income on happiness.[35]

A survey of the people on *Forbes's* wealthiest Americans list finds that those individuals were not significantly happier than other Americans and that, in fact, 37 percent reported being less happy than the average American, a statistic Myers and Diener also report.[36] Even as personal income in the United States has climbed from roughly $4,000 (in 1990 dollars) in 1930 to approximately $16,000 (in 1990 dollars) in the early 1990s, the percentage of people describing themselves as "very happy" generally has hovered in the low- to mid-30s.[37]

Researcher Angus Campbell reports that in 20 years' surveys "the proportion of 'very happy' people is higher as we move from low- to high-income levels," but he is careful to note that this is a "very stable relationship, but by no means an exclusive one. Even among the most affluent, there are a large majority who describe themselves as less than very happy and a sizable minority of the least affluent claim that they are very happy."[38] As he summarizes, "Happiness is far from the exclusive domain of the well-to-do."[39]

Studies of the country's well-being show that economic growth does not significantly affect happiness (though at any given time the people of poor countries are generally less happy than those of wealthy ones). As Worldwatch Institute researcher Alan Durning states, "People living in the nineties are on average four-and-a-half times richer than their great-grandparents were at the turn of the century, but they are not four-and-a-half times happier. Psychological evidence shows that the relationship between consumption and personal happiness is weak."[40] In addition, it has been reported that while per-capita disposable (after-tax) income in inflation-adjusted dollars almost exactly doubled between 1960 and 1990, 32 percent of Americans reported that they were "very happy" in 1993, almost the same proportion as did in 1957 (35 percent). Although economic growth slowed since the mid-1970s, Americans' reported happiness was remarkably stable (nearly always between 30 and 35 percent) across both high-growth and low-growth periods. Moreover, in the same period, from the late 1950 to the early 1990s, rates of depression, violent crime, divorce, and teen suicide have all risen dramatically.[41]

Recent psychological studies have made even stronger claims: that the *more* concerned people are with their financial well-being, the *less* likely they are to be happy. One group of researchers found that "[h]ighly central financial success aspirations . . . were associated with less self-actualization, less vitality, more depression, and more anxiety."[42]

Another scholar, Robert Lane, pointed out that

. . . most studies agree that a satisfying family life is the most important contributor to well-being. . . . [T]he joys of friendship often rank second. Indeed, according to one study, an individual's number of friends is a better predictor of his well-being than is the size of his income. Satisfying work and leisure often rank third or fourth but, strangely, neither is closely related to actual income.[43]

Increases in individual income briefly boost happiness, but the additional happiness is not sustainable because the higher income level becomes the standard against which people measure their future achievements.[44]

These and other such findings raise the following question: If higher levels of income do not buy happiness, why do people work hard to gain higher income? The answer is complex. High income in consumer-based capitalist societies "buys" prestige; others find purpose and meaning and contentment in the income-producing work *per se*. There is, however, also good reason to suggest that the combination of artificial fanning of needs and other cultural pressures, manifest through such vehicles as the aggressive American marketing industry, maintains people in consumer-based roles when these are not truly or deeply satisfying. As social historian Robert Bellah has stated, "[t]hat happiness is to be attained through limitless material acquisition is denied by every religion and philosophy known to man but is preached incessantly by every American television set."[45]

Voluntary simplicity works because consuming less, once one's basic creature-comfort needs are taken care of, is not a source of deprivation, so long as one is freed from the culture of consumerism and the artificial "needs" it induces. Voluntary simplicity represents a new culture, one that respects work (even if it generates only low or moderate income) and appreciates conservation and modest rather than conspicuous or lavish consumption, but does not advocate a life of sacrifice or service (and in this sense is rather different from ascetic religious orders or some socialist expressions, as in kibbutzim). Voluntary simplicity suggests that there is a declining marginal satisfaction in the pursuit of ever-higher levels of consumption. And it points to sources of satisfaction in deliberately and voluntarily avoiding the quest for ever-growing levels of affluence and consumption and making one's personal and social project the pursuit of other purposes. These purposes are not specifically defined other than that they are not materialistic. Indeed, just as some people intrinsically find satisfaction in work and savings rather than in purchasing power, so some voluntary simplicity followers find satisfaction in the very fact that they choose (and have not been forced to choose) a simpler lifestyle and are proud of their choice. Moreover, as they learn to cultivate other pursuits, simplifiers gain more satisfaction out of lifelong learning, public life, volunteering, community participation, sports, cultural activities, and observing or communing with nature.

In each of these areas, some simplifiers slip back into consumerism, promoted by marketeers. Thus, those engaged in sports may feel they "need" a large variety of expensive, ever-changing, fashionable clothing and equipment to enjoy their sport of choice. But a considerable number of members of the affluent classes in affluent societies—especially, it seems, societies that have been well off for a while—find that they can keep consumerism under control and truly learn to cultivate lower-cost sources of contentment and meaning. They enjoy touch football, a well-worn pair of sneakers, doing their own home repairs and cooking, or take pride in their beat-up car.

The obsessive nature of some consumerism is evident in that people who seek to curb it often find doing so difficult. Many people purchase things they later realize they neither need nor desire, or stop shopping only after they have exhausted all their sources of credit. (This reference is not to the poor but to those who have several credit cards and who constantly "max" them out.) In short, the conversion of a large number of people to voluntary simplicity requires taking into account the fact that constant consumption cannot simply be stopped, that transitional help may be required, and that conversion is best achieved when consumerism is replaced with other sources of satisfaction and meaning.

Abraham Maslow, the Haves and the Have-Nots, and Voluntary Simplicity

We have seen that there is reason to suggest that the continued psychological investment in ever-higher levels of consumption has an unpleasant addictive quality. People seek to purchase and amass ever more goods whether they need them (in any sense of the term) or not. It follows that voluntary simplicity, far from being a source of stress, is a source of a more profound satisfaction. This point is further supported by examining the implications of Maslow's theory to these points.

The rise of voluntary simplicity in advanced stages of capitalism, and for the privileged members of these societies, can be assessed in light of a psychological theory of Abraham Maslow, detailed especially in his work *Towards a Psychology of Being*. There he suggested that "the basic motivations supply ready-made an hierarchy of values which are related to each other as higher needs and lower needs, stronger and weaker, more vital and more dispensable," and ordered "in an integrated hierarchy . . . that is, they rest one upon another."[46] At the base of the hierarchy are basic creature comforts, such as the need for food, shelter, and clothing. Higher up are the need for love and esteem. Self-expression crowns the hierarchy. Although there are some connections, these needs are disassociated from the classical Freudian concept of "instincts."

Maslow theorized that people seek to satisfy lower needs before they turn to higher ones, and that healthy people have sufficiently gratified their basic needs for safety, belong-ingness, love, respect and self-esteem so that they are motivated primarily by trends to self-actualization (defined as ongoing actualization of potentials, ca-pacities and talents, as fulfillment of mission [or call, fate, destiny, or voca-tion], as a fuller knowledge of, and acceptance of, the person's own intrinsic nature, as an unceasing trend toward unity, integration or synergy within the person).[47]

Maslow's theory does not, however, postulate that basic needs are superseded by higher pursuits. As he states, "[g]rowth is seen then not only as progres-sive gratification of basic needs to the point where they 'disappear,' but also in the specific growth motivations over and above these basic needs. . . . We are thereby helped also to realize that basic needs and self-actualization do not contradict each other any more than do childhood and maturity."[48] The primary issue relevant here is whether or not people continue to invest themselves heavily in the quest for "creature comforts" long after they are quite richly endowed in such goods, and if in the process other needs, such as emotional interaction and care for others, are ignored or undervalued.

Maslow's thesis is compatible with the suggestion that voluntary simplic-ity may appeal to people after their basic needs are well satisfied. Once they feel secure that these needs will be attended to in the future, they are objec-tively ready to focus on their higher, "self-actualizing" needs—even if their consumeristic tendencies blind them to the fact that they are read to shift upward, so to speak. Voluntary simplicity is thus a choice a successful cor-porate lawyer, not a homeless person, faces; Singapore, not Rwanda. Indeed, to urge the poor or near poor to draw satisfaction from consuming less is to ignore the profound connection between the hierarchy of human needs and consumption. Consumption becomes an obsession that can be overcome only after basic creature-comfort needs are sated.

Consumerism has one often-observed feature that is particularly relevant here. Consumerism sustains itself, in part because it is visible. People who are "successful" in traditional capitalist terms need to signal their achieve-ments in ways that are readily visible to others in order to gain their appre-ciation, approval, and respect. They do so by displaying their income by buying expensive status goods, as social critic Vance Packard demonstrated several decades ago.[49]

People who are well socialized into the capitalist system often believe that they need income to buy things they "need" (or that without additional in-come they "cannot make ends meet"). But examinations of the purchases of those who are not poor or near poor shows that they buy numerous items not needed for survival but needed to meet status needs. This is the sociological role of Nike sneakers, leather jackets, fur coats, jewelry, fancy watches, expensive cars, and numerous other such goods, all items that are highly visible to people who are not members of one's community, who do not know one personally. These goods allow people to display the size of their income and wealth without attaching their accountant's statement to their lapels.

In such a culture, if people *choose* a job or career pattern that is not income-maximizing but is voluntarily simplistic, they have no established means of signaling that they choose such a course rather than having been forced into it and that they have not failed by the mores of the capitalist society. There are no lapel pins stating "I could have but preferred not to." Voluntary simplicity responds to this need for status recognition without expensive conspicuous consumption by choosing lower-cost but visible consumer goods that enable one to signal that one has chosen, rather than been coerced into, a less affluent lifestyle.

Voluntary simplicity achieves this by using select consumer goods that are clearly associated with a simpler life pattern and are as visible as the traditional status symbols *and/or* cannot be afforded by those who reduced consumption merely because their income fell. Which specific consumption items signal voluntary simplicity vs. coerced simplicity change over time and from one sub-culture to another. Some refer to this practice as "conspicuous non-consumption."[50] In this way, voluntary simplifiers can satisfy what Maslow considers another basic human need, that of gaining the appreciation of others, without using a high—and ever escalating—level of consumption as their principle means of gaining positive feedback.

This idea is of considerable import when voluntary simplicity is examined not merely as an empirical phenomenon, as a pattern for social science to observe and dissect, but also as a set of values that has advocates and that may be judged in terms of the moral appropriateness of those values. As I see it, voluntary simplicity advocates addressing those who are in the higher reaches of income, those who are privileged but who are fixated on the creature-comfort level; it may help them free themselves from the artificial fanning of these basic needs and assist them in moving to higher levels of satisfaction. The same advocacy addressed to the poor or near poor (or disadvantaged groups or the "have-not" countries) might correctly be seen as an attempt to deny them the satisfaction of basic human needs. Consumer*ism,* not consumption, is the target for voluntary simplicity.

Oddly, a major development brought about by technological innovations makes it more likely that voluntary simplicity may be expanded and that the less privileged and have-nots may gain in the process. In considering this development, I first discuss the nature of nonscarce objects and then turn to their implications for the reallocation of wealth.

Voluntary Simplicity in the Cyber-Age

Developed societies, it has been argued for decades, are moving from economies that rely heavily on the industrial sector to economies that increasingly draw on the information industry.[51] The scope of this transition and its implications are often compared to those societies that experienced as they moved from farming to manufacturing. It should be noted that there is a measure of overblown rhetoric in such generalizations. Computers are, for instance, classified as a major item of the rising knowledge industry rather than of traditional manufacturing. However, once a specific computer is programmed and designed, a prototype tested and debugged, the routine fastening of millions of chip boards into millions of boxes to make personal computers is not significantly different from, say, the manufacturing of toasters. And while publishers of books are now often classified as part of the knowledge industry and computers are widely used to manufacture books, books are still objects that are made, shipped, and sold like other non-knowledge industry products. Acknowledging these examples of overblown claims is not to deny that a major transformation is taking place, only that its growth and scope are much slower and less dramatic than was originally expected. Indeed, given this slower rate of change, societies are able to face the ramifications in a more orderly manner.

The main significance of the rise of the cyber-age is that the resulting shrinking of scarcity enhances the possibility for the expansion of voluntary simplicity. This important point is surprisingly rarely noted. Unlike the consumer objects that dominated the manufacturing age—cars, washers, bikes, televisions, houses (and computers)—many knowledge "objects" can be consumed, possessed, and still be had by numerous others—that is shared—at minimal loss or cost. Hence, in this basic sense, *knowledge defies scarcity,* thus reducing scarcity, a major driving principle behind industrial capitalist economies. Compare, for instance, a Porsche to Beethoven's Ninth Symphony (or a minivan to a folk song). If an affluent citizen buys a particular Porsche (or any other of the billions of traditional consumer objects), this Porsche—and the resources that were invested in making it—is unavailable to any others (if one disregards friends and family). Once the Porsche is "consumed," little of value remains. By contrast, the Ninth (and a rising number of other such objects of knowledge) can be copied millions of times, enjoyed by millions at one and the same time, and is still available in its full, original glory.

Perhaps there is a measure of snobbism in showing a preference for the Ninth over a Porsche. But this is hardly the issue here; the same advantage is found when one compares an obscene rap song to a Volkswagen Beetle, or a pornographic image on the Internet to a low-income housing project. The criterion at issue is the difference between the resources that go into making each item and the extent to which it can be copied, consumed, and still be "possessed" and shared.

True, even knowledge-related objects have some minimal costs, because they need some non-knowledge "carrier"; they have some limited material base, a disk, a tape, or some paper, and most require an instrument—a radio, for instance—to access them. However, typically the costs of these material carriers are minimal compared to those of most consumer goods. While many perishable goods (consumer objects such as food or gasoline) are low in cost per item, one needs to buy many of them repeatedly to keep consuming them. In contrast, "knowledge" objects such as cassette tapes or laser discs can be enjoyed numerous times and are not "consumed" (eaten up, so to speak). In that sense, knowledge objects have the miraculous quality of the bush Moses saw at Mount Sinai: It burned but was not consumed.

What is said for music also holds for books and art. Shakespeare in a 99-cent paperback edition is no less Shakespeare than in an expensive leather-bound edition, and above all, millions can read Shakespeare—his writings are still available, undiminished, for millions of others. Millions of students can read Kafka's short stories, solve geographical puzzles, and study Plato, without any diminution of these items. That is, these sources of satiation are governed by laws that are the mirror opposite of those laws of economics that govern oil, steel, and other traditional consumer objects from cellular phones to lasers.

Numerous games (although not all) are based on symbolic patterns and hence, like knowledge objects, are learned but not consumed, with minimal costs. Children play checkers (and other games) with discarded bottle caps. Chess played by inmates, using figures made of stale bread, is not less enjoyable than a game played with rare, ivory hand-carved pieces. (One may gain a secondary satisfaction from the aesthetic beauty or expense of the set, but these satisfactions have nothing to do with the game of chess per se.)

Similarly, bonding, love, intimacy, friendship, contemplation, communion with nature, certain forms of exercise (yoga, for example, as distinct from step aerobics), all can free one, to a large extent, from key laws of capitalist economies. In effect, these relationship-based sources of satisfaction are superior from this viewpoint to knowledge objects, because in the kind of relationships just enumerated, when one gives more, one often receives more, and thus both sides (or, in larger social entities such as communities, all sides) are "enriched" by the same "transactions." Thus when two individuals are getting to know one another as persons and become "invested" in one another during the ritual known as dating, often both are richer for it. (This important point is often overlooked by those who coined the term "social capital" to claim that relations are akin to transactions.) Similarly, parents who are more involved with their children often (although by no means always) find that their children are more involved with them, and both draw more satisfaction from the relationship. Excesses are far from unknown—for example, when some parents attempt to draw most of their satisfaction from their children, or in sharply asymmetrical relations in which one side exploits the other's dedication or love. Nonetheless, mutual "enrichment" seems much more common.

The various sources of nonmaterialist satisfaction listed here were celebrated by counterculture movements. However, voluntary simplicity differs from these counterculture movements in that voluntary simplicity, even by those highly dedicated to it, seeks to combine a reasonable level of work and consumption to attend to creature-comfort needs with satisfaction from higher sources. The counterculture movements of the past tried to minimize work and consumption, denying attention to basic needs, and hence became unsustainable. To put it more charitably, they provided an extreme, path-blazing version for the voluntary simplicity ideology that followed. While much more moderate than the lifestyle advocated by the counterculture, the voluntary simplicity approach, because it fosters satisfaction from knowledge rather than consumer objects, reduces the need to work and shop. As a result, it frees time and other scarce resources for further cultivation of nonmaterialistic sources of satisfaction, from acquiring music appreciation to visiting museums, from slowing down to enjoy nature to relearning the reading of challenging books or watching classic films.

None of the *specific* sources of nonmaterialistic satisfaction are necessarily tied to voluntary simplicity. One can engage in a voluntarily simple life without enjoying music or nature, being a loving person or a consumed chess player, an Internet buff or a domino aficionado. However, voluntary simplicity does point to the quest for *some* sources of satisfaction other than the consumption of goods and services. This statement is based on the elementary assumption that people prefer higher levels of satisfaction over lower ones; hence if higher satisfaction is not derived from ever-higher levels of consumption, their "excess" quest, that which is not invested in the unnecessary pursuit of creature comforts, seeks to be invested elsewhere. It follows that while the specific activities that serve as the sources of nonmaterialist satisfaction will vary, some such must be cultivated or voluntary simplicity may not be sustainable.

A Voluntarily Simplistic Society

The shift to voluntary simplicity has significant consequences for society at large, above and beyond the lives of the individuals who are involved. A promising way to think about these effects is to ask what the societal consequences would be if more and more members of society, possibly an overwhelming majority, engaged in one kind or another of voluntary simplicity. These consequences are quite self-evident for environmental concerns; however, they are much less self-evident for social justice and thus warrant further attention.

The more comprehensively voluntary simplicity is embraced as a lifestyle by a given population, the greater the potential for realizing a fundamental element of social justice, that of basic socioeconomic equality. Before this claim is justified, a few words are needed on the meaning of the term "equality," a complex and much-contested notion.

While conservatives tend to favor limiting equality to legal and political statutes, those who are more politically left and liberal favor various degrees of redistribution of wealth in ways that would enhance socioeconomic equality. Members of the left-liberal camp differ significantly in the extent of equality they seek. Some favor far-reaching, if not total, socioeconomic equality in which all persons would share alike in whatever assets, income, and consumption are available, an idea championed by the early kibbutz movements. Others limit their quest for equality to ensuring that all members of society will at least have their basic creature comforts equally provided, a position championed by many liberals. The following discussion focuses on this quest for socioeconomic and not just legal and political equality, focusing on equality at the basic, creature-comfort level rather than comprehensive overall equality. (The debate about whether or not holistic equality is virtuous, and if it entails undercutting both liberty and the level of economic performance on which the provision of creature comforts depends, is an important subject. However, it need not be addressed until basic socioeconomic equality is achieved, and so far this has proven to be an elusive goal.)

If one seeks to advance basic socioeconomic equality, one must identify sources that will propel the desired change. Social science findings and recent historical experience leave little doubt that ideological arguments (such as pointing to the injustices of inequalities, fanning guilt, introducing various other liberal and socialist arguments that favor greater economic equality), organizing labor unions and left-leaning political parties, and introducing various items of legislation (such as estate taxes and progressive income tax) have thus far not effected the desired result—namely, significant wealth redistribution—in democratic societies. The most that can said for them is that they helped prevent inequality from growing bigger.[52] Additionally, in recent years, many of the measures, arguments, and organizations that championed these limited, rather ineffectual efforts to advance equality could not be sustained, or were successful only after they had been greatly scaled back.[53] Moreover, for these and other reasons that need not be explored here, economic *inequalities* seem to have increased in many parts of the world. The former communist countries, including the Soviet Union, where once a sacrifice of liberties was associated with a minimal but usually reliable provision of subsistence needs, have moved to a socioeconomic system that tolerates, indeed is built on, a much higher level of inequality, one in which millions have no reliable source of creature comforts. Numerous other countries that had measures of socialist policies, from India to Mexico, have been moving in the same direction. And in many Western countries social safety nets are under attack, being shredded in some countries and merely lowered in others. When all is said and done, it seems clear that if basic socioeconomic equality is to be significantly advanced, it will need some new or additional force.

Voluntary simplicity, if more widely embraced, might well be the best new way to foster the societal conditions under which the limited reallocation of wealth needed to ensure the basic needs of all could become politically possible. The reason is as basic and simple as it is essential: To the extent that the privileged (those whose basic creature comforts are well sated and who are engaging in conspicuous consumption) will find value, meaning, and satisfaction in other pursuits, ones that are not labor or capital intensive, they can be expected to be more willing to give up some consumer goods and some income. These "freed" resources, in turn, can be shifted to those whose basic needs have not been sated, without undue political resistance or backlash.

Enhancing basic equality in a society in which voluntary simplicity is spreading is rather different from doing so in a society in which the same cause is served by coercive measures. First, the economically privileged are often those who are in power, who command political skills, or who can afford to buy support. Hence, to force them to yield significant parts of their wealth often has proven impractical, whether it is just or theoretically correct or not. Second, even if the privileged can somehow be made to yield a significant part of their wealth, such forced concessions leave in their wake strong feelings of resentment that often have led the wealthy to nullify or circumvent programs such as progressive income taxes and inheritance taxes, or to support political parties or regimes that oppose wealth reallocation.

Finally, the record shows that when people are strongly and positively motivated by nonconsumerist values and sources of satisfaction, they are less inclined to exceed their basic consumption needs and more willing to share their "excess" resources. Voluntary simplicity provides a culturally fashioned expression for such inclinations and helps enforce them, and it provides a socially approved and supported lifestyle that is both psychologically sustainable and compatible with basic socioeconomic equality.

A variety of public policies, especially in Holland but also in France and Germany, seek to transfer some wealth and income from the privileged to those who do not have the resources needed to meet their basic needs has been introduced recently. A major category of such policies are those that concern the distribution of labor, especially in countries in which unemployment is high, by curbing overtime, shortening the work week, and allowing more part-time work.

Another batch of policies seeks to ensure that all members of society will have sufficient income to satisfy at least some of their basic needs, approaching the matter from the income rather than the work side. These include increases in the minimum wage, the introduction of the earned income tax credit, attempts at establishing universal health insurance, and housing allowances for the deserving poor.

In short, if voluntary simplicity is more and more extensively embraced as a combined result of changes in culture and public policies by those whose basic creature comforts have been sated, it might provide the foundations for a society that accommodates basic socioeconomic equality much more readily than societies in which conspicuous consumption is rampant.

Notes

I am indebted to Natalie Klein, Rachel Mears, and Barbara Fusco for their research assistance on this version of this chapter.

1. See Frank Musgrove, *Ecstasy and Holiness: Counter Culture and the Open Society* (Bloomington: Indiana University Press, 1974), 17–18, 40–41, 198.

Musgrove notes the paradox that although the counterculture is "marked by frugality and low consumption," it arises specifically in wealthy societies: 17.

2. United Nations Environment Programme, *Global Environmental Outlook–1; Chapter 2: Regional Perspectives.* http://unep.unep.org/unep/eia/geo1/ch/ch2_12.htm

3. Duane Swank, "Modernization and Postmodernization: Cultural, Economic, and Political Change in 43 Societies," *Comparative Political Studies* (April 1998): 247.

4. Ibid.

5. Paul R. Abramson and Ronald Inglehart, *Value Change in Global Perspective* (Ann Arbor: University of Michigan Press, 1995): 19. Similar shifts occurred in most developed nations: 12–15.

6. Ibid., 12–15.

7. *Public Agenda,* "Consumer Debt Rising in Recent Years," 1998. Available: http://www.publicagenda.org:80/CGI/getdoc . . . 168994x0y64&pg=economy _factfiles13.html.

8. U.S. Bureau of the Census, *Statistical Abstract of the United States, 1996* (116th ed.) (Washington, D.C.: U.S. Bureau of the Census, 1996), table 695.

9. U.S. Bureau of the Census, *Statistical Abstract of the United States, 1994* (114th ed.) (Washington, D.C.: U.S. Bureau of the Census, 1996), table 695.

10. Alan Durning, *How Much Is Enough? The Consumer Society and the Future of the Earth* (New York: Worldwatch Institute, 1992), 33.

11. Duane Elgin, *Voluntary Simplicity: Toward a Way of Life That is Outwardly Simple, Inwardly Rich* (New York: William Morrow, 1981).

12. See, for instance, Charles Handy, *The Hungry Spirit: Beyond Capitalism: A Quest for Purpose in the Modern World* (New York: Broadway Books, 1998).

13. Pilar Viladas, "Inconspicuous Consumption," *New York Times Magazine,* April 13, 1997, 25.

14. Rita Henley Jensen, "Recycling the American Dream," *ABA Journal* (April 1996): 68–72.

15. Trends Research Institute, cited in Stephanie Zimmerman, "Living Frugal and Free," *Chicago Sun-Times,* April 20, 1997, 6.

16. "Choosing the Joys of a Simplified Life," *New York Times,* September 21, 1995, C1; Merck Family Fund, *Yearning for a Balance: Views of Americans on Consumption, Materialism, and the Environment, Executive Summary* (The Harwood Group, 1995).

17. John Martellaro, "More People Opting for a Simpler Lifestyle," *The Plain Dealer* (Kansas City), February 10, 1996, 1E.

18. "Boomers Would Pay To Simplify," *USA Today,* November 7, 1997, 1A.

19. "Voluntary Simplicity," *NPR Morning Edition,* February 26, 1997.

20. "Is Greed Dead?" *Fortune,* August 14, 1989, 41.

21. "More Mothers Staying at Home," *Boston Globe,* December 18, 1994, NW1.

22. "More Career-Switchers Declare, 'Those Who Can, Teach,'" *Wall Street Journal,* April 8, 1997, B1.

23. Barry Schwartz, *The Costs of Living: How Market Freedom Erodes the Best Things in Life* (New York: W.W. Norton and Company, 1994), 235–36.

24. Elgin, *Voluntary Simplicity,* 34.

25. Ibid., 51.

26. Ibid., esp. 27–28.

27. David E. Shi, *The Simple Life: Plain Living and High Thinking in American Culture* (New York: Oxford University Press, 1985), 4.

28. Duane Elgin, *Voluntary Simplicity,* 201.

29. United Nations, *The Rio Declaration on Environment and Development,* 1992, Principle 8.

30. Paul H. Ray, "The Emerging Culture," *American Demographics* (February 1997): 29, 31.

31. Frank M. Andrews and Stephen B. Withey, *Social Indicators of Well-Being: Americans' Perceptions of Life Quality* (New York: Plenum Press, 1976), 254–55.

32. Jonathan L. Freedman, *Happy People: What Happiness Is, Who Has It, and Why* (New York: Harcourt Brace Jovanovich, 1978).

33. David G. Myers and Ed Diener, "Who Is Happy?" *Psychological Science* 6 (1995): 13.

34. Ibid.

35. Ed Diener and R. J. Larsen, "The Experience of Emotional Well-Being," in M. Lewis and J. M. Haviland, eds., *Handbook of Emotions* (New York: Guilford Press, 1993): 404–415. Cited in Myers and Diener, "Who Is Happy?."

36. Myers and Diener, "Who Is Happy?," 13.

37. Data culled by Myers and Diener, ibid., from various sources.

38. Angus Campbell, *The Sense of Well-Being in America: Recent Patterns and Trends* (New York: McGraw-Hill, 1981), 56–57.

39. Ibid.

40. Durning, "How Much Is Enough?," 23.

41. Myers and Diener, "Who Is Happy?," 12–13; see also Ed Diener, E. Sandvik, L. Seidlitz, and M. Diener, "The Relationship Between Income and Subjective Well-Being: Relative or Absolute?" *Social Indicators Research* 28 (1993): 208.

42. Tim Kasser and Richard M. Ryan, "A Dark Side of the American Dream: Correlates of Financial Success as a Central Life Aspiration," *Journal of Personality and Social Psychology* 65 (1993): 420.

43. Robert E. Lane, "Does Money Buy Happiness?" *Public Interest,* (Fall 1993): 58.

44. Ibid., 56–65.

45. Robert Bellah, *The Broken Covenant: American Civil Religion in Time of Trial* (New York: Seabury Press, 1975), 134.

46. Abraham H. Maslow, *Toward A Psychology of Being* (Princeton: Von Nostrand, 1968), 172.

47. Ibid., 25.
48. Ibid., 26–27.
49. Vance Packard, *The Status Seekers: An Exploration of Class Behavior in America and the Hidden Barriers That Affect You, Your Community, Your Future* (New York: D. McKay Co., 1959).
50. David Brooks, "The Liberal Gentry," *The Weekly Standard,* December 30, 1996, January 6, 1997, 25.
51. Alvin Toffler, *Future Shock* (New York: Random House, 1970). Daniel Bell, *The Coming of Post-Industrial Society: A Venture in Social Forecasting* (New York: Basic Books, 1973).
52. Joseph A. Pechman, *Federal Tax Policy* (Washington, D.C.: The Brookings Institution, 1987), 6.
53. For instance, note the changes in the Labour Party in the United Kingdom and the Democratic Party in United States in the mid-1990s.

PART II

Emerging Models of the Firm

CHAPTER 6

Enterprise in the Information Age

*Sten A. Thore, Luso-American Development Chair,
Instituto Superior Tecnico, Lisbon, Portugal*

For some time economists have realized that many of the laws of the market economy are being rewritten by a growing reliance on software and knowledge-based products. Toward the end of the twentieth century, a new kind of economic goods and services made its appearance in the marketplace that has the potential of revolutionizing the workings of the entire capitalist economy. These are the *digital products*—communication, education, and entertainment in digital form. The appearance of the *digital economy* represents the current high-water mark of this development of a knowledge-based economy, with knowledge encoded in digital form.

In the text to follow, I argue that a new kind of economic analysis is needed to study the knowledge-based economy. I sketch the outlines of a new economic paradigm that traces the rapid transformation of the market economy in the information age.

The new paradigm is based on the recognition of the following four points:

1. The life cycles of knowledge products are often short, due to intense product development. As new and advanced products are launched on the market, the earlier generations become obsolete. Typically, the new generation of a product embodies not only upgraded technological and marketing characteristics but also a wider array of attributes.

Defining a product by the vector of services it delivers, the dimensionality of this vector increases all the time. Products become more *complex*.

2. Those corporations that successfully market and sell the most advanced products at any given time will experience spectacular growth rates—so-called *hypergrowth*. Economists have been late in recognizing this phenomenon, so characteristic of the knowledge economy. Conversely, corporations clinging to product laggards can see their markets collapse overnight, with disastrous results. The knowledge-based economy can become polarized into two camps: swarms of small start-up companies growing at phenomenal rates and stumbling giants.

3. The high-tech corporation typically is embarked on a dynamic path that is located far from equilibrium all the time. The orbit is nonlinear. It harbors the possibility of *chaos*.

4. In the resulting setting of industrial turmoil, there will occur rapid *technological evolution*. A kind of balance will be established between creativity and oblivion, between the commercialization of new products, the launching of new start-up companies, mergers and acquisitions, and bankruptcies.

Whereas conventional economics assumes optimizing behavior, equilibrium, and the stability of equilibrium, *the dominant mode of operation of the new knowledge-based corporations is suboptimal behavior and disequilibrium*. To back up these claims, I shall report on an extensive empirical study of the U.S. computer industry.

The chapter ends with some comments on the long-term perspectives of the U.S. economy. During the last two decades, the knowledge industry has been an important driver of the U.S. economy at large. The pivotal role of the U.S. knowledge-based corporations seems destined to continue well into the next century, as they are now expanding their markets globally. Corporations like Disney and Time Warner are becoming global digital powerhouses, enjoying not just domestic economies of scale but global economies of scale.

The Digital Economy

Toward the end of the twentieth century, a new kind of economic good and service has emerged that is changing the nature of the entire economic system. A *digital product* is information, entertainment, or education that is delivered in digital form, often communicated over great distances. Digital communication occurs when sound waves or light waves are converted to digital (binary) codes, transmitted, and finally converted back to sound or pictures. Early instances of digital communication are the word processor, the CD disk, and fiber-optic cables. In fiber-optic cables, sound or pictures encoded in binary form are transmitted by a pulse laser beam through a glass filament. Here are some examples of digital products that are here already or just around the corner:

- Personal communication services (PCS) will be Star Trek–like communicators that can be tucked into a coat pocket or into a small purse. They are tiny cordless phones with computing, faxing, and video features.
- Electronic commerce with electronic malls on the Internet where consumers can browse the goods that they are interested in and buy them.
- Distance learning, where you can be a student in a virtual classroom and do homework graded by famous professors at Harvard or MIT.
- Newspapers, radio, or movies accessed over the Internet.
- Telecommuting, where the employees of a company do their work at a computer workstation at home and are connected with the main office via videoconferencing.

A Brief Chronology of Events

Let me go back to the beginnings. As a convenient starting point, I choose the date of January 1, 1984, when American Telephone & Telegraph Co. was deregulated and split up. The seven Baby Bells (Ameritech, Bell Atlantic, BellSouth, Nynex, Pacific Telesis, Southwestern Bell, and U.S. West) were each handed a monopoly on their local lines. Deregulation opened the door to relentless product innovation and cutthroat competition, first in the long-distance market using fiber-optic cables to improve the quality of the sound dramatically, but soon also in cellular phone service. Then AT&T had to battle not only private long-distance carriers like MCI and Sprint but also a growing cellular phone industry. To stem the onslaught from the cellular communication companies, both the Baby Bells and AT&T acquired cellular services of their own. In 1993 AT&T bought the largest of them all, McCaw Cellular.

The pioneer in the cable industry was Ted Turner, a self-made television tycoon who in 1976 had started sending signals from his Atlanta "Superstation" to a satellite hovering 22,000 miles above Earth. The signals returning to Earth could be received by the fledgling cable TV market over all of North America and beyond. A couple of years later Turner turned to his next idea: an all-news program called Cable News Network (CNN) beamed to the world. It merged TV, satellites, cable, and international news operations.

Apple Computer also was born in 1976, as Steven Jobs and Stephen Wozniak got to work in Jobs's sister's bedroom, putting together their first 50 machines. Four years later, Apple went public. The price of the stock increased so rapidly that the state of Massachusetts temporarily stopped people from buying it. By the end of the day, the company had reached the list of the Fortune 500. The stock market placed Apple's value at $1.7 billion, which at the time was larger than that of Ford Motor Company. Apple came to pioneer some remarkable features in the PC industry, including the mouse and a windowslike software.

Ted Turner and Steven Jobs were the archetypes of a new breed of entrepreneurs, creating the first digital consumer products. Others were Craig O. McGaw (of McGaw Cellular) and Seymour Cray (of Cray Research). Several of the start-up companies founded by the first generation of digital entrepreneurs grew explosively. They were the first cases of a phenomenon that we may call hypergrowth—total revenues of a corporation growing at an annual rate of 50 percent or more, year after year. An industry like this had never been seen before.

To sustain their growth, these companies drew on several new sources of financing. A new breed of venture capitalists invested in Silicon Valley start-ups. New waves of initial public offerings (IPOs) hit Wall Street. And to raise necessary financing, many of these companies turned to a new debt instrument, the so-called junk bond (corporate bonds below investment grade). Timely junk issues enabled Compaq, Silicon Graphics, Cray Research, and others to survive dangerous industry downturns. The U.S. hard disk industry was saved by junk, including $250 million for Seagate Technology. Similarly, McGaw and Turner got a helping hand in their early days from Michael Milken (junk bond king) of Drexel, Burnham Lambert Inc. Seeing the advent of the new information economy earlier than others, Milken financed large buildings blocks of the new "information superhighway."

A new wave of digital products arrived in the early 1990s with the development of new computer networking technology. An early leader was Sun Microsystems, founded in 1982 as a Stanford University start-up, pioneering local networks of computer workstations. So-called local area networks (LANS) are common in today's corporate environment, leading to an explosive growth in the demand for networking software and hardware (manufactured by Cisco Corporation and others). As a local networks grows, it turns into a so-called intranet, that is, an all-inclusive corporate communication network joining together all the employees of a company, enabling them to exchange documents, file them, retrieve them, and work on them.

The Internet grew out of an early network of U.S. university computers called NSFNET, created in 1984. It was patterned on a design by the Rand Corporation for building a decentralized network of computers that could resist a nuclear attack. The commercialization of the Internet started in January 1990, and since then the net has grown at an astronomical rate. Today it comprises tens of thousands of computer nodes and features many millions of home pages. Increasingly, consumers are able to tap into the net from NCs ("network computers") or even from their regular TV sets. The first generation of NCs currently is being built by Sun, Oracle Computer, and Netscape Communications.

Another kind of digital network will be put in place in the late 1990s: satellite networks, circling the globe 400 to 700 miles up in so-called low-earth orbit (LEO) and delivering digital TV, fax, and phone services, and data transmission. The first will be the Iridium network launched by Motorola and comprising 66 satellites. Other satellite networks on the drawing board include the Globalstar to be launched by Lockheed Martin and Qualcomm (48 satellites) and a projected network dreamed up by Bill Gates consisting of 840 satellites.

So far I have mainly discussed digital technology as a means of communication. But it is more. It is also "content," that is, the message communicated. This ranges from digital libraries to entertainment and education in digital form. In the early 1990s an interesting trend surfaced of "content providers" buying controlling interests in the digital communications industry; an example is Time buying Warner Communications in 1990 and Time Warner six years later buying Turner Broadcasting, creating the world's largest media company. Similarly, Disney bought Capital Cities/ABC Television in 1995. That same year NBC and Microsoft announced plans to launch a 24-hour news channel with interactive features. These entertainment and communications giants will control the flow of information from its source (the recording studio or the movie studio) to its final delivery to the consumer (the TV screen). The content provider in this vertical chain is seen increasingly as the main profit generator, with the communication service rapidly becoming just a standardized "commodity."

Still, there will be room in the entertainment industry for the small and independent animation studio or the special effects studio. It is no contradiction to find in the industry at one and the same time both disintegration (splitting up large corporations into smaller ones, such as the recent partitioning of AT&T into three separate corporations, and in the form of subcontracting) and integration (in the form of vertical acquisitions).

Introduction of Knowledge-Based Products

In the intensely competitive climate of the 1990s, a firm needs to bring to the marketplace a continuous stream of new product designs, each generation being superior to the preceding one. Consider the case of videoconferencing equipment, the personal computer, or electronic cameras. New designs hit the market every month. But the change from one "vintage" to the next is often minute.

Each generation or vintage of a product goes through a characteristic life cycle, starting with product development and subsequent commercialization. If the product is successful, it will experience a phase of growth, quite rapid at first, but decelerating as the product gains market share. Finally there is a phase of falling sales and eventual obsolescence, as competitors introduce new and more sophisticated products embodying more advanced technology.

The introduction and marketing of an economic good is an example of a diffusion process. The standard diffusion process starts out growing at an exponential rate but eventually flattens out approaching a saturation level. The diffusion curve has a characteristic S-shape. Figure 6.1 illustrates the diffusion curve resulting from a series of successive generations of a given consumer product. The life cycles of those individual product generations have been indicated with stippled lines. During the upswing phase of the diffusion curve, new product cycles rapidly enter the market. During the maturing phase, they arrive at a slower pace.

During the upswing of each product life cycle, a new and superior demand pattern is diffused among the purchasing public. The ranks of the first "innovating" buyers who accept the new product on their own are joined by "imitating" buyers, that is, people who are influenced in their new product purchasing decisions by other people. The purchases of both categories swell under the barrage of advertising efforts, promotion, and a falling price.

The downswing of the life cycle sets in when the product is not able to match the features of its competitors. Consumers, restlessly looking for superior consumption alternatives, turn to more advanced product designs. Brand loyalty is a fickle thing. As the buyers desert the product and sales dwindle, the life cycle races downhill. The more sophisticated the technology, the shorter the life cycle.

Figure 6.1 Stylized Diffusion Curve and Product Life Cycles

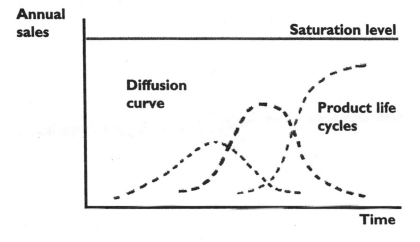

The agony of bringing on-line a never-ending series of ever more advanced technological products has become highlighted by the efforts the U.S. semiconductor industry. Intel Corporation introduced its 486 microprocessor in 1989; at the time it was the most powerful chip available. But behind Intel was a pack of competitors, led by Advanced Micro Devices (AMD). Three years later AMD announced the successful cloning of the 486. The next generation of microprocessors was the 586 chip, named Pentium, introduced in late 1993. The economic life span of each new wave of technology in the semiconductor industry is about three years. That adds up to a lead time of eight or nine years from the start of research to market introduction. Peak output of the Pentium is expected to be reached about the year 2000. And that is not the end. The Pentium is a 64-bit microprocessor, meaning that it addresses 2^{64} locations of memory. Research is already in full swing for the development of the 256-bit chip generation. At the same time, preparations are being made for entirely new types of microprocessors with even more stupendous capabilities.[1]

To stay on top of these complex dynamic processes, a new kind of management is needed: product-cycle management. A corporation needs to bring on-line a continuous stream of new product designs, each in some sense "better" than the preceding, just in order to survive. There must be a second and a third generation of the current models under development. Some of these will fail; a few will survive. Those that do survive have only a limited life span and will need to be replaced soon by superior models. The scheduling problem consists of determining when each vintage should hit the market (commercialization) and when it should be withdrawn (technological or economic obsolescence).

Such concepts as "technology," "progress," and "economic growth" are directly tied to the diversity or heterogeneity of economic goods and services. Managers perceive a discrepancy between the list of attributes that current technology is able to deliver and a list of attributes that lies within the realm of possibilities. It is this discrepancy that prompts current efforts at product development and new commercialization. In the final analysis, it is this discrepancy that drives progress. The driver of progress is disequilibrium: the leap between what is and what could be.

Technological Evolution

The mathematics of successive generations of species was developed by the Italian mathematician Vito Volterra in the 1930s. His classical treatise is entitled *Lecons sur la Theorie Mathematique de la Lutte pour la Vie,* which translates as Lessons on the Mathematical Theory of the Struggle for Life. Here one finds the origin of the modern nonlinear mathematical theory of evolution. But Volterra had to conduct his pioneering research with a severe handicap: He had no electronic computer. He never became aware of the amazing numerical possibilities to which I now turn.

In 1975 the mathematician J. Yorke was playing around with a diffusion equation of the type originally studied by Volterra, tracking its path over time with the help of a computer. With suitable parameter values, he found that the time path of the diffusion process was indeed a neat cycle over time. Upon varying the parameter values, however, Yorke found that the path sometimes would become jittery and bifurcate, or split into two.[2]

Figure 6.2 plots the results from a simple computer simulation, assuming that there are three consecutive product cycles.[3] Sales of the first generation of the product take off almost immediately, reaching a peak level of 0.117 in month 10, and then slowly taper off. Already in month 23, sales of the first generation of the product have virtually vanished. The second generation comes on-line a little bit later, reaching a peak of 0.309 in month 12. Sales of the third generation of the product, finally, appear in month 5 and grow steadily at first, hitting 0.403 in month 18. Then something unexpected happens: The monthly sales statistics starts zigzagging, breaking up into two different paths, one upper path and one lower path. In other words, the sales curve bifurcates.

Figure 6.2 Computer Simulation: The Possibility of Bifurcation

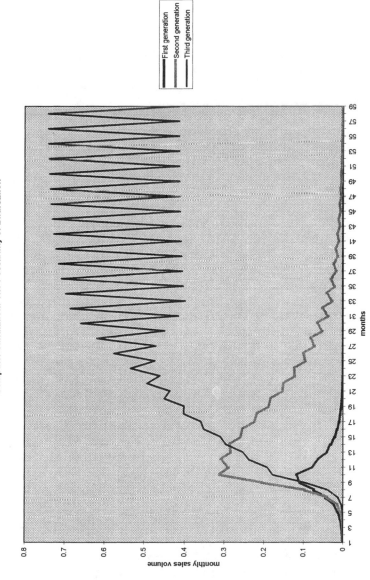

Computer Simulation: The Possibility of Bifurcation

monthly sales volume

months

First generation
Second generation
Third generation

An even more remarkable case is illustrated in figure 6.3.[4] This time the numerical parameters have been varied slightly, enough to tip the dynamics of the system into full-blown *chaos*. Sales of the two first generations follow the same kind of life cycles as before, with the total sales volume slightly smaller. Sales of the third generation start gaining ground in month 5; from there on sales grow rapidly, reaching 0.558 in month 12. But the subsequent statistics should be a nightmare for any market analyst. In one month a glorious upturn; in another, the pits. Notice the lull during the months 20 to 25. But, as it turns out, this brief interlude of stability is just the calm before the storm.

Is chaos the same thing as randomness? In the computer simulation, chaos is produced by a few simple (nonlinear) mathematical equations. The sales curve in figure 6.3 is determined, point by point, by an exact mathematical formula. In the terminology of mathematical statistics, it is deterministic. Randomness, on the other hand, is the result of probability drawings, like the throw of dice or the spinning of a roulette wheel. Chaos *looks* random, but there is order hidden behind the apparent whimsicalness.

One characteristic of high technology is its complexity. All living systems are complex. The economy, too, is a living system, with all the spontaneity and complexity of molecular biology. DNA or the genetic blueprint is a kind of molecular-scale computer that directs how the cell is to build and repair itself and interact with the outside world. In a similar manner, technologies are blueprints for the production of economic goods and services. A technology can be thought of as a kind of computer that directs the organization of a particular industrial or marketing activity. It includes instructions on how the technology can interact with other technologies, how it can be managed, and how it can be developed under the aegis of various corporate entities: in other words, how it can evolve.

In a way, the modern conception of evolution is still Darwinian. The survival of the fittest is still seen as a driving mechanism. But there is more. During the last 30 years, a large body of knowledge has been brought together concerning the evolution of dynamic systems in general. At its core, this theory is mathematical, dealing with the behavior of nonlinear systems, such as water dripping from a faucet or the rising morning mist.

The basic premise of chaos theory is the universal tendency toward disorder, dissolution, and decay. The rise and the fall, the bankruptcy, and the death of corporations. Mergers and acquisitions, corporate raiders, and corporate vultures. Be it a piece of machinery, a living organism, or a corporation: For a brief moment, life is a triumph over death. But the triumph is forever evanescent. Life has to be reestablished every second.

Figure 6.3 Computer Simulation: Chaos

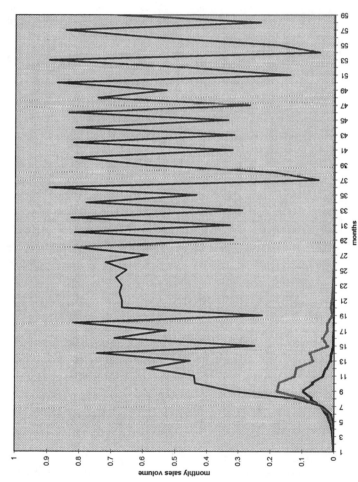

141

Complex systems have at their heart a great number of "agents" such as molecules or neurons or species. In economic systems the agents are managers and corporations. To fight the cosmic compulsion for disorder, agents constantly are organizing and reorganizing themselves into larger structures through the clash of mutual accommodation and mutual rivalry. Molecules form cells, neurons form brains, species form ecosystems, corporations form industries. At each level, entirely new properties appear. And at each stage, entirely new laws, concepts, and generalizations are necessary. Each system has many niches. The very act of filling one niche opens up more niches. The system is always unfolding, always in transition. New technologies and start-up companies representing new ways of doing things are forever nibbling away at the edges of status quo, and even the most entrenched old production methods eventually have to give way.

Emergent technologies are those that are rising above the horizon of technological and commercial feasibility. Often there is a competitive race among many companies seeking to exploit a new technology, such as the race among computer companies a couple of years ago to develop laptop computer technology or the current race to develop high-definition television. Emergent industrial structures are new ways of organizing research and development (R&D), production, distribution, and/or marketing. New technologies often prompt dramatic changes of industrial organization, such as when advances in telecommunication make it possible to have employees telecommuting.

Perhaps the most important characteristic of emergent technologies is the inherent risk and uncertainty—the risk that the technology won't work and the uncertainty over how the components of the new technology are going to fit together. Consider "multimedia"—the marriage of computers, video, TV, and audio. Obviously it is going to come. Obviously it will entail an electronic revolution. Billions of dollars will be made. But what is it going to look like precisely? Is it going to be transmitted via the cable networks' optic fibers, or is it going to be broadcast over the airwaves? And which are the corporations that stand to benefit: cable companies or Hollywood? Software companies like Microsoft, or the manufacturers of "smart" boxes to be put on top of all the TV sets in the land? A new industrial structure will emerge. In retrospect, no doubt it will look perfectly compelling, orderly, and logical.

To understand the nature of the emerging industrial state, consider the computer superstars of the 1980s that humbled the once-mighty IBM. They were all start-ups like Apple, Sun Microsystems, Compaq, Silicon Graphics, and Dell. The workstations and personal computers that they pioneered were more than just new computer products that reordered the product mix of the computer industry; these new products wrought fundamental changes in the economics and the structure of the computer industry. These companies maintained low overheads, and they outsourced many components to save R&D expenses. Smaller companies, such as Cyrix, MIPS and Tseng Labs, could be viewed as design houses or design boutiques farming out the manufacturing to outside companies.

What will the never-ending quest for technological innovation bring us? The surprising answer of modern nonlinear mathematics is that the tendencies to order and chaos—to build and to destroy, to invent the new and to discard the old—somehow can keep each other in balance, never locking into a fixed pattern nor ever dissolving into uncontrolled turbulence. That balance is called "the edge of chaos." At the edge, the system has enough stability to sustain itself and enough creativity to evolve.[5]

Furthermore, at that edge there is self-organization, an aspect of evolution that not even Darwin understood. It goes beyond the principle of survival of the fittest. As a storm picks up speed, it may evolve into a hurricane. The eye of the hurricane travels along some path, from the Bahamas toward Florida. Eventually the hurricane dissolves. Migrating birds develop the ability to find their way over half the globe. Land-based animals develop organs like the lungs. General Dynamics develops into one of the major defense contractors in the United States, and eventually, in 1992, a decision is made to sell out most of its divisions and to redistribute the cash proceeds to the stockholders. Structures form spontaneously as order battles chaos.

Evolution never proceeds at an even and predictable pace. There are bursts of creativity interspersed with long periods of inactivity or even collapse. One such burst of technological creativity occurred in the early nineteenth century—the industrial revolution. To use the terms of dynamic theory, it represented a phase transition. Are we now, in the early 1990s, heading toward yet another such economic metamorphosis, a phase transition to an age of instant communications, robotics, and biotech? If so, the transient state would be characterized by order and chaos intertwined in an ever-changing dance of evanescent corporate structures. Eventually, from the shakeout, a new state of capitalism will arise.

Empirical Analysis of the U.S. Computer Industry

Productivity data for companies producing and distributing digital products reflect the industry's turmoil. Some companies enjoy a much faster productivity growth than others. As we shall see, there may exist no tendency in a digital industry for data to group themselves around central values such as averages. Instead, this analysis will focus on the *technology frontier* or *envelope,* defined by the best-performing companies in the industry. Technological progress occurs as the envelope is being pushed forward.

The frontier can be determined by a mathematical technique called data envelopment analysis, invented in the late 1970s by A. Charnes and W. W. Cooper. A company located on the technology frontier is cost effective, that is, it generates its outputs with a minimum expense on inputs. This is "efficiency." Since the days of Adam Smith and Alfred Marshall, economics has been the science of the behavior of "economic man," some fictitious rational individual who, weighing all possible courses of action, chooses the one that maximizes "utility" or profits or whatever. A widely used definition of economics states that it is the science of allocating given means to obtain a set of desirable ends.

But suboptimal companies are not very good at solving that optimizing problem. And yet they are very much part of the reality that economists need to come to grips with. Thes companies are not very good at maximizing profit. Their engineers may not see or understand the technological opportunities. Their managers may simply be poor managers. In order to understand the real world, we need a theory of management operating at the cutting edge of technology *and* we also need a theory of management that is falling behind.

The possible existence of "noneconomic man," of companies that fall behind the technology frontier, has, of course, been recognized from time to time. Nobel laureate Herbert Simon speculated that many companies may not minimize costs but rather choose to adopt a stance of "satisficing behavior," that is, aiming for "satisfactory" rather than maximal profits. Nevertheless, data envelopment analysis has brought about a revolution in economics. For the first time, economists can measure these matters empirically. Companies located at the frontier are assigned an efficiency value of 1. Units located behind the frontier are given an efficiency rating less than unity.[6] To illustrate, we shall here take a quick look at some results obtained for the U.S. computer industry between 1980 and 1991. The envelopment calculations are based on standard financial data from earnings statements and balance sheets of 120 publicly traded corporations. A computer program gauges the relative performance of each computer stock.[7]

First, a number of indicators of performance (outputs) were chosen, such as total sales, earnings, and stock capitalization (the market value of a company's outstanding shares). Other indicators measure inputs into the productive process, such as employment, selling and administrative expenditure, capital investments, and expenditure on research and development. While this may seem like a long list, it nevertheless represents only a first cut at the problem.

The results of the envelopment calculations show that a few corporations systematically obtained top scores in terms of their productive efficiency. The winners are listed in table 6.1. Among these 11 corporations, Apple Computer, Compaq Computer, and Seagate Technology stand out. Apple was at the frontier every single year except 1989. A few of the winners (such as Dell, listed on Wall Street since 1987) are recent start-ups and have a briefer track record.

But these were the exceptions. The great majority of the 120 companies investigated were inefficient, that is, falling behind the frontier, most of the time. They did not use best available practice. They represented suboptimal management. The list includes households names in the computer industry such as Amdahl Corp., Data General Corp, Digital Equipment, Hewlett Packard, Sun Microsystems, Unisys, and Wang. IBM had been at the frontier in the early 1980s but fell behind by 1984.

One of the great stars of the computer industry was Sun Microsystems, formed in 1982. After its introduction on Wall Street in 1985, Sun saw its sales multiply more than 20-fold during the next five years. And yet Sun was subefficient every single year, falling solidly behind the cost-effectiveness frontier. How can that be? The answer is that the Sun management consciously sacrificed short-term cost efficiency in order to achieve rapid long-term growth. Sun was riding the wave of its line of immensely successful computer workstations, built around the UNIX software (originally developed by AT&T).

The modern history of computers is the history of a few immensely successful companies, such as Apple, Cray, Microsoft, and Sun, that during the opening phases of their life cycles all grew at unbelievable rates. These were

Table 6.1   Computer Companies with Long Sequences of Top Efficiency Scores,
              1980–1991

Apple Computer	Dell Computer Corp.	Quantum Corp.
Atari Corp.	Floating Point Systems	Seagate Technology
Compaq Computer Corp.	National Computer	Silicon Graphics
Conner Peripherals	Systems	Stratus Corp.

Note: To be included in this table, a company was permitted to have an efficiency rating less than 1.00 only once.

wildly divergent disequilibrium processes. These companies revolutionized their industry. And yet during that phase of explosion, they were not able to move up to the static frontier. The great technology revolutions are disorderly, flaunting the narrow bookkeeping concept of cost effectiveness!

So, who is leading the advance into the technological unknown? Is it those companies at the cost-effectiveness frontier, or is it those along the second line of assault, shoving and pushing to get ahead? As the reader will realize, the dynamics of the battle is complex. There is no field marshal in command, field tube in hand, astride his white horse, pointing out the lines of attack to his soldiers. It is every chief executive officer for himself. There is only one certainty: Those who fall too far behind will falter.

Discarding the standard notions of equilibrium, economists working at the Santa Fe Institute have developed a new kind of economic system with "positive feedback," such as real estate booms and stock market crashes. Once such systems get rolling, they keep snowballing and feed on themselves, up to a point. Positive feedback arises in an economy when there are increasing returns to scale. If the average production costs of some firms fall with increasing output, the managers of these firms will find it profitable to expand their scale of operation. Outputs and market shares of individual firms will embark upon some dynamic path of growth.[8]

A rapid turnover of product cycles is self-reinforcing in that it tends to speed up the rate of product development even further. As managers watch their competitors flood the market with new and advanced product designs, they realize that their own brands will become obsolete even faster than originally expected. To maintain their market share, each competitor will need to pour even more resources into research and development and to accelerate their various projects already under development.

The envelopment analysis described earlier presents an opportunity to determine the possible presence of increasing returns to scale. It turns out that the returns to scale tend to vary systematically over the life cycle of a technology. In the beginning of the cycle typically there will be large returns to scale. Young and expanding start-up companies enjoy increasing earnings. But as the technology matures, it soon needs to be replaced by a later technology generation. If the company lags behind in updating its technology, it will be stuck in a position with decreasing returns to scale. At that point, the choice is to scale back or to make an all-out effort to regain the technological initiative.

Increasing returns are quite common in the beginning of the corporate life cycle, immediately upon introduction on Wall Street. There were 33 computer companies in the database in 1980; out of the remaining 87 companies that entered the base in 1981 or later, 29 exhibited increasing returns to scale at market introduction and fully 44 exhibited constant returns to scale. In either case, these companies entered the database in a mode of potential growth. Decreasing returns to scale at the moment of the initial public offering perhaps would be a contradiction in terms; they are not common.

As a corollary, it may be noted that companies with increasing returns are quite small. The largest company with increasing returns in 1991 was CMS Enhancements, with sales of $130 million. Many had sales of less than $10 million.

Several companies go through prolonged periods of increasing returns, as depicted in table 6.2. Note in particular Symbol Technologies. Starting out with several years of increasing returns (with sales growing from $2.4 million in 1980 to $8.7 million in 1984), this company thereupon entered a phase of efficiency and rapid growth ($13.9 million in 1985, booming to $319.4 million in 1991).

The archetype of a successful life cycle for a company manufacturing a single product seems to be this: market introduction at increasing returns, followed by a stabilized growth path with constant returns to scale.

Briefly characterizing the empirical results, one word comes to mind: polarization. Apart from the efficiency leaders—that is, the companies at the efficiency envelope—the industry breaks up into two distinct camps: those companies that have increasing returns to scale and those with decreasing returns to scale. The first camp consists of small and young companies, recent

Table 6.2   Long Time Spans of Increasing Economies of Scale

	Present in Sample Since	Years with Increasing Returns to Scale
Astro-Med	1980	1984–88
Datasouth Computer	1983	1984–88
Genisco Technology	1980	1980–81, 1985, 1987–91
IX Systems	1987	1987–91
PCPI	1984	1985–90
Scan Graphics	1987	1987–91
Symbol Technologies	1980	1980–84
Tridex	1984	1985–91
Vertex Industries	1987	1987–91

Note: To be included in this table, a company was required to display increasing returns to scale for at least five consecutive years.

start-ups located at the beginning of their life cycles. Since they have increasing returns to scale, they face a financial incentive to grow. (Remember that the output variables are all financial.)

During the time period considered, a great number of new computer corporations were started. Out of the 102 corporations participating in the sample in 1991, only 28 existed back in 1980. (Five additional companies existing in 1980 eventually folded.) And, as we have seen, most of the start-ups displayed at least in the beginning of their corporate life cycle nondecreasing returns to scale. Many start-ups were able to stay in that growth phase throughout the period considered. For instance, IX Systems entered the database in 1987 and continued posting very low weight sums in the following years. Other start-up companies displaying nondecreasing returns to scale in every single year were Alpharel, Datasouth Computer, Masstor Systems, Mylex, Scan Graphics, Science Accessories, Sulcus Computer, and Vertex Industries.

Start-up companies concentrate their activities around one or just a few products; the sales of each of these presumably go through a characteristic diffusion curve, eventually leaving the start-up phase and entering market growth and subsequent maturity. As they do so, further growth depends on the corporation's ability to launch in a timely fashion new successor generations of the original product. That is, the strategic factor determining success or failure is product-cycle management. If the company is not able to generate a continuous series of cost-effective new vintages of its technologies, it will fall behind its competitors. Its efficiency rating will fall, and there will now be decreasing economies of scale—the company has grown too fast and has overextended itself.

The other camp in the industry consists of established and mature companies that typically have achieved considerable size and that manufacture and market a wide range of products. They have decreasing returns to scale, that is, theoretically they should be able to assume a neoclassical optimum. But with an efficiency rating less than unity, the analysis tells us that they have failed to do so, and many of them display signs of acute distress (falling sales, negative profits).

The aging corporations face a formidable task: Marketing a wide range of products, they need to upgrade or renew a large number of entries in their product line every year. The evidence indicates that most large companies have difficulties staying cost effective while they accomplish such a broad-based R&D program. In a narrow sense there may well exist economies of scale in running a larger R&D operation rather than a smaller one (better utilization of researchers, spreading the risk among a larger number of development projects), but small companies occupying highly specialized niches of technology nevertheless often are able to outcompete the corporate giants. One reason may be that there are strong *economies of specialization* in R&D. Another reason, of course, is that niche companies that do not succeed are rapidly eliminated from the marketplace, so that only the successful ones are left. In our study 13 computer companies had left the sample by 1991; only 2 of these existed back in 1980.

To conclude: The companies in the camp of decreasing returns to scale were eclipsed and outperformed by swarms of small start-up companies.

The kind of observations that we have just documented fly in the face of conventional neoclassical economic theory. There is no apparent "equilibrium" in this industry. Of 120 companies, only 2 stayed at the theoretical equilibrium frontier throughout the years (Apple and Cray Research). The industry is characterized by turbulence. It is our contention that the basis of this turbulence is a confrontation between individual products and technologies located at different phases of their life cycles. Indirectly, it is a confrontation between individual corporations, some being more effective than others in their product-cycle management: Some companies are riding on the upswing of their cycles, others struggling as their products are reaching maturity and eventual obsolescence.

The Future of the Knowledge-Based Economy

Many observers, watching how the developed economies of the world are now being driven by an unparalleled growth of knowledge capital, ask themselves whether this rapid growth can continue. Will the new millennium usher in an era of continued tumultuous but sustained growth, or will it eventually see a major collapse, on the order of the depression of the 1930s? As we have seen, when self-reinforcing mechanisms are at play, there is little reason to expect the resulting growth path to be orderly and linear. Even granting that a major phase transition of the economy is now under way, what comes next, boom or bust? Can the stock markets of the world continue to climb to ever loftier heights, driven by the digital revolution, or is a major reversal in store?

There are two extreme, and opposite, views. Up to the present, the economies of the United States and of other Western economies have relied on a plentiful supply of resources such as coal, oil, natural gas, iron ore and other minerals, hydroelectric power, arable land, and forests suitable for logging. Because the availability of such resources is limited, the prices of the resources would shoot up when the economy accelerates, leading to cyclic movements in resource prices and ultimately providing a break on the feasible rate of growth of the macroeconomy. As knowledge capital becomes the major driver of the modern economy, however, and since there are no apparent limitations to the formation of new knowledge capital, it is easy to argue that now many restrictions placed on the earlier industrial economy are being removed. The marginal productivity of knowledge capital actually may be increasing rather than decreasing. In principle, therefore, it should be possible to sustain a growth path of the entire economy with knowledge capital and knowledge output (i.e., the portion of gross national product ascribable to knowledge capital) increasing *in tandem,* with no limit in sight.

The other view would point at the disorderly nature of a knowledge economy. A nonlinear economy can possess a multiplicity of solutions, that is, a multiplicity of alternative future courses. There may exist many candidates for long-term self-reinforcement; the cumulation of small random events can push the system onto an orbit that is bound for eventual collapse. Just as individual products eventually enter an orbit of obsolescence and decline, the system as a whole also may be pushed onto a path of concurrent decline. That is what happened in the semiconductor industry in 1984–85, as it was hit by worldwide overcapacity. It takes no great imagination to spell out the possibility of a concurrent crash of all digital industries at the same time, from the communications industry to the computer industry.

While pondering these matters, one issue that needs to be dealt with is that of "overinvestment." Can there be an overinvestment in knowledge capital, a glut of knowledge capital that eventually depresses markets? In order to answer this question, let me first review some well-known features of overinvestment in conventional "hard" capital, such as in the steel industry, in shipping, and in construction. Overinvestment occurs because it takes time to construct and build hard capital (e.g., shipyards and ships) in response to an increase in demand. As the excessive capital eventually is completed and hits the market, prices collapse and a supply surplus develops. (Ships are being laid up.) Both changes in demand and changes in price tend to amplify as we travel upstream in the vertical production chain: Small variations in the markets for consumer goods tend to generate large variations in the markets for capital. Small increases in consumer demand lead to an excessive formation of capital, thus setting the stage for an eventual market glut.

To a degree, these classical mechanisms still seem to apply to the digital industry; consider the previous example of the semiconductor industry. And it is easy to construct other examples. An increase in the sales of "video on demand" (cable subscribers calling up a video over an interactive network), for instance, might lead to excessive production of movies, and the formation of new movie studios in Hollywood that may not be viable in the long run. An increase in the demand for educational Internet programming may lead to an excessive buildup of electronic libraries. Another striking example can be seen in the field of biotech. In the early 1990s the demand for new genetically engineered pharmacy products led to an avalanche of new biotech start-ups in the United States. Many of the new initial public offerings foresaw no immediate sales and no earnings; they were pure research companies. An excess supply of biotech research capital was offered on the market. The result soon became apparent: depressed stock prices throughout the entire biotech industry.

Ultimately, demand is the driver of the formation of knowledge capital: the demand for information, for education, and for entertainment. An explosion of demand for knowledge products is what drives the explosion of the knowledge industry. Can this explosion of demand be sustained, or will there eventually be satiation and stagnation?

To a large extent, this is a management problem, a question of directing the efforts of product development and marketing in directions that respond to consumer desires. Corporate survival in a turbulent industry is possible, but it requires a new kind of management that is more perceptive than ever of the market, its evolving potentials, and its limitations.

Many high-tech products are "luxuries" in the sense that they have high-income elasticities. But a surprising number of knowledge products rather seem to be in the nature of necessities that consumers even at low-income levels want to buy: TV sets, CD players, VCR machines, videocassettes. Also, I would surmise that the Engel elasticities of knowledge products such as CD-ROMs and electronic games are rapidly falling. The result would be an increase in total demand for these products.

The greatest demand potential for the knowledge industry is located overseas. The United States is the global leader in the development of computer software, in telecommunication, and in digital entertainment. The entire world is the market for U.S. knowledge products. In a very real sense, the demand facing U.S. knowledge companies is therefore infinite. There seems to be an insatiable global demand for U.S. news, movies, TV sitcoms, and educational programming.

We may speculate that the reason for the U.S. global leadership in the knowledge industry somehow is tied to American optimism and a can-do attitude. No other country can match the proliferation of small startup companies in the United States. In any case, the United States obviously enjoys strong "comparative advantages" in the creation and dissemination of knowledge capital, in the sense of the classical doctrine of comparative advantage. If, as I believe, this advantage is rooted in basic national characteristics, there is reason to believe that this global advantage will be retained long into the twenty-first century.

It is easy to imagine a future scenario with the United States as the tumultuous driver of global technological progress, disseminating knowledge capital to the world. Obviously, such a picture does not preclude a rapid product development of knowledge capital in other countries (e.g., the rapid progress of telecommunications in France) on the model of a driving center and secondary developments along the periphery. In any case, as the knowledge sector grows, nationally and internationally, the paradigm of disequilibrium will become the key to understanding future events.

Notes

This chapter is based on an inaugural lecture that the author gave at the Institute Superior Tecnico, Lisbon, on March 18, 1997, assuming a newly created chair in the Commercialization of Science and Technology, donated by the Luso-American Development Foundation.

1. J. Yorke and T.-Y. Li, "Period Three Implies Chaos," *American Mathematical Monthly* 82 (1975): 985–992. Empirical sequences of life cycles like those illustrated in figure 6.1 can be found in J. A. Norton and F. M. Bass, "A Diffusion Theory Model of Adoption and Substitution for Successive Generations of High Technology Products," *Management Science* (September 1987): 1069–1086 (for computer chips), and in J. A. Norton and F. M. Bass, "Evolution of Technological Generations: The Law of Capture," *Sloan Management Review* (winter 1992): 66–77 (disk drives, recording media, beta blockers).
2. The computer simulation illustrated in figure 6.2 was set up as follows. Let X be the sales of the first-generation, Y the sales of the second-generation, and Z the sales of the third-generation product. The initial values were put at X = 0.001, Y = 0.0001, Z = 0.00001. Furthermore, sales in any subsequent month (subscripted +1) was assumed to be related to sales in the previous month by the equations $X_{+1} = 2X(1-X-Y-Z) - 0.1X$, $Y_{+1} = 3Y(1-X-Y-Z) - 0.25Y$, $Z_{+1} = 3.75Z(1-X-Y-Z) - 0.4Z$. See further S. Thore, *The Diversity, Complexity, and Evolution of High Tech Capitalism* (Boston: Kluwer Academic Publishers, 1995), chapter 7.
3. The numerical assumptions for figure 6.3 are the same as for figure 6.2, but sales for the third generation product have this time been set at $Z_{+1} = 4.35(1-X-Y-Z) - 0.4Z$.
4. On the "edge of chaos," see M. M. Waldrop, *Complexity: The Emerging Science at the Edge of Order and Chaos* (New York: Simon and Schuster, 1993), and R. Lewin, *Complexity: Life at the Edge of Chaos* (New York: Macmillan, 1993).

5. For a recent survey of data envelopment analysis, see the introductory chapter in A. Charnes, W. W. Cooper, A. Y. Lewin, and L. M. Seiford, eds., *Data Envelopment Analysis: Theory, Methodology and Applications* (Boston: Kluwer Academic Publishers, 1994).

6. The study of the U.S. computer industry mentioned in the main text is described in S. Thore, G. Kozmetsky, and F. Phillips, "DEA of Financial Statements Data: The U.S. Computer Industry," *Journal of Productivity Analysis* 5 (1994): 229–248, and S. Thore, F. Phillips, T. W. Ruefli, and P. Yue, "DEA and the Management of the Product Cycle: The U.S. Computer Industry," *Computers and Operations Research* 23 (1996): 341–356.

7. See W. B. Arthur, "Competing Technologies, Increasing Returns, and Lock-in by Historical Events," *Economic Journal* (March 1989) and "Positive Feedbacks in the Economy," *Scientific American* (February 1990): 92–99.

8. The results regarding economies of scale in the U.S. computer industry were reported in S. Thore, "Economies of Scale in the U.S. Computer Industry: An Empirical Investigation Using Data Envelopment Analysis," *Journal of Evolutionary Economics* 6 (1996): 199–216. The data in table 6.2 and in the main text are all drawn from this publication.

CHAPTER 7

Cellular-Network Organizations

Raymond Miles, University of California;
Charles C. Snow, Pennsylvania State University;
John A. Matthews, University of South Wales; and
Grant Miles, University of North Texas

Since the time of the industrial revolution, the U.S. economy has moved through the machine age into the information age and now stands at the threshold of the knowledge age. In the process, the locus of organizational exemplars has shifted from capital-intensive industries such as steel and automobiles, to information-intensive industries such as financial services and logistics, and currently toward innovation-driven industries such as computer software and biotechnology, where competitive advantage lies mostly in the effective use of human resources.

This evolution has been powered and facilitated simultaneously by the invention of a succession of new organizational forms—new approaches to accumulating and applying know-how to the key resources of the day. Each new organizational form has allowed firms to use their expanding know-how to adapt to market opportunities and demands, first for standardized goods and services, then to increasing levels of product and service customization, and, today, toward the expectation of continuous innovation.

We believe that certain trends are currently visible in the coevolution of markets and organizations—trends that make it possible to predict the shape and operation of the twenty-first-century organization. Moreover, we believe that a number of pioneering firms already are demonstrating the organizational characteristics suggested by those trends, especially a growing reliance on entrepreneurship, self-organization, and member ownership of firm assets and resources.

The Evolution of Organizational Forms

Conceptually, an organizational form is an overall logic shaping a firm's strategy, structure, and management processes into an effective whole. In each historical era, market forces "pull" forth new organizational forms as managers seek new ways of arranging assets and resources to produce the products and services that customers want and expect. At the same time, in each era some companies accumulate more know-how than their current operating logic allows them to utilize. Those excess capabilities "push" managers to experiment with new organizational arrangements, which, in turn, stimulate the search for new markets and/or new products or services. As we will describe, the continuing interaction of these push-pull forces has been visible in the major eras that have characterized the U.S. economy over the past 100-plus years. (See table 7.1.)

Era of Standardization

The era of standardization saw hierarchical forms of organization used to apply know-how primarily to the utilization of physical assets, such as raw materials, capital equipment, plant facilities, and so on. In the late nineteenth and early twentieth centuries, pioneering companies learned to mass-produce efficiently standardized products (e.g., steel and automobiles) and services (e.g., transportation and communications).[1] The period's dominant organizational form, the functional organization, used a centrally coordinated, vertically integrated structure to manage employees in highly specialized jobs. By focusing on limited product and service lines, firms moved down the learning curve, using their accumulating know-how to produce time and cost reductions that constantly added value to employed resources and allowed the United States to mass-produce its way to a position of global economic power.

Early Customization

As illustrated in figure 7.1, the era of customization actually began during the earlier period of standardized production. That is, by the middle of the

Table 7.1 Organizational Evolution

Historical Era	Standardization	Customization	Innovation
Dominant Organizational Form	Hierarchy	Network	Cell
Key Asset	Capital goods	Information	Knowledge
Influential Manager	Chief operating officer	Chief information officer	Chief knowledge officer
Key Capability	Specialization and segmentation	Flexibility and responsiveness	Design creativity

twentieth century (and even before in industries such as automotive and retailing), markets generally had become more demanding, and some firms had accumulated know-how that could not be fully utilized in the production of their existing goods and services. Thus markets "pulled" companies to diversify their offerings, and their underutilized know-how and resources "pushed" them toward new markets where expansion was possible.[2] Those forces coalesced in the invention of a new organizational form, the divisional, which allowed companies to serve related markets with differentiated goods and services. In the divisional form, know-how accumulated in one market could be utilized by a newly created, semiautonomous division to provide products or services to different but related markets. Corporate-level executives sought new market opportunities for the creation of new divisions and used the current revenue streams to invest know-how and resources in these new arenas. Although each division typically produced a standard product (e.g., autos at General Motors), the divisional form enabled companies to achieve limited amounts of customization (market segmentation).

The movement from standardization to customization continued into the late 1960s and 1970s as firms adopted mixed organizational forms, such as the matrix, that allowed a dual focus on both stable and emerging market segments and clients.[3] For example, by employing a matrix organization, an aerospace firm such as TRW could produce differentiated but standard products for the civilian and military markets in one or more divisions while simultaneously transferring some resources from those units into project groups that designed and built prototypical products for space exploration. The matrix organization provided companies with a more finely grained

Figure 7.1   TCG's Cellular Organization

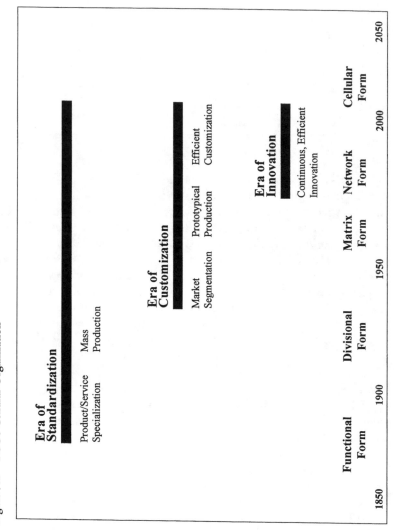

mechanism for exploiting their know-how across a wider range of both standardized and customized products and services.

Full, Efficient Customization

By the 1980s the "pull" toward customization intensified as a rapidly growing number of firms around the world used their know-how to enter an increasingly deregulated global marketplace.[4] New entrants competed for customer attention with lower prices, improved quality and distribution, and seemingly endless choices among styles and models. However, many existing companies initially found it difficult to unleash their competencies and know-how to meet the new market opportunities and pressures. Divisional and matrix organizations, designed for less challenging and turbulent markets, were better suited to internal coordination needs than to rapid forays into new markets. Once again, a new organizational form was needed in order to help firms use and extend their capabilities. The model that evolved from the late 1970s into the 1990s was the network organization.[5]

The key contribution of the network form was not just its ability to rapidly respond to market demands for differentiated products and services but to do so efficiently by extending the customization process backward and forward along the entire industry value chain, from raw materials, to parts and component production, to manufacture and assembly, to distribution and final sale. In their search for flexibility and responsiveness, most traditional companies began by downsizing and then refocusing on those areas where their assets and know-how added the greatest economic value. As companies downsized and reengineered, they began to outsource noncore operations to upstream and downstream "partner" firms whose capabilities complemented their own. As multifirm networks proliferated, numerous potential partners around the world began to occupy points along industry value chains, offering increased overall flexibility and therefore more opportunities for customization. The expanded number of competent firms kept prices in check, improved product and service quality, and pressured all firms to adopt better information and production technologies.

Most important from an organizational point of view, companies began to realize that success in the age of efficient customization again demanded a higher level of know-how and resource utilization than existing internal management processes allowed. Increasingly, firms turned to network structures in which empowered teams managed not only their internal work processes but external relationships with upstream and downstream partners as well. In many networks of the 1990s, it became difficult to determine where one organization ended and another began as cross-firm teams resolved interface issues, representatives of important customers were invited to participate in new product development processes, and suppliers were given access to large firms' scheduling and accounting processes through electronic data interchange systems.

Summary

In little more than a century, the pull of market forces and the push of underutilized company know-how carried the U.S. economy through the era of mass standardization into the era of efficient customization. Throughout this period, firms faced increasingly complex market and technological environments. In response, firms themselves became more complex, by creating new organizational means of adding economic value.

Functional firms, as shown in table 7.2, primarily utilized increased operating know-how to add economic value, with only top managers providing coordination and entrepreneurial direction. The divisional form utilized operating knowledge but also developed and applied knowledge of how to invest money, people, and systems in related markets—so-called diversification know-how. In the process, divisional firms brought not only corporate managers but an expanding group of divisional managers into organizational and business decision processes.

Matrix organizations were designed to add value not only through the application of operating and investment know-how but also through their adaptation capabilities—the frequent refocusing of underutilized assets on the needs of temporary projects and new market opportunities. In those organizations top managers, division managers, and project managers all were involved in entrepreneurial and organizational decisions.

Table 7.2 Location of Managerial Know-how in Alternative Organizational Forms

	Operational Know-how	Investment Know-how	Adaptation Know-how
Functional	Top, middle, lower	Top	Top
Divisional	Top, middle, lower	Top, middle	Top
Matrix	Top, middle, lower	Top, middle	Top, middle
Network	Top, middle, lower	Top, middle	Top, middle, lower
Cellular	Top, middle, lower	Top, middle, lower	Top, middle, lower

The network form allowed value to be added not only within but across firms along the value chain, combining the operational, investment, and adaptation know-how of individual firms and achieving higher levels of overall utilization through their freedom to link rapidly with numerous upstream and downstream partners. The network organization's dependence on decision-making teams, both within and across firms, dramatically increased involvement in organizational and entrepreneurial decisions in all firms at all levels.

In sum, across this entire period of organizational evolution, certain trends are clearly evident. First, as each new organizational form was created, it brought an expectation that more and more organization members would develop the ability to self-organize around operational, market, and partnering tasks. Second, each new form increased the proportion of members who were expected to perform entrepreneurial tasks—identifying customer needs and then finding and focusing resources on them. Third, each new organizational form increased member opportunities to experience psychological ownership of particular clients, markets, customized products and services, and so on. Also, because performance measurement now occurred at more points and organizational levels, the opportunity for reward systems to promote financial ownership increased, mostly in the form of bonuses and stock-purchase plans. These key trends, we believe, can be used to forecast the main characteristics of twenty-first-century organizational forms.

The Twenty-First Century: Era of Innovation

In tomorrow's business world, some markets still will be supplied with standard products and services, while other markets will demand large amounts of customization. However, the continued pull of market forces and the push of ever-increasing know-how honed through network partnering is already moving some industries and companies toward what amounts to a continuous process of innovation. Beyond the customization of existing designs, product and service invention is becoming the centerpiece of value-adding activity in an increasing number of firms. So-called knowledge businesses such as design and engineering services, advanced electronics and biotechnology, computer software design, health care, and consulting not only feed the process of innovation but feed upon it in a continuous cycle that creates more—and more complex—markets and environments.[6] Indeed, for companies in such businesses, both by choice and by the consequences of their choices, organizational inputs and outputs become highly unpredictable.

For example, according to the chief executive officer of a biotechnology firm, the potential inputs to the firm are spread across hundreds and even thousands of scientists worldwide. Around each prominent researcher is a cluster of colleagues, and each cluster is a rich mix of talent held together by a set of connecting mechanisms including shared interests, electronic mail systems, technical conferences, and so on. Connecting devices are not coordinated by plan but rather are self-organizing, reflecting the knowledge needs and data-sharing opportunities recognized by members of the various clusters. The overall challenge of the biotechnology firm is to maintain close contact with as much of this continuously evolving knowledge field as it can. A similarly complex pattern is visible at the firm's output interface, as myriad alliances and partnerships are formed to take partially developed products (and by-products) through the stages of final design, testing, and marketing. Clearly, a biotechnology firm that is rigidly structured will not be able to muster the internal flexibility required to match the complexity of its environment.

A New Organizational Form for a New Economic Era

Similar elements of complexity are visible in a growing number of industries. For example, in computer software, there are few limits on potentially profitable product designs, and a vast array of independent designers move in and around software companies of every size. The choices firms face at both the input and output ends of their operation are thus large and constantly changing. Faced with these opportunities, and projecting the evolutionary trends just discussed, one would expect the organization of the twenty-first-century to rely heavily on clusters of self-organizing components collaboratively investing the enterprise's know-how in product and service innovations for markets that they have helped create and develop.

Such firms, in our view, can best be described as cellular.[7] The cellular metaphor suggests a living, adaptive organization. Cells in living organisms possess fundamental functions of life and can act alone to meet a particular need. However, by acting in concert, cells can perform more complex functions. Evolving characteristics, or "learning," if shared across all cells, can create a higher-order organism. Similarly, a cellular organization is made up of cells (self-managing teams, autonomous business units, etc.) that can operate alone but that by interacting with other cells, can produce a more potent and competent business mechanism. It is this combination of independence and interdependence that allows the cellular organizational form to generate and share the know-how that produces continuous innovation.

Building Blocks of the Cellular Form

We believe that in the future, complete cellular firms will achieve a level of know-how well beyond that of earlier organizational forms by combining *entrepreneurship, self-organization,* and *member ownership* in mutually reinforcing ways.

Each cell (team, strategic business unit, firm) has an entrepreneurial responsibility to the larger organization. The customers of a particular cell can be outside clients, or they can be other cells in the organization. In either case, the purpose is to spread an entrepreneurial mind-set throughout the organization so that every cell is concerned about improvement and growth. Indeed, giving each cell entrepreneurial responsibility is essential to the full utilization of the firm's constantly growing know-how. Of course, each cell also must have the entrepreneurial skills required to generate business for itself and the overall organization.

Each cell must be able to reorganize continually in order to make its expected contribution to the overall organization. Of particular value here are the technical skills needed to perform its function, the collaborative skills necessary to make appropriate linkages with other organizational units and external partner firms, and the governance skills required to manage its own activities. Application of this cellular principle may require the company to strip away most of the bureaucracy that is currently in place and replace it with jointly defined protocols that guide internal and external collaboration.

Each cell must be rewarded for acting entrepreneurially and operating in a businesslike manner. If the cellular units are teams or strategic business units instead of complete firms, psychological ownership can be achieved by organizing cells as profit centers, allowing them to participate in company stock-purchase plans, and so on. However, the ultimate cellular solution is probably actual member ownership of those cell assets and resources they have created and that they voluntarily invest with the firm in expectation of a joint return.

Toward the Cellular Organization

Examples of cellular organizations, in which the individual cellular principles and their interconnectedness are clearly seen, are rare. We have attempted to identify and track those companies that appear to be at the leading edge of organizational practice, and our interviews and observations to date have uncovered one example of a complete cellular organization, Technical and Computer Graphics of Sydney, Australia. Also, The Acer

Group, a rapidly growing personal computer company, is a significant user of cellular principles on a global scale. Lastly, there are many examples of companies around the world that are partial users of the cellular form, relying on one or more of its key building blocks to achieve impressive innovative capabilities.

TCG: A Complete Cellular Organization

Technical and Computer Graphics (TCG), a privately held information-technology company, is perhaps the best example of the cellular approach to organizing. TCG develops a wide variety of products and services, including portable and hand-held data terminals and loggers, computer graphics systems, bar-coding systems, electronic data interchange systems, and other information technology (IT) products and services. The 13 individual small firms at TCG are the focus of cellularity. Like a cell in a larger organism, each firm has its own purpose and ability to function independently, but it shares common features and purpose with all of its sister firms. Some TCG member firms specialize in one or more product categories, while others specialize in hardware or software.

At TCG, the various firms have come into the group with existing high levels of technical and business competence. However, the operating protocol at TCG assures that systemwide competence will continue to grow. The process is called "triangulation," and it is the means by which TCG continually develops new products and services.[8] Triangulation is a three-cornered partnership among (1) one or more TCG firms, (2) an external joint-venture partner (e.g., Hitachi) that also provides equity capital to the venture, and (3) a principal customer (e.g., Telstra, the Australian telephone company) whose large advance order wins it contractual rights as well as provides additional cash to the venture. (See figure 7.2.)

Each TCG firm is expected to search continually for new product and service opportunities. When a particular venture shows concrete promise, the initiating firm acts as project leader for the remainder of the venture. The first step in the triangulation process is to identify and collaborate with a joint-venture partner, a firm with expertise in the proposed technology. TCG receives partial funding for the project from the joint-venture partner, and it also gains access to technical ideas and distribution channels. Next, the project leader firm identifies an initial large customer for the new product. TCG also collaborates with the customer in the sense that it agrees to custom-design a product for that client. By working together with the joint-venture partner and the principal customer, TCG is able to develop

Figure 7.2   Coevolution of the Economic Era and Organizational Form

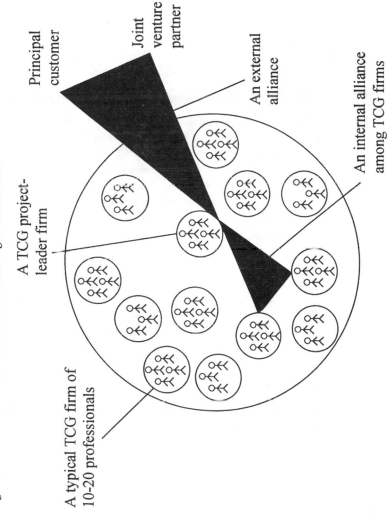

Principal customer

Joint venture partner

An external alliance

An internal alliance among TCG firms

A TCG project-leader firm

A typical TCG firm of 10-20 professionals

efficiently a state-of-the-art product that is tailor-made to the principal customer's specifications.

According to TCG's governance principles, the project leader firm also is expected to search among the other TCG companies for additional partners—not only because they are needed for their technical contribution, but also because the collaboration itself is expected to enhance overall organizational know-how. The process of "internal" triangulation thus serves a dual purpose. It produces direct input to the project, and it helps to diffuse competence in areas such as business development, partnering, and project management.

The three principles of cellularity are tightly interconnected at TCG, mutually reinforcing each other and producing a strong overall organization. First, acceptance of entrepreneurial responsibility is required for admission to the group and is increasingly enhanced by the triangulation process. Second, self-organization gives the individual firm both the ability and the freedom to reach deeply into its own know-how to create responses to a continuously evolving set of customer and partner needs. Third, each firm's profit responsibility, as well as its opportunity to own stock in other TCG firms, provides an ongoing stimulus for know-how growth and its utilization.

To this point, TCG has pushed its version of the cellular organizational approach to a modest size (approximately 200 staff in 13 small firms). Whether TCG's particular approach can be used to propel its growth to medium or large size is not yet clear. It may well be that some modification of its self-organizing abilities and reward system may be required.

Acer: A Global Cellular Company

An attempt to build a large-scale cellular organization is evident at The Acer Group, where cofounder Stan Shih has created a vision of a global personal computer company.[9] As at TCG, Shih's design calls for a federation of self-managing firms held together by mutual interest rather than hierarchical control. Shih's driving slogan is "21 in 21"—a federation of at least 21 independent firms located around the world by the twenty-first century, each operating in what Shih calls a "client-server" mode. That is, each firm, depending on the type of transaction involved, is either a client or a server of the other firms in the federation. Some firms, called Regional Business Units (RBUs), are operated primarily as marketing organizations—advertising, selling, and servicing computers according to particular national or regional needs. Other firms, called Strategic Business Units (SBUs) are primarily

R&D, manufacturing, and distribution units. For the most part, RBUs are clients that receive products from servers, the SBUs. However, RBUs are required to submit on an ongoing basis short-, medium-, and long-term forecasts of their product needs. In this mode, the SBUs are the clients of the RBUs—depending on each RBU's knowledge of its local market to provide information that will drive product development and manufacturing.

Although each firm has a core task to perform, new product concepts can and do originate anywhere in the federation. For example, Acer America (an RBU) wanted a stylish yet affordable PC for the North American market. It contracted with Frog, an outside industrial design firm, to assist it in the development of the highly acclaimed Acer Aspire. Manufacturing was done by Acer SBUs, and the marketing campaign was developed jointly by Acer America and Acer International, another RBU based in Singapore. Other Acer units are free to borrow from the Aspire design or to create unique designs suited to their respective markets. Every new-product proposal is evaluated as a business venture by the federation's partner firms.

Shih's vision for the Acer federation of companies, however, appears to go one step beyond that of TCG in terms of reinforcing both the responsibility of the individual firm for its own destiny and the responsibility of all firms for the long-term success of the total organization. At TCG, the value of each of the member firms is calculated through an internal stock market, and firms are free to leave the group if they so choose. At Acer, the firms are each owned jointly by their own management and home-country investors, with a (usually) minority ownership position held by Acer, Inc., the parent firm. Shih intends that Acer firms around the world will be listed on local stock exchanges and be free to seek capital for their own expansion. He believes that local ownership unleashes the motivation to run each business prudently.

With all Acer firms enjoying the freedom to both operate and expand, the value of their membership in the federation is the capacity of the "cells" to continue to serve one another in an increasingly competitive global marketplace. Acer has developed the competence to produce all of its products efficiently for just-in-time assembly and distribution. With minimal inventories, the latest models are available at all times at every sales site.

As yet, Acer's operating protocols are not geared as explicitly to the diffusion of know-how as is the case at TCG. Nevertheless, Acer's business model provides the opportunity for each firm to draw on federation partners as preferred providers or clients. Currently, Acer's worldwide training programs are being used to translate Shih's global vision into action programs at the local-firm level.

Partial Uses of the Cellular Approach

Even those firms that have not yet moved to a complete cellular model appear to obtain benefits from using one or more of its three main building blocks. For example, Kyocera relied heavily on the principle of self-organization to improve its manufacturing process. In that company, each cell consists of a small group of machines and a team of highly trained employees who collaborate in the production of a well-defined set of products for a specific group of customers. As opposed to the functional organization of manufacturing, where machines are grouped according to task performed, and products or parts are produced through specialized batch methods, the cellular approach divides the stream of production into parallel flows, giving the members of each cell responsibility for planning their own operations, ensuring that the quality of their output meets specified performance standards, interfacing with their suppliers and customers, and responding to unusual circumstances.[10]

Alternatively, Oticon, the Danish hearing aid manufacturer, has thoughtfully reengineered its organization using approaches similar to the cellular principles of self-organization and entrepreneurship. First, it dramatically and systematically removed many of the bureaucratic barriers that plagued organization members. It eliminated rules, reports, and forms, achieving in the process a paperless workplace. It reduced the need for planning and supervision by allowing employees to choose the project teams on which they worked. Such voluntarism also served to stimulate entrepreneurship, as the most successful projects were those that were widely regarded as compelling ideas.[11] Thus self-managing teams now have responsibility for both the identification and organization of new business projects.

At Semco, the Brazilian industrial-equipment manufacturer, management places great emphasis on the principles of member ownership and entrepreneurship. For example, work teams within all of Semco's plants have a standing invitation to take their operations outside the company and form their own business firms. Semco will lease its equipment to the new outside firm at very favorable rates. If the new firm provides a product or service desired by Semco, it can do business with its former employer. Even if the new firm later wishes to rejoin Semco, it can propose to do so, and the decision will be treated just like any other business proposal. All of these actions are encouraged because Ricardo Semler, Semco's former chief executive officer, believes that employee ownership is the best means of achieving a competitive business. Although it is a privately held company, Semco shares almost a quarter of its profits with managers and employees.[12]

Adding Value by Using the Cellular Form

A close examination of cellularly structured firms such as TCG and Acer indicates that they also share some of the features of earlier organizational forms. Indeed, each new form, as we noted earlier, incorporates the major value-adding characteristics of the previous forms and adds new capabilities to them. Thus the cellular form includes the dispersed entrepreneurship of the divisional form, customer responsiveness of the matrix form, and self-organizing knowledge and asset sharing of the network form.

We believe, however, that the cellular organizational form offers the potential to add value even beyond asset and know-how sharing. In its fully developed state, we envision the cellular organization adding value through its unique ability to create and utilize knowledge. For example, knowledge sharing occurs in networks, but as a by-product of asset sharing, not as a specific focus of such activity. Similarly, matrix and divisionalized firms recognize the value that may be added when knowledge is shared across projects or divisions, but they must create special-purpose mechanisms (e.g., task forces) in order to generate and share new knowledge.

By contrast, as illustrated at TCG, the cellular form lends itself to sharing not only the explicit know-how that cells have accumulated and articulated but also the tacit know-how that emerges when cells combine to design unique new customer solutions.[13] Such learning focuses not on the output of the innovation process but on the innovation process itself—it is know-how that can be achieved and shared only by doing.

Beyond knowledge creation and sharing, the cellular form has the potential to add value through its related ability to keep the firm's total knowledge assets more fully invested than do the other organizational forms. Because each cell has entrepreneurial responsibility and is empowered to draw on any of the firm's assets for each new business opportunity, high levels of knowledge utilization across cells should be expected. Network organizations aspire to high utilization of know-how and assets, but upstream firms ultimately are dependent on downstream partners to find new product or service uses. In the cellular firm, the product/service innovation process is continuous and fully shared.

Implementing the Cellular Organization

Many organizational variations using some or all of the cellular principles are likely to emerge in the years ahead.[14] However, while the direction of the evolution is clear, companies that attempt implementation of the complete cellular form face several significant challenges. Certainly, cellularly structured firms will not just happen. Our interviews with leaders of cellular firms make it clear that they are the product of a bold managerial vision and, even more important, a unique managerial philosophy.[15] The ability to envision and build the entrepreneurial, self-organizing, and ownership components of cellular organizations must be undergirded with a philosophy that emphasizes *investment in human capabilities* and the *willingness to take substantial risks* to maximize their utilization.

The first requirement is a willingness to invest in human capability that goes well beyond simply providing for current education and training. The concept of investment calls for expenditures to build the capabilities needed to respond to the future demands that will be placed on the organization, even those that cannot be forecasted easily. Training to meet current needs is not an investment because the requirement is clear, and the costs and benefits can be calculated easily. Building competencies for future needs is an investment because risk is involved—not every return can be predicted and, moreover, not everyone whose skills are enhanced will remain with the firm.

For example, companies such as Chaparral Steel make heavy investments in building know-how even though not all returns can be measured easily. Chaparral invests up to one-third of every member's time annually in one form or another of continuous education and skill development. Chaparral views growing know-how as the basic source of members' ability to add economic value in a highly competitive industry.[16] The competencies visible in firms such as Kyocera, Oticon, Semco, Acer, and TCG are the products of similar investments.

It is worth noting that the basic notion of achieving competitive advantage through people is far from new. In the late 1950s Edith Penrose focused on managerial competence as the principal engine of organizational growth, and in the 1960s Rensis Likert advocated careful accounting for investments in human resources and the costs of managerial actions that might deplete them. The 1990s have brought a renewed awareness among managers and management scholars that building know-how is the primary means by which firms create economic value.[17] The difference today, however, is that continuing investment in the competence of organization members is no longer merely an option; it is an economic must.[18]

The concept of investment always involves risk. Moreover, risk is usually proportional to the level of possible return. Therefore, the biggest challenge facing most firms that are considering the use of a cellular form of organization is not just the investment required to build key competencies, it is the willingness to allow the levels of self-governance necessary to utilize that competence fully. For example, Oticon takes what many firms would view as an extraordinary risk in allowing members to choose their own work assignments on projects where their capabilities can be used most effectively. Others would regard the firm (cell) autonomy allowed at TCG and Acer to involve even bigger risks, since coordination is largely voluntary and agreed-upon protocols and responsibilities are used instead of hierarchical controls.

Perhaps even more challenging than making investments and taking risks, however, is the long-term requirement for *sharing with organization members the returns of their knowledge utilization.* That is, if organization members are to accept professional levels of responsibility, traditional reward schemes such as bonus plans are not likely to be sufficient. Perhaps the future structure of return-sharing will follow the philosophies expressed by Stan Shih and Ricardo Semler—that the long-run pursuit of an increasingly competent organization may require innovative mechanisms providing real ownership and profit-sharing—mechanisms that give members' intellectual capital the same rights as the financial capital supplied by stockholders.

Given the required levels of investment, risk-taking, and member ownership, many companies will not—and need not—move completely to the cellular organizational form. For example, firms that produce standard products or services to forecast or order still may be most productive if arranged in at least shallow hierarchies. Groups of such firms may be linked into networks for greater speed and customization. The push toward cellular approaches, as noted earlier, is appearing first in firms focused on rapid product and service innovation—unique and/or state-of-the-art offerings. However, while cellular firms are associated most easily with newer, rapidly evolving industries, the form lends itself to firms providing the design initiative in virtually any type of industry. For example, within a network of companies in a mature business, it is the cellularly structured firms that are likely to provide leadership in new product and service development.

Conclusion

Across national and regional economies, the overlapping eras of standardization, customization, and innovation will continue to evolve, and new variations of hierarchical, network, and cellular organizational forms will continue to emerge. Decades of experimentation honed the functional, divisional, matrix, and network forms, clarifying their operating logics and highlighting their costs and benefits. A similar pattern can be expected to occur with the cellular form.

Throughout the evolutionary process of organizational form, one constant has been the search for ever-increasing effectiveness and efficiency in the ability to fully apply know-how to resource utilization. Firms willing to take the risk of leading this search have been and will continue to be most successful.

Notes

This chapter reflects the authors' continuing conversations with managers in leading-edge firms in the United States, Europe, Asia, and Australia. We wish to thank those managers for their insights into the process of building cellular organizations. We are also grateful for research funding from the Carnegie Bosch Institute for Applied Studies in International Management. Important contributions to our understanding of knowledge-management processes have been made by Professor Henry J. Coleman, Jr., of St. Mary's College of California.

1. For excellent accounts of the evolution of organizational forms during this period, see A. D. Chandler, Jr., *Strategy and Structure: Chapters in the History of the American Industrial Enterprise* (Cambridge, Mass.: MIT Press, 1962); and P. R. Lawrence and D. Dyer, *Renewing American Industry* (New York: Free Press, 1983).

2. A discussion of "excess managerial capacity" as the engine of corporate growth can be found in E. T. Penrose, *The Theory of the Growth of the Firm* (Oxford: Basil Blackwell, 1959). A new edition of this book, with a foreword by Professor Penrose, was published in 1995.

3. For a discussion of matrix organizations, see S. M. Davis and P. R. Lawrence, *Matrix* (Reading, Mass.: Addison-Wesley, 1977).

4. For a discussion of the globalization process, see M. E. Porter, ed., *Competition in Global Industries* (Boston, Mass.: Harvard Business School Press, 1986).

5. The multifirm network organization was first identified and described by R. E. Miles and C. C. Snow, "Fit, Failure, and the Hall of Fame," *California Management Review* 26, no. 3 (1984): 10–28. For descriptions of the major types of network organizations used today, see R. E. Miles and C. C. Snow, *Fit, Failure, and the Hall of Fame: How Companies Succeed or Fail* (New York: Free Press, 1994), chaps. 7–9.

6. S. Kauffman, *At Home in the Universe* (New York: Oxford University Press, 1995).

7. We did not invent this term. The concept of cellular structures has been discussed at least since the 1960s. For a review, see J. A. Mathews, "Holonic Organisational Architectures," *Human Systems Management* 15 (1996): 1–29.

8. J. A. Mathews, "TCG R&D Networks: The Triangulation Strategy," *Journal of Industry Studies* 1 (1993): 65–74.

9. J. A. Mathews and C. C. Snow, "The Expansionary Dynamics of the Late-comer Multinational Firm: The Case of The Acer Group," *Asia Pacific Journal of Management,* In Press.

10. M. Zeleny, "Amoebae: The New Generation of Self-Managing Human Systems," *Human Systems Management* 9 (1990): 57–59.

11. L. Kolind, "Creativity at Oticon," *Fast Company* vol. 18, no. 3 (1996): 5–9.

12. R. Semler, *Maverick* (New York: Time Warner Books, 1993).

13. I. Nonaka and H. Takeuchi, *The Knowledge-Creating Company: How Japanese Companies Create the Dynamics of Innovation* (New York: Oxford University Press, 1995).

14. Many of these experiments will involve various forms of strategic alliances and/or joint ventures. See A. C. Inkpen, "Creating Knowledge Through Collaboration," *California Management Review* 39 (1996): 123–140.

15. J. A. Mathews and C. C. Snow, "A Conversation with Stan Shih on Global Strategy and Management," under review.

16. G. E. Forward, D. E. Beach, D. A. Gray, and J. C. Quick, "Mentofacturing: A Vision for American Industrial Excellence," *Academy of Management Executive* 5 (1991): 32–44.

17. Penrose, *Theory of the Growth of the Firm;*3d ed. (New York: Oxford University Press, 1995). R. Likert, *The Human Organization* (New York: McGraw-Hill, 1967); and J. Pfeffer, *Competitive Advantage Through People* (Boston: Harvard Business School Press, 1994).

18. For an example of a firm that seriously and creatively attempted to calculate the value of its intellectual capital and other intangible assets, see L. Edvinsson and M. S. Malone, *Intellectual Capital: Realizing Your Company's True Value by Finding Its Hidden Brainpower* (New York: HarperBusiness, 1997).

CHAPTER 8

The Internal Market Economy

*Russell L. Ackoff, Professor Emeritus,
University of Pennsylvania*

The state of management practice today is highlighted by the fact that there are more panaceas than problems. Downsizing, reengineering, total quality management (TQM), benchmarking, outsourcing, scenario planning, and so on represent only a partial list of the panaceas in good currency at the moment. However, there is a growing literature about their failure. Well-known studies by Arthur D. Little and Ernst and Young consulting firms showed that about two-thirds of TQM efforts have been disappointing.[1] Other studies show that most downsizing efforts eventually increase costs.[2]

The Need to View Organizations as Systems

Panaceas fail because they are antisystemic. A system is a whole that cannot be divided into independent parts. Its essential (defining) properties derive from the interactions of its parts, not their actions taken separately. If an automobile were disassembled, for example, it would lose all its essential properties even if all its parts were kept in one place. A disassembled automobile is no longer an automobile because it cannot function as one.

All the panaceas deal with parts or aspects of a system taken separately. It turns out that when we improve the parts of a system taken separately, we very seldom improve the performance of the system as a whole. This can be rigorously proven in system science, but it is not necessary. An example will do.

Suppose we gather in one place one of every automobile that is available in the United States. Then we have a group of the best automotive engineers determine which car has the best motor, then the best transmission, then the best distributor, and so on until we know for each essential part of an automobile which is the best available. Then suppose we have these parts removed from their source and try to assemble them into an automobile that consists of only the best parts available. We don't even get an automobile, let alone the best one, because *the parts don't fit.*

What can we conclude? The performance of a system depends on how its parts interact, not on how they act taken separately. Yet today's panaceas focus on improving parts considered independently of the system of which they are part. Doing so may improve the performance of the part but seldom the performance of the whole.

Another fundamental problem is the important distinction Peter Drucker made between doing things right and doing the right thing. It is much better to do the right thing wrong than the wrong thing right. The righter we do the wrong thing, the wronger it becomes. For example, we continue to put more and more money into outmoded approaches to education and health care and succeed only in making them worse. But if we do the right thing wrong, we have the opportunity to learn from an acknowledged mistake and improve the next time around.

There are many other examples of doing the wrong thing right, of increasing the efficiency with which we pursue the wrong objectives. For instance, the automobile is clearly a dysfunctional solution to the urban transportation problem. A visit to most major cities—for example, Mexico City, Santiago, Caracas, or New York—reveals why. Mexico City recently suffered a traffic jam that tied up thousands of cars for hours. During it several people died because of the inability to get medical attention to them. Mexican children frequently are kept home for school because air pollution makes it dangerous for them to walk outside. Trees on the beautiful Avenida de Reforma have died of the same pollution.

The automobile is gradually destroying the quality of urban life around the world. Automobiles are designed to carry four to six people but carry only 1.2 on average. They are designed for speeds in excess of 100 miles per hour but travel in cities at about 17 miles per hour on average. Passengers face forward when it has been shown that their safety is maximized when they sit facing backward. But we keep improving automobiles as currently conceived; hence continue to do the wrong thing righter.

All panaceas are concerned with changes in the existing system, reform. In contrast, I want to talk about a change in the very *nature* of the system—transformation. There is a fundamental difference between reforming an existing system and transforming it. Reformation simply produces a modified version of the existing system. Transformation produces a system different in form and function. Panaceas reform, never transform, an organization.

A Systemic View of Corporate Economies

A number of problems facing enterprises that cannot be dealt with by any one or set of panaceas but can be treated effectively by transforming the organization into one with an internal market economy. The apparent need for downsizing and benchmarking is eliminated in such an economy. It dissolves the need to use TQM to improve quality and the need for process reengineering to increase productivity. Dissolving these needs is a lot better than trying to solve the problems they create.

Many of the problems panaceas address derive from the fact that most units within organizations do not obtain their income from those they serve but are subsidized from above. For example, personnel, finance, and data processing units are examples of units whose services normally are not paid for directly by the units they serve. They are budgeted from above out of funds obtained by taxing the units served, much like government agencies. There are two principal consequences. First, serving units are not nearly as responsive to those they serve as they are to those who subsidize them. Second, because they are subsidized monopolies, they tend to bureaucratize. Bureaucracies tend to grow without limit because they believe that doing so provides maximum protection against downsizing. Yet the fact is that they maximize the need for downsizing because their principal mode of growth is make-work, work that has no useful product.

The need to downsize can virtually be eliminated by destroying internal bureaucratic monopolies, and this can be done by converting an enterprise's internal economy from one that is centrally planned and controlled to a market economy. At the national (macroeconomic) level we are dedicated to pursuit of a market economy, as originally formulated by Adam Smith in *Wealth of Nations*. But at the (microeconomic) level of the enterprise, we usually employ the same kind of economic system as the Soviet Union used before its transformation—one that is centrally planned and controlled.

This inconsistency often is rationalized by reference to the difference in size between the nation-state and even a large corporation. But this is nonsense. The Associated Press recently identified the 20 largest economies in the world, 6 of which were corporations. AT&T has a larger economy than more than 100 nations. Scale has nothing to do with it. The real reason for this inconsistency is that chief executives of our public and private institutions and enterprises are not willing to give up their power over others. Unfortunately, we have learned that the more educated subordinates are, the less effective power-over is as a means for getting them to do what we want them to. To exercise power-over is to employ command and control; to exercise power-to is to *lead*.

An internal market economy requires reduction of executive power-over but increases its power-to, and it enables executives to manage systemically, that is, to manage the interactions of units rather than their actions taken separately. Without these changes it is, and will become, more and more difficult for enterprises to compete effectively in the increasingly turbulent and competitive global economy.

An Internal Market Economy

What does a corporation that is transformed from a centrally planned and controlled economy to one that is based on a free market look like?

First, almost every unit, including the executive office, becomes a profit center. The exceptions are those units that, for one reason or another, cannot be permitted to serve external customers; for example, the corporate secretary and the corporate planning department. Such units are treated as cost centers but are assigned to profit centers.

The requirement that most units be profit centers does not mean that they must be profitable. For example, Corning has retained Steuben Glass despite what I have been led to believe is its low profitability because it lends considerable prestige to the corporation. One university that employed an internal market economy retains its linguistic department despite the fact that its graduates are the most expensive for the university to turn out. The reason is that the department is one of the most prestigious in the world. On the other hand, departments that have been profitable but of low quality have been discontinued.

Although profitability is not necessarily required of every part of the enterprise, the profitability of each part is taken into account when evaluating its performance and considering how to treat it.

Second, subject to a constraint to be described, each profit center is free to sell its output to whomever it wants, internally or externally, at whatever price it wants. In addition, it can buy whatever it wants from whatever internal or external sources it wants. For example, a unit that needs accounting services can either buy them from an internal or external supplier or provide them to itself. The same is true for data processing, other services, acquisitions of parts to be assembled, and even products.

Third, these rules are subject to a few mild constraints. One is lawlike, intended to protect the ability of the enterprise to compete. For example, during the Cold War the U.S. government prevented IBM from selling mainframe computers to the Soviet Union. A company that has a product based on a secret formula, such as Coca Cola, is not likely to permit its product to be made by an external producer.

The other type of constraint is specific rather than general: A corporate executive may override a particular lower-level decision to buy or sell a product or service from or to an external source. However, when this increases the cost or decreases the profitability of a transaction, the executive who does the overriding must compensate the unit affected for this loss. It is the executive's decision and he or she must pay for it. Since overriding executives are also a profit centers, they must balance the cost of their overrides with the benefit their part of the organization obtains from them. In effect, the exercise of overrides is the management of interactions of units, not their separate actions.

When an internal unit wants to buy something externally for which there is an internal supplier, the internal supplier is given the opportunity to bid for the order. However, the consuming unit is free to choose an external unit even if the internal supplier quotes a lower price. Price is not the only reason for selecting a supplier; other reasons are time to delivery, reliability, quality, and so on.

Asking for prices from external suppliers can create a problem that can and should be avoided. If one repeatedly asks them for quotes but never places an order with them, the sources may come to suspect that there is no possibility of a sale and therefore deliberately inflate the prices quoted. To avoid this, some business should be given to at least some of those from whom price quotes are sought.

Fourth, one of the fundamental differences between a conventional organization and one employing an internal market economy is that every unit in the latter must pay for all services and supplies it receives, for rent of the space it occupies, and, most important, interest on the capital it employs either for operating or investment. Higher-level management acts like an investment bank for lower-level units. It provides capital but at a cost. Paying all costs enables every unit to be evaluated using its return on the capital employed. Payment may be in the form of interest if the capital supplied is treated as a loan or as dividends if the capital supplied is treated as stock ownership.

Fifth, units are permitted to accumulate profit up to a specified limit. The limit is set based on an estimate of the amount that the unit can invest at a return equal to, or greater than, that which the higher-level unit can obtain. Up to that limit units can use the money accumulated however they see fit as long as it does not affect any other unit. If it does affect another unit, the affected unit must agree to the use; if it does not, all the units affected together must go to the lowest level of management at which they converge for resolution of the difference—again management of interactions.

Money accumulated above the limit goes to the next higher level of management, which pays interest on it to the unit from which it comes. This requirement elevates the status of "cash cows" that supply the enterprise with the capital it requires for development and growth.

The Executive Office as a Profit Center

As noted earlier, the chief executive's office and the executive office of any business unit operate as profit centers. They incur costs for personnel, services, supplies, capital acquired by borrowing or investment, and costs of their overriding decisions. They derive income from the services and capital they provide units or dividends paid by them. Government taxes on corporate profit is allocated to units that are profit centers proportional to their contribution to that profit.

Since the executive office also must operate as a profit center, its costs tend to decrease dramatically under such a transformation. For example, when an internal market economy was introduced at Clark Equipment, its corporate overhead came down greatly because its headquarters shrank from about 450 people to about 50. Those displaced were reassigned to productive activities in subordinate units.

The requirement that the executive office operates as a profit center helps assure that it sees itself as having a value-adding function. It makes executives conscious of the quality and responsiveness of their decisions and the services they provide. Furthermore, their dependence on the performance of subordinate units is made explicit and measurable.

Examples

An increasing number of corporations have implemented internal markets successfully. I describe some of the more dramatic cases to illustrate the power of the concept.

A Major Oil Company

This company had one of the largest computing facilities in the United States. Projections of the cost of computing showed that in a very few years, the company would be spending more on computers than on people. The new CEO did not know whether this was good or bad. He asked my group if we could determine whether the money being spent on computing was justified. We naively said we thought we could.

We found that the computers were used mainly to prepare schedules for refineries and for the shipping of crude oil from the Middle East to the refineries. We designed an evaluative experiment and went to discuss it with the refinery managers. We explained that some of these managers selected at random would be asked to prepare schedules manually while others would use the computer-generated schedules. They told us the latter was not possible since they never used the computer-produced schedules without modification. They explained that the model used by the computers left out some important qualitative variables that they had to take into account. Therefore, they always adjusted the computer-generated schedule given to them. We said that if we were given a record of their changes, we still might be able to go ahead as planned. They told us that their changes often were made daily or within a day and no record of them was kept.

We learned much the same thing when we talked to those responsible for scheduling the shipping. After several months of complete frustration, we found it impossible to evaluate the outputs of computing.

One day, out of desperation, we invoked Hitch's principle. Charley Hitch was a distinguished operations researcher at the RAND Corporation during and after World War II who eventually was demoted to presidency of the University of California. He once said: "If you can't solve the problem you're facing, you must be facing the wrong problem." We began to look for a different formulation of the problem.

Sure enough, when we reflected on what we were doing, we saw that we were trying to evaluate a product consumed by someone else. They were obviously better equipped to evaluate it than we. This led to a different formulation of the problem and different kind of proposed solution. We asked the CEO: "Why don't you make the corporate computing department a profit center? Let it charge its users whatever it wants for its services. But it should be free to solicit customers externally as well as internally. On the other hand, internal users should be free to use external computing services if they so desired." The CEO liked the proposal and implemented it.

In the next six months the computing center reduced the number of its computers by about half. Nevertheless, it continued to do almost all of the internal work because internal demand was significantly reduced once the users had to pay directly for the work they requested. The center still had time left over, which it began to sell to external users. Over time it generated a very profitable data-processing business while improving the quality and reducing the cost of its services. Such improvement and reduction were necessary if it was to attract and retain customers. The executive who had computer oversight responsibilities no longer had to be concerned with benchmarking the services provided; he had a much better way of evaluating it.

An Electrical Equipment Manufacturer

A very good example of the power of an internal market economy, even though applied only to a part of a corporation, is provided by a large manufacturer of electrical and electronic equipment. One of its business units was a major manufacturer of small motors used mostly in large household appliances. A few very large manufacturers of such appliances bought most of its output. Another business unit supplied electrical wholesalers with replacement parts used primarily on production equipment. Included were small electric motors. The corporation's executives required the motor-producing unit to supply the other, and the other to use no other source of supply. Since both units were profit centers, a transfer price for the motors was established. All hell broke loose.

The wholesaler-supply unit often needed electrical motors at a time when the producing unit was operating at capacity and preferred to supply its major customers who paid a higher price for the motors than the transfer price. Therefore, compliance with the corporate directive required it to sacrifice profit.

On the other hand, the wholesaler-supply unit frequently was offered equivalent motors by external manufacturers at a lower-than-transfer price. It could not buy them, a fact that increased its costs and lowered its profit.

Little wonder each unit hated the other. The intensity of this hate led to overt conflict that disrupted corporate activity and set a poor example for other units. The CEO asked us if we could find a way to reduce the conflict by adjusting the transfer price. We told him there was no such thing as a permanently fair transfer price, that sooner or later every transfer price would produce conflict. We suggested that he allow each unit to buy and sell wherever it wanted, but give the executive to which both units reported the ability to override these decisions. However, he should pay for the increased costs or lost profits incurred because of his overrides. The CEO agreed.

In the first year the executive responsible for oversight constrained the two business units to the tune of $3 million. At the end of the year the corporate executive office met to evaluate this expenditure and decided it was not justified; it bought no tangible synergy. The constraints were removed the following year. Profitability of both business units and the corporation were increased and the conflict between the units was eliminated. They became completely cooperative.

An Ivy League University

As indicated earlier, a major university applied an internal market economy to its departments. As a result two unprofitable and less-than-high-quality units were discontinued, but one unprofitable unit was retained because of its prestige. However, the major effect of this transformation was on the behavior of other departments. Previously, growth had been the major objective of almost all departments because they took stability to be positively correlated with size. But now, for the first time, they had to worry about the effects of size on their profitability. Unconstrained growth no longer appeared to be an effective means to their ends.

In one department faculty members were treated as profit centers. Their income was associated with the number of student credits their teaching produced and the amount of billable research in which they engaged. A faculty member who did not end up the year in the black could not receive an increase in salary. Professors were amazed when they learned how much teaching they had to do to break even, much more than they were used to. For example, each academic year a full professor had to teach five courses of 37 students each in order to break even. Before the new economy was installed, most were teaching only two seminars per year with an average of about 8 students in each. Their orientation toward teaching and research changed abruptly.

Professors now wanted to teach large first-year required courses in order to earn enough to enable them to conduct their advanced seminars without sacrificing future income. Contractual research was no longer viewed as academic prostitution. Competition for grants and contracts increased dramatically, and participation in research was much easier to obtain.

Internal Markets in the Public Sector

The use of an internal market economy is by no means restricted to private for-profit organizations. It can be, and has been, used effectively in the public sector, by government. For example, the use of educational vouchers, suggested by Christopher Jenks of Harvard University and publicized by Milton Friedman, involves a conversion to a market economy. In this system schools receive income by cashing in vouchers obtained from students who have a choice of public schools to attend. The vouchers are supplied by government. They also can be used to pay all or part of the tuition required by nonreligious private schools. This system requires schools to compete in order to survive, and this, in turn, requires they be responsive to the needs of those they service.

In one version of the voucher system, every public school must accept all applicants from the area for which it is responsible. Students who are accepted at and attend schools in different areas must be compensated for their transportation costs by the schools in the areas in which they live. In such a system if schools are required to select at random from among applicants living outside their area, segregation in schools becomes a nonissue.

To take another example, a large centralized licensing bureau in Mexico City had a terrible record of inefficiency and poor service. It was divided into small offices that were placed in each section of the city. These offices were compensated for each license they issued, and they had no other source of income. Those who wanted a license could use any of the offices. Unlike the centralized bureaucratic monopoly they replaced, the small offices could survive only by providing good service inexpensively. Service time decreased, the quality of service increased, and the corruption that had permeated the service previously virtually disappeared.

It should be noted that privatizing a public service does not necessarily convert it to a market economy. Privatization can preserve a monopoly; which is antithetical to a market economy in which competition is essential.

Objections to an Internal Market Economy

Proposals for the introduction of an internal market economy usually are received with four types of concern.

First, skeptics argue that the additional amount of accounting required would be horrendous. Not true! The amount of accounting required actually is reduced. Most of the accounting currently required of organizational units is done to facilitate control by higher-level organizational units. In an internal market economy, however, only profit-and-loss statements and balance sheets need to be provided to others in the organization. They should pay for any additional information they request. Paying for such services has a strong tendency to reduce the amount of unnecessary accounting information flowing within organizations, particularly up.

Second, some argue that an internal market economy will increase conflict and competition between parts of the organization. Again, not true! Transfer pricing, which is a surrogate for market pricing in a centrally planned and controlled economy, produces intense internal conflict and competition. Peter Drucker once observed that there is more competition within firms than between them, and it is a lot less ethical.

Most organizational units have much better relations with external suppliers that they choose than with internal suppliers that they can't. The competition that is stimulated by an internal market economy is between external and internal suppliers of the same goods or services, not between internal supplying and supplied units. Moreover, internal suppliers who must compete with external suppliers for internal customers are much more responsive to their customers' needs than monopolistic internal suppliers.

Consider the case of a large food producer that had a substantial market research unit, a monopolistic subsidized supplier of its services to other organizational units. It was held in low regard by its users because it was considered to be unresponsive and inferior to outside market research organizations. Corporate management converted it into a profit center, and permitted it to market its services externally and its users to obtain market research services externally. Using units were required to pay for whatever services they used whatever its source. All internal users initially moved to external suppliers, forcing the internal supplier to look for external work. Eventually it succeeded, but only after it had improved the quality of its services significantly. It became a thriving business. Internal units began to wonder why it was so successful and tried it out. This time they found it responsive and competent. Internal demand became so great that the market research unit had to turn down some work offered by external organizations.

A third argument is that an internal market economy cannot be installed in only one part of an organization, only in the whole. A partial internal market, it is claimed, may be very difficult, if not impossible. Difficult, yes, but not impossible! About three years ago, one of a company's two manufacturing arms, one that produces copiers, cameras, X-ray and other medical equipment converted to an internal market economy. The containing company was not willing to adopt the same type of economy. Therefore, the division had to operate as a market-oriented unit within a centrally planned and controlled economy.

The containing company continued to charge the division for all corporately provided services through an overhead allocation. The division could not break these charges down into those for services it received and those it did not. Therefore, the unit developed surrogate costs for the services it received and treated unaccounted for charges from the company as a tax. It continued to report to the corporation in the conventional way but operated with two sets of books.

One year after its conversion, the division's effectiveness had increased so much that the corporation and other parts of it began to wonder what was happening. When the corporation found out, it did not convert to a similar system but it did change the information required of and provided to the division. This change enabled the division to operate more easily with its internal market economy. Other units subsequently followed suit.

A similar case involved the R&D unit of Esso Petroleum Canada. It also converted to an internal market economy within a centrally controlled corporate economy. But in this case the parent company tried to facilitate the conversion, as a trial that could lead to a similar transformation in other units and possibly the whole corporation.

A fourth reason given for not seriously considering an internal market economy is that certain internal service functions cannot "reasonably" be expected to attract external customers. Frequently cited examples are accounting and human-resource departments. One corporation headquartered in the Midwest converted both these departments into profitable business units. Many local small and medium-size businesses that could not afford internal accounting and human resource services of high quality welcomed the availability of such services.

Another company that occupied a number of buildings in a suburb of a major city converted its facilities-and-services department (buildings, grounds, and utilities) into a profit center that operated within a corporate internal market economy. All of its internal users shifted to external suppliers from whom they obtained better services at a lower cost. As a result, the facilities-and-services department gradually shrank and eventually was eliminated with a considerable saving to the company.

Advantages of an Internal Market Economy

A number of the benefits of an internal market economy have been identified already, in particular, increased responsiveness of internal suppliers, better quality and reduced cost of internally supplied services and products, continuous right-sizing, debureaucratization, and so on. A few other advantages are worth mentioning.

First, because almost every corporate unit operating within an internal market economy becomes a profit center, similar measures of performance can be applied to all of them. This makes it possible to compare the performance of units that were previously not comparable, for example, manufacturing and accounting.

Second, managers of profit centers within an internal market are necessarily general managers of semiautonomous business units. This provides them with opportunities to acquire, improve, and display their general management skills. Therefore, executives are better able to evaluate the general management ability of their subordinates.

Third, when units are converted to profit centers and are given the autonomy that goes with it, their managers are in a much better position to obtain all the information they require to manage well. They become more concerned with providing themselves with the information they need than with providing their superiors with the information they want.

Conclusion

Conversion to an internal market economy obviously raises a number of issues. Therefore, it is not a task to be undertaken lightly; it is not for the fainthearted. The conversion requires courageous managers, *transformational leaders*. The potential payoff, however, is an order-of-magnitude increase in effectiveness. The transformation of corporations into internal market economies, corporate perestroika, is as important to our country on the microeconomic level as it was to the Soviet Union on the macroeconomic level.

Notes

Russell Ackoff is Professor Emeritus, University of Pennsylvania, and one of the deans of modern management thought. He co-founded the first U.S. graduate program in Operations Research at the Case Institute of technology and the Social Systems Sciences Program at the University of Pennsylvania. He is the former president of the Operations Research Society and the Society for General Systems Research. Dr. Ackoff has authored 20 books and hundreds of articles, and consulted to more than 400 corporations and governments. His most recent book is *The Democratic Corporation* (NY: Oxford University Press, 1994).

1. See: Arthur D. Little, "Companies Continue to Embrace Quality Programs, but TQM Has Generated More Enthusiasm Than Results," press release, March 1992; Ernst & Young and American Quality Foundation, "Best Practices Report," Preliminary Report (May 14, 1992), and Final Report (October 1, 1992); and Fuchberg, Gilbert, "Quality Programs Show Shoddy Results," *Wall Street Journal*, June 14, 1992, B1 and B7.

2. American Management Association, "1994 AMA Survey on Downsizing," research report, July 20, 1995; Andrea Knox, "Most Cuts in Jobs Don't Help Forms, Survey Indicates," *Philadelphia Inquirer,* March 9, 1992, D1; J. Pourdehnad, W. E. Halal, and E. Rausch, "From Downsizing to Rightsizing to Selfsizing," *Total Quality Review,* July/August 1995, 43–50; Ted J. Raksis, "The Downsizing Myth," *Kiwanis,* April 1994, 46ff; and Bernard Wysocki Jr., "Some Companies Cut Costs Too Far, Suffer 'Corporate Anorexia,'" *Wall Street Journal,* July 5, 1995.

CHAPTER 9

Business and the Environment: The Economics of a Clean Business

Paul Ekins, Keele University, England

Introduction

The purpose of a business is to create wealth. This is sometimes interpreted as increasing the value of shareholdings. However, such private accumulation is justifiable only from a wider social perspective if it proceeds having internalized into its structure of costs and prices any social and environmental impacts resulting from the business activity.

It is widely perceived that business as a whole is generating environmental costs that are not reflected in market prices and that are therefore a source of economic inefficiency, resulting in a loss of human welfare. Thus the Report of World Commission of Environment and Development, in its chapter on industry, stated: "It is evident that measures to reduce, control and prevent industrial pollution will need to be greatly strengthened. If they are not, pollution damage to human health could become intolerable in certain cities and threats to prosperity will continue to grow. . . . If sustainable development is to be sustainable over the long term, it will have to change radically in terms of the quality of that development."[1]

There is now an impressive consensus that the scale and intensity of the environmental challenge are such as to make business as usual a response that is both inadequate and potentially disastrous. Thus the World Resources Institute (WRI), in collaboration with both the Development and

Environment Programs of the United Nations, concludes on the basis of one of the world's most extensive environmental databases that "The world is not now headed toward a sustainable future, but rather toward a variety of potential human and environmental disasters."[2]

The United Kingdom Royal Society, in an unprecedented joint statement with the U.S. National Academy of Sciences, concluded in its message to the 1992 Rio Summit: "Unrestrained resource consumption for energy production and other uses . . . could lead to catastrophic outcomes for the global environment. Some of the environmental changes may produce irreversible damage to the earth's capacity to sustain life. . . . The future of our planet is in the balance."[3]

An important, indeed indispensable, condition for meeting this environmental challenge successfully is the transformation of the way goods and services are produced, a transformation of business into "clean business." The Brundtland Report broadly characterized this transformation as the development of industries and industrial operations "that are more efficient in terms of resource use, that generate less pollution and waste, that are based on the use of renewable rather than nonrenewable resources and that minimize irreversible adverse impacts on human health and the environment."[4] This chapter develops some ideas as to how business can, and how far business should, move in this direction.

I start by presenting a model of wealth creation, equally applicable to a business or the macroeconomy, in order to understand the range of contributions made by the environment to business activity and the economy. I then place this contribution in the context of the emerging concept of environmental sustainability, which is becoming a major organizing principle of environmental policy. Next I consider how businesses are starting to monitor, measure, report, and account for their environmental impacts, a necessary precondition to being able to manage them. Then I discuss the extent to which it is currently financially feasible for businesses to move toward environmental sustainability and present the results of some case studies that suggest that substantial progress is, in fact, possible. Finally, I set out some of the changes that need to be made to the current business context to encourage more businesses down this route, by ensuring that it is environmentally sustainable businesses that are the most profitable.

The transformation of industrial production into "clean business," a process that sometimes is called "ecological modernization," will not be easy. As the Business Council for Sustainable Development noted: "The requirement for clean, equitable, economic growth remains the single biggest difficulty with the larger challenge of sustainable development. Proving that such growth is possible is certainly the greatest test for business and industry."[5] This chapter suggests how the test might be approached in a way that makes the most of the opportunities that are offered and also points out the problems.

Understanding Wealth Creation

The process of wealth creation is characterized most commonly as one in which different kinds of asset, or capital, are brought together to produce goods and services. It is evident that one of the most fundamental stocks of capital is that provided by nature, here called ecological or natural capital. The model that follows emphasizes the role of this kind of capital, so that the natural environment's place in and contribution to business activity and the economy may be better understood.

Figure 9.1 portrays four kinds of capital stock: ecological (or natural) capital, human capital, social and organizational capital, and manufactured capital. Each of these stocks produces a flow of "services" from the environment (E), from human capital (L), from social/organizational capital (S), and from physical capital (K). These services are inputs into the productive process, along with "intermediate inputs" (M), which are economic outputs used as inputs in a subsequent process.

Manufactured capital comprises material goods—tools, machines, buildings, infrastructure—that contribute to the production process but do not become embodied in the output and, usually, are "consumed" in a period of time longer than a year. Intermediate goods, in contrast, either are embodied in produced goods (e.g., metals, plastics, components) or are immediately consumed in the production process (e.g., fuels). Human capital comprises all individuals' capacities for work; while social and organizational capital comprises the networks and organizations through which the contributions of individuals are mobilized and coordinated.

Ecological capital is a complex category that performs three distinct types of environmental function, two of which are directly relevant to the production process.[6] The first is the provision of resources for production (E), the raw materials that become food, fuels, metals, timber, and the like. The second is the absorption of wastes (W) from production, both from the production process and from the disposal of consumption goods. Where these wastes add to or improve the stock of ecological capital (e.g., through recycling or fertilization of soil by livestock), they can be regarded as investment in such capital. More frequently, where they destroy, pollute, or erode, with consequent negative impacts on the ecological, human, or manufactured

Figure 9.1 Stocks, Flows, and Welfare in the Process of Production

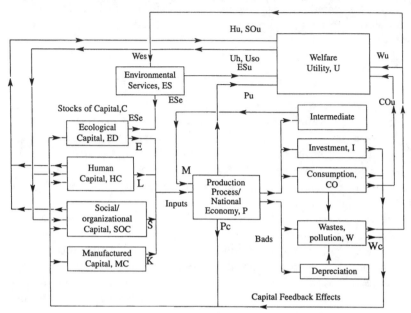

Note: In the flow descriptors, the upper-case letters denote the source of the flow, the lower-case letters denote the destination.

Key

Stocks of Capital, C

EC	Ecological capital
HC	Human capital
SOC	Social/organizational capitals from SOC
MC	Manufactured capital
K from MC	

Flows from the Capital Stock

E	(resources) from EC
L	(labor) from HC

Other Flows

Ees	Flows of environmental services (ES) from EC
Ese	Effects of environmental services (e.g., climate) on EC
M	Flows of intermediate goods into the production process, P
Pc	Effects of P on the various components of the capital stock, C
Wc	Effects of wastes (pollution) on C
Pu	Effects of P on welfare, U
Wu	Effects of pollution on U
Wes	Effects of pollution on environmental services, ES
Esu	Effects of environmental services, ES, on U
Cou	Effects of consumption, CO, on U
Hu, Sou	Effects of human and social/organizationalcapital on U
Uh, Uso	Effects of welfare, U, on human and social/organizational capital

capital stocks, they can be regarded as agents of negative investment, depreciation, or capital consumption. Either way, the wastes contribute to the capital feedback effects identified in figure 9.1.

The third type of environmental function does not contribute directly to production, but in many ways it is the most important because it provides the basic context and conditions within which production is possible at all. It comprises basic environmental services (ES), including survival services, such as those producing climate and ecosystem stability, shielding of ultraviolet radiation by the ozone layer, and amenity services, such as the beauty of wilderness and other natural areas. These services are produced directly by ecological capital independently of human activity, but human activity certainly can have an (often negative) effect on the responsible capital and therefore on the services produced by it, through the capital feedback effects discussed earlier.

The outputs of the economic process can, in the first instance, be categorized as "Goods" and "Bads." The Goods are the desired outputs of the process as well as any positive externalities (incidental effects) that may be associated with it. These Goods can be divided in turn into consumption, investment, and intermediate goods and services. The Bads are the negative effects of the production process, including capital depreciation and polluting wastes and other negative externalities, which contribute to environmental destruction, negative effects on human health, and so on. Insofar as they have an effect on the capital stocks, the Bads can be regarded as negative investment.

The necessity for a matter/energy balance on either side of the production process means that all matter and energy used as inputs also must emerge as outputs, either embodied in the Goods or among the Bads. At the end of this process, therefore, all former inputs are returned to the environment, as the stock of ecological capital, where they may have a positive, negative, or neutral effect.

Human welfare, or utility as economists call it, is generated at many points of the overall process of wealth creation. It is derived from consumption (COu); it can be generated through work satisfaction (Pu); it is derived from social and organizational structures (SOu); it is a function of human capital itself (Hu); and, most important for this chapter, it is affected by the quality of the natural environment (ESu) and by the nature and level of wastes (Wu).

Wastes and pollution from production and consumption affect utility directly (Wu, e.g., litter, noise) and through their mainly negative feedback into the stocks of environmental, human, and manufactured capital. These feedbacks, Wc, can reduce the productivity of environmental resources (e.g., through pollution) and affect the ecological capital that produces environmental services (e.g., by engendering climate change or damaging the ozone layer); they can damage human capital by engendering ill health; and they can corrode buildings (manufactured capital). They also can affect environmental services directly (Wes, e.g., by reducing the appreciation of natural beauty).

Figure 9.1 emphasizes feedback effects. One that has not yet been mentioned is the joint relationship between the stock of ecological capital (EC) and the environmental services (ES) deriving from it. In a stable ecosystem, EC and ES will tend to be symbiotically balanced.

Through this model it is possible to characterize more clearly the environmental attributes of a "clean business." First, however, it is necessary to explore briefly the concept that is becoming the organizing principle of much environmental policy, environmental sustainability.

Business and Environmental Sustainability

The basic meaning of sustainability is the capacity for continuance more or less indefinitely into the future. As discussed in the introduction, it is now clear that overall, current ways of life do not possess that capacity, either because they are destroying the environmental conditions necessary for their continuance, or because their environmental effects will cause unacceptable social disruption and damage to human health. The environmental effects in question include climate change, ozone depletion, acidification, toxic pollution, the depletion of renewable resources (e.g., forests, soils, fisheries, water) and of nonrenewable resources (e.g., fossil fuels), and the extinction of species.

A way of life is a complex bundle of values, objectives, institutions, and activities, with ethical, environmental, economic, and social dimensions. While current concern about unsustainability largely has an ecological basis, it is clear that human situations or ways of life can be unsustainable for social and economic reasons as well. The pertinent questions are: for the environment, can its contribution to human welfare and to the human economy be sustained? for the economy, can today's level of wealth creation be sustained? and for society, can social cohesion and important social institutions be sustained? In what follows the focus is on the environmental-economic dimensions of sustainability.

Economic sustainability is most commonly interpreted as a condition of nondeclining economic welfare projected into the future. As has been seen, economic welfare derives from, among other things, income and the environment. The environment performs various functions, some of which contribute to production, and therefore income, others of which contribute to welfare directly. Income is generated by stocks of capital, including manufactured, human, and natural capital. Natural capital also performs the welfare-creating environmental functions. Nondeclining economic welfare requires, *ceteris paribus,* that the stock of capital be maintained.[7]

An important question is whether it is the total stock of capital that must be maintained, with substitution allowed between various parts of it; or whether certain components of capital, particularly natural capital, are *nonsubstitutable*—they contribute to welfare in a unique way that cannot be replicated by another capital component. "Weak" environmental sustainability conditions derive from a perception that welfare is not normally dependent on a specific form of capital and can be maintained by substituting manufactured for natural capital. "Strong" sustainability conditions derive from a different perception that substitutability of manufactured for natural capital is seriously limited by such environmental characteristics as irreversibility, uncertainty and "critical" components of natural capital that make a unique contribution to welfare.[8] Those who regard natural capital as a complement to man-made capital place an even greater importance on it.[9]

To some extent it is possible to view the process of industrialization as the application of human and social capital to natural capital to transform it into human-made capital. But it is now clear that such substitutability is not complete. If our current development is unsustainable, it is because it is depleting some critical, nonsubstitutable components of the capital base on which it depends. To safeguard such critical natural capital, conditions such as the following need to be applied if the environment is to be used sustainably:

1. Destabilization of global environmental features such as climate patterns or the ozone layer must be prevented. Most important in this category are the maintenance of biodiversity (see condition 2), preventing climate change by stabilizing the atmospheric concentration of greenhouse gases, and safeguarding the ozone layer by ceasing the emission of ozone-depleting substances.
2. Important ecosystems and ecological features must be protected to maintain biological diversity. Importance in this context comes from a recognition not only of the perhaps as-yet unappreciated use value of individual species but also of the fact that biodiversity underpins the productivity and resilience of ecosystems.

3. Renewable resources must be renewed through the maintenance of soil fertility, hydrobiological cycles, necessary vegetative cover, and the rigorous enforcement of sustainable harvesting. The latter implies basing harvesting rates on the most conservative estimates of stock levels for such resources as fish, ensuring that replanting becomes an essential part of such activities as forestry, and using technologies for cultivation and harvest that do not degrade the relevant ecosytem.

4. Depletion of nonrenewable resources should seek to balance the maintenance of a minimum life expectancy of the resource with the development of substitutes for it. On reaching the minimum life expectancy, its maintenance would mean that consumption of the resource would have to be matched by new discoveries of it. To help finance research for alternatives and the eventual transition to renewable substitutes, all depletion of nonrenewable resources should entail a contribution to a capital fund. Designing for resource efficiency and durability can ensure that the practice of repair, reconditioning, reuse, and recycling (the "four Rs") approach the limits of their environmental efficiency.

5. Emissions into air, soil, and water must not exceed their critical load, that is, the capability of the receiving media to disperse, absorb, neutralize, and recycle them, nor may they lead to life-damaging concentrations of toxins. Synergies between pollutants can make critical loads very much more difficult to determine. Such uncertainties should result in a precautionary approach in the adoption of safe minimum standards.

6. Because of their rarity, aesthetic quality, or cultural or spiritual associations, landscapes of special human or ecological significance should be preserved.

7. Risks of life-damaging events from human activity must be kept at very low levels. Technologies that threaten long-lasting ecosystem damage should be done away with.

It is clear that these are aggregate conditions and that comparable conditions for individual businesses cannot simply be derived from them. However, they do establish a context within which the characteristics of a clean business can be defined. A business is clean if:

- Its emissions to air, soil, and water are both well within local thresholds of ecosystem and human vulnerability, and it does not make a disproportionate contribution to aggregate emissions, where these have an effect beyond the local scale.

- It does not deplete the stock of resources that feed into its production process, either because its resources are renewable and are being renewed or because it is increasing the efficiency of its nonrenewable resource use at a greater rate than the decline of the resource stock.
- Its products and processes do not entail risks, even at a very low level, of large-scale or irreversible negative impacts on people or the environment.

Such concerns fall well outside traditional systems of business management. Before companies can begin to address them, they must measure and monitor their environmental performance as carefully as they do any other core business outcome.

Measuring Corporate Environmental Performance

From an environmental point of view, what matters is the nature and volume of a business's inputs of energy and other natural resources, its emissions to air, water, and land; the use of energy and materials by its products during their useful life; and the environmental implications (for example, the reuseability, recyclability, or biodegradability) of the disposal of its products at the end of their lives. The laws of thermodynamics (conservation of matter/energy, law of entropy) state that ultimately all matter/energy taken from the environment as "resources" will be returned to it as "wastes" and that the process of converting resources into wastes will inevitably increase overall entropy (disorder) in the system in which it is taking place. Figure 9.2 gives a schematic illustration of the transformation of matter/energy into products and thence wastes. Environmental impacts are associated with the extraction of matter/energy and the emissions of wastes that result from each stage.

It is a truism to say that, in order to know the environmental impact of a business, the flows of matter/energy as a result of its activities must be measured. For those impacts recognized as environmentally serious, there is increasingly a legal requirement for them to be measured. However, such requirements currently fall far short of what would be necessary for businesses to construct mass/energy balances (i.e., tables of material and energy inputs and outputs) for their operations, far less account for the environmental implications of their products' use and disposal. Yet if the impact of business on the environment is to be understood and managed effectively, the development of such an information system cannot be avoided.

198

Figure 9.2   Inputs of Matter and Energy into the Life Cycle of a Product

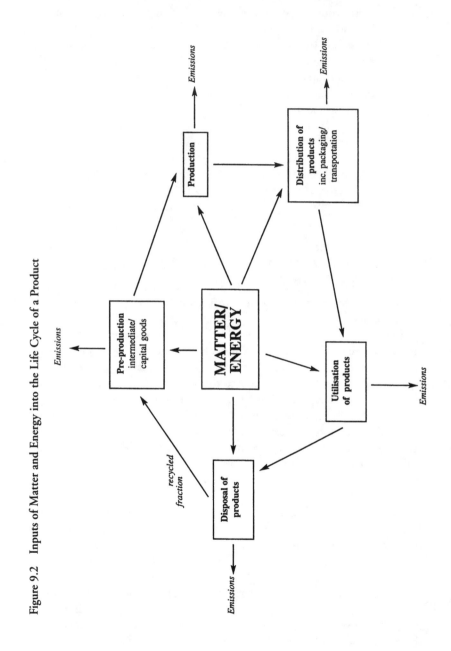

The desirability of measuring corporate environmental throughput, over and above what is legally required, has been recognized by a significant number of companies as a necessary precondition of effective environmental management and is being reflected in the growth of voluntary corporate environmental reporting. By 1993 over 100 companies had published environmental reports on a voluntary basis,[10] with the number growing rapidly, partly at least as a result of encouragement from business associations (including the International Chamber of Commerce and the Confederation of British Industry), business-environment networks (such as the World Business Council for Sustainable Development), and the European Commission, with its voluntary Environmental Management and Auditing System (EMAS). While many of the early corporate environmental reports were largely descriptive and textual, there is a clear trend toward quantification in the assessment of environmental impacts.

It is interesting to compare these new efforts at environmental reporting, considering where they might lead, with the systems of financial accounting that have been adopted for the management of business and the economy. Business accounts are entirely analogous to mass balances. Money flowing into a business is balanced by money flowing out and a change in the value of net assets. Economywide, the national accounts are constructed explicitly on an input-output basis, so that interactions between industries can be identified as can be the producers and composition of final demand. Attempts to construct integrated environmental-economic accounting at the national level use the same techniques for environmental resources.[11] If moving toward environmental sustainability really is an imperative, then it seems likely that companies will need to account to society at large for their use of the environment with as much rigor as they do to their shareholders for the use of their money. Certainly this was the view expressed by Deloitte Touche Tohmatsu International, which identified the final stage in corporate environmental reporting as one "based on the extensive use of quantitative methods such as life cycle assessments and mass balances."[12]

Once the physical flows to and from the environment have been calculated, it becomes possible to consider a business's performance in relation to sustainability. Initially the information enables the business to set targets for environmental improvement, which has been perceived as important stages in the development of corporate environmental reporting.[13] Ultimately, if sustainability is the objective, the targets for improvement must comply with standards of sustainability. R. Gray, J. Bebbington, and D. Walters consider that a sustainable organization is one that leaves the biosphere no worse off at the end of the accounting period than it was at the beginning."[14] It is important to recognize that such a zero-pollution criterion is not the same as zero emissions, because of the environment's ability to absorb and neutralize a certain quantity of waste, but it is a demanding criterion nevertheless.

Gray and coauthors also have proposed that the notional expenditure required for the firm to make good any biospheric damage caused during the accounting period, which they call the "sustainable cost," be identified in the company accounts as a measure of the firm's contribution to natural capital depreciation, analogously to the figures for depreciation of other assets. While a challenging task in practice, this valuation of the "restoration cost" is also the technique recommended by the United Nations as a means of linking the physical with the monetary accounts at the national level. It offers the intriguing prospect of enabling the firm, by deducting the sustainable cost from the operating profit, to arrive at a "sustainable profit" figure that takes account of the environmental degradation caused by the company's activities.

In addition to identifying and accounting for their environmental impacts, it is just as important that businesses identify and correctly account their actual environmental expenditure, whether this is for abatement, source reduction, monitoring, or regulatory compliance. Unless firms know how much they are paying to prevent or monitor environmental damage, they will not feel the correct incentive to move toward products and processes that are inherently less environmentally damaging—and that could save them money. D. Ditz, J. Ranganathan, and R. D. Banks report on nine case studies carried out on five large and four medium-size firms, to see whether their environmental expenditures were reported correctly in their management accounts.[15] In each case the authors found that they were not; because environmental expenditures sometimes were subsumed under nonenvironmental headings, real environmental expenditures were substantially larger than they appeared in the accounts, financially justifying environmental improvement measures that before had not appeared economic.

Such revised accounting procedures have been called Total Cost Assessment.[16] Table 9.1 shows one application of TCA to an investment that converted a solvent/heavy metal to an aqueous/heavy metal-free coating at a paper-coating company. The company analysis column shows how the company's conventional accounting system assessed the project's costs and benefits. The TCA column includes costs and benefits that were accounted for in the company analysis under headings that obscured their relation to the project. These hidden, or indirect, costs and benefits included costs of waste management, utilities (energy, water, sewerage), pollution control/solvent

Table 9.1 Financial Data for a Project Comparing Conventional Company
Analysis with a Total Cost Assessment (TCA)

	Company Analysis	TCA	Difference
Total capital costs	$623,809	$653,809	6%
Annual savings (BIT)	$118,112	$216,874	84%
Net present value, years 1–10	($98,829)	$232,817	336%
Net present value, years 1–15	$13,932	$428,040	2,972%
Return on investment, years 1–10	12%	24%	12%
Return on investment, years 1–15	16%	27%	11%
Simple payback (years)	5.3	3.0	–43%

Source: T. Jackson, ed., *Clean Production Strategies: Developing Preventative Environmental Management in the Industrial Economy* (Boca Raton, Fla.: Lewis Publishers, 1993), 203.

recovery, and regulatory compliance. It can be seen that the project under TCA was substantially more profitable than with the conventional company analysis.

Moving Business toward Environmental Sustainability

For companies that aspire to move toward environmental sustainability, environmental accounting and reporting are only two of several necessary management initiatives. Others include the adoption of a corporate environmental policy, of an environmental strategy and action plan to give it effect, and appropriate communication of environmental outcomes, both internally and externally. The whole environmental management process needs to be integrated as in figure 9.3.

It may be imagined that the development and implementation of such an environmental management system, seeking to meet targets of continual environmental improvement, would be expensive and damaging to competitiveness. This can be true. However, there is now substantial evidence that this need not be the case.

The natural resources that are used in economic processes normally have to be purchased. The discharge of wastes during or at the end of a process represents a failure to use productively all the purchased inputs. The waste resource is also wasted money. Moreover, often disposal of the waste will have to be paid for. Waste management costs, while vital once wastes have been generated, are also a waste of money in that they add

202

Figure 9.3 Stages in the Pursuit of Environmental Excellence

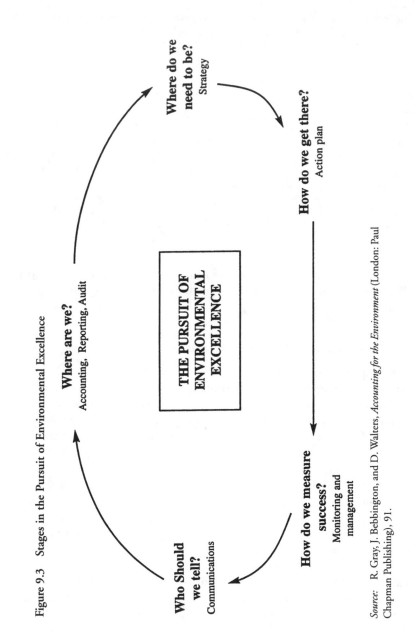

Where are we?
Accounting, Reporting, Audit

Where do we need to be?
Strategy

How do we get there?
Action plan

THE PURSUIT OF ENVIRONMENTAL EXCELLENCE

Who Should we tell?
Communications

How do we measure success?
Monitoring and management

Source: R. Gray, J. Bebbington, and D. Walters, *Accounting for the Environment* (London: Paul Chapman Publishing), 91.

nothing to the service delivered by a product. Finally, where the processes or products involved are potentially toxic or otherwise hazardous, they will be subject to regulations and controls, compliance with which also may be costly. Therefore, environmental management systems actually can result in net savings and improve competitiveness, if they lead to changes in company practices that save money in excess of the cost of implementing the management systems.

B. Smart gives five reasons why moving "beyond compliance" with regulations in their environmental performance can benefit corporations:[17]

1. Preventing pollution at the source can save money in materials and in end-of-pipe remediation.
2. Voluntary action in the present can minimize future risks and liabilities and make costly retrofits unnecessary.
3. Companies staying ahead of regulations can have a competitive edge over those struggling to keep up.
4. New "green" products and processes can increase consumer appeal and open up new business opportunities.
5. An environmentally progressive reputation can improve recruitment, employee morale, investor support, acceptance by the host community, and management's self-respect.

Smart gives many examples of firms that have benefited financially for these reasons from voluntary environmental management initiatives:

- Between 1975 and 1992, the 3M Corporation saved more than $530 million from all the projects in its 3P (Pollution Prevention Pays) program.[18]
- Feeling exposed because of his firm's status as highest reporter of listed substances in the Toxic Release Inventory of the U.S. Environmental Protection Agency, Dupont's chief executive officer reported that the company embarked on an ambitious emissions reduction program. "The result is a total air emission reduction of 80 percent within one year. Our investment of just over $250,000 results in annual savings of $400,000—instead of a $2-million investment for an incinerator that would have cost an additional $1 million annually to maintain and operate."[19]
- Under its Tank Integrity Program, Chevron replaced all its old underground gas tanks with double-walled fiberglass tanks, although this was not strictly required. However, a Chevron vice-president noted: "Making right contamination from a leaking tank could cost the company

$250,000 or more. If such a liability could be prevented with an expenditure of $25,000 to $50,000, then it's well worth it."[20]
• Pacific Gas and Electric adopted a program on Customer Energy Efficiency, which involved it investing in the more efficient use of energy by its customers and sharing in the resulting financial savings. Its 1991 measures under this program reduced emissions of nitrogen oxides by 445 tons, of sulfur oxides by 120 tons, and of carbon dioxide by 340,000 tons, and earned the company $45.1 million before taxes.

The Smart "beyond compliance" studies were of U.S. corporations, but very similar results were reported in a recent study of U.K. business:

> The main benefits reported from investment in cleaner production systems were cost savings through improved waste management, improved public image for the company and staff motivation, cost savings through better energy management, improved process efficiency, and increased profitability. Substantial savings could be made though energy management systems and relatively simple "housekeeping" modifications to production processes. Longer term gains in competitiveness were expected by many firms, mainly large corporations with sophisticated strategies for environmental management."[21]

Generalizing Best Environmental Practice

In a market economy, the price system is the single most important mechanism for allocating resources. Where prices include all the relevant costs of production, and providing basic conditions of market competition are fulfilled, the price system will ensure an efficient (although not necessarily an equitable) allocation of resources, in the sense of achieving an outcome such that it is not possible to make anyone better off without making someone else worse off.

However, impacts from economic activity on the environment routinely escape the price mechanism, affecting people who are not involved in and do not benefit from the activity. This "externalization" of some of the costs of production and consumption is both inefficient and inequitable and provides the basic rationale for governmental environmental policy and intervention.

The companies whose experiences of environmental management have been reviewed here briefly have shown how far it is possible to improve environmental performance alongside conventional business goals through voluntary commitment. Their actions are equivalent to the voluntary internalization of costs that before were escaping their management systems and reducing the welfare of others. The case studies show the extent to which these companies have been able to turn such internalization to their competitive advantage in order to remain profitable in an economic context that currently permits the externalization of costs to continue.

However, there is little prospect that the necessary transformation to "clean business" can be achieved through voluntary action alone. Companies such as those discussed are in a small minority in business as a whole. Most do not proceed voluntarily down the route of environmental improvement. Indeed, I. Christie, H. Rolfe, and R. Legard report a widespread view among the environmentally leading companies they surveyed that "diffusion [of cleaner production systems] so far was patchy and disappointing given the imperative of the transition towards sustainable development, and the fact that cleaner production techniques hold out the prospect of integration of business goals with environmental protection and of major new opportunities for product and process innovation."[22] The diffusion is slow and patchy due to organizational and market failures, especially in the small-business sector. But it also seems likely that, in competitive markets, if the option of externalizing costs is available, the baseline for business profitability will be set by taking advantage of that option. Only exceptional companies will be able to maintain profitability where others routinely externalize costs. The purpose of government intervention in such a situation is to change the competitive rules, enforcing the internalization of environmental costs, so that the firms that achieve it most efficiently have a competitive advantage rather than the reverse.

This is not the place for a detailed exposition of the possible ways government may seek cost internalization. T. Jackson lists regulatory programs; economic instruments; the provision of training and information; including ecolabeling systems, voluntary agreements with industrial sectors (usually backed up by the threat of regulation); the imposition of liability for environmental damage; and insistence on full disclosure.[23] Government also can seek to use its power as a major purchaser by applying environmental conditionalities to its contracts.

Both Jackson and Christie and coauthors agree that regulations are the most important factor in the promotion by government of clean or cleaner production. Regualtion is also generally desired by firms that are committed to proactive environmental management themselves. In a survey of environmental leaders it was found that "Very few user-company respondents wanted to see voluntary approaches in place of legislation: they wished to see environmental requirements apply to all firms in order to avoid the problem of free-riding."[24] Other firms tend to be nervous about stringent regulations, believing them to impose costs and damage business competitiveness. Such fears are transmitted to politicians, who worry in turn about closures, corporate relocation, and unemployment.

There is, in fact, very little evidence that environmental regulations to date have harmed competitiveness in any way. Not only is there the experience cited earlier of the firms that had gone beyond regulatory requirements and improved their competitive position, in addition, a number of studies have sought but failed to find significant evidence of economic disadvantage from environmental regulation. Surveying these studies, the Organization for Economic Cooperation and Development (OECD) reports: "The trade and investment impacts which have been measured empirically are almost negligible."[25] Similarly, R. De Andraca and K. McCready of the Business Council for Sustainable Development dismiss fears that environmental regulation can damage an economy: "Concerns about pollution havens, free riders or an exodus of capital and jobs from countries with tough standards are unsubstantiated."[26] They emphasize in contrast the competitive benefits to be gained by innovation and ecoefficiency induced by stringent regulations and high prices of environmental resources.

M. Porter has explored in detail the factors that seem to contribute to competitive advantage. He is in no doubt about the potential benefits for competitiveness of corporations pushing themselves, or being pushed by regulations, toward improved environmental performance:

> Stringent standards for product performance, product safety, and environmental impact contribute to creating and upgrading competitive advantage. They pressure firms to upgrade quality, upgrade technology and provide features in areas of important customer (and social) concern. . . . Particularly beneficial are stringent regulations that *anticipate* standards that will spread internationally. These give a nation's firms a head start in developing products and services that will be valued elsewhere. Social concerns such as the environment are increasingly differentiating factors in advanced markets, and regulation influences the response of a nation's firms to them. . . . Firms, like governments, are often prone to see the short-term cost of dealing with tough standards and not their longer-term benefits in terms of innovation. Firms point to foreign firms having a cost advantage. Such thinking is based on an incomplete view of how competitive advantage is created and sustained. Selling poorly performing, unsafe, or environmentally damaging products is not a route to real competitive advantage in sophisticated industries and industry segments, especially in a world where environmental sensitivity and concern are rising in all advanced nations."[27]

It is indisputable that the environmental protection industry that has sprung up at least partly as a result of environmental regulation is now a major industrial sector in its own right; it is valued at $70 billion to $100 billion in OECD countries and probably half as much again worldwide.[28] It is not implausible that there should be a first-mover advantage to environmental regulation, in that those countries that develop new technologies early in response to stringent domestic regulations will be well placed in world markets if those regulations are imposed in other countries. Porter gives examples where Japan, Germany, the United States, and Switzerland have, in different instances, all benefited from first-mover advantages and thereby improved their national economic performance.[29]

Even though regulations may have a broadly neutral or even positive economic effect overall, there is widespread agreement among economists and policy analysts that they are a less-efficient way of achieving many environmental goals than the use of economic instruments, such as environmental taxes and charges, tradable permits, and other means of direct financial incentives for environmental improvement. There are several reasons for their greater efficiency:

- They equalize the marginal cost of abatement across polluters, so that all the cheapest options for abatement are implemented first.
- They can be as effective for diffuse sources of pollution, which are difficult to regulate, as for point sources.
- By becoming incorporated into the prices of products, environmental taxes in particular give incentives to consumers as well as producers to shift away from environmentally intensive consumption.
- Because environmental taxes are payable by everybody (unlike regulations that permit its free use once the regulatory requirements have been met), they give an incentive for continual environmental improvement at all levels of use.
- By raising revenue, environmental taxes provide the means to give earmarked subsidies, where appropriate, to achieve environmental improvements beyond those arising from the price effect or to reduce distortionary taxes elsewhere. Where these are labor taxes, greater employment may result.

A variety of environmental taxes and charges have been implemented, especially in North European countries, in recent years.[30] Although they allow society as a whole to achieve environmental goals more cost effectively than total reliance on regulation, in one way environmental taxes and charges raise more serious competitiveness issues than regulations for firms that are in particularly environmentally intensive sectors. This is because, as noted earlier, after compliance with regulations, firms may use the environment without further payment; with environmental taxes firms pay for *all* use of the environment, even that which is within regulatory limits. Of course, provided the revenues from environmental taxes are used to reduce other business taxes, overall effects on business competitiveness from the tax will be negligible, and clean businesses actually will benefit from it.

While, as with regulations, there is no evidence that environmental taxes do have a negative effect on competitiveness, most countries that have introduced such taxes have sought to reduce even the possibility of such an effect by giving vulnerable firms or sectors exemptions or concessions. These reduce the economic efficiency of the environmental tax and reduce the economic advantage to be gained from clean production systems. It is arguable, however, that they are justified if they prevent companies' relocation to countries with lower environmental standards.

The Western European experience of environmental taxation could develop in one of several different directions. Several countries clearly desire to push ahead with more ambitious schemes, but what they are likely to enact unilaterally is bound to be constrained by concerns about national competitiveness and distortions in the European Union single market. However, if the European Union were to introduce minimum energy taxes, as the European Commission has proposed recently, a further range of opportunities for unilateral innovation and experimentation would open up, and some of the more ambitious schemes might start to be implemented. But it is still not clear whether this or any other proposal on common energy taxation in the European Union will be adopted. For the present, it seems certain only that governments will continue to introduce environmental taxation bit by bit, attracted by the combination that such taxation seems to offer of cost-effective environmental policy and a source of government revenue.

The imposition of environmental taxes is not the only way the prices of goods and services may be made to reflect environmental costs or environmental risks (which relate to a possibility of environmental costs in the future). Two other ways that are gaining an increasing profile in environmental policy, and that have a fundamental impact on business operations, are the assignation to firms of liability for the environmental impact of their operations and of responsibility for their products through to their disposal.

Environmental liability refers to the legal responsibility of a firm for any environmental impact it may cause and its consequent obligation to pay compensation to parties injured by the damage and/or for any environmental restoration that may be required. The current trend is away from fault-based liability to "strict" liability, which attaches to the perpetrator of damage irrespective of fault. Strict environmental liability has applied for some time to certain activities in the United States, and there have been ongoing discussions in the European Union for a number of years around a possible directive in this area, although so far without effect.

In principle, environmental liability should be insurable, as with other risks, converting possible future environmental costs into present financial costs, and so providing an incentive to firms to reduce their risks, and therefore their insurance premia, to a socially satisfactory level. In practice, the uncertainties associated with environmental impacts, and the size of potential costs, have caused many insurers to withdraw from underwriting liability for environmental damage.[31] Unavailable, or very expensive, insurance may in turn have the effect of deterring producers from business of certain kinds altogether. Where the potential environmental liabilities relate to past activities, as with much contaminated land, this may result in an inability to find private-sector companies, or finance, either to decontaminate or to redevelop such sites. Thus although strict environmental liability provides powerful incentives to firms to manage and reduce their environmental risks, its possible deterrent effects on desirable activities also should be borne in mind, and guarded against, when legislation on environmental liability is introduced.

Producer responsibility, the second way of internalizing environmental costs—in this case especially the costs of disposal—operates by making producers responsible for their products disposal at the end of the products' useful lives. The first application of producer responsibility was the German Packaging Ordinance of 1991, which required producers to take back their packaging waste and mandated minimum recycling levels. Since then the approach has been, or will be, extended to electronic goods, batteries, and automobiles.[32] Combined with the current trend of waste disposal becoming more expensive through the imposition of waste disposal taxes, and subject to increasingly strict regulations designed to increase the proportion of waste that is reused and recycled, the application of producer responsibility can be expected to exert a powerful influence on every aspect of product development, from their initial design to the way they are marketed.

Conclusions

This chapter has proceeded from the perception that sustainable development is increasingly becoming a fundamental objective of government policy and that the general transformation of business into clean business is an imperative of sustainable development.

For firms to contribute to national goals of sustainable development, they first of all require an environmental management system that enables them to measure and monitor their environmental impacts. Several such systems now exist and are increasingly being employed and reported on by companies. There is now substantial evidence that the disciplines of adopting an environmental management system and the more efficient use of resources to which this can lead can result in net financial savings. Leading companies that use environmental management and accounting systems to become clean businesses may well save money and gain competitive advantage from doing so.

Despite this potential for savings, the diffusion of cleaner production methods is slow and will remain slow without determined government policy. There is general agreement both within business and outside that legislation is both necessary and desirable if ambitious environmental objectives are to be pursued. So far government regulations have been the principal driving force to improve environmental quality. However, the same environmental goals can be achieved more cost effectively, and with greater stimulus to innovation to develop cleaner production methods, if other policy instruments, including environmental taxes, are used as well.

Because they allow other taxes on business to be reduced, environmental taxes are of particular benefit to clean businesses. Without taxes on environmentally harmful products and processes, or some other means of ensuring that the price mechanism reflects the environmental benefits of clean business, it is hard to imagine clean businesses being generally more competitive and commercially successful than businesses that can reduce their costs by failing to exercise similar environmental care. However, where environmental taxes are introduced in such a way that other business taxes are reduced, the overall competitiveness of an economy can be increased. While there may be a trade-off between the environment and the performance of environmentally intensive sectors, there is no evidence that this is so for the economy as a whole. On the contrary, it seems likely that a tax shift from other factors of production to the use of natural resources will lead to modest increases in employment and output.

Clean business has become an environmental imperative and can be profitable. The fast-growing environmental business sector has become a major business opportunity. Well formulated environmental policy can yield economic as well as environmental benefits. Clearly this combination of circumstances does not make the achievement of sustainable development simple. But, at the very least, it makes it feasible.

Notes

1. World Commission on Environment and Development (WCED), *Our Common Future* (The Brundtland Report) (New York: Oxford University Press, 1987), 211, 213.
2. World Resources Institute, with United Nations DP and United Nations EP, *World Resources, 1992–93* (New York: Oxford University Press, 1992), 2.
3. Royal Society and National Academy of Sciences, *Population Growth: Resource Consumption and a Sustainable World* (New York: National Academy of Sciences, 1992), 2, 4.
4. WCED, *Our Common Future*, 213.
5. S. Schmidheiny, with the Business Council for Sustainable Development, *Changing Course: A Global Business Perspective on Development and the Environment* (Cambridge, Mass.: MIT Press, 1992), 9.
6. D. Pearce and R. K. Turner, *Economics of Natural Resources and the Environment* (Hemel Hempstead: Harvester Wheatsheaf, 1990), 35ff.
7. J. Pezzey, *Sustainable Development Concepts: An Economic Analysis,* World Bank Environment Paper 2 (Washington, D.C.: World Bank, 1992), 14ff.
8. D. Pearce and G. Atkinson, "Are National Economies Sustainable?: Measuring Sustainable Development," CSERGE Discussion Paper GEC 92–11 (London: University College, 1992); K. Turner, "Speculations on Weak and Strong Sustainability," CSERGE Working Paper GEC 92–26 (Norwich: University of East Anglia/CSERGE, 1992).
9. H. Daly, "From Empty World to Full World Economics," in R. Goodland, H. Daly, and S. El Serafy, eds., *Population, Technology and Lifestyle: The Transition to Sustainability* (Washington, D.C.: Island Press, 1992), 27ff.
10. J. Elkington and N. Robins, "The Corporate Environmental Report," Discussion Paper (London: New Economics Foundation, 1993), 5.
11. See, for example, United Nations, *SNA Draft Handbook on Integrated Environmental and Economic Accounting,* provisional version (New York: UN Statistical Office, 1992).
12. Deloitte Touche Tohmatsu International (DTTI), International Institute for Sustainable Development, and SustainAbility, *Coming Clean: Corporate Environmental Reporting* (London: DTTI, 1993), 9.
13. DTTI et al., *Coming Clean,* 60–61. R. Gray, J. Bebbington, and D. Walters, *Accounting for the Environment* (London: Paul Chapman Publishing, 1993), 73.
14. Gray et al., *Accounting for the Environment,* 273.
15. D. Ditz, J. Ranganathan, and R. D. Banks, *Green Ledgers: Case Studies in Corporate Environmental Accounting* (Washington, D.C.: World Resources Institute, 1995).
16. T. Jackson, ed., *Clean Production Strategies: Developing Preventive Environmental Management in the Industrial Economy* (Boca Raton, Fla.: Lewis Publishers, 1993), 200ff.

17. B. Smart, ed., *Beyond Compliance: A New Industry View of the Environment* (Washington, D.C.: World Resources Institute, 1992), 3.
18. Ibid., 13.
19. Ibid., 191.
20. Ibid., 103.
21. I. Christie, H. Rolfe, and R. Legard, *Cleaner Production in Industry: Integrating Business Goals and Environmental Management* (London: Policy Studies Institute, 1995), xi.
22. Ibid., 216.
23. Jackson, *Clean Production Strategies*, 301ff.
24. Christie et al., *Cleaner Production in Industry*, 218.
25. Organization for Economic Cooperation and Development (OECD), *Implementation Strategies for Environmental Taxes* (Paris: OECD, 1996), 45.
26. R. De Andraca and K. McCready, *Internalizing Environmental Costs to Promote Eco-Efficiency* (Geneva: Business Council for Sustainable Development, 1994), 70.
27. M. Porter, *The Competitive Advantage of Nations* (New York: Free Press/Macmillan, 1990), 647–648.
28. OECD, *The State of the Environment* (Paris: OECD, 1991), 198; Business International, *Managing the Environment: The Greening of European Business* (London: Business International, 1990), 157.
29. Porter, *Competitive Advantage of Nations*, 648–649.
30. For a survey, see OECD, *Environmental Taxes in OECD Countries* (Paris: OECD, 1995).
31. P. Simmons and J. Cowell, "Liability for the Environment," in Jackson, ed., *Clean Production Strategies*, 345–364, 356.
32. F. Meyer-Krahmer, "Industrial Innovation Strategies: New Concepts and Ex Experiences—Towards an Environmentally Sustainable Industrial Economy," Paper prepared for the Six Countries Program Workshop "Innovation and Sustainable Development—Lessons for Innovation Policies?" mimeo., Fraunhofer Institut, Karlsruhe, November 1996, 8.

CHAPTER 10

Case Study of Lufthansa

Mark Lehrer,
University of Rhode Island

hile the airline industry never has been an easy arena to compete
in, the task of airline managers was made even more difficult in
the 1980s and 1990s by deregulation, market turbulence, and
technological change. One of Lufthansa's top managers put the dilemma as
follows: "We are used to thinking in terms of certainty and safety for passengers and production. But the competitive environment has become unstable and uncertain. This results in a dialectic. We produce safety and
certainty for our passengers, but not for the career prospects of our managers. We have had to give up the promotions of past eras in which managers
were guaranteed an automatic climb up the corporate ladder. Now it's more
a matter of individual initiative."[1]

In 1995 Lufthansa instituted an internal market system in order to master this complex challenge. As a result, the passenger, cargo, maintenance,
and data processing divisions of Lufthansa are now legally separate units that
transact business with one another as customers and suppliers.

Turning the Company Around

Lufthansa's internal markets actually come at the tailend of an exciting turnaround process. Since the European Commission began its liberalization of
European civil aviation in 1987, there have been clear winners and losers

among Europe's national flag carriers. "Aided" by the Gulf war and excess capacity in the 1990s, Europe's aviation authorities did succeed in creating a truly competitive market for aviation services. So competitive, in fact, that without the injection of state aid, a large number of the national carriers would no longer be solvent. While the liberalized market drove a visible performance wedge between the stronger and weaker carriers, one national carrier managed to find the inner strength to move without state aid into the winners' category. This was Lufthansa.

On the brink of financial disaster in 1992, Lufthansa managed an astounding turnaround that enabled it to post record profits in 1994 and 1995. Its chief executive officer, Jürgen Weber, became a household name in Europe. The turnaround was a bloodless cultural revolution, a corporate-wide team effort during which the phrase "mental change" (in English!) became a permanent fixture in Lufthansa's corporate vocabulary. In a spurt of organizational energy and brainstorming, costs were sharply reduced, operations were restructured, and the company strategically repositioned itself from being the German flag carrier to being the European anchor of a global alliance that included United States, Thai, SAS, and other regional airlines. Thanks in part to the indefatigable Weber's series of "town meetings" with Lufthansa employees all over the globe, the company was able to realize major productivity improvements and personnel reductions through voluntary departures without a strike.

Planning the New Corporate Structure

By late 1993 Lufthansa's efforts had put it out of the danger zone—for the short term. But Weber and his colleagues knew that in the longer term, yields would continue to decline. An ever greater share of Lufthansa's revenues was generated outside of Germany, yet its cost base was still largely in the expensive *Standort Deutschland*. As further wage concessions could not be expected, Weber pinned his hopes on a new corporate structure of internal markets to create greater cost transparency, responsibility, and initiative in company operations. The idea was to split Lufthansa into several legally separate companies: Cargo, Technik (maintenance), Systems (data processing) would all be separated from the mother company Lufthansa AG. The goal was to generate additional annual savings of 500 million to 700 million deutsche marks (DM) by 1997. The Supervisory Board approved the restructuring in January 1994. Then in September it approved the business plans for three units to become legally independent companies on January 1, 1995: Lufthansa Cargo AG, Lufthansa Technik AG, and Lufthansa Systems GmbH.

Lufthansa's approach can be characterized by the three concepts of irreversible commitment, adaptive implementation, and overarching management guidance. Lufthansa has signaled *irreversible commitment* to internal markets by setting up its three new units as independent subsidiaries that by German law must submit accurate balance sheets, profit-and-loss statements, and reports to shareholders. The Lufthansa group's *adaptive implementation* means corporate structures are in place that, as will be described, guide the overall reform process as the new subsidiaries find their footing as market-facing units. Finally, the idea of *overarching management guidance* expresses Lufthansa's recognition that internal markets are not a panacea that will create all needed solutions in a vacuum; for internal markets to have their intended effect of fostering entrepreneurship and accountability at lower levels, the new corporate structure has to be complemented by strong leadership at the top of Lufthansa and by informal networking at lower levels. To prepare for January 1, 1995 deadline, a cross-unit project team began deliberations in April 1994 on how to structure relations among the business areas. In addition to the three new units just mentioned, Lufthansa for a time had investigated the feasibility of setting up two further units, Ground Service and Flight Operations, as subsidiaries or profit centers distinct from the Passenger Division. Furthermore, much of corporate overhead was compiled in a cost center for the corporate functions. To set up an internal market among all of these potential units required each area to establish, first, an inventory of the "products" it exchanged. An 8-by-8 matrix was set up to detail what the units would buy and sell to each other, as shown in table 10.1.

The next step was to examine the interactions and decide on the pricing criteria to be applied and the degree to which transactions would be truly arm's length. Although the separation of Ground Service and Flight Operations ultimately appeared unfeasible for legal and technical reasons, the accounting systems for transactions between all other units were in place by early 1995. As one can imagine, establishing accounting systems to handle transactions between so many different units was a major undertaking. The three new subsidiaries also had to work at break-neck speed to install systems enabling them to issue complete information for external and internal accounting purposes.

What did the new structure enable the new corporate units to do? First of all, it gave them greater freedom to grow their businesses by finding outside customers. All three new subsidiaries had achieved world-class competence in their areas.

Even prior to the new corporate structure, Lufthansa was renowned for its maintenance operations; Technik AG did almost half of its work for

Table 10.1 Input-Output Table of Lufthansa's Internal Enterprise Units

Product Transfer	Marketing	Operations	Maintenance	Flight Operations	Ground Operations	Cargo	Systems	Central Functions
Marketing		1	1	1	1	3	1	1
Operations	3		1	1	1	2		1
Maintenance		3		2	2			
Flight Operations		3				2		
Ground Operations	3	2				2		1
Cargo	1	1	2	1	1			1
Systems	3	1	2	1	3	2		2
Central Functions	2	2	2	2	2	2	2	

Degree of Interaction: 3 = high, 2 = medium, 1 = low

outside customers right from the start. Lufthansa has been the world's largest cargo carrier since 1987, and thus the creation of Cargo AG was a natural step in its business development. While leasing the bellies of the Passenger Division's aircraft on the internal market, Cargo AG acquired greater flexibility to build up its web of international alliances to provide global coverage at the lowest possible cost. Finally, changes in the global airline industry have made information processing systems as important a competitive tool as aircraft themselves, vital for computer reservation systems, cost accounting, flight scheduling, yield management, and frequent flyer programs. Upon updating its systems to leading-class levels, Lufthansa knew its expertise could be marketed on world markets. Electronic Data Systems (EDS), eager to gain a foothold in the lucrative aviation market, took a 25 percent stake in Lufthansa's new data processing subsidiary, Lufthansa Systems. By expanding the business in the third-party market, System's ultimate goal was to reduce the in-house share of its revenue to 50 percent.

Managing the New Corporate Structure

At the beginning of 1995, 16,000 of Lufthansa AG's 44,000 employees were transferred to the new units (about 10,000 in Technik, 5,000 in Cargo, and 1,000 in Systems). Given the speed with which the new structure was implemented, Lufthansa had to design a way to monitor the functioning of the internal corporate market. The top-level guidance mechanism involved an ingenious change in the allocation of roles on Lufthansa's Executive Board, the *Vorstand*. The Vorstand traditionally had been composed of a chairman and five functional heads (finance, personnel, maintenance, marketing, operations) who decided policy on a collegial basis. Although remaining a collegial decision-making body, the Vorstand was henceforth composed of two distinct roles. (See figure 10.1.) On one hand, three members (chairman, finance, personnel) retained corporate-wide mandates, while the other two (marketing, operations) had functional responsibility for the activities of the Passenger Division. The idea was that while the Passenger Division would transact with the newly formed subsidiaries on a largely arm's length basis, the Vorstand would monitor the overall process to ensure that the unleashed corporate dynamics worked to the benefit of the Lufthansa group as a whole.

In other words, under the new corporate structure, the mother company Deutsche Lufthansa AG was left with only the Passenger Division and the corporate functions: the formal Vorstand functions finance and personnel continued to be headed by a Vorstand member, while others (corporate controlling, strategy, and government relations) reported to the chairman. Figure 10.1 depicts Lufthansa's highly innovative Vorstand structure.

However, structure is only one part of the story. Lufthansa recognized that leadership and culture were equally indispensable to undergird the change process. In 1995 Weber intensified his worldwide series of town meetings in order to impress upon employees that Lufthansa's environment required cost reduction and adaptation to become a way of life. Weber emphasized that Lufthansa's internal markets were a valuable instrument in the struggle for greater flexibility and initiative, but the instrument could work only as well as the motivation of employees and the culture of the company allowed them to. As one marketing manager put it: "Many employees see Lufthansa making a decent profit in 1995, and think they can sit back and relax. That's why Weber is so keen to spread the message: 'People, that was only the beginning!' The turnaround and the new corporate structure are not one-time events, but part of a permanent effort. That's why *Überzeugungsarbeit* [the work of persuading people] is so important."

In addition to the need for overarching leadership, Lufthansa's new subsidiaries have recognized that exchange through internal markets needs to be supplemented by informal networking between units in many cases. For example, while passenger and cargo operations are now administered separately, many foreign countries prefer to deal with Lufthansa as a single entity and not as separate companies. Thus, internal markets paradoxically create the need for "soft" forms of cooperation such as networking and culture. Corporate leadership will become ever more critical, Lufthansa managers point out, as there are now more corporate units that are going their own way, as indeed they were instructed to.

Within middle management, more responsibility has been delegated downward with more initiative being taken in many areas. The challenge for Lufthansa's management therefore is to encourage greater responsibility at lower levels in such a way that managers retain a view of the interests of the Lufthansa group as a whole.

Going Global

The peculiarly German twist to Lufthansa's internal markets resides in the company's global strategy. Like many German companies, Lufthansa had been reluctant to internationalize its operations and management, preferring to rely on a high-wage, high-quality, upscale-segment made-in-Germany

219

Figure 10.1 New Structure of Lufthansa Group

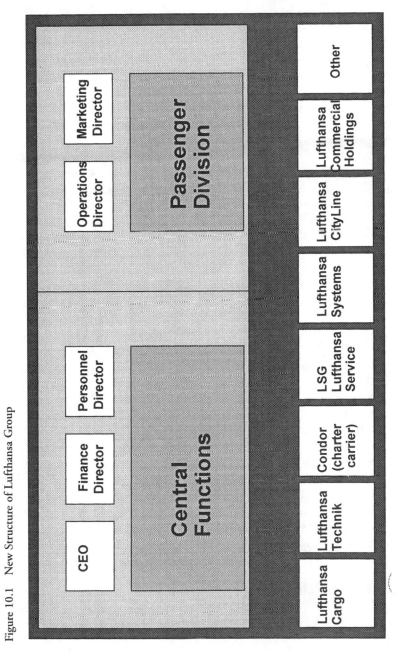

Source: Lufthansa, June 1996.

policy. "Aided" again by the Gulf war, Lufthansa was in the vanguard of German companies to abandon this policy in the 1990s.

Lufthansa's global strategy began with the goal of coming closer to the customer worldwide. In 1994 Lufthansa and United Airlines put together the world's first comprehensive global alliance of airlines with Thai Airways and a host of smaller carriers; SAS joined in 1995. The route networks, frequent flyer programs, and many other customer amenities were shared and a range of commercial activities more closely coordinated.

Yet there was a cost side to globalization as well, and this is where internal markets became so crucial to Lufthansa's competitiveness. Like other German companies, Lufthansa had to find ways to reduce the burden of its home-country cost case, with its high wages, costly social benefits, and an ever-appreciating deutschmark. In 1995 Lufthansa repositioned itself in international competition with a wide-ranging program under the slogan "Going Global." Lufthansa's units and subsidiaries were invited to internationalize their operations further and thereby dilute the high cost of paying their expenses in deutschmarks. With the spinoff of Technik AG, Cargo AG, and Systems GmbH, these new companies acquired greater operational independence to step up their international activities, to forge links and acquire equity holdings in foreign countries, and to expand existing alliances. Weber stated quite openly: "Internationalizing our cost structure obviously means concentrating employee growth to a greater extent outside Germany—and not only because a global economy like Lufthansa needs a cosmopolitan workforce. Expanding our staff abroad also reduces costs and so safeguards jobs at home. The trade unions and staff councils are aware of this. We aim to pursue our strategy of "Going Global" in concert with them."

Thus Lufthansa Cargo AG set up a subsidiary in India and established secondary hubs in Sharjah and Bangkok. Lufthansa Technik AG shifted some of its work to its Irish joint venture Shannon Aerospace. Indeed, Lufthansa AG itself moved some of its data processing tasks to India and concluded an agreement with its unions in 1995 allowing it to hire up to 10 percent of its cabin crew in foreign countries at the lower prevailing wages. What internal markets allow Lufthansa to do is give different parts of the company both an incentive and the flexibility to adopt the globalization strategy that will best help them to reduce costs. As Weber put it: "While Lufthansa generates only about half its income in deutschmarks, it has to pay for more than two-thirds of its expenditure in the strong German currency. We aim to lessen the risk stemming from this imbalance by shifting an appropriate portion of expenses out of the deutschmark and into softer currencies. That will make us less vulnerable to exchange rate fluctuations, which in 1995 alone cost the Company some DM 650 million in lost revenue."

Within this overall general deutschmark predicament that Lufthansa faces, the exchange-rate disadvantage varies by unit. While Systems GmbH started out selling most of its business to other units of the group, Cargo AG received 99 percent of its revenue outside Lufthansa and about 75 pecent outside of Germany in 1995. Technik AG received about 40 percent of its revenue outside of Germany and outside of Lufthansa. For the Passenger Division of Lufthansa AG, about half the revenue is generated outside of Germany. The "German" aspect of Lufthansa's internal markets, then, lies is allowing each company to adapt its global strategy to its own cost/revenue predicament. What "Going Global" implies in parallel to just solving the deutschmark problem, of course, is the human resource challenge of developing the Lufthansa "global manager." Yet this concept too is being implemented in different ways among the units.

Needless to say, this diversity of cost/revenue predicaments also led to major management challenges in internal pricing between Lufthansa units. In a globalizing company, what is the proper market price to apply? Are the prices charged to Technik AG's internal company customers to be based on comparable market prices within Germany? within Europe? in the Third World? These are difficult questions and were raised frequently. One of the principles that Lufthansa did try to apply in its first year of internal markets was to put a ceiling on the amount of energy devoted to arguments over pricing. As one top manager at Cargo AG put it:

"If you have (say) 50 network managers from the Passenger Division and 20 from Cargo who busy themselves fine-tuning the transfer pricing between the units on every flight, there is a danger of our management capacities becoming focused on this task instead of the external market. How nice it is to argue with one's former colleagues! But whether the total transfer price is DM 10 million more or less really only concerns an internal corporate optimum. For me it's more important to position ourselves in the market: where can I reduce costs, where can I earn more revenue? So the priority was to identify the most important economic factors, like the schedule, and then find a compromise."

The First Year of Internal Markets in Practice

Having finished our overview of the rationale and framework for Lufthansa's internal markets, how did the new units fare in their first year? To answer this question, let us examine the three cases separately.

Technik AG

When the new corporate structure was being designed in 1994, many Lufthansa managers were concerned about whether the maintenance side of Lufthansa would be placed at a relative disadvantage if it had to transact on a market basis with the rest of the airline. Competition in the maintenance business intensified after the end of the Cold War, as cuts in defense spending led to excess capacity in maintenance facilities for military aircraft; many of these facilities then were converted to civilian uses.

To make matters worse, the major jet engine manufacturers recently have made increasing incursions into the maintenance field, thereby making the industry even more crowded. Technik's willingness to take the plunge was based on great productivity strides it had made through process reengineering and on the courage of the division's designated head, who believed that lean management and aggressive pursuit of external business would allow the division to make profits.

Under the new corporate structure the Passenger Division and Cargo wasted no time in demanding lower prices for maintenance services based on selected market comparisons. As foreseen from the beginning, these negotiations required the mediation of the three Vorstand members with corporate-wide responsibilities. The chief executive officer and finance director had to ensure that actions taken by one part of Lufthansa to improve profitability did not reduce the profitability of the Lufthansa group as a whole. The personnel director had to ensure that industrial relations within the Lufthansa group remained intact.

In practice, mediation of discussions over transfer pricing and outsourcing for maintenance services involved the periodic arbitration of the corporate controller reporting to Weber. Corporate Controlling was summoned, first, to assess the appropriateness of the market price comparisons presented by Cargo and the Passenger Division. The second task of Corporate Controlling was to suggest remedies to the conflicts. This usually involved setting precise targets for cost and price reductions of given maintenance services over a specified number of years. As one Lufthansa manager put it: "A consequence of the new corporate structure is that the corporate controller is called upon to play a more sophisticated role than ever before."

Cargo AG

The most important immediate consequence of the new corporate structure was the way it did business with the Passenger Division. In prior times, a fixed tonnage/mile cost was calculated on the bellies of passenger planes, irrespective of when the planes flew. The new internal market system created the need to assess the value of aircraft bellies on a flight-by-flight basis, taking into account the specific equipment, day of the week, and time of day of the flight. "Flights from Tokyo at noon provide almost no cargo value," explained Cargo's vice president for controlling. "The lucrative business comes early in the morning or at the end of the business day."

The final outcome was very favorable to Cargo. The final lump sum it paid to the Passenger Division for aircraft bellies in 1995 was hundreds of million DM less than charged under the old system. (The exact figures are confidential.) In return, the Passenger Division was guaranteed a minimum level of cargo business for 1996.

In addition to this cost advantage, the interviewed Cargo managers stressed the emotional and political benefits of their newfound independence. Being "set free" reportedly liberated a lot of latent energy in the managerial ranks. It also created a platform to lobby for even more entrepreneurial freedom within the Lufthansa group. As one top Cargo manager put it: "On the revenue side we're in the Wild West. But on the cost side, many expenses are occasioned by Lufthansa. It's the very opposite of the Wild West. If you have your revenues in the Wild West, you must also be allowed to have your costs in the Wild West. Loosening these regulations on the cost side is an absolute precondition for the continued success of Cargo."

Systems GmbH

In its first year (1995) Systems received 97 percent of its revenue from units within the Lufthansa group (Lufthansa AG, Technik AG, Cargo AG, and the charter and catering subsidiaries Condor and LSG). In 1996 this figure fell to 95 percent of its revenue of about 500 million DM, and by finding additional outside customers the in-house share of its revenue was supposed to fall to 50 percent. The Australian airline Ansett had signed up as Lufthansa's first major external airline customer for its network scheduling tools. The managing director of Lufthansa Systems reported:

> So far the new corporate structure has not been an excessive strain on us. We agreed with the Vorstand to reduce our unit prices on 80 percent of our business by 5 percent annually for the first three years. . . . We have drawn up finer-grained invoices for services than we used to, and there is greater transparency in costs and contracts. The new structure also has a psychological effect. Out-

lays for data processing are now seen as real payments by our customers, whereas we increasingly have to justify the added value of what we do in relation to external suppliers.

The Challenge Ahead

Under the new structure, Lufthansa's managers are more directly exposed to market realities in their particular operating domain. Two of these realities—high German exchange rates and intensifying competition in aviation—have promoted a common awareness among managers and employees that the company can prosper only on the basis of continual productivity improvement and innovation.

The spinning-off of Cargo, Technik, and Systems was a critical step in diffusing the spirit of enterprise across the airline, but Lufthansa managers stress that it was only one step in the struggle to create a more dynamic, self-renewing organization. By bringing its managers into closer proximity to the laws of the marketplace, Lufthansa's reform has helped instill in them the understanding that the new corporate structure of internal markets is not just a one-time reform but part of a dynamic process of change.

Notes

This chapter draws on three published case studies: two INSEAD case studies written by the author with Professor Heinz Thanheiser, *Lufthansa: The Turn-around* (INSEAD, 1995) and *Internal Markets at Lufthansa* (INSEAD, 1996), and one written by students of London Business School under Professor Sumantra Ghoshal, *Lufthansa: The Challenge of Globalization* (LBS, 1996).

1. All quoted material was drawn from interviews conducted by the author.

PART III

*Between Laissez-Faire
and Industrial Policy*

CHAPTER 11

Toward Developing a Twenty-First Century Economic Paradigm: Lessons from Myrdal, Schumpter, and Hayek

James Angresano, Albertson College of Idaho

Introduction

A useful economic perspective is one that offers normative propositions and a conception of the socioeconomic reality that are shared by a growing number of social scientists.[1] If formal methods of analysis and coherent theories also are provided and accepted by a number of practitioners, the perspective can be considered a paradigm.[2] In order for a new perspective to establish itself as a serious, viable alternative to the neoclassical perspective, and thereby become part of *the* paradigm for social science practitioners in the academic community, it must provide a more realistic conceptualized reality than the neoclassical perspective currently provides. Doing so would enable its proponents to offer colleagues, students, and laypersons an alternative understanding of an economy's principal institutions and working rules than that which is currently provided by neoclassical economics as well as a basis for developing public policies for achieving its normative propositions. The objective of this chapter is not to set forth a new paradigm but to provide a starting point toward its development.

Our heritage of economic thought can serve as a guide toward developing a new economic perspective. A useful place to begin is to draw from three prominent economic philosophers: Gunnar Myrdal, Joseph Schumpeter, and Friedrich Hayek. While it is true that some of their normative propositions were diametrically opposed and they held significantly different positions regarding the efficacy of economic planning, they had much in common. Studying and articulating principal aspects of their conceptualizations of reality, criticisms of neoclassical economics, methods of analysis, and conclusions can serve as a solid foundation from which to begin building a new economic paradigm.

What Did Myrdal, Schumpeter, and Hayek Share?

While the early part of their respective careers was devoted entirely to technical aspects of economics, especially monetary and trade theory, all three devoted most of their professional lives to analyzing the dynamic process of change within an economy, accounting for social, philosophical, political as well as psychological aspects of societal growth and development.[3] Despite their having provided pathbreaking analysis of many pressing economic issues, their contributions have become tangential to mainstream economic analysis, primarily because they deemphasized pure economic theory while providing their own political philosophy. However, each has been considered among the greatest social science analysts of this century due to the striking breadth and depth of their theories and analyses and the innovative nature of their significant contributions to methodology, economic theory, history of economic thought, and economic history.

All three relied heavily on history in their analysis, and each was influenced by (and sought to account for) the economic, political, and social conditions of the era in which he was writing.[4] Each looked at particular economies over different time periods, and retrospective analysis indicates that each of them was "right" regarding his analysis, conclusions drawn, and policy proposals offered for the particular economies he analyzed. History also demonstrates that none of them offered policy proposals and predictions that would be correct for all economies over a long period. This should not be surprising, for no one is always right regarding the predictions of the path economies will follow. Viewed from an evolutionary-institutional perspective, over time economic institutions have a different impact on the performance of an economy, and the change in performance results in new attitudes which, in turn, lead to new institutions and new types of economy.[5] For example, prior to 1932 Sweden was not flourishing under laissez-faire policies. The nation grew and developed rapidly thereafter under a democratically controlled social economy with considerable contributions from both social insurance and welfare programs as well as entrepreneurs whose multinational corporations stimulated an export boom. However, the same government policies designed to alleviate poverty and create a more egalitarian society also contributed to the demise of the economy in the late 1980s and to partial abandonment of those policies. Similar paths of prosperity followed by recession under one set of institutions and policies can be identified for nearly all economies.

Other common features can be identified for two of these masters. As did Myrdal, Hayek received a law degree and doctorate in economics. Both published general works that included methodology of social science, and they shared the 1974 Nobel Prize in Economics. Schumpeter and Hayek were Austrians who placed the entrepreneurial personality and function at the center of their analysis. For those interested in predicting the path economies will follow in the early twenty-first century, it is noteworthy that Schumpeter and Hayek appear correct concerning their predictions that an economy with relatively little government interference in which entrepreneurial activity is permitted to flourish will prosper.[6] This is evident by the recent rapid economic growth of the East Asian economies, as well as growth in Poland and the Czech Republic compared to the rest of Europe.

Gunnar Myrdal

Despite being imbued with the neoclassical paradigm during his graduate education and macroeconomic policy development work during the early 1930s, Gunnar Myrdal (1898–1987) realized this paradigm was inadequate for analyzing broad social problems. He began to develop his own normative propositions, conception of the socioeconomic reality, critique of neoclassical economics, and method of analysis. In doing so he conceived an alternative approach to social science analysis that is consistent with such heterodox approaches to economics as institutional economics and social economics.[7] With his approach Myrdal was instrumental not only in promoting macroeconomic stabilization policy for Sweden during the early 1930s depression but also in laying the foundation for the social insurance and welfare programs that the nation gradually implemented thereafter. He also applied his interdisciplinary method of analysis (which incorporates history, politics, social psychology, and sociology with economic principles) to his landmark examination of race relations in the United States, implementation of economic recovery measures in Europe after World War II, and investigation of the causes of poverty in underdeveloped nations'.

Normative Propositions

Myrdal's goals are similar to those established for society during the optimistic era of Enlightenment. He believed economics should not be simply a discipline used to promote economic growth, efficiency, or macroeconomic stability. Instead, his interest in reforming society led him to believe that economics also should be an instrument for social and economic reform. The ideal Myrdalian society would be experiencing development, which to Myrdal meant the movement upward of the entire "social system." This system is comprised of attitudes and institutions whose condition or performance consists of both economic indicators (production, income, work conditions, consumption levels) and noneconomic indicators (attitudes toward life and work, levels of education and health, distribution of power throughout society). Myrdal advocated state intervention to correct outcomes where unregulated market mechanisms foster results that are undesirable. Each family would be guaranteed at least a simple and decent standard of living—with the ultimate goal being equalization of living and working conditions. Myrdal was not content with implementing policies that would establish a "welfare state" in Sweden but extended his vision to the establishment of a "welfare world" founded on social insurance and welfare schemes policies similar to those he proposed for Sweden.[8]

Conceptualized Reality

Myrdal's conceived socioeconomic order consists of a wide set of social relations. There are a number of relevant, interrelated economic and noneconomic conditions that constantly interact to generate social change. Among the relevant economic conditions are the level and methods of production, productivity of labor, distribution of income, and level of consumption. Important noneconomic conditions he accounted for in his analysis include the nature of educational and health facilities and attitudes toward life and work—especially as influenced by religion. Other conditions were social mores and principal economic, social, and political institutions, particularly those that influence the stratification of power in society, and the working rules established by authorities for these institutions.[9] Consequently, Myrdal believed "economic" problems could not be studied in isolation but only in their demographic, social, and political setting.

Myrdal believed other forces besides self-interest (including emotion and interpersonal relationships such as trust) influence economic decisions of societal members. Further, he did not view inequality as a prerequisite for economic efficiency and growth. Instead, he believed that greater equality can stimulate efficiency and growth, as was the case for Sweden from the early 1930s to late 1980s. A commitment to shared values such as equality is felt to foster cooperation, rather than competition, among nonmarket institutions by achieving a consensus among decision makers. He would agree that institutions and processes such as Japan's Ministry of International Trade and Industry and France's indicative planning illustrate that nonmarket allocation and distribution schemes have been capable of promoting efficiency, growth, and greater equality.[10]

Unlike recent advisors to Central and East Europe, Myrdal did not believe that a large number of profit-oriented entrepreneurs offering supply-side innovations can be expected to emerge quickly in every nation—particularly in a nation whose economy is performing poorly and that suddenly seeks to stimulate investment while transforming its principal economic, political, and social institutions. Citing differences in conditions such as availability of raw materials, climate, population growth, government honesty and stability, and social motives and mechanisms between Western industrialized nations and the rest of the world, he argued against expecting the existence of some latent entrepreneurial class that will respond spontaneously and rationally to investment opportunities in all nations.

In Myrdal's conception of reality there existed a causal interrelatedness among technological, attitudinal, and institutional factors during the process of societal change. Unlike most economists, he argued that the original stimulus for initiating cumulative change within a complex social mechanism will stem from changes in attitudes and institutions rather than from technology or economic variables, such as prices or interest rates. Those seeking to direct the transformation of an economy, he argued, must recognize that attitudinal and institutional change have to precede changes in economic variables. He was adamant that there are no "economic problems" but rather that social systems have mixed and complex problems with economic, political, social, and cultural components—all aspects of which are highly interrelated and which needed to be studied in their cultural context. It is necessary for the analyst to identify causal relationships among these variables and propose policies consistent with a society's attitudes and institutions. He cited the "Green Revolution" (introduction of hybrid wheat and rice seeds that, under ideal conditions, would boost land productivity by about two to four times) as an example where his conception was ignored.

Technological change preceded attitudinal and institutional change, with unfavorable results for decades in terms of a majority of poor farmers realizing few benefits from introduction of the new seeds without complementary changes (e.g., better access to water, fertilizer, or credit) being provided as well.

Myrdal recognized significant attitudinal and institutional differences among societies and therefore argued that no single set of policies would provide a panacea for any nation. Current advisors to Central and Eastern Europe, nearly all of whom do not share Myrdal's conceptualized reality, purport that their sweeping macroeconomic stabilization and privatization policies are, in fact, a panacea for all nations throughout the region. Myrdal would soundly criticize such policies, based on narrow, closed economic models that emphasize easily quantifiable variables to the neglect of noneconomic factors such as attitudes, health, and education as inappropriate and misguided, for they ignore the primary impediments to societal transformation and development. In the case of Central and Eastern Europe, these impediments include absence of achievement-oriented individualistic competitiveness, lack of a civic culture by which people willingly adhere to laws concerning commerce, absence of a business culture wherein people would be consumer oriented, and corrupt political authorities.

Criticism of Neoclassical Economics

Myrdal's criticism of neoclassical economics was extensive.[11] He recognized the inadequacy of its static equilibrium approach for analyzing societal problems, especially its assertion that the process by which changes in one basic, endogenous economic factor generates subsequent adjustments in other economic factors is typical of social change.[12] In particular, he was critical of the narrow neoclassical notion of economic determinism that holds that there is one "basic factor" that predominates to the extent that significant economic and social transformations are expected to ensue following a change in one factor, such as a change in relative prices or privatization of previously state-owned enterprises. As a result Myrdal chides most economists (including those holding a Marxist ideology or laissez-faire advocates) for failing to account adequately for noneconomic factors while placing emphasis on some basic factor to which all other economic and noneconomic variables are expected to adjust once the basic economic factor has been altered. The experiences of underdeveloped countries and post-1989 Central and Eastern European nations where favorable adjustments to promote growth were expected following high levels of investment or wide-scale privatization have both demonstrated the fallacy of the economic determinist view and its belief in a fatalistic tendency for society to adjust in a predictable manner to changes in economic variables without prior introduction of necessary changes in pertinent noneconomic conditions.

Myrdal also criticized neoclassical economics for being ahistorical, with proponents advancing their theories as universal propositions valid for every time, place, and culture. He was openly opposed to neoclassical economists' strong technical bent (to the neglect of the noneconomic factors he argued were important), especially its overemphasizing mathematics in analyzing and explaining societal behavior, and policy prescriptions that had their roots in traditional neoclassical theory—both of which were inappropriate for nearly all nations not belonging to the Organization for Economic Cooperation and Development (OECD). In particular, he chided neoclassical policymakers for reducing all problems to a matter of optimum allocation of resources and for assuming that efficiency and favorable economic growth would ensue following the establishment of competitive markets.

Method of Analysis

Myrdal's method of analysis contains three distinctive aspects, each of which stands in sharp contrast to methods practiced by neoclassical economists: his positions regarding objectivity in the social sciences, interdisciplinary approach to analyzing issues, and theory of social change. Taken together, they comprise an analytical method that contains a useful theory that can serve as a basis for understanding the nature of a society's economy.

Myrdal argued that a social scientist was not able to hide his ideological persuasion. Rather, he believed the particular criteria chosen as the basis for evaluation by an analyst, the method of measuring these criteria, and the relative importance attached to each would be influenced by the analyst's viewpoint. Myrdal was fond of stating that "every view [conception of the socioeconomic reality and conclusions] has a viewpoint [normative propositions]." By this he meant that results of analysis are influenced by the normative propositions held by the analyst. Analysts may purport to be engaging in value-free, positive analysis, but all have "hidden values" that influence their conclusions and policy prescriptions. This, he argued, is particularly true of neoclassical economists, who seem to have a preference for free trade and laissez-faire domestic policy. Failing to state one's normative propositions explicitly leads to analysis and conclusions that Myrdal believed to be "biased"—systematically twisted in an opportunistic direction. For example, Myrdal would argue that the goals and policy prescriptions of

Western advisors to Central and Eastern Europe have been riddled with the ideology inherent in neoclassical theory.

To reduce such bias in what generally is presented as "objective" analysis, Myrdal proposed that analysts accept that economics is a moral science and thereby identify explicitly their viewpoint, or normative propositions, so as to purge the analysis (to the extent possible) of distorting biases. He refuted the positivist claim of neoclassical economists that economic theory can prove certain norms exist. Instead he argued social scientists should accept that these normative propositions are extrascientific and do not emerge from the analysis itself, and that social laws do not exist as do physical laws of the universe. His method of analysis began with the specification of his explicit normative propositions, which he believed were relevant to the problems he analyzed.[13] Doing so, he argued, enabled him "(1) to purge as far as possible the scientific investigation of distorting biases which are usually the result of hidden biases; (2) to determine in a rational way the statement of problems and the definitions of terms for the theoretical analysis; (3) to lay a logical basis for practical and political conclusions."[14]

Myrdal's interdisciplinary approach to analyzing issues integrated history, politics, social psychology, and sociology with economics.[15] It was a departure from the traditionally rigid boundaries between separate social science disciplines as they had developed pragmatically to accommodate pedagogical purposes and the desire for research specialization. Such an approach made for a wider range of empirical observations and required common sense, rather than adherence to a strict theoretical framework, to choose or develop an appropriate theoretical framework for analysis of the issue in question. Although Myrdal relied on his theory of social change to structure his thinking, his approach featured a reduced emphasis on precision and formal analysis than that which characterizes of economic theory in the neoclassical tradition.

Myrdal applied his interdisciplinary approach to analyze and propose policies for Sweden, the United States, post–World War II Europe, and underdeveloped nations.[16] He began each analysis with an in-depth review of the history, attitudes, and institutions of the nation or region in question, seeking to identify the causal relations between social facts—particularly the impact of noneconomic variables on development. In analyzing Sweden's low population growth and poverty problems during the early 1930s, Myrdal sought to determine factors causing the secular trend in migration, cyclical fluctuations of migration, and how business cycles were reflected in migration.[17] His objective was to determine not only the interrelations between the movements of the factors affecting migration but also the relations between these factors and all other changes of an economic, social, or political character that influenced the low level of living then experienced by many Swedish families. In doing so Myrdal recognized that it was not possible to analyze migration as an isolated phenomenon but that it had to be studied in connection with all other factors determining the population size and composition. He viewed population as an interdependent mechanism influenced by cultural, economic, social, and political factors. Among his conclusions was that the roots of the poverty problem were the prevalent Swedish attitudes and institutions, particularly the tendency to blame the poor for their own plight and faith in the "do-nothing" laissez-faire policies. These findings served as the basis for his advocating planned, egalitarian reforms that became the basis for the Swedish democratically controlled social economy. Not only did these reforms succeed in alleviating poverty, but Sweden became one of world's wealthiest nations by the late 1980s (albeit while encountering significant economic problems since then).

Recognizing that a theory of societal change was necessary before an analyst could observe the facts, and finding neoclassical theories lacking as a means for analyzing the problems he chose to study, Myrdal developed his own theory. To him theory was a broad vision of what essential facts are (conceptualized reality) and the causal relations between the facts (theory of social change). His theory of social change identified the principle of circular and cumulative causation. It is a dynamic causation process in which he recognized both the interrelationship among all relevant economic and noneconomic factors involved in the process of social change as well as the interlocking nature of the circular and cumulative aspects of change. In the Myrdalian methodology, the process of social change stems from changes in all relevant factors necessary to induce circular causation such that a social process would tend to become cumulative and often to gather speed at an accelerating rate. First, a change in one endogenous condition will include a response in secondary endogenous conditions. These changes, in turn, are likely over the long run to generate further changes as the interrelationships among conditions and changes create a cumulative causation process with the social system continuously moving away from any equilibrium position. Myrdal argued that changes which occur stimulate social change in one direction (positive or "spread effects," negative or "backwash effects") and that the ultimate resting place of the system is not easily predicted. This is because "coefficients of interrelation between all conditions in the social system . . . and time lags . . . usually are unknown . . . [therefore] our knowledge of them is utterly imprecise."[18] Tendencies can be identified for the purpose of policymaking, but precision in forecasts cannot be expected.

Whether a policy's impact initiates a positive or negative movement depends if its initial impact has a favorable or unfavorable effect on any of Myrdal's six key variables to development: production and income, conditions of production, levels of consumption, attitudes toward life and work, institutions, and public policy. To each variable he assigned an equal value so any change upward or down in one necessarily pulls the other in the same direction. Positive changes in one condition (e.g., increased level of consumption) would result in secondary changes, thereby improving another condition (worker productivity), which, in turn, would promote greater output and income, which would complete the circle by reinforcing further increased consumption, the initial condition affected.

Myrdal was adamant that his theory of circular causation justified active state involvement to promote development; he argued that a tendency toward inequality was the outcome of the interplay of unfettered market forces—particularly so when the level of economic development was low so that a segment of the population could be characterized as in poverty.[19] He was particularly in favor of educational and institutional reforms, arguing that such reforms not only would prevent further povert, but also would stimulate productivity of the needy so that development would ensue in a positive direction. Rather than suggesting a cookbook recipe of reforms for all societies, Myrdal's method relied on developing policies in an ongoing, instrumental manner (much as one plays chess) based on findings from an in-depth, interdisciplinary analysis of the society or region in question.

Joseph Schumpeter

Joseph Schumpeter (1883–1950) spent the formative and middle part of his professional life in Austrian academic and business circles. In 1932 he received an appointment to Harvard, where he remained for the rest of his career. Among his many major contributions, he is best known for his comprehensive, insightful analysis of economic growth and the dynamic properties of capitalist development and concurrent societal transformation, especially during the period 1870 to 1930 in the United States.

Normative Propositions

Although his normative propositions were not as extensive and explicit as those proposed by either Myrdal or Hayek, Schumpeter was not a "value-free" economist. He held that society's interests were best served through rule by an elite entrepreneurial class. This position was based on his "explicit belief in the 'supernormal quality' of the bourgeoisie," especially the daring entrepreneurs and capitalists who provided the necessary financing.[20] His conceptualized reality contains further support for this view.

Conceptualized Reality

Schumpeter's conception of capitalism's socioeconomic reality is embodied in his long-run view of capitalism's development. He views capitalism and competition "as a dynamic process, not a set of structural conditions or a static, equilibrium end-state."[21] He argued that "without . . . development the capitalistic society cannot exist, . . . without innovation there are no entrepreneurs, without entrepreneurship there are no capitalist profits and no capitalist momentum . . . The atmosphere of industrial revolution—of progress—is the only atmosphere in which capitalism can survive."[22]

Schumpeter recognized the evolutionary nature of economies with industries in various stages of rise and fall. He believed economic development comes from "within the economic system . . . it occurs discontinuously . . . it brings qualitative changes or 'revolutions,' which fundamentally displace old equilibria and create radically new conditions. Economic development is accompanied by growth . . . But mere quantitative growth does not constitute development."[23] To illustrate this, Schumpeter pointed out that an economy could grow by adding many horse-drawn carriages, but such growth would not lead to the development of an automobile industry.

Rather, the forces that stimulate development are new technologies in the form of innovations of new or previously existing inventions, that are deemed successful by market participants, when applied to the market place by an entrepreneur. The key factor is innovation—"the commercial or industrial application of something new—a new product, process, or method of production; a new market or source of supply; a new form of commercial, business, or financial organization."[24] The process of innovation, initiated by the entrepreneur, revolutionizes the economy from within, thereby destroying parts of the old structure while creating new structures. If this occurs on a broad scale, the process will generate a "perennial gale of creative destruction." Schumpeter's creative destruction manifests capitalism's achievements, for the new goods and services typically are not only of higher quality but also are available at a much lower cost. The primary beneficiary are members of the working classes who could afford items such as silk stockings or automobiles that, prior to the innovation that ultimately led to their being massed-produced, were affordable only to the wealthy class.

Schumpeter argued that capitalism would be characterized by overlapping business cycles that were irregular in length and varied in direction. Each business cycle would be influenced by some initial entrepreneurial innovations, then followed by "swarms" of subsequent innovations as the economy adapted to the original innovation. The reason other entrepreneurs are likely to copy or adapt to the initial innovation is their being stimulated by "animal spirits." Schumpeter, who coined this term before John Maynard Keynes made it famous, argued that these spirits consisted "of inexplicable impulses which inspire entrepreneurs to give free rein to their willfulness and which in this way enable the whole economy to develop and change."[25] As a result, prices fall, and eventually the competitive process will lead to establishment of a new equilibrium state where the typical firm receives low profits. At this point what had been an upswing may turn into a recession or depression due to overoptimistic or overpessimistic judgments that, given the "animal spirits" of entrepreneurs, tend to occur in swarms that coincide with the upswing and downswing cycle. That a recession inevitably follows the surge in economic growth and development, however, did not indicate to Schumpeter that "capitalism" is weak. Rather, he viewed the cycle of economic surges and recessions as part of the capitalist development process—a price paid for economic freedoms and for receiving greater choices of higher-quality goods and services.[26]

Schumpeter's conception of development places the entrepreneur in the heroic role of bearing the mechanism, innovation, that is the generator of the evolutionary process of development. Schumpeter shared Friedrich Nietzsche's view concerning the extraordinary powers of certain individuals to shape society. Nietzsche distinguished between the "overmen" and the "mass" or "herd," with the "overmen symboliz[ing] the rejection of any kind of conformism: they are a rare breed striving toward 'higher ends' and personifying the antithesis to mediocrity and stagnation."[27] Schumpeter held a similar view, describing entrepreneurs as "the leaders who emerge vigorously from the mass."[28] The Schumpeterian entrepreneur not only must possess vision and daring but also must be driven to become a captain of industry. This special individual needs to be willing to move forward and innovate based on intuition. Only a few gifted persons can be successful entrepreneurs, for in addition to the aforementioned character traits, they also must be able to overcome difficulties faced, such as imperfect information about future demand and resource availability and costs, institutional resistance to any form of change, and the "antagonism of non innovators to the pioneer—in the form of legal and political obstacles, social mores, customs, and the like."[29]

Schumpeter recognized that an unequal income distribution would ensue from the capitalist development process but acknowledged this condition as the price of innovation and economic development. The price of not permitting such a condition was a static economy without either growth or development. The lures of high profits and status are required to attract entrepreneurial talent, without which capitalism could not survive and prosper. While development following entrepreneurial innovations creates extraordinary incomes for a few, Schumpeter argued that in the long run, capitalism tends to reduce income inequalities. It does so

> first, by increasing equality of opportunity relative to earlier, more class-bound societies; second, by the creation of mass-produced products that benefit working masses more than they do any other sector of the economy; third, by philanthropy and social legislation underwritten by the process of capitalist economic growth; and fourth, because although inequality is necessary for the sustenance of capitalism, "absolute poverty" falls as capitalist development proceeds."[30]

In the Schumpeterian conception of development capitalists are also vital, for it is they who finance many entrepreneurs' innovations in return for a portion of the expected profits. A well-developed financial system therefore is a prerequisite for capitalist development. Schumpeter was among the first to recognize this imperative, and argued that capitalists acting as "financial intermediaries are essential for technological innovation and economic development."[31] Contemporary analysis supports his view.[32]

Criticism of Neoclassical Economics

Neoclassical economics was too static, according to Schumpeter, overly concerned with "the derivation of theorems from given technological, institutional, and motivational assumptions."[33] His challenge to economic orthodoxy therefore was quite fundamental. "Because capitalism is a dynamic system . . . [he argued] it cannot be understood with the same theoretical apparatus used for examining the stationary economy. There are, in short, two domains—the stationary and the evolutionary—requiring two different organizing principles. " . . . the weakness of orthodox neoclassical economics exposed by Schumpeter's analysis lay, not in its incompleteness, but in its attempt to force dynamic elements into the static mold."[34] In opposition to the neoclassical view in which change within an economy is gradual, on the margin, not very disruptive, and heading toward some equilibrium via a process that is not painful, Schumpeter viewed societal transformation as being "rapid, large scale, disruptive, disequilibrating, and at times heroic but painful socioeconomic change."[35] In response, he synthesized a method analysis that focused on institutional change using his theory of capitalist development.

Method of Analysis

As an analyst Schumpeter was "a special blend of eclectic and innovator" demonstrating both "methodological independence and creative insight."[36] He was among the first economists to recognize that "reality is always and everywhere an ideologically and normatively tinted phenomenon in the literature of innovative economics."[37] That is, he argued that his own conception of reality, or what he called "vision," was the basis for his analysis.[38] Ideology thereby entered Schumpeter's analysis "on the very ground floor, into the preanalytic cognitive act."[39]

Schumpeter's conception of a theory included "the actual sequence of the economic process as it goes on under its own steam, in historic time, producing at every instant that state which will of itself determine the next one."[40] From his early works it was clear "that his vision of the economic system was one where static equilibrating forces (explainable in terms of the general equilibrium theory) are confronted by dynamic forces of disequilibrium. These latter he sought to explain by constructing an original [dynamic] theory of development."[41] Schumpeter believed that "the pulsating processes of real-world economic life are better explained from an explicitly dynamic and evolutionary perspective."[42]

Schumpeter's method of describing the dynamic process of capitalist development is similar to Myrdal's circular and cumulative causation approach. Another method in common with Myrdal was the emphasis Schumpeter placed on economic sociology, which he considered to be "the interpretive description of economically relevant institutions, including habits and all forms of behavior in general, such as government, property, private enterprise, customary or 'rational' behavior."[43]In *Capitalism, Socialism and Democracy,* his "major work on economic sociology," Schumpeter argues "that capitalism will decline because its economic success will prepare social circumstances unfavorable to it should not be interpreted as historical determinism. It has nothing to do with a historical hypothesis or prediction. It is a theoretical hypothesis derived from certain assumptions about the interaction between economic and social factors, and its validity rests on instrumentalist methodology."[44]

Friedrich Hayek

The contemporary influence of Friedrich Hayek (1899–1992) could be considered more widespread than that of Myrdal or Schumpeter because two recognized schools of thought continue to embrace and refine his theories and normative propositions: the Austrian School (of which Hayek was an integral contributor while in Vienna, having developed and articulated some of its basic tenets) and monetarism at the University of Chicago, where Hayek was a faculty member late in his career. He believed his influence would increase after his death, once informing a student that "he was writing for the next century."[45] Perhaps he believed this because he devoted the mature phase of his career designing a system of rules to protect individual liberty. In the process he "sketched out a sweeping theory of social change that was broadly evolutionary in its structure."[46]

Normative Propositions

Hayek was avowedly in favor of individual freedom, exercised within a laissez-faire market economy, while adamantly opposed to any form of government intervention in economic matters—particularly economic planning. He was convinced that "[t]he guiding principle that a policy of freedom for the individual is the only truly progressive policy remains as true today as it was in the nineteenth century."[47] In his ideal economy individuals would have the right to pursue their own ends, especially in regard to producing and selling what they wish if they violated no one else's property rights. Therefore, an important imperative for the Hayekian society was protection of property rights and recognizing the need to remove impediments to entrepreneurial action so as to permit spontaneous human reason and the pursuit of individual gain to flourish.

Strong preference for a laissez-faire market economy was logical and necessary for societal development, according to Hayek. In defense of this belief he wrote his greatest work, *The Road to Serfdom,* "a political book . . . [in which] all I shall have to say is derived from certain ultimate values [and that] the beliefs set out in it are not determined by my personal interests."[48] Expressing a deep concern "with fundamental questions and ultimate values,"[49] Hayek warned free societies that there was a slippery slope from introducing some government intervention policies to the development of a totalitarian state. While recognizing that temporary monopolies are created due to the creativity of entrepreneurial innovations, he argues that in the absence of free competition, only government intervention can sustain a real monopoly (by inhibiting entry). Therefore, he held that only a laissez-faire market environment was conducive to the emergence of entrepreneurs and that it is the only economy capable of preserving individual freedom.

He was adamantly opposed to the large-scale, planned reordering of any society's social and economic institutions by the state. Naturally, he offered strong criticism of democratically controlled social economies, such as Sweden. Over 50 years ago he lamented about "[t]hat hodgepodge of ill-assembled and often inconsistent ideals which under the name of the Welfare State has largely replaced socialism as the goal of the reformers needs very careful sorting-out if its results are not to be very similar to those of full-fledged socialism."[50]

Conceptualized Reality

Hayek's conception of reality are contained in his "presuppositions," which he believed were a priori true.[51] The two most important were his conception of competition and the entrepreneur and of government intervention and planning. Together they formed the building blocks of his dynamic theories and policy prescriptions.

Hayek believed competition was "first and foremost a discovery procedure. The economy is never in perfect equilibrium: there are always gaps to be filled by alert, profit-seeking entrepreneurs. Economic progress can . . . never become wholly automatic: invention can never become a routine."[52] Entrepreneurs who "outperform the masses in mental power and energy"[53] were the primary agents involved in this process of discovering new and better ways to organize resources, a process that, while fraught with errors, was being improved constantly. Entrepreneurs would be alert to profit opportunities, see a discrepancy between existing production costs and future selling prices, then act to take advantage of that discrepancy. Using their knowledge and foresight, and exhibiting a willingness to take risks while pursuing their own self-interest, entrepreneurs would behave as arbitrageurs of profit opportunities they had discovered. In the process the Hayekian entrepreneur was a "long-distance rational planner" who manifested "the success of human reason in human action."[54]

The political ideals of a people and its attitude toward authority were affected by their political institutions, according to Hayek. Therefore, extension of government authority gradually would undermine and destroy any spirit of freedom. He believed that "discretionary [government] power is dangerous and is bound to be abused sooner or later," arguing that what such "control produces is a psychological change, an alteration in the character of the people."[55] To further emphasize this point, he argued that extensive government intervention that constantly restrained people from acting, in the name of preserving state control, "compresses, enervates, extinguishes, and stupefies a people, till each nation is reduced to be nothing better than a flock of timid and industrial animals of which government is the shepherd."[56]

Hayek believed individuals could possess only a limited range of knowledge, particularly as it pertained to prices of goods and services and resource costs as well as consumer tastes and that there are very high information costs to obtaining such knowledge. While entrepreneurs could be informed about relative scarcities and profit opportunities solely by market prices, any planning authority would lack such information since prices were not market determined and therefore are not what they "ought to be."[57] He lamented the tendency for a "fatal conceit" to prevail in society—"the idea that the ability to acquire skills stems solely from reason . . . that humankind can shape the world according to wish . . . or that evolutionary products can always be improved by human ingenuity."[58] He was quick to respond that given the limitations of human knowledge about the future and the impossibility of making many decisions concerning prices that would equate the desired behavior patterns of producers and consumers, "[a]ttempts to replace a spontaneous order with a conscious, comprehensive plan for society simply cannot work according to the planners' expectations."[59]

Criticism of Neoclassical Economics

By not relying on mathematical models of the economy or suggesting ways that government policies can improve an economy's performance, Hayek purported to be more realistic and more socially scientific than practitioners of neoclassical economics. He did not attempt to create abstract models of a macroeconomy that include the view that capital is homogeneous, that competition is a static end-state, that in the long run normal profits are earned and equilibrium achieved, that an economist can identify some grand welfare function that measures society's welfare, and that these assumptions and models can be used for public policy. Along with other members of the Austrian School, Hayek believed that such unrealistic models were the hallmark of conventional economic methods.

Method of Analysis

Hayek's analysis became increasingly interdisciplinary as he sought to integrate his views of economic history, theory, and philosophy. In doing so he chose not to rely on mathematical models, holding that an economist cannot collapse the complexity of market arrangements into enormous aggregates. Instead he relied on verbal logic as his primary methodological tool. Further, while predicting the course societies would follow if government intervention were permitted unabated, Hayek believed that the future is so uncertain that the job of precise forecasting was not that of the economist but that of entrepreneurs. The latter need only predict specific price and cost changes arising from disequilibrium, enabling them to take advantage of profit opportunities.

Lessons

Social scientists seeking a new paradigm for analysis of twenty-first century economic problems should be encouraged by the contributions of Myrdal, Schumpeter, and Hayek.[60] Studying their major works, particularly *An American Dilemma* and *Asian Drama, Capitalism, Socialism and Democracy*, and *The Road to Serfdom* will demonstrate there can be an alternative to the reductionist neoclassical economic perspective—an alternative that yields more accurate predictions of the path and extent of societal development. These three scholars demonstrate a more realistic understanding of economies, and their respective methods of analysis are capable of providing a sound basis for policy formulation.[61]

What particular lessons can students and practitioners who seek a new economic perspective for the twenty-first century learn from Myrdal, Schumpeter, and Hayek? First, their conceptualized realities, criticisms of neoclassical economics, and methods of analysis indicate that there is an important place for dynamic, long-run analysis that is interdisciplinary—accounting for historical, political, and social aspects of the society being studied. Next, Schumpeter's and Hayek's normative propositions and conceptualized realities are consistent with recent evidence that indicates inefficient economic performance coincides with extensive government intervention. Therefore, Myrdal notwithstanding, there is the imperative of maintaining an economic environment conducive to entrepreneurial innovations, especially through establishing low income tax rates.[62] Certainly Schumpeter and Hayek would agree that

"[e]ntrepreneurship may be, in large measure, a function of an institutional sociopolitical structure which permits protection . . . to the innovator and the generation of pure economic profits through the manipulation of price, quantity, and quality variables via techniques which in the short run appear restrictive and monopolistic. Thus, the possibility of retention, at least temporarily, of above-normal profits from innovations may well stimulate a higher rate of innovation and technological improvement."[63]

Finally, the normative propositions and methods of analysis of these three economists demonstrate that analysts can avoid hidden biases and subjective value judgments (and therefore ideologically loaded analysis) by openly stating their value premises. Each man dealt explicitly with the "political element" inherent in his research, thereby enabling readers to evaluate the consistency of his conclusions without facing hidden biases. By not purporting to be "objective" and value free, Myrdal, Schumpeter, and Hayek provide analysis and conclusions that are more intellectually honest, and useful, than those offered by many practitioners of the neoclassical perspective. Those seeking to overcome this and other deficiencies of the neoclassical perspective by developing an alternative paradigm for analyzing twenty-first century economic problems would do well to use Myrdal, Schumpeter, and Hayek, among other heterodox contributors to economics, as their foundation.

Notes

1. The term "conceptualized reality" is used to represent the idealized image of the socioeconomic order as perceived by the analyst, an image conditioned by the cultural patterns of the society within which the analyst lives. It consists of two interrelated views: one involving a perceived relationship between social and economic forces within a society; the other pertaining to an interpretation of human behavior. A conceptualized reality gives direction to the analyst's work by influencing both the problems chosen for investigation as well as the conceived interrelationships between economic and noneconomic factors.

2. A paradigm is a universally recognized scientific achievement that provides model problems and methods of analysis for a community of practitioners.

3. Myrdal and Schumpeter sought to articulate the methodological foundation of neoclassical economics early in their careers with pathbreaking analysis of monetary theory. Yuichi Shionoya, "Schumpeter on Schmoller and Weber: A Methodology of Economic Sociology," *History of Political Economy* 23, no. 2 (1991): 193–219.

4. For example, Enrico Santarelli and Enzo Pesciarelli argue that Schumpeter was influenced by the "particular cultural climate of the early 20th C, especially the importance then of the great entrepreneurs." See "The Emergence of a Vision: The Development of Schumpeter's Theory of Entrepreneurship," *History of Political Economy* 22, no. 4 (1990): 677–696.

5. James Angresano, *Comparative Economics* (Englewood Cliffs, N.J.: Prentice-Hall, 1996).

6. This assumes that in evaluating and comparing the performance of economies, emphasis is placed on criteria such as economic growth, low unemployment, low inflation, and economic freedoms.

7. See James Angresano, "Gunnar Myrdal as a Social Economist," *Review of Social Economy* 44, no. 2 (1986): 146–148; and Gunnar Myrdal, "Institutional Economics," *Journal of Economic Issues* 12, no. 4 (1978): 771–783.

8. Gunnar Myrdal, *Against the Stream: Critical Essays on Economics* (New York: Vintage, 1975), 50.

9. For a presentation of a model of these interrelated factors as they comprise an economy, see Angresano, *Comparative Economics*.

10. For a detailed presentation of these institutions and their impact on the economy's performance, see ibid., chaps. 9–13.

11. For detailed criticisms of neoclassical economics, see the following works by Myrdal: *Rich Lands and Poor* (New York: Harper, 1957); *Value in Social Theory: A Selection of Essays on Methodology*, ed. Paul Streeten (London: Routledge & Kegan Paul, 1958); *Asian Drama: An Inquiry into the Poverty of Nations*, 3 vols. (New York: Pantheon, 1968); *The Political Element in the Development of Economic Theory* (Cambridge, Mass.: Harvard University Press, 1969); *An American Dilemma: The Negro Problem and Modern Democracy* (New York: Pantheon, 1975); *Against the Stream*; and "Institutional Economics."

12. Myrdal viewed the neoclassical perspective as too simplistic in its formulation of policies and representative of a monolithic, deterministic vision of the behavior of an economy. This vision viewed development as occurring in a linear, mechanical, simplified manner by which neoclassical economists assumed that once certain economic conditions had been established (i.e., privatization of previously state-owned enterprises or liberalizing rules pertaining to free trade), the market mechanism would emerge and prosperity would inevitably ensue.

13. For example, for the study of race relations and poverty in the United States, he selected the "American Creed." See Myrdal, *An American Dilemma*, 3–25. For poverty in underdeveloped nations, he identified his "modernization ideals." See his *Asian Drama*, 49–69.

14. Myrdal, *An American Dilemma*, lxxviii.

15. One Swedish social scientist paid tribute to Myrdal, arguing that "[a]t one time or another . . . [Gunnar Myrdal] has worked seriously at history, politics, and sociology. . . . It is hard to think of any other economist of our generation who would have had the courage, competence, and energy to carry through such studies of such sweeping scope, in which the purely economic component is kept always in proper perspective." Erik Lundberg, "Gunnar Myrdal's Contribution to Economic Theory: A Short Survey," *Swedish Journal of Economics* 74, no. 4 (1974): 472–478; quoted on 480.

16. For a classic presentation of his method, see Myrdal, *Asian Drama* and *An American Dilemma*, particularly the appendixes.

17. This study was carried out with his wife, Alva. See Myrdal with Myrdal, *Kris I befolkningsfragan* (Crisis in the population question) (Stockholm: Bonnier, 1934).

18. Gunnar Myrdal, "What is Economic Development?" *Journal of Economic Issues* vol. 8 (1974): 729–736.

19. Gunnar Myrdal, *Rich Lands and Poor* (New York: Harper & Brothers), 1957.

20. Robert Heilbroner, "Was Schumpeter Right After All?" *Journal of Economic Perspectives* 7, no. 3 (1993): 87–96; quoted on 94.

21. John E. Elliott, "Joseph A. Schumpeter at 100 and the Theory of Economic Development at 72," Paper presented at the meeting of the Southwestern Economic Association, Houston, TX, 1983, 27.

22. E. Ray Canterbery, *The Literate Economist* (New York: HarperCollins, 1995), 269.

23. Elliott, "Schumpeter at 100," 10.

24. Ibid.

25. Santarelli and Pesciarelli, "Emergence of a Vision," 688.

26. Some analysts argue that "Schumpeter hypothesizes a Walrasian-type adjustment mechanism [in which] . . . innovations first spread within a certain sector, and then through the entire system. . . . Thus once these innovations have spread to all production sectors, the economic system returns to equilibrium. The cyclical pattern of development is due to the irregular pattern of occurrence of innovations in certain markets, where equilibrim is restored by means of an endogenous adjustment mechanism." Ibid., 688–689.

27. Ibid., 689.

28. Ibid.

29. Elliott, "Schumpeter at 100," 12.

30. Ibid., 26.

31. Robert G. King and Ross Levine, "Finance and Growth: Schumpeter Might Be Right," *Quarterly Journal of Economics* 108, no. 3 (1993): 717–738; quoted on 716.

32. Ibid. King and Levine's analysis presents cross-country evidence that supports the Schumpeterian view "that the financial system can promote economic growth." They conclude that there is a strong empirical link between a range of indicators of financial development and economic growth—and that "The data are consistent with the view that financial services stimulate economic growth by increasing the rate of capital accumulation and by improving the efficiency with which economies use that capital." Further, they cite their empirical findings to "conclude that Schumpeter might have been right about the importance of finance for economic development." They argue that he was right not only regarding the role of the entrepreneur as innovator of new technology, but also his emphasis on the key roles for financial intermediaries "as

entrepreneurial selection and the financing of tangible and intangible investments that lead to innovation.

33. Elliott, "Schumpeter at 100," 20.
34. Ibid., 40–41.
35. Ibid., 42.
36. Ibid., 5.
37. Hans A. Jensen, "J. A. Schumpeter as a Forerunner of T. S. Kuhn," Paper presented at the meeting of the Eastern Economic Association, April 1978, Washington, D.C., 16.
38. Heilbroner, "Was Schumpeter Right?" 88. Schumpeter argued that "In every scientific venture . . . the thing that comes first is Vision. That is to say, before embarking upon analytic work of any kind we must first single out the set of phenomena we wish to investigate, and acquire 'intuitively' a preliminary notion of how they hang together or, in other words, of what appear from our standpoint to be their fundamental properties."
39. Jensen, "Schumpeter as a Forerunner," 10.
40. Everett Johnson Burtt, Jr., *Social Perspectives in the History of Economic Theory* (New York: St. Martin's Press, 1972), 162.
41. Santarelli and Pesciarelli, "Emergence of a Vision," 678.
42. Elliott, "Schumpeter at 100," 10.
43. Ibid., 21.
44. Shionoya, "Schumpeter on Schmoller and Weber," 217. Schumpeter did not believe mid-twentieth-century capitalist economies would continue to repeat the pattern of development of the late nineteenth and early twentieth century. Instead he argued that capitalism would be weakened by the bureaucratization of economic life, especially rent-seeking behavior by mature, gigantic monopolies and the emergence of an intellectual elite—both of which would generate political and social attitudes that sought capitalism's destruction. He predicted that in the absence of innovations, economic development of the capitalist economy would settle into the "routine of the circular flow in stationary general equilibrium." Elliott, "Schumpeter at 100," 6. It is noteworthy that following the growth and development of what would become United States Steel under the guidance of the quintessential entrepreneur of the nineteenth century, Andrew Carnegie, subsequent bureaucratized management and labor unions brought it down in absolute and relative economic strength as the firmed failed continually to introduce innovative cost-cutting measures—a practice Carnegie had championed. Meanwhile, foreign producers that emulated Carnegie's entrepreneurial practices were successful in capturing a large share of the world's steel market from their American competitors.
45. Norman Barry et al., *Hayek's "Serfdom" Revisited* (West Sussex, UK: Institute of Economic Affairs, 1984), lx.
46. Ibid., 123.

47. Friedrich A. Hayek, *The Road to Serfdom* (Chicago: University of Chicago Press, 1944), 240.
48. Ibid., xvii.
49. Barry et al., *Hayek's "Serfdom" Revisited*, xi.
50. Hayek, *Road to Serfdom*, viii.
51. Chiaki Nishiyama and Kurt R. Leube, eds., *The Essence of Hayek* (Stanford, Calif.: Hoover Institution Press, 1984), xlviii.
52. Barry et al., *Hayek's "Serfdom" Revisited*, 11.
53. Canterbery, *Literate Economist*, 262.
54. Ibid., 263.
55. Hayek, *Road to Serfdom*, xi, xii.
56. Ibid., xiii.
57. Hayek was highly critical of Oscar Lange's belief that "market socialism" in which planners could set prices in an efficient manner, arguing that "Lange appears to have been so confused between the knowledge possessed in day-to-day economic life by the individuals whose actions economics attempts to ex plain and the knowledge which the economist must pretend to possess in order to be able to do so, that he represents the latter as if it were something obviously perceivable to any observer of the economy." Nishiyama and Leube, *Essence of Hayek*, 57.
58. Frederic L. Pryor, "Review of *The Collected Works of F. A. Hayek*," *Journal of Economic History* 49, no. 4 (December 1989): 1072–1073; quoted on 1072.
59. Barry et al., *Hayek's "Serfdom" Revisited*, 122. Hayek believed that planners' minds cannot replace the knowledge and signals generated by the market, partly because millions of pricing decisions would be necessary and beyond the capability of any bureaucratic scheme with top-down authority. Therefore, Hayek concluded that "on the whole, societies which rely for this purpose on competition have achieved their aims more successfully than others. This is a conclusion which the history of civilisation seems eminently to have confirmed." Nishiyama and Leube, *Essence of Hayek*, 255. Schumpeter would agree.
60. Studying Myrdal's intellectual development would demonstrate the possibility for an economist trained in the neoclassical tradition to shift successfully toward the socioeconomic approach. Students and practitioners of economics seeking a paradigm that includes a multidisciplinary approach to broad social problems are likelier to avoid offering inadequate, inappropriate policies—not only for the United States but for foreign nations. Myrdal also serves as an example for those teaching economics—particularly if they are interested in reforming their programs to offer an alternative to the dominant neoclassical paradigm.
61. One scholar argues that "Schumpeter's conceptualization of economic leadership and internally-generated processes of revolutionary, qualitative change are pregnant with implications transcending his own particular historical setting

and social perspective." Elliott, "Schumpeter at 100," 42. Others would offer the same conclusion for both Myrdal and Hayek.

62. The recent economic problems encountered by two of Europe's most advanced "welfare states," France and Sweden, demonstrate that Hayek may have been correct when he argued that "the idea of a stable 'middle way' must be judged a mirage. It could happen only by a sheer (and continuously recurring!) fluke. Far more plausible is that such a system, given the fundamental processes involved, will become either a road to serfdom or a form of loophole capitalism with no guarantee of providing a secure basis for large-scale capitalist enterprise. The source of these ganders is the presumption that an elected government in a majoritarian democracy has an unlimited right to intervene in the voluntary arrangements of citizens. All such interventions are, of course, always labeled as being in the interests of 'social justice,' 'the public good,' 'compassion,' and so on. In practice, however, government intervention always creates losers as well as gainers, and it is to attract the support of the latter that the measures are undertaken." Barry et al., *Hayek's "Serfdom" Revisited*, 115.

63. Elliott, "Schumpeter at 100," 28.

CHAPTER 12

The Road to Ruin: Neoclassical Hegemony in Transition Economies

Robert J. McIntyre, United Nations University, Helsinki

ejection of the Soviet-type economic-political system has led a broad spectrum of Eastern and Central European intellectuals and new government functionaries to embrace a starkly ideologized and empirically ungrounded version of free-market capitalism. To what extent did neoclassical theory per se contribute to this outcome? This chapter argues that while the crucial decision makers and advisors in country after country walked and talked like neoclassical adepts, it was not the body of theory they carried that explained the devastation they caused but an accompanying neoclassical mind-set and hidden political agenda. These ideological correlates of neoclassical thinking had the effect of both preventing the actual application of market logic to these situations and foreclosing clear discussion about what was being done, why, and in whose name.

Some warned against the dangers of constructing transitional strategy on the basis of textbook simplifications. The arguments offered all called for a carefully modulated and evolutionary approach to the transformation problem.[1] When Douglass North accepted the Nobel Prize for work developing a new institutional economics, he went so far as to assert that neoclassical training had the effect of disabling economists from being able to deal intelligently with issues involving the initial construction or transformation of institutions.[2]

These warnings can be given a slightly sharper reading—that virtually nothing expected to occur in perfectly (or nearly perfectly) functioning markets, within established capitalist market-type economies, should be taken on faith as a guide to the complex tasks of simultaneously expanding the scope of markets (already there, legally, under the old system) and creating the formal and informal institutions able to allow their "self-organizing" features to emerge.

The transformation process is different because it mixes together normal "commodity transactions" with institutional invention, called by Daniel Bromley "institutional transactions" and also known as *Ordnungspolitik,* or "bargaining over choice sets."[3] Of course, even a carefully orchestrated and evolutionarily inspired "new system" would from its first moment set off market dynamics in an iterative cascade. Knowing about how markets operate would be a useful guide to many aspects of policy conduct, but it is worthwhile to pause and ask directly which if any institutional design choices would be well served by values that could be called neoclassical. Why, indeed, should a neoclassical market analysis perspective be expected to have anything at all to say about the proper allocation of ownership and other rights, *before* the market game begins.

I argue that the neoclassical perspective led to a failure to think clearly about the short-run selection mechanisms and the divergence of short-run from long-run survival characteristics under the peculiar circumstances of the transformation process. The hegemonic position of this school of thought thereby fostered a nearly catastrophic reticence on the part of governments in Eastern Europe and in the former Soviet Union, which have focused their attention on creating the superficial aspects of market modernity to the near exclusion of serious attention to the requirements for success under conditions actually existing in the contemporary capitalist world market.

The failure to mobilize effective industrial policy in the "transition" process closes off potentially promising growth paths and systematically creates forms of dependency that hold little promise for integration into the broader European economy on favorable terms. Much-heralded Western investment has been mostly "assets swaps" changing the ownership of existing productive resources, but even in the best cases of actual new investment, it has tended to produce what Gernot Grabher calls "cathedrals in the desert."[4] These failed hopes for the transformational effects of Western investment, along with deskilling, technological regression and provision of virtually uncontrolled market access for Western producers, together create a nearly impossible menu of policy choices. Under such conditions only very large countries that are aided by distance and risk filters can exercise independent economic policy even in principle. China has done so. Russia, operating from much more favorable initial conditions, has not.

Ideological Hegemony and No-Third-Way Maxims

Rather than being a simplified summary of a scientifically tenable set of conclusions, which has been assembled by careful weighing of evidence and experience, the No Third Way presuppositions are simply ideological assertions. These seductive arguments directly contradict the developmental lessons to be drawn from diverse Eastern European experience before 1989, historical patterns found in advanced capitalist countries for the last century, and rapidly accumulating evidence from the period after 1989 in Eastern Europe and the former Soviet Union. They lack any serious scientific content yet lie at the base of the standard transition strategies (transition orthodoxy) prescribed for ex-Soviet-type economies.

Apologists for conventional approaches often argue that shock therapy is a dead issue, either having occurred as an earlier but no longer relevant event or never really occurring. This is no more than an evasion, since slower or step-by-step application of the same fundamentally wrong policy produces comparable but more drawn-out disaster. The first rush of excitement with shock therapy is long past, and many pragmatic compromises have emerged despite the absolutist dynamics of the policies it inspires, but the logic of the approach remains at the core of much of the policy-relevant discussion by both governmental and international organizations of what to do next in these countries. Not by accident did the new (retreaded) Chubais-Nemtsov team in Russia in 1997 immediately echo the assumptions and rhetoric of the Gaidar policy disasters of 1991–1992. Soon after their eviction from power, following the August 17, 1998 financial collapse, they were again talking of doing "shock therapy" more fully and thoroughly when they had their next chance to govern.

A firmly established conventional wisdom about markets and market reform provides the intellectual grounding for policies applied across a broad range of countries and conditions. The rejection-of-transplants analogy lying behind this approach has two distinct subpoints that: only large reforms can work, and mixed institutions cannot survive. Because most Western analysis has adopted this perspective, the mixed nature of Soviet-type systems and the special characteristics of production/settlement units have been misunderstood or simply not considered. When systems-level structural adjustment policies are applied in this manner, without taking account of the special working arrangements of the old system, they result in largely destructive micro- and mesolevel effects. The destruction caused by these marketization and privatization policies is capricious, failing to preserve those aspects of the old system that have future development potential, encouraging a short-term speculative mentality and use of resources, while building up political tensions unlikely to be consistent with continued democratic process.[5]

Orthodox "transformation" measures also have failed to deal coherently with the relationship among internal markets, world market conditions, and the motives of the multinational firms that tend to emerge as the sole interested "investors" when valuable assets are being privatized. This combination of internal and external incompetence in the transition strategies, pushed from the West and often eagerly accepted by the new government leadership in the East, has led to the failure either to correctly understand what was valuable under the old system or to bring to bear developmental wisdom accumulated from outside the Anglo-American free-market experience to construct a coordinated short-, medium-, and long-run strategy that would permit entry into the world market on noncatastrophic terms.

It must be admitted that, given the political path chosen, there is need for local experts who are able to placate foreign institutions qua governments. Sounding like a modern Western-trained economist effectively means professing total ignorance of the policy issues raised by modern development experience, ignoring the ethical/normative content of those same choices, talking of privatization and capitalism as inseparable means and ends, and being able to offer early-Thatcher period platitudes with sincerity. When Yegor Gaidar called for a government of economists who "spoke good English and knew how to tie their ties," his meaning was clear.

Preventing Open Discussion of Alternatives

Serious public discussion of economic policy choices is strongly discouraged, partly by arguing that, in "normal" economies, such policy choices are safely entrusted to experts. Few pause to note that both Austria and Mobutu-period Zaire were normal economies by this standard, and both capitalist to boot. Constitutional issues are treated as matters for expert determination within a prelimited universe of choice whose boundaries and categories are never discussed openly. No one speaks candidly about the costs and distribution of benefits that will result from the economic policies being pursued.

Some will benefit, but few would choose this path in the name of their societies if they had full information about the implications of the "shock therapy" and "shock privatization" regimes.

Under the banner of "no more experiments," wild social surgery was performed without informed consent. For example, in Moscow, arrangements for privatization are made exclusively by presidential decree, with no parliamentary debate. The secrecy and contempt for public opinion at the heart of all shock privatization methods are also the source of most of the corruption endemic to the years after 1989 everywhere "in transition" but most vivid in Russia.

The effect of this propaganda fog has been to silence debate about profound issues at a moment of unusual system fluidity, during which societies are being altered permanently. With the lifting of the restraints on debate under the old system, the new ruling elites in each of the Eastern and Central European countries have prevented emergence of a real, open discussion of what is to come next. Both domestic and foreign advocates have used the no-third-way argument to attempt to stampede these societies in the direction of a nineteenth-century liberal phantom, perhaps secretly expecting a less-extreme, real-world outcome. Unfortunately, regardless of motive, this tactic destroys the institutional bridges that could lead to viable mixed alternatives.

Multiple Channels and Real Choices

It is useful to begin a brief analysis of the stability of institutional combinations within Soviet-type and advanced capitalist economies. Comparative analysis of both erstwhile camps shows that a wide variety of institutional arrangements—a veritable profusion—has survived in each others' presence. The variety of management and incentive forms is so great that a tempting countermaxim poses itself: Almost anything can be made to work with proper investment and policy support.

In the pre-1989 Soviet-type economies of Eastern and Central Europe, the mixture of property types (state, cooperative, and purely private) and organizational forms was different in each case. Mixed systems with different proportions between large state and small cooperative or private enterprises developed, and in some cases prospered, in various parts of Eastern Europe. In both urban and rural contexts, societies operating with Soviet-type large institutions and central planning found diverse ways of integrating smaller-scale and more market-oriented components.[6]

When these systems failed, it was not because of their mixed characteristics. Agriculture in Hungary, Czechoslovakia, and Bulgaria; entrepreneurial small-enterprise development in Bulgaria; and purely private small-scale industry in the old German Democratic Republic (GDR) provide relevant examples. In each case some kind of nonadversarial relationship emerged between the large state institutions and these other "peripheral" bodies. No ideologically gratifying way can be found to say which worked best, except perhaps to note that Soviet-type forms always performed worst at home, often while functioning reasonably well under institutionally and legally similar conditions elsewhere.

The variety of economic arrangements that modern economists are willing to certify as being fundamentally "capitalist" is even larger, ranging from Japan and South Korea, to Scandinavia; from the West German social market over to the Anglo-American model of not-quite-jungle capitalism. The central dynamic forces of capitalism are able to mobilize relatively effective economic performance in the presence of vast differences in: business cultures; financial systems, and market structures; levels of governmental regulatory and operating "intrusion"; and the realities of democratic political institutions.[7] It even could be argued that the best growth records tend to be found in those capitalist states that deviate the most from the classical liberal policy vision of perfect competition in an economy of thousands of small, powerless producers and minimal government intervention. In the capitalist world as well, stable institutional arrangements have arisen with very different constituent parts. Together these experiences show or at least suggest that there are stopping places at many points on the institutional continuum, if and when there is a will to create them.

Motivational Illusions: Many Paths to Excellence

The nature of individual motivation in Soviet-type systems is never omitted from the litany of causes of the decline or collapse of Soviet-type economic institutions. Inconsistency between equity and efficiency now is commonly cited as if it were a tragic fact of nature. If only the rest of Eastern Europe and the Soviet Union could develop the admirable tolerance of Polish and Hungarian policymakers for sharp income inequalities and mass unemployment, the market would soon work its magic. Again, within both capitalist and socialist worlds, small income differentials have not led automatically to poorer growth performance nor have increasing differentials (from any level) led systematically to improved performance.

If growth is all that matters, some of the most impressive national growth trajectories of the last 130 years have been achieved by countries such as Sweden, Japan, and Korea, which have rather narrow earnings differentials.

(The latter two compound the perplex by emphasizing group rather than individual performance rewards and seniority as the basis for advancement within professional categories.) There are obviously other paths to improved worker and manager effort. So much for the irremediable core of human nature in the work place, we might be tempted to say.

The real problems in the Soviet Union and some Eastern European countries were the lack of proper feedback mechanisms and poorly focused or inconsistent incentives, not their absence. Principal-agent and other incentive problems are features of large formal organizations regardless of their ownership form. It is often forgotten that large material performance rewards were a core feature of the Stalin-period economic model that was reversed under Nikita Khrushchev. Twenty-five years later Mikhail Gorbachev called consistently for reversal of the leveling trend of the Khrushchev-Brezhnev period.

An aspect of questionable legitimacy lay behind the unwillingness (or, in the Polish case, inability) to ask Eastern European populations for serious short-term sacrifice. For overall growth to slow down and consumption to continue to rise as it did for much of the decade from 1979–1989, capital accumulation obviously had to lag. This sacrifice of capital formation in support of consumption was an important contribution to the problems that came to be viewed as untreatable in 1989. It should, however, be noted that if the range of consumer goods available becomes inadequate, the motivational effects of cash wages are weakened. This deterioration in incentives reflects primarily investment and other resource allocation priorities and does not, by itself, demonstrate the absence of sufficiently large earnings differentials within or between labor force groups.

It also true that market incentives do not only have meaning in, or logically require, pure market systems. In the Canadian (or some other non-U.S.) health care system, the desire for more physicians may well lead to their recruitment by higher salaries, but both the financing and the distribution of the care provided by the system could not be further from the pure market outcome. The failure to consider such distinctions is normal practice in Eastern Europe today—neither the subtle facts of institutional differentiation in real advanced capitalist countries nor the connection of these differences to performance seems to be playing a significant role in contemporary discussions of systems design. This failure allows the new "market-oriented" elites to support pernicious policies by blandly asserting that in order to draw the benefits of marketlike incentives and behavior, the whole, pure system in an extreme (and imaginary) eighteenth- and nineteenth-century form must be accepted.

New Ideologically-Driven Elites and Popular Culture

Incentive rhetoric, which underlies much of the currently prevalent marketization and shock therapy thinking in previously state socialist countries, leaps from unexamined premises to socially destructive and probably politically impossible remedies without explication of its inner logic or implications. Comprehensive and rapid privatization is presented as the only path to systems mobilization and achievement of the "optimality" intrinsic to market capitalist polyarchy. Favorable results are alleged to be available in no other way—a view made manifest by the ferocious hostility to the idea that Third (or Fourth) Ways *might* exist. Although optimality is a question of achieving the best possible outcome under the circumstances, given the goals of the decision makers, reports of reform in Eastern Europe systematically cloud the question of who makes the decision about goals and what the assumed consequences of those choices are.[8]

Also missing from discussions of the early transition period has been attention to the long history before 1989 of market-reform thinking among Eastern European intellectuals, the narrow base of popular support for such measures anywhere, and the extent to which the socialist model of entitlement and citizens' economic rights struck deep roots into the culture of "ex-real, existing socialist" states, despite popular hostility to the word "socialism." Time requires no amendment to the acidic clarity of Peter Wiles's characterization of this divergence in Eastern and Central Europe: "Being very often of bourgeois origin and nearly always of bourgeois aspirations, the technocrats, scientists, doctors, teachers, etc., have quite simply wanted to re-establish the income differentials their fathers enjoyed; and they have tried it on in the name of incentives."[9] Following Amartya Sen, I suggest that a heavier weight should be placed on the lack of effective democratic supervision and oversight than on economic unsustainability in explaining why all of these systems crashed. In the central case of the Soviet Union, David Kotz and Fred Weir have argued that a subsection of the ruling elite simply decided personally to seize social property and were prepared to destroy the system to do so.[10]

Unlimited Market Ideology and Strictly Limited Policy Competence

This distinction between popular values and the ideologically driven radical-liberal program of the reform intellectuals simultaneously explains why events are reported as they are in the West and why nevertheless it is possible to be somewhat optimistic about the prospects for the emergence of mixed institutions compatible with popular values. The shock-reform programs regularly applauded in the West are politically viable only as long as the population is either bamboozled or given no role in deciding what will happen. This background political reality has been drowned out thus far by the self-reinforcing, reciprocal flow of happy talk between Western market advocates and new elites.

The transition orthodoxy is extreme and embodies a strong Friedmanite all-or-nothing analysis, in part hanging on the assumption that without a new price structure generated by a totally free market, nothing else will work. In a series of policy areas, groundless neoclassical optimism about the speed of adjustment and the relatively smooth movement to a new competitive equilibrium has driven out the counsel of caution and care in making society-transforming policies.

The irony of doubly subsidized German butter (large production subsidies from the Federal Republic, plus European Economic Community surplus commodity export subsidies) underselling Polish farmers (who had lost all their subsidies after 1991) is substantial, although it did prove Polish free-market purity. The virtual domination of urban Russian retail food supplies by foreign production also is heavily, but not exclusively, the result of concealed subsidies. Cases like these unfortunately seem to be the music of the future. The ill-conceived jump to exclusively convertible currency trade resulted in large and possibly permanent losses of Russian and Chinese markets, losses even capitalist Finland came to regret deeply. The old quasi-barter links, which had a logic at least in the short run and soon forcibly reasserted themselves, did not pass ideological muster.

Roads to Unnecessary Ruin

Almost all of the society-wrecking advice given to the Eastern European countries points them in the opposite direction of successfully developing capitalist countries. An extreme and naive application of free-market ideology has produced structure-determining policy decisions that do not engage product- or input-market realities.[11] As a result the "new democracies" are being directed onto a path that no countries have followed successfully, since the free-market and minimal government experiences of the United Kingdom and the United States during the eighteenth and first half of the nineteenth centuries.[12]

Western proponents of shock transition methods must know that no Western capitalist economy has such a pure system, and might even admit that those that come closest—the United States and the United Kingdom— have functioned toward the lower end of the performance scale for much of the last century. Yet they present these pure, stark options to Eastern European policy makers, who labor under the added inconvenience of dealing with populations having a very strong sense of social entitlement. The size of the disjunction between reality and policy advice raises questions about the motives of both advice givers and receivers. This intensely ideological approach has proved persuasive in the short run, allowing the new "market-oriented" elites to support pernicious policy by asserting blandly that to draw the benefits of marketlike incentives and behavior, the whole system must be accepted in an extreme (even then imaginary) eighteenth- or nineteenth-century form. Ill-thought-out "incentive" arguments are often at the core of these "reform" philosophies. The absence of grounded discourse on the realities of economic development has been remarkable. Alternative perspectives and methods of analysis are available, all of which begin by requiring an understanding of how the old system "worked."

Four Agriculture Lessons with Universal Structural Implications

Agriculture provides a set of powerful examples of the importance of understanding embedded relationships in transitional economies. It provides a four-fold lesson of the way in which seemingly familiar surface situations can work in unexpectedly different and complex ways; can achieve considerable success on this basis; and can suffer unanticipated disasters when their reorganization is approached from within the universe of assumptions and policy conclusions of orthodox economic analysis. Each of these points is directly relevant to the urban sector, but agriculture provides a good starting point and vivid lessons because of the total unexpectedness of its Eastern European successes.

The Ghost of the Transition: Why No Spontaneous Decollectivization?

Western expectations were formed on the basis of a generalized worst-case picture of Soviet agriculture. As a result, the absence of interest in or pressure for decollectivization coming from the rural populations of Eastern European and the former Soviet Union is a puzzling feature of the post-1989 period. Collective agriculture has been collapsing only where active measures (initiated from outside agriculture) are taken to destroy it. The simple explanation of the anomaly is that as both a social and an economic institution, the Soviet-type collective farm has been relatively successful wherever it has been tried in Europe outside the Soviet Union (and it improved dramatically at home as well during the period from 1958 to 1985).

After the agricultural management policies of the Stalin period were reversed, and without any significant changes in organizational or legal structure, the Soviet-type collective farm achieved improved economic performance on the basis of a period of high investment, favorable procurement prices, professionalization and specialization of agricultural management, and comprehensive adoption of scientifically grounded cultivation practices in a big-field context. Together these factors explain the improvement in purely economic performance, but understanding the success of these arrangements as a rural social system requires consideration of a whole layer of supplementary conditions and practices.[13]

Nonwage Features of Collectives: Social and Private Cost

In all of the European countries that adopted the Soviet-type agricultural model, the collective farm supported local schools, built local housing, and provided local transportation and other services. These duties reflected a quasi-constitutional division of functions that made the collective or cooperative farm effectively both an economic actor and a political entity similar to the local government in a Western society. Provision of these urban-type services was part of an implicit post-Stalin social bargain to treat (or at least move toward treating) farmers like factory workers in terms of living standards and amenities, in return for their continued acceptance of the collective arrangements.

As part of this new social contract, agricultural workers were brought to approximately urban levels of income stability and economic integration, with 8- to 9-hour days, 40- to 50-hour weeks (and hence, weekends), regular paid vacations, social security, and a full array of social support programs (day care and after-school care, maternity leave, health insurance, retirement and disability benefits, cultural events, and continuing education opportunities). Acting as local government, the collectives provided universal access for the rural population to a broad range of services and goods.

The quality-of-life improvements, combined with high earnings from direct employment, resulted in the evaporation of urban-rural income differentials and explain the solid acceptance of collectives that built up over time. This service-supply dimension, and its transparent financing, also explains the lack of interest in returning to an economy in which these services are bought in a market environment (which would mean, in fact, that most would disappear). This was a relatively high labor cost environment because the extensive array of social provisions and protections that developed as "constitutional" rights of rural workers were counted as production costs of the collective.

Since most of the active farm population came to be quite happy with collective agriculture, pressure to break up collectives came either from urban reformers (unaware of agricultural realities but driven by free-market ideology to assume that the logic of privatization they proposed for industry and city services must apply in the countryside as well) or from individuals hoping to make short-term speculative gains from acquiring and then selling off land (few of whom prove to be interested in going into small-scale agricultural production themselves).

The results of an April 1997 attempt to reorganize a collective farm near Moscow, which were "disappointing" to the foreign organizers (the International Finance Corporation of the World Bank and the British Know-How Fund), illustrate both the logic and continuing nature of this problem. Of 689 individuals or families with participation rights, 688 chose to place their share of collective farms assets back into common cultivation—the one exception was a schoolteacher, not a farm worker, whose only payoff was a better private residence.[14]

Disinformation with "Personal-Plot" Statistics

A separate aspect of the problem of appreciating the performance realities of Eastern European collective agriculture comes from the pervasive misuse of data reporting the "proportion of output from private plots." The mixture of large-scale collective agriculture with the backyard gardening and livestock raising of the member households proved to be successful because it broke down the Stalin-period barriers between private and social production.

The state provided fodder, seeds, fertilizer, baby pigs, services (plowing, veterinary, seeding, and harvesting), and technical advice in exchange for an agreed-upon share of personal plot output, which then was sold through the state distribution network. The success of the private-plot component was thus the result of working through, rather than in competition with, the socialized agriculture sector. The symbiotic relationship between collective and garden-plot production altered the meaning of "private." The routine assignment of workers in the course of their collective farm duties to cultivate, fertilize, or deliver supplies to the family plots of other collective farm members makes the relationship manifest.

Once the issues of improper (single-factorial) productivity measurement, failure to count the bulk of input costs, and missassignment of output, are understood correctly, the same data lead to the conclusion that private plots represent very useful activity but one that is of extraordinarily low productivity.[15] This point is almost never presented correctly in either popular or professional discussions. Fredric Pryor gets the agricultural output side of this situation correct, although he does not deal with the input and nonagricutural output aspects.[16]

Findings of "Inefficiency" Without Facts

Attempts to measure the efficiency of agriculture in different systems generally have been based on the crudest type of statistical aggregation, which leave out this entire realm of social-cultural externalities and misallocates both production totals and input use between the social and private parts of collective agriculture. The systematic omission of these costs and activities always and everywhere overestimates the use of inputs and underestimates or fails to count many outputs in all Soviet-type agricultural systems.

In addition, when explicit comparisons are made with Western European agriculture, labor inputs in the West are greatly underestimated due the failure to count unpaid work by family members.[17]

Systematic inefficiency did occur in Soviet-type agriculture as the result of political (macrolevel) decisions to achieve agricultural self-sufficiency. This approach arose from a particular political situation and created literal inefficiency, which again is not evidence of dysfunctional production (microlevel) behavior. Criticism of the political decision to subsidize rice growing in California simultaneously neither indicts the microlevel production skills of the farmers nor indicates that they lack the skill, motivation, and equipment that would allow them success in other activities, given time to adjust and restructure. As marginal land or climatically inappropriate crops are used to achieve self-sufficiency, output per input falls below what otherwise would have been achieved. Efficiency losses occurred in industry for exactly the same reason, where output of products that were difficult (due to resource endowment, insufficient scale, or lack of access to world technology markets) lowers the apparent efficiency of enterprise and systems performance, but not as a function of operating inefficiency or lack of skill and motivation.

Industrial Sector Parallels: Four Case Studies

The confusion resulting from finding boundaries located at unexpected places applies equally to the rest of the system, since the Soviet-type industrial enterprise was responsible for provision of a broad array of social services that extended beyond its own employees and, in effect, carried out major functions of local and regional government. Often it is only in discussion of the unexpected resistance to enterprise privatization (or commercialization) that these arrangements are acknowledged openly. This major consideration must distort any empirical measure of performance based on ratios of inputs to outputs, whether the calculations are done at a micro-, sectoral or systems level.[18]

Simon Clarke, P. Fairbrother, V. Borisov, and P. Bizyuko and Simon Clarke, Fairbrother, M. Burawoy and P. Korotov provide a series of careful studies of the privatization experiences of four healthy and well-managed enterprises, which entered the process during the late Gorbachev period. This fascinating and complicated set of experiences cannot be summarized easily, but one aspect is especially relevant here. The early start of these enterprises meant that there was some time for reflection and planning before they were swept up in the whirlwind of administrative and legal change/chaos of the Yeltsin period.[19]

Each of these large enterprises initially set off on a distinctive path, but as the disorder resulting from the collapse of previously stable markets in Eastern Europe and the other parts of the former Soviet Union grew and as mutual nonpayments and supply irregularities became endemic, each enterprise fell back toward the old structural and political relationships that had characterized the pre-1991 system. Each converged back to a classic Soviet-type pattern of close dependence on local and regional (*oblast*) government, returned to nonmonetized transactions, and abandoned attempts to alter the actual methods of work and remuneration within the enterprise.

The World Bank View and Embedded Rationality

Often explanations of the need for drastic marketization and privatization are phrased in terms of extreme models of atomized individual decision makers operating in perfectly competitive markets. There is the familiar tendency to use the model of perfectly functioning markets as if it were real or about to be real. Much of the material from the World Bank on the transition reads like self-parody—assuming that: (1) successful small and medium-scale family enterprises will emerge en masse; (2) large enterprises will be privatized in a competitive process with many bidders and clear information; (3) the resulting new system will both emerge and function under perfectly competitive conditions (which exist nowhere in Western Europe). Enterprises, managers, and workers in urban and rural sectors are modern and "fit to survive" if they behave in ways that would be functional if they were in such a model. Since it is unlikely that the inmates of this experiment are living under such conditions (or expect to be), judging the rationality or efficiency of their conduct on this basis is not possible in any simple way. No one knows what will work or survive under the new conditions, in part because it is not clear that the new conditions themselves will survive. While it may be admitted that, of course, markets are not perfect "during transition," researchers are totally mystified about what is rational or efficient behavior under the actual conditions being considered. Perhaps "transition" is forever.

Social Embeddedness and Squandered Foundations

While it does not directly overlap with the externality discussion, a parallel and perhaps equally important feature of Soviet-type organizations are institutional coping mechanisms. The significance of these institutional features can be particularly well illustrated by reference to the first years of the Treuhand activities in the ex-GDR.

In the "kombinate" the strategy and tactics of survival (with intermittent flashes of pure excellence) under extremely difficult conditions were managed by highly competent specialist departments, organizational forms, and informal structures. Gernot Grabher provides a subtle and convincing explanation of these relationships, on the basis of research being conducted by the Science Center Berlin, using a longitudinal interview approach to study the hidden forces that made the old GDR system function as well as it did under adverse circumstances.[20] These key structures turned out to be early victims of the first stages of "commercial" reorganization because their importance cannot be recognized when the enterprises are approached with a Western market economy orientation (and the resulting set of assumptions about how organizational structures work).

Given the legendary role of "overstaffing" in the standard Cold War picture of how these organizations operated (and ignoring for the moment the role of back-door deals, insider trading, and other forms of conflicts of interest in directing the behavior of the Treuhand itself), an immediate effort to produce leaner organizations by cutting employment is understandable, but such cuts can be made intelligently only if the organizations themselves are clearly understood.

The GDR and most of the other Soviet-type economies adopted the production association form of organization, in which a number of related plant (sometimes geographically concentrated, sometimes, in the Soviet case, thousands of miles apart and in multiple republics) were grouped under the control of a headquarters plant. The headquarters plant of the combine, *kombinate*, or production association concentrated specialist functions (especially research, design, and engineering) and in its coordinating role with the branch plants took over much of the detailed planning responsibilities of the branch ministry. Both horizontal and vertical integration took place under this form of organization, which often was pushed further than would be expected on purely technical grounds by the forces (supply unreliability and a highly asymmetric incentive/reward system) that had long encouraged "universalism."

In the GDR this production association approach was adopted as early as 1962 and carried further than in the Soviet Union, so that nearly every production unit of any size was incorporated in one. This arrangement (absent the industrial ministry and Gosplan) is very similar to the structure of headquarters and research departments in American and other large corporations. Indeed, in the Soviet Union the production association reform (in 1967, 1969, and 1972) was heralded internally and externally as an adoption of "American" models of enterprise organization.

The incompetence of the West German trusteeship organization (Treuhand) in dealing with this East German organizational form was so large that it is hard to understand as anything other than deliberate. The sharp, indiscrimnant staffing cuts and reorganization the Treuhand imposed as the first stage of "commercialization before privatization" simply wiped out these specialist departments. Yet all of the special formal and informal networks that had held the organizations together centered in or required the major participation of these specialist headquarters departments. The Treuhand's actions destroyed the value of many of the organizations involved and left most of the surviving parts irreversibly crippled.

Market-Access Disasters: The Missing Category of Wholesale Trade

One seldom considered aspect of the collapse of many Eastern European and former Soviet Union producers has been loss of access to market channels within their own countries. State monopoly (or price-controlled duopoly) distribution channels either have been sold as a unit (all outlets to one Western buyer) or have been allowed to make side deals with Western suppliers that provide them with all or most shelf space. There are quality differences in many consumer and food products, but not all. Even those of clearly comparable quality suffer this fate. It also should be noted that lower quality (even when simply involving packaging) is exposed to consumer choice only if these goods remain available for comparison after the period of initial infatuation with new products from the West.

Double-subsidized European Union (EU) foodstuffs also play a role in demonstrating an illusory (i.e., exaggerated) Eastern preference for West products. EU subsidies provide classic cases of market outcomes that satisfy long-standing prejudices but do not reflect either short-run or long-run production cost realities. What they do reflect are the strange effects of EU butter mountains and milk lakes on neighboring markets that have not taken fundamental measures to protect their own producers until conditions stabilize sufficiently to allow real judgments to be made about economic viability. Lack of self-protection often can be explained partly by Western political blackmail, connected first to "membership" in the North Atlantic Treaty Organization (NATO) and then in the European Union, but there are other reasons as well.

Incompetence, Corruption, or Simple Excess of Ideology

Several different forms of avoidable destruction rise out of rapid marketization and privatization in the absence of adequate social and technical preparation. First, Treuhand-like direct destruction occurs in all cases where commercialization is pushed forward without a careful, in-depth, and subtle analysis of the existing circumstances. Second, when Eastern Europe moves rapidly toward "capitalism," what it gets, even in the absence of corruption, are highly monopolistic market structures. Freeing prices from the existing system of state-supervised controls was economically indefensible, even if it does sop up surplus purchasing power and create the appearance of successful anti-inflation results. Markets always work in that sense, which says nothing about the longer-term economic development effects. Price liberalization was simply a cover for a massive theft of social property and private savings, all of which ended up in the hands of the worst, least socially responsible elements of the old elite.

Use of the discipline of the world market to offset local market power implies massive collateral destruction, if it is allowed to occur rapidly. But once the price "liberalization" approach is undertaken, the other alternative—monopoly without price controls, effective antitrust measures, or prospects for market entry—is also unpalatable. Partial or full foreign ownership of retail and consumer goods firms makes monopoly prices seem more plausible to the local population, and the "new" products escape inclusion in the price indices used to measure inflation.

The already capitalist market economies of Spain, Portugal, and Ireland enjoyed decade-long buffer periods when they joined the Common Market and continuing special preferences and exemptions after that. But a "destroy-to-save" mentality is real and pervasive in Eastern Europe, perhaps resulting from the belief that this is the only way to please international lenders and achieve salvation from the outside in the form of debt relief and new credits. Latin American and Third World parallels should not be ignored in Eastern Europe, World Bank protestations to the contrary not withstanding. Structural adjustments policies often lead to sharp and sustained declines in living standards and produce serious resistance from the general population. As the inevitable corruption attendant on these particular privatization and marketization policies is brought into the open, in the presence of sharply growing unemployment and income inequality, maintaining popular support without openly repressive measures becomes more difficult.

The free-market incompetence or naïveté suggested by the earlier discussions of social externalities and efficiency, the role of embedded structures and informal structures in organizational success, and the Treuhand-style privatization disasters also are revealed in the problems that have emerged in practice with nonagricultural privatization in other countries. Many of the purchase or joint-venture arrangements with foreign firms that were reported initially as triumphs for the new strategy and system later turned out to be profoundly flawed due to corruption or incompetence. The Ikarus-Ganz and Tungsram cases in Hungary and the aborted Liaz-Avia-Mercedes plan in the Czech Republic are different vivid examples of these problems. When there is not a wealthy foreign buyer more home-grown, internal buyers are selected on the basis of corruption and fraud. Russia provides only the most comprehensive and extreme example of what is a bloc-wide phenomenon.

Systemic patterns of insider and other corruption showed up as early as 1986 in the Soviet small cooperatives, then emerged in different forms in Hungary, Poland, Czechoslovakia, and Bulgaria. The characteristic "nomenklatura cooperative" in Poland has not trifurcated into old, new, and newer varieties. In Czechoslovakia the domination of dirty money and money from abroad in the early and generally successful small privatizations led to a public outcry and the wonderfully revealing free-market line of defense that, since there was no way to make clean money under the old system, what was the difference? The need to create the appearance of fast success for privatization policies leads to poor negotiating tactics and results (even when the process is not subject to side-door corruption), but the number and speed of privatizations seems to be more convincing evidence of seriousness than does their quality. Here as elsewhere a "free-market" definition of normality looms in the background and controls political discourse.

In evaluating the overpraised privatization in Czechoslovakia, it is important to remember that even in the relatively noncontroversial first small-enterprise (mostly retail) privatization wave, employees of state-owned small enterprises were excluded as a matter of principle from participation in these privatization auctions, which were rushed through with no apparent effort to allow other forms of financing (e.g., small-enterprise loan funds and sweat-equity schemes) to emerge. The "principle" in this case turned out to be that such arrangements were not part of normal (i.e., American-style) market capitalism. Under these conditions, policy manipulation by a self-serving elite is pushed through under the cloak of expediency, to applause from abroad.

The problems of maintaining public support for privatization on these terms is obvious and already at the time of the first Czechoslovak enterprise auctions in January 1991 had played a major role in the de facto suspension of the Hungarian privatization program during 1990. The Hungarian program was resumed in a reformulated, more deliberate from, but problems of spontaneous privatization also quickly reemerged. Despite an abundance of optimistic reports about medium- and large-size enterprise privatization in these and many similar cases, corruption has been their hallmark, not simply an unfortunate fiction. Even apparently seriously worked out programs, such as the large-enterprise coupon privatization in the Czech Republic, are driven to reporting superficial manipulations as thoroughgoing reorganizations.

Social Values, Privatization, and Economic Performance

Shock-therapy prospects in Eastern Europe ultimately are undermined by the deeply ingrained acceptance of socialist distribution norms and values (despite hostility to the political system that put them in place and the terminology) and the trade unions that have survived and remain strong. Local loyalties, a history of low geographical mobility, and the unique Soviet-type settlement pattern combine to produce an especially sharp focus on the effects of market reforms on communities and groups of workers who already have an organizational from, complete with newly elected popular leadership.

The widespread assumption that Eastern Europe and ex-Soviet populations enthusiastically await the movement to recognizable forms of market capitalism have been based, to a large degree, on a simple mistranslation: In the West the word "privatization" has been understood to mean "private" ownership in the American sense of the word, while in Eastern Europe and the former Soviet Union it is understood to mean "no longer totally owned by the national-level government." Robert McIntyre provides a discussion of the case of the Kama River Truck Factory (Kamsky Avtomobilny Zavod), which was widely cited as an example of successful privatization in the Russian Republic even though it had no private owners.[21]

Under these conditions, only an opening up of discussion and toleration of diverse, mixed outcomes is consistent with the coexistence of popular support for transformation and the continuation of democratic functioning. Market Stalinism is neither a graceful phrase nor a socially viable path on the edge of Western Europe. Clearly the exaggerated emphasis of the new Eastern European market-oriented elites on joining the European Economic Union will founder if they adopt authoritarian measures to maintain domestic control. Only with an openly negotiated social compact on the terms and character of marketization can such repression by avoided. This social dialogue is a dangerous dialectical process; the risk of dire results is already quite high because of shock therapy per so.

Conclusion

To the extent that the process of constructing a new market-oriented system remains open to local political influence (and redirection), it will be very interesting to watch. When local opinion can have a significant effect on the privatization process, reality moves far from the assumptions of the free-market economists who currently dominate national-level decision making. Opinion polls throughout Eastern Europe show very little interest in pure forms of capitalism, whenever the survey instruments include any option that includes social protections of the type features under the old system. The rampant corruption of privatization and marketization policies carried out under current rules has created resistance that will require either systemic compromise or repression.

If the more hopeful alternative obtains, a new type of social compromise is likely to emerge that includes an institutional mixture different from classical European capitalism. Consistent with correctly defined economic rationality, evaluation of the system's success will include consideration of its provision of nonindividual and nonmaterial goods (such as those described in the discussion of special social-cost characteristics of Soviet-type enterprises under the old systems).[22]

Notes

1. Austrian Academy of Sciences, *Agenda '92 for Socio-Economic Reconstruction of Central and Eastern Europe* (Vienna: Austrian Academy of Sciences, 1992);

Kenneth Koford, "Why the Ex-Communist Countries Should Take the 'Middle-Way' to the Market Economy," *Eastern Economic Journal* vol. 23, no. 1 (1997): 31–50; Robert McIntyre, "The Phantom of the Transition: Privatization of Agriculture in the former Soviet Union and Eastern Europe," *Comparative Economic Studies* 34, nos. 3–4 (1992): 81–95; Murrell 1992 *Eastern European Politics and Societies* vol. 6, no. 1 (1992): 3–24.

2. Douglass North, "Economic Performance Through Time," *American Economic Review* 84, no. 3 (June 1994): 359–368.

3. See the following works by Daniel Bromley: *Economic Interest and Institutions: The Conceptual Foundations of Public Policy* (Oxford: Basil Blackwell, 1989); and "Reconstituting Economic Systems: Institutions in National Economic Development," *Development Policy Review* vol. 11 (1993).

4. See the following works by Gernot Grabher: "Eastern 'Conquista': The 'Truncated Industrialization' of East European Regions by Large West-European Corporations," in Huib Ernste and Verena Meier, eds., *Regional Development and Contemporary Industrial Response* (London: Belhaven/Pinter, 1992), 219–232; and "The Dis-Embedded Economy: Western Investment in Eastern German Regions," in A. Amin and N. Thrift, eds., *Globalization, Institutions, and Regional Development in Europe* (Oxford: Oxford University Press).

5. Alice Amsden, Michael Intriligator, Robert McIntyre, and Lance Taylor, "American Expert Report: Strategies for a Viable Transition: Lessons from the Political Economy of Renewal," Paper presented in Moscow, June 13–16, 1995. Published in *Russia and the Contemporary World* (Moscow), 10, no. 1 (1996): 64–95. Reprinted as "Strategies for a Viable Transition: Lessons from the Political Economy of Renewal," *Theoretical and Practical Aspects of Management* (Moscow), 14, no. 2 (1996): 30–37. Robert McIntyre, "Structural Roots of Reform Failure," *Problemy Upravleniya* 14, no. 5 (1966): 8–13.

6. See the following works by Robert McIntyre: "The Small Enterprise and Agriculture Initiatives in Bulgaria: Institutional Invention Without Reform," *Soviet Studies* 40, 4 (1988): 602–615; and "Economic Changes Without Conventional Reform: Small-scale Industrial and Service Development in Bulgaria and the GDR," in Reiner Weichardt, ed., *The Economics of Eastern Europe Under Gorbachev's Influence* (Brussels: NATO Economics Directorate, 1989), 80–104.

7. Robert McIntyre, "Eastern European Success with Socialized Agriculture: Developmental and Sovietological Lessons," *RRPE* vol. 23, nos. 1–2 (Summer): 177–186.

8. See the following works by Alice Amsden: "Taiwan's Economic History: A Case of Etatisme and a Challenge to Dependency Theory," in Robert H. Bates, ed., *Toard a Political Economy of Development: A Rational Choice Perspective* (Berkeley: University of California Press, 1988), 142–175; *Asia's Next Giant: Late Industrialization in South Korea* (New York: Oxford University Press, 1989); and "Diffusion of Development: The Late-Industrializing Model and

Greater East Asia," *American Economic Review* 81, no 2 (1991): 282–286. See also: Alexander Gerschenkron, "Economic Backwardness in Comparative Perspective" and "Postscript," in Alexander Gerschenkron, *Economic Backwardness in Historical Perspective* (Cambridge, Mass.: Harvard University Press, 1962), 5–30, 353–364; and Tom Kemp, *Industrialization in Nineteenth-Century Europe*, 2d ed. (London: Longman, 1985).

9. See the following works by Amartya Sen: "What Did You Learn in the World Today?" Paper presented at the University of Pennsylvania, October 19, 1990; and *Inequality Reexamined* (Cambridge, Mass.: Harvard University Press, 1996).

10. David Kotz and Fred Weir, *Revolution from Above: The Demise of the Soviet System* (New York: Routledge, 1997).

11. Alice Amsden, Jacek Kochanowicz, and Lance Taylor, *The Market Meets Its Match* (Cambridge, Mass.: Harvard University Press, 1994); Lance Taylor, "The Market Met Its Match: Lessons for the Future from the Transition's Initial Years," *Journal of Comparative Economics* 19, no. 1 (1994): 64–87; and Grigory Yavlinsky and Sergei Braguinsky, "The Inefficiency of Laissez-Faire in Russia: Hysteresis Effects and the Need for Policy-led Transformation," *Journal of Comparative Economics* 19, no. 1 (1994): 88–116.

12. Amsden, "Diffusion of Development"; Robert McIntyre, "Structural Roots of Reform Failure," *Theoretical and Practical Aspects of Management* (Moscow) 14, no. 5 (1996): 8–13.

13. McIntyre, "Small Enterprise and Agricultural Initiatives in Bulgaria"; "Economic Changes Without Conventional Reform."

14. "Land Auction Reaffirms Collective," *Moscow Times,* April 12, 1997, 11. This is a general pattern, not an isolated incident. An earlier illustration was the widely praised and publicized (similarly unsuccessful) IFC effort in Nizhny Novgorod-Gorky five years earlier, discussed in McIntyre, "Phantom of the Transition," 90–91, and in Robert McIntyre, "Regional Variations on Russian Chaos: Price Controls, Regional Trade-Barriers, and Other Neo-Classical Abominations," *Communist and Post-Communist Studies* 29, no. 1 (1996): 95–102; and "Regional Stabilization Policy under Transitional Period Conditions in Russia: Price Controls, Regional Trade Barriers and Other Local-level Measures," *European-Asia Studies* 50, no. 5: 859–871.

15. See the following works by McIntyre: "Small Enterprise and Agriculture Initiatives in Bulgaria," 609–613; and, 182–183.

16. Frederic Pryor, *The Red and the Green: The Rise and Fall of Collective Agriculture in Marxist Regimes* (Princeton, N.J.: Princeton University Press, 1992).

17. See the following works by McIntyre: "Small Enterprise and Agriculture Initiatives in Bulgaria"; and "Phantom of the Transition."

18. A more detailed discussion of the urban manifestations of this relationship is provided in the following works by Robert McIntyre: "Intermediate Structures and Shock Transition: Squandered Foundations and Capricious Destruction,"

Human Systems Management 12, no. 4 (1993): 325–332; and "Structural Roots of Reform Failure."

19. See: Simon Clarke, P. Fairbrother, V. Borisov, and P. Bizyukov, "The Privatisation of Industrial Enterprises in Russia: Four Case Studies," *Europe-Asia Studies* 46, no. 2 (1994): 179–214; and Simon Clarke, P. Fairbrother, M. Burawoy, and P. Korotov, *What About the Workers?* (London: Verso, 1993).

20. Grabher, "Eastern 'Conquista'" and "The Dis-Embedded Economy." See Andreas Pickel, "Jump-starting a Market Economy: A Critique of the Radical Strategy for Economic Reform in Light of the East German Experience," *Studies in Comparative Communism* 25, no. 2 (1992): 177–191.

21. McIntyre, "Intermediate Structures and Shock Transition" and "Structural Roots of Reform Failure."

22. Sen, "What Did You Learn in the World Today?"

CHAPTER 13

Japan Faces the Twenty-First Century

Koji Taira, University of Illinois, Champaign

T he prediction of the future of a national economy is an inexact science of extrapolations and inferences from less than ideal, hardly exhaustive data and information. It is by and large an art of scenario painting based on images born of impressions, imaginations, and insights.

Images of Japan

In the last half century, images of Japan in the minds of Americans have changed wildly. Likewise, attitudes toward Japan have fluctuated over a wide gamut of emotions. This volatility of images and attitudes reflects a lack of durable perspectives and paradigms that can help generate a sound understanding of Japan's internal dynamics. It also implies that "Japanese studies," or any area studies for that matter, is a very soft science lacking the ability to predict.

Right after World War II, the United States had a punitive attitude toward Japan. This attitude quickly changed into condescending paternalism when Japan was drawn into the Cold War as a junior partner of the United States. With U.S. aid and encouragement, Japan recovered from the ravages of war and went on to achieve the "Japanese miracle" of rapid economic growth in the 1950s and 1960s. Japan stealthily pulled off this *economic* feat by lying low politically, diplomatically, and militarily. In the 1960s only a few seers sensed that Japan was on its way to a "superpower" status.[1] The "Japanese miracle" induced a period of U.S. admiration for Japan. A model of Japanese-style macroeconomic performance arose in its wake, further diversifying into stylizations of subsectors such as economic policy, organization and management, production methods, employment relations, labor movement, and so on, all capped by Japanese style or Japanese type.

The elaboration of Japanese style for a variety of phenomena became a minor growth industry. In the meantime, Japan's economic, political, and social realities kept changing in unpredictable fashion, under pressures of unanticipated changes, external as well as internal. The heavy and chemical industrialization of Japan during the 1960s produced enormous pollutions of all kinds, which turned the suffering public against the official growth-first policy. The first oil shock of 1973 derailed the Japanese model of rapid economic growth, and the restructured Japanese economy settled at growth rates half as much as before. Nevertheless, there was growth, and the Japanese economy steadily moved on to become an economic superstar. Aided by America's own internal malaise, U.S. attitudes toward Japan around 1980 were changing from Japanophilia to Japanophobia, which in the course of the 1980s developed into revisionism and Japan bashing.

A positive by-product of U. S. Japanophobia was the rise of a defensive mechanism to learn and apply the secrets of Japanese strengths. "Learn from Japan" intensified alongside Japan bashing. The learning effects contributed to a sophistication of U.S. industrial policy and a restructuring of industrial organization, management processes, production methods, labor-management relations, and many other microeconomic aspects with favorable effects on macroeconomic performance.[2] The U. S. efforts to learn from Japan during the 1980s yielded a handsome dividend in the form of sustained economic growth in the 1990s. With economic strength, U. S. confidence returned; Japan bashing changed into "Japan passing." The United States once again is asserting its global leadership as the sole hegemon in the post–Cold War world. Japan has dimmed in the American perception, while something new suddenly has loomed large and menacing over the East Asian horizon—China, where an economic "miracle" on a scale unheard of has been taking place.

A Closer Look at a Failed Prediction

When Ezra Vogel's *Japan as Number One* was selling briskly in Japan, the twenty-first century appeared to be preempted as the Japanese century.[3] But Vogel also contributed to the search for strategies to bring about an American resurgence to beat Japan.[4] He went on to examine the possibility of U.S.-Japan hegemonic competition.[5] During the 1980s there were many signs of Japan's ascendance in contrast to numerous signs of the United

States' decline. Studies of world history and theories of hegemonic power created an intellectual climate in the late 1980s in which the end of the U.S. hegemony appeared all but certain, even if Japan's ability or willingness to succeed the United States as a new world hegemon was unclear or only tentatively acknowledged.[6]

In hindsight, the idea of Japan and the United States engaged in hegemonic competition for world leadership and the prediction of the twenty-first century as a Japanese century sound preposterous. During the 1980s many comparative analyses of the United States and Japan that emphasized economic performance chalked up Japan's strengths one after another against contrasting U. S. weaknesses. A most glaring contrast was the rise of Japan as the world's biggest creditor nation together with the United States' becoming the world's biggest debtor nation. This gave rise to speculations that it was only a matter of time before Japan's economic power would translate into awesome political and military power, while the overstretched United States would have to close down its economic and military operations in many areas of the world. It looked as if one hegemon was retreating and another taking its place. Since hegemonic succession historically has never been peaceful, some observers of the U.S.-Japan relations even speculated on the outbreak of a shooting war between them to determine who should rule the world.[7]

Such a war for world hegemony is certainly an ill-advised conjecture at its extreme. In the closing years of the twentieth century, the United States still amply demonstrates its will and capability to manage the post–Cold War world. By itself the United States does not have enough resources, economic or military, to enforce Pax Americana in the traditional hegemonic way, as in the case of Pax Britannica. The world has grown too big and too diverse, economically, politically, and militarily, for any one nation-state to rule. The key word that makes post–Cold War U.S. hegemony different from the past hegemonies is *management*—the creation and maintenance of a durable institutional infrastructure of international relations ("public goods") and the orchestration of the roles and activities of the world's nation-states to maintain peace, preventing or pacifying localized international conflicts instigated by some rogue states. This is a different kind of hegemony from its historical predecessors. In this kind of world order, Japan, with its considerable economic resources but with little else, can contribute to the world peace and stability as a good number two working together with the United States.[8]

The 1990–1991 Gulf war was in many ways symbolic of the new U.S. hegemony, especially of the U.S.-Japan relations in a U.S.-led world order.

The United States succeeded in mobilizing international military forces by diplomatic leadership. With respect to Japan, which is constitutionally barred from military participation, the United States assessed a huge peace-making/keeping "tax." The receipt of this tax temporarily balanced the deficit-ridden U.S. current account of international trade in goods and services. Japan's role as the supplier of resources and auxiliary paramilitary services under the U.S. leadership has been in practice in East Asia under the U.S.-Japan Mutual Security Treaty for nearly 50 years. This bilateral alliance can be expected to last at least another quarter century, setting the immediate international context Japan is beholden to. Any prediction of what the twenty-first century holds in store for Japan must acknowledge the existence of this U.S.-Japan alliance as an institutional context. The illusion of a Japanese century has evaporated. Japan is a junior partner of the United States in Pax Americana.

The Dimming of Japan: Macroeconomic Trends

In the light of widely publicized comparative growth rates of the gross national products of various national economies (routinely published by the United Nations, the World Bank, and other international organizations), it is puzzling that Japan was perceived, until recently, as a country of exceptional economic growth. In the last 25 years Japanese economic growth has been paltry in comparison with that of many other countries, especially that of Asian countries. The mother of all economic miracles is taking place in China, a nation whose population makes up one-fourth of the human race. Japan's low economic growth rate implies that its weight in the world economy, especially in the Asian, is declining.

In the late 1990s the popular perception of Japan finally has caught up with comparative economic realities, and attention is shifting from Japan to China. How to relate to and profit from China's spectacular economic growth is now a priority in foreign economic policies of many countries, including Japan. There is a rush of foreign investment in China. In other words, China has become a magnet for the world's economic adventures and a centerpiece in the discussion of the world's future. The twenty-first century may well be a Chinese century. Thus Japan no longer commands much weight in thinking about the world's future.

Away from the popular spotlight, sober reevaluations of comparative performances of national economies have made a quiet progress in recent years. For the international comparison of incomes and productivities, values expressed in units of diverse national currencies must be converted to values in units of a common yardstick, such as the U.S. dollar. For this purpose, purchasing power parity (PPP) has come to be regarded as a more defensible conversion rate than the conventional foreign exchange rate.[9] The use of PPP for international income or productivity comparisons has exposed crucial structural weaknesses of the Japanese economy that have been hidden by the pervasive euphoria over the (now somewhat illusory) economic power of Japan based on the use of foreign exchange rates.

How figures diverge according to the conversion rates used for comparison may be illustrated by differences between the results of conversion based on foreign exchange rates and those based on PPP. The 1993 Japanese gross national product (GNP) per capita converted by the dollar-yen exchange rate was $31,490. The U.S. GNP per capita for the same year was $24,740, more than 30 percent below the Japanese figure.[10] However, when the conversion is based on PPP, the 1993 Japanese gross domestic product (GDP) per capita was only $20,660, while that of the United States was $24,680, nearly 20 percent *above* the Japanese figure.[11] (Some, although only a small, difference should be expected between GDP and GNP as seen here for the United States.) These figures imply that the use of the foreign exchange rate results in a more than 50 percent overestimate of Japan's "real" GNP or GDP. In other words, the Japanese domestic price level is 50 percent higher than the international price level. This is the well-known internal/external price gap of Japan, which implies that the Japanese markets are extensively protected against price-equalizing international competition. Various estimates of nontariff barriers that limit foreign access to the Japanese markets often turn up astounding internal/international price gaps for tradable goods.[12]

The reversal in the relative positions of Japan and the United States depending on which conversion rate is used, foreign exchange rate or PPP, makes all that 1980s excitement about Japan's ascendance to a hegemonic status sound rather silly. On the basis of PPP, Japan has not yet caught up with the United States in terms of per-capita national income. Americans are still better off than the Japanese. Even the Japanese now admit that their standard of living, when compared with that of the United States, is not particularly enviable despite the decades of fabled economic growth. Thus a popular saying has arisen: "Japan is powerful, but life in Japan is painful." (This "contradiction" between the *country's* power and wealth on one hand and the *people's* welfare and comforts on the other has been a perennial problem in Japan).[13] This contradiction arises from the unusual degree of autonomy that the state bureaucracy enjoys in policy formulation and enforcement without sufficient attention or sensitivity to the social cost of policy suffered by the general public other than the favored beneficiaries. The consequences of toxic emissions and effluents from nationally promoted industries are a case in point. Thus the saying: "The *nation* prospers (by industrialization), but the *people* perish (under pollution)."

Lately the Japanese government has come to realize the contradiction between the nation's economic power and the people's living conditions and begun to take measures for overcoming it. The slogan adopted for the purpose is "Japan as a lifestyle superpower." This English phrase is an eye-catching, but it's an opaque translation of a somewhat untranslatable Japanese original, *seikatsu taikoku*.[14] It may be paraphrased as "a country where people live it up in a grand style." The image of living it up implied is none other than the conventional "all-American" lifestyle (fast disappearing in the United States itself): bigger houses, shorter work and school weeks, more vacations, more leisure and comforts, more family togetherness and recreation, freedom from stress and inconveniences, and so on. It also implies a shift in values from loyalty to the company to the autonomy of the individual, which is no easy matter in a country of weak individualism and strong groupism, as the theories of Japanese-style management have propounded relentlessly.

Even so, if Japan currently is retreating from an aspiration to national glory by maximizing economic growth, this turnaround should be important in thinking about the nation's future. Macroeconomic implications of the policy that accords priority to living would be more consumption and less saving, reducing the potential growth rate of the economy in the long run. Even without the official lifestyle policy, however, Japan's saving ratio has been declining over time.[15] A conceivable extrapolation from this, with the help of economic theory, would be that in the remote future, savings would decline to the level just enough to replace the wear and tear of capital stock. As forces slowly move in this direction, the predominant source of economic growth would have to be technological progress. But since Japan has reached the world's technological frontier, more technological progress would have to be generated from within. Doing this would be costly compared with imitative technological progress, Japan's trademark until recently, based on imported technologies at bargain prices from other "advanced" countries. All this implies that as we move deeper into the twenty-first century, the Japanese economy will increasingly become a typical textbook case of "steady state" at a high level of per-capita income growing at a rate permitted only by largely endogenous technological progress.[16] Indeed, many Japanese economists already are talking about a growth rate of 3 percent as the best that the Japanese economy would achieve in the years to come. This is the historical rate of growth of the U.S. economy. While growth rates converge, the existing differential in the *level* of income and productivity not in favor of Japan will persist.

The preceding paragraph must be qualified by considering how another variable behaves. The above assumes that, in Japan, all savings are invested in capital formation. But the problem, already present in the Japanese economy in the last fifteen years, is that domestic capital formation is weaker than the people's propensity to save; that is, domestic savings are not fully channeled into capital formation, so that a portion of the savings are exported and invested in foreign economies. Eventually, then, the domestic demand for a net addition to the capital stock would diminish to zero, and the portion of domestic savings that exceed the need for replacement investment would be exported to the rest of the world. The upshot of this process is that the Japanese people would increasingly become rentiers living off the earnings of their capital, supplemented no doubt by some paid work. Their living conditions will be rich, comfortable, and relaxed. Japan then may indeed be considered a "lifestyle superpower."

This scenario of Japan's convergence toward a high-income steady state becomes more credible if we consider demographic trends. In 1992 the Ministry of Welfare estimated that the Japanese population would peak at 130 million in 2011 and decrease to below 100 million by 2074. According to the ministry's projections based on the 1990 census, the Japanese population 65 years or older would exceed 25 percent of the total by 2020 and 30 percent by 2030. In the last five years, the decline in the birth rate has turned out to be greater than assumed in the 1990-based projections. The new estimates move up the peaking of the population to 2007 at 127 million and the date of decline to 100 million to 2050.[17] According to these latest estimates, in 2050 32.3 percent of the population will be 65 years or older. In the phraseology much liked by the Japanese, this would make Japan a *koreisha taikoku* (Aged Superpower, a country that is great by the number and proportion of the elderly population). Since the Japanese do not seem to be alarmed by these demographic projections, one might assume that they are gracefully resigned to the inevitability of their society's aging and the decline in vitality that aging brings about.

Cycles and Microeconomic Responses

Japan's economic growth stopped twice in the last 50 years: in 1974 and 1993. The slightly negative growth rate of 1974 (minus 0.7 percent) was like a racecar coming to a screeching halt. In the late 1960s, the Japanese economy was growing at 11 percent. This high growth rate, apparently unsustainable, faltered for internal reasons, but more dramatically, it was brought down by two major exogenous shocks; the Nixon shock of 1971, which revalued the exchange rate for the yen by 17 percent and the first oil shock of 1973, which revolutionized the cost of energy. In the rest of the 1970s, Japan's growth rate ranged between 4.0 percent and 5.5 percent, less than half as high as in the late 1960s. This lowered growth rate was further aggravated by the second oil shock in 1979; the growth rates from 1980 to 1985 ranged between 3.2 and 4.8 percent, lower than in the preceding five years. The Plaza Accord of September 1995 among the Group of Seven countries brought about a sharp appreciation of the Japanese yen and induced a short-lived recession in 1986. A new policy to stimulate the domestic demand then created an economic boom celebrated as "the Bubble," which burst in January 1990, giving rise to a prolonged five-year recession.

The growth rates during the Bubble were not spectacular. From 1987 to 1990 they ranged between 4.5 and 6.0 percent, modest but the best since the collapse of rapid growth in the mid-1970s. The extraordinary characteristics of the Bubble appeared in the real-estate markets and stock markets, stimulated by monetary expansion and low interest rates. The Tokyo Stock Price Index (TOPIX), which equaled 100 in 1983, peaked at 394 at the end of 1989, while the land prices in six major cities peaked at 488 in the following year.[18] During this short period, an unusually bullish psychology took hold of the Japanese: Many apparently believed that the boom would last forever. On the U.S. side, Japan's apparently unstoppable economic aggression struck terror into American hearts: The Japanese were buying up America.[19] However, a lone author was able to see through the tangles of "irrational exuberance" and warned the public that "The Sun Also Sets."[20]

Between 1987 and 1989 Japanese corporations found money easy to borrow for investment in capacity expansion and for stock market speculation. They also raised funds in stock markets, where their shares quickly sold and appreciated, reducing the cost of capital to zero or below. Individuals also briskly borrowed money and bought securities, land, and houses. Wealthier Japanese bought up classic Western paintings, driving up the auction prices in the art markets. During this period or from a little earlier, the Japanese government privatized major public corporations (Japan National Railways, Nippon Telephone & Telegraph, and other public monopolies) and, fortunately at the beginning, the eager public immediately bought their shares at outrageous prices.

The Bank of Japan raised the official discount rate in steps in 1989 but kept the money supply increasing. Monetary expansion slowed in 1990, stopping altogether two years later. As a consequence, the Bubble burst and kept shrinking. Stock and property prices began turning down at the beginning of 1990. After a lag, industrial production followed suit. According to the government, the recession began in April 1991 and ended in October 1993. The GNP growth rate decreased from 5.3 percent in 1990 to 0.1 percent in 1993. The recovery in 1994 and 1995 was anemic, not yet reaching even 1 percent. The rate of unemployment, which usually lags behind the business cycle, kept increasing, from a low of 2.1 percent in 1990 to an all-time high of 3.4 percent in 1996.[21] (Although the figure is low, the "real" unemployment rate—the rate one would, for example, obtain by using the U.S. labor force concepts and methods—is generally considered twice as high as the official Japanese rate.) The year 1996 chalked up a GNP growth rate of 3.1 percent, suggesting that for the first time in six years, the Japanese economy was returning to normal. Still, it was widely believed that the encouraging growth rate of 1996 was a one-time effect of massive fiscal and monetary stimuli which would quickly dissipate. (I present a different view later.)

The stock prices bottomed out in 1995 at less than 40 percent of the peak prices of 1989; in the spring of 1997 they were fluctuating around 45 percent of the peak. In 1996 land prices apparently bottomed out at a 12-year low. It is extraordinary that these asset price indices have been unable to return to their previous peak levels. Together with the record level of unemployment, they are signaling that the Japanese economy is still morbid. One bright sign, which can be internationally troublesome, is that Japanese exports are increasing, aided by a weak yen, which has depreciated more than 50 percent since its peak strength in the spring of 1995. The Japanese trade surplus is beginning to rise, foreboding trade conflict with the United States and other countries. Already the charge is being heard that Japan again is trying to export itself out of the recession.

The boom, bust, and stagnation cycle of 1987 to 1996 is unusual in the postwar chronicle of Japanese business cycles. Economic woes since the burst of the Bubble in 1989–1990 have been complicated by domestic and foreign pressures for institutional, organizational, and structural reforms. Foreign pressures (*gai'atsu*), principally from the United States, led Japan's reform movement. Annoyed by a chronic bilateral Japanese trade surplus and having failed to remedy it by the conventional measures of trade protection and exchange rate manipulations, the United States in 1985–1986 engaged Japan in the Market Oriented Sector Specific (MOSS) negotiations targeted at the opening of specific markets. In 1989–1990, the U. S. Structural Impediments Initiative (SII) demanded Japanese action on a series of regulatory and competition issues that were thought to be obstacles to increased foreign sales in Japan. Japan, a regulatory superpower (*kisei taikoku*), thus was prompted into deregulation, initially unwillingly, but gradually embracing it as a national priority. The year 1990 was informally declared the Deregulation Year 1. The SII negotiations were succeeded by talks based on the Framework for a New Economic Partnership jointly announced in July 1993. The talks covered macroeconomic as well as sectoral and industrial policies.

Foreign pressures have become a domestic policy instrument in Japan providing excuses and support for actions that otherwise would be difficult to enforce due to opposition from domestic vested interests. Foreign pressures are unpleasant to any government, but in the 1990s the Japanese have been surprisingly receptive to the U.S. demands for far-reaching changes in the rules of running their economy. In a sense, the United States represents voices of the Japanese consumers in national economic policymaking, which hitherto has been dominated by the producer interests. The 1996 *Economic Report of the President* mentions that the United States and Japan had concluded 20 trade agreements, the latest being in automobiles and auto parts, financial services, and investment. These agreements are said to have produced faster growth of U.S. exports to Japan in the covered sectors than the overall growth of U.S. exports to Japan.[22] "Foreign pressure" is prying open the "closed" Japanese markets.

The previously mentioned internal/external price gap in Japan now is widely admitted to be due to overregulation of private economic initiatives and the government's stranglehold on domestic and international market forces. Deregulation and market opening would streamline production and distribution in concert with global market forces and contribute to macroeconomic growth. Deregulation strikes at the heart of the "systemic" forces that have made postwar Japanese economic growth a world-renowned success story. Economists are aware, however, that 1945 was a long time ago and that the "Japanese system" that produced miracle growth during the first half of the post-1945 period, roughly up to the early 1970s, has increasingly ossified, restraining growth and efficient resource allocation.[23] Numerous structural anomalies of the Japanese economy as measured by standards of major industrial countries have surfaced since the 1980s. The upshot is the impression that Japan is not a "normal" country and that all sorts of reforms are needed to make it so. In 1993 politics of normalization (as it were) brought down the long one-party rule that earlier had overseen Japan's miracle growth and later became a nest of special interests and scandals.[24]

Of course, Japan is not standing still. Rule making is a continuous process. Deregulation does not come in the form of wiping the slate clean at one stroke. In Japan, progress has been slow but steady.[25] The Economic Planning Agency from time to time has measured the effects of deregulations. The latest estimates for the period from 1990 to 1996 covering 11 sectors (gas and electricity, telecommunications, oil refining, airlines, auto inspection, etc.) put the annual gains to the general public at 0.97 percent of GDP.[26] This seems to imply that but for the deregulations, GDP growth from 1993 to 1995 would have been negative. Further, it may imply that when such economic growth from deregulation is combined with the cyclical upturn of the economy, the GDP growth rate might rise to a respectable level, say more than 3 percent over a medium term, enabling Japan to cross into the twenty-first century smiling all the way to the bank. Eventually the process of deregulation will come to an end, and the deregulated Japanese economy will have to rely on the strength and rationality of the market forces that completed deregulation brings about.

The End of "Japan, Inc."

The Japanese system that produced all the great economic achievements earlier and that currently is blamed for many recent failures is known as "Japan, Inc." In the 1990s Japan, Inc. has been greatly weakened and in need of reform or overhaul. Japanese receptivity to restructuring and deregulation in the 1990s is part of the general climate of change in reaction to visible failures of the established institutions that until recently had guided Japanese economic successes. Japan, Inc. was based on the "iron triangle" of the ruling conservative Liberal Democratic Party (LDP), the permanent State Bureaucracy, and the Business Community comprised of a few major peak business/employer organizations. The LDP ruled Japan since 1955 but lost control of the Diet (parliament) in 1993 due to internal dissensions and public disaffection. Irregularities in election financing and seamy deals with special business groups have weakened public support for the LDP. State bureaucrats, traditionally thought to be incorruptible, also have fallen prey to influences of special interests, resulting in several high-profile bribery cases. Sections of the business community also have been rocked by major scandals of influence peddling, bid rigging, and improper transactions in stocks, bonds, and foreign exchange.

Even without scandals, Japan, Inc. has developed numerous inefficiencies in the structure and process of policymaking that signal the need for restructuring and reorganization. A laundry list of desired reforms may be summarized as follows: (1) economic structural reform (which is understandably preempted by the "notorious MITI"—Ministry of International Trade and Industry), (2) reform of public finance, (3) reform of the monetary/financial system (so-called Big Bang), (4) administrative reform, (5) structural reform of social security, and (6) educational reform. The LDP, the largest of minority parties, recovered the privilege to govern solo in January 1996, and Prime Minister Ryutaro Hashimoto (in office beginning January 1996) has proposed a number of far-reaching reform programs. His particular concern is administrative reform. Previous non-LDP governments since 1993 made deregulation (*kisei kanwa*) a household word.

Over the years, there have grown up too many state ministries, agencies, commissions, committees, and councils with fierce commitments to sectional interests, losing sight of the overall national interest. There is a definite need for administrative reform. Ministries and agencies need to be consolidated and reconfigured to eliminate current functional or jurisdictional overlaps. Many commissions, committees, and councils simply have to go. The overly centralized administrative structure needs to distribute power to prefectural and local governments. The prime minister has expressed a desire to cut the 22 extant ministries and agencies, each headed by a minister of state, to 11.

Besides numerous regulations, the mother of all regulations, called "administrative guidance," is based on the discretionary power of the bureaucracy to make extra-legal, sometimes arbitrary, intrusions into the strategies and operations of individual firms. The Japanese bureaucrats have been above the law in this sense. Bringing bureaucrats "under" the law alone would constitute a major administrative reform. A new Administrative Procedure Law, recently passed, for the first time requires that administrative guidance be justified by reference to relevant laws and communicated to the targeted firms in writing. This does not sound much by general standards but is lauded in Japan as landmark legislation that may at least restrain arbitrary bureaucratic intrusions into private business. Much more is needed to bring about civilized "transparency" (a concept suddenly popular in Japan) in government-economy or government-society relations.

Reforms that are of special importance to economic policymaking are those of the Ministry of Finance (MOF) and the Bank of Japan (BOJ). In addition to the conventional treasury functions involving revenue, expenditure, and budget deficit or surplus, the MOF controls or supervises the Bank of Japan (BOJ), banks, securities brokerages, public investment programs, and so on. Nothing monetary or financial escapes the MOF's attention. Naturally, the MOF has become the prime target of criticism for its "regulatory failures" that permitted the Bubble in the first place and then failed to get Japan out of the post-Bubble recession quickly. With the collapse of the stock and property markets, banks, housing loan companies (created by banks), brokerage houses, credit unions, and cooperatives ended up with staggering volumes of nonperforming loans. Rescue of these financial institutions has been a top priority on the policy agenda, and politicians have become serious about reforming the MOF.

The reform ideas include an independent BOJ, a securities and exchange commission, a banking oversight commission, and other agencies taking over the budget and treasury functions.[27] These ideas imply a breakup and demise of the MOF as the Japanese have known it. Naturally MOF bureaucrats have mounted a massive counteroffensive with their own reform ideas. Out of the melee, there first emerged a bill for a more independent BOJ. The bill was passed by the parliament in June 1997, ensuring the autonomy of the BOJ's Policy Committee in decision making regarding monetary policy. However, MOF representatives were allowed to be present as occasions justified, although without voting rights, at the committee's meetings.

Closely following the new BOJ law, the parliament also enacted a law to detach from the MOF and to consolidate in a new agency the functions of overseeing banks and financial institutions. The new unit, called the Financial Supervisory Agency, was to be placed organizationally in the prime minister's office. But the MOF has since been scheming to (physically) keep the agency in its own building for the ease and closeness of working relationships. Thus some important functional responsibilities are being moved out of the MOF, although informal, dotted-line relationships might be devised so that the MOF would still continue to influence the spun-off units.

Another area for reform is the Fiscal Investment and Loan Program (FILP) controlled by the MOF.[28] Reform here would be extremely difficult, because it involves more than 100 public corporations and the largest "savings bank" in the world, called Postal Savings System. Currently the Postal Savings System is run by the Ministry of Posts and Telecommunications (MOPT), the social security trust funds, and the MOF as the investment program's managing, operating, and overseeing agent. The ideal reform would be a total dismantling of the FILP by a full privatization of the public corporations and postal savings. As a consequence, the MOF's Trust Fund Bureau, which is in charge of the FILP, will have to be abolished. The process of privatization of the public corporations will come up against the problem of what to do with the chronic losses and accumulated debts of these enterprises, which the FILP currently cleverly covers up. Further, the MOPT would not willingly let go of its Postal Savings System. People's savings under this system are in essence a national debt; if clearly recognized as such, they would horrify anyone sensitive to the national debt problem. In 1996, Japan's bond-financed national and local government debt already reached as high as 88 percent of the nation's annual GDP.[29] In April 1997 the Administrative Reform Council, under prodding by Prime Minister Hashimoto, produced some rough plans to privatize the Postal Savings System along with other reform plans, including reorganization of the entire executive branch of the government, implementation of a "Big Bang," and other measures. The prime minister's aim is to put the Japanese government and economy on an entirely new footing by the year 2001.

The Japanese financial system is well known for its extreme Glass-Steagall type of segmentation by function and purpose (encouraged during General Douglas MacArthur's administration during the occupation). The MOF has been quite successful in divide-and-rule over Japan's financial sector, but its very success in the past has now become a major liability. The reform envisaged here is an imitation of the British Big Bang, enabling all financial enterprises to enter competitively into any kind of financial transactions—commercial banking, long-term credit, brokerage, insurance, trust funds, foreign exchange, and so on. For some time the Big Bang was only talk without any serious consequences, but lately sentiments appear to be drifting toward an eventual acceptance of some version of it as inevitable in the near future.

At the level of general competition policy to strengthen the sinews of the market economy, the role and place of the Fair Trade Commission that enforces the Anti-Monopoly Law has been questioned. The commission first must be protected against interference by the Ministry of International Trade and Industry (MITI), which long has dabbled in industrial structure policy, often by subverting the market forces. The MITI's industrial policy by and large succeeded in guiding structural changes for the Japanese economy during the catchup (rapid-growth) period prior to the oil shock of 1973. During those days, the MITI picked the right industries to encourage (heavy and chemical industries) and the right industries to discourage (coal mining, textiles, etc.).

In the 1980s, however, the MITI made a few high-profile errors: It picked and encouraged wrong industries, such as computer hardware (fifth-generation computer) while neglecting software development, high-definition television (analog design) at the expense of digital HDTV. The business community also felt the MITI was making too many concessions to the United States in trade and investment policies. Today the MITI's influence over Japanese firms and industries is considerably weaker than in the 1950s and 1960s. Oddly enough, if the MITI tends to fail in picking winners to lead economic growth, it is still highly effective in regulating and orchestrating the downsizing of firms caught up in declining industries as well as organizing "recession cartels" for an equitable sharing of shrinking markets among the existing firms.

Under MITI administrative guidance, Japan's industrial policy does not operate in a vacuum. It works through close collaboration with "private governments"—the well-known *keiretsu* (major firms from a broad cross-section of industries in "horizontal" alliance and generally perceived to be capable of cooperation verging upon collusion) and trade associations that regulate entry and pricing in various industries.[30] In fact, the MITI promoted *keiretsu* formation in reaction to what it considered "excessive competition" brought about by General MacArthur's trust busting. At the national policymaking level, business interests are overrepresented on the MITI's Industrial Structure Council.[31] In August 1997 the Administrative Reform Council announced a number of suggestions, including a new Economic Ministry to be cobbled out of the MITI, parts of the EPA, and parts of the MOPT.

If working relationships among the member firms of the above "horizontal" *keiretsu* are rather opaque, the hierarchical supplier/distributor network around a major firm ("vertical" *keiretsu*) is tightly organized and work flow within the network is more efficient than that in an integrated firm (e.g., "just-in-time" delivery systems in manufacturing.) In construction, however, the *keiretsu* is a collusive grouping of firms capable of raising costs and prices. There a handful of general contractors allocate work among themselves by secret consultation (*dango*), and each distributes work down the hierarchical chain of subcontractors. In recent years the Fair Trade Commission has discovered and prosecuted several cases of *dango* as violations of the Anti-Monopoly Law. In other industries such as transportation and utilities, regional monopolies are the rule, and interregional coordination of operations as well as the regulation of entry is effected through consultation and cooperation of all the affected parties. These and other anticompetitive practices are entrenched, and enforcement of rules of competition has been generally lax. There seems to be a strong undertone in Japanese business behavior that shuns open, transparent competition in favor of secret deals and agreements. Ubiquitous "trade associations" as private regulatory mechanisms are expressions of the deep-seated propensity for "clans" as desirable organizations.[32] Official regulations often maintain and further strengthen the entrenched anti-competitive behavior of the private sector.[33]

A short, illuminating definition of a *keiretsu* is offered by C. Fred Bergsten and Marcus Noland: "A *keiretsu* might consist of a group of large core firms horizontally linked across markets, together with their vertically linked input suppliers, and possibly a captive distribution network."[34] Six large *keiretsu* conform to this description. They comprise about 200 core firms in total; their subsidiaries and affiliates, in which the core firms own at least 10 percent of shares, number about 1,200 firms. These six *keiretsu*, also known as Six Big Enterprise Groups or, in short, Big Six, account for one-third of Japan's paid-in capital, one-fourth of its assets, and one-fourth of sales.[35] The cited proportions seem large for "only six" business groups, but it should be remembered that the number of firms involved is also rather large.

Aggregative ideal/typical descriptions of *keiretsu* tend to give the impression of a monolithic entity pursuing "monopoly profit." Within a *keiretsu*, each member firm is from a different industry, and member firms favor interindustry business as much as possible. But between *keiretsu*, interfirm competition within the same industries, especially in manufacturing, is extremely keen. At least in manufacturing, firms from different *keiretsu* competing in the same industry do not get together in the interest of anticompetitive practices. Inter*keiretsu* collusion does not exist in manufacturing. Six *keiretsu* means that there are at least six major (core) firms competing vigorously in the same product markets, such as steel, machinery, automobiles, electronics; *keiretsu* loyalties ensure inter*keiretsu*, interfirm competition.

Vertical *keiretsu* often is perceived as a mechanism by which the core firm exploits its subsidiaries, affiliates, subcontractors, sub-subcontractors, and so on down the line. The vulnerability of a subordinate firm to the core firm's exploitation depends to a large extent on the proportion of the core firm's orders in the subordinate's total business. The usual stereotype of a vertical *keiretsu* assumes that this proportion is 100 percent. But there is no constraint on a supplier's effort to diversify customers so long as capacity is large enough to produce more than the *keiretsu* leader's orders. Besides, the relationships between the core firm and its subcontractors are not always exploitative. The core firm often assists the subcontractors with capital, personnel, and technology.

The internal cohesion of the horizontal *keiretsu* is likely to weaken in the days of globalization. The principal agents of change are the manufacturing members of the *keiretsu*. Each of them is now a very large, multinational firm with its own national and international vertical *keiretsu* and alliances. For example, it means little for the Toyota Motor Company (leading the Toyota Group, a vertical *keiretsu*) to be a member of the Mitsui *Keiretsu*, or for Nissan Motor (leading the Nissan Group) to be a member of the Fuyo

Keiretsu. The *keiretsu* bank, which is conventionally the hub of the group as a "main bank" for its members, is undergoing restructuring under pressures for diversification, which will accelerate under the government's reform plans. The *keiretsu* trading company, which used to be an exclusive export agent for member firms of the group, has lost that historic function, simply because each manufacturing member is now quite capable of handling its own international trade (as Toyota or Nissan is).

Even among the Big Six, group solidarity differs. Three older groups, such as Mitsui, Mitsubishi, and Sumitomo, most closely fit the ideal type of *keiretsu*. The other three are relatively new and were put together as *keiretsu* by the core banks taking on willing applicants from other industries. On the whole, they practice a relatively open membership policy with rather free entries and exits. Double or triple memberships with other *keiretsu* are also tolerated. These may be considered a harbinger of future business groupings that would be only a shadow of today's *keiretsu*. Foreign firms in Japan would find the door open for future *keiretsu* membership, although the benefits of such membership would then be rather uncertain.

The Japanese-Style Management System

Inside firms, a distinct type of human resource management (HRM) and industrial relations (IR) developed during the period of "miracle growth" (no doubt in response to contingencies of growth under the then-unusual conditions such as recovery from the devastations of war and the requirements of catching up to Japan's own past and the new standards set by advanced countries) and has since been entrenched. It too is in for reform. When the U.S.-Japan comparison of productivity became popular in Japan in the late 1970s (apparently largely motivated by the Japanese desire to watch when precisely Japan would overtake the United States in terms of productivity), a few structural anomalies of human resource utilization (products of the Japanese-style HRM and IR) became well known.

1. Productivity in manufacturing on the whole was coming very close to the U.S. level, but the productivity gap between export-oriented front-runner industries/firms and protected domestically oriented laggards was astoundingly large.[36]
2. Even in the best-run firms, productivity on the shop floor was high, but white-collar productivity was low relative to U.S. firms. The secrets of shop-floor productivity were later discovered and christened "lean production."[37]

3. The female and aged labor force was vastly underutilized because of the mechanism of discrimination built into the fabled Japanese-style management.
4. The overall trend toward fewer working hours came to a halt in the late 1970s. Since then contradictory trends have developed: Employed persons have been working harder and longer, while the rate of unemployment has been on the rise. In the course of the 1980s, "death from overwork" (*karoshi*) became not only a novel statistical heading but also a legal category of injury and death on the job, entitling the victims and their survivors to workers' compensation.

These imbalances or contradictions in the structure of productivity implied faults Japanese-style HRM/IR system. Remedies required a full opening of Japanese industries, firms, and products to international competition so that the economy and industry might be restructured on the basis of comparative advantage and efficiency. This meant that the MITI's traditional structural policy had to be redesigned. Equal employment opportunity had to be ensured to all participants in the labor force, regardless of age, sex, or other differences. Working hours had to be limited, while extended periods of leave from work had to be encouraged. All that required new laws, which were enacted, if piecemeal, in the late 1980s after many years of debate and discussion. The results, however, have been rather modest so far.

The discussion of the Japanese-style HRM/IR system traditionally has turned on the "three treasures" of lifetime employment, wage determination by length of service, and the enterprise union (ideally, one union for all the employees of a firm). Management practices that used to make the three treasures an efficient system have come under strain as the Japanese economy has "matured"[38] and heads for an unknown technological future under intensified global competition. There are limits to the continued effective learning and skill growth on the part of employees, some of whom burn out long before their "lifetime" company employment comes to an end. Weeding them out in their 40s and 50s, instead of keeping them on the ever-rising age-wage profile, has become a managerial priority.

Hiring only a roughly homogeneous cohort of new employees fresh out of school or college every year and training them in stages as they move up on job ladders throughout their lifetimes of employment have become too cumbersome under rapid technological development. Strategic flexibility often requires immediately usable new skills, which are increasingly available by mobile specialists obtainable from the labor markets or worker loaning firms (created under a new law that authorizes labor market intermediation).

Lifetime employment used to be lauded for an optimal combination of a "rigid" implicit lifetime employment contract with the "flexibility" of lifetime learning and skill improvements.[39] Yet rapid technological change has increased the required flexibility many times faster than before, and not all employees can advance year after year in lock-step. Midcareer workers who drop out of their "main" careers join the ranks of mobile workers with less job security. Periods between jobs lengthen, which show up as a trend increase in the aggregate unemployment rate.

Major firms now openly advocate and increasingly practice a contractual diversification of their workforces. They retain only the best for lifetime employment. Many employees are terminated at various stages of their careers (of course, with sweetened inducements for early retirement and generous help for transfers and outplacements, never by brute force). Specialized temps are used in increasing numbers. Compensation is tied increasingly to individual performance. Ultimately, work processes and job ranks are "reengineered," implying the fall of the Japanese icon of *ringisei*, a slow upward spiral of a strategic initiative originating at the "bottom" as a preferred decision-making process. All this further implies a more active, agile top management, which together with a newly found need for attention to the stockholder interest would spell a minor revolution in company governance and management style.

Major firms' ability to employ is being reduced by their own need to invest in overseas production under the pressures of high labor costs at home and the strong yen. They thus contribute to a hollowing out of the Japanese economy. Overseas production by Japanese firms is still a small proportion of their total production. This bodes ill for the future of Japanese employment, for in the near future an increased outflow of Japanese capital, technology, and entrepreneurship is expected, which would exacerbate the weakened demand for labor at home. The outflow of Japanese capital may be made up for in part by an inflow of foreign capital. Receiving such an inflow, however, requires a major effort on Japan's part to open its market to inward foreign investment, which is naturally part of the ongoing drive for deregulation. A harder part of it is that Japan's traditional "neomercantilist" trade and investment policy (encouraging exports while controlling imports) must give way to more two-way interactions with the rest of the world in trade, investment, services, and technology.

If the traditional Japanese-style employment system breaks down and there is no need to maintain the steeply rising age/wage profile, the problem of age discrimination in employment under the system of mandatory retirement at a certain age will solve itself. So long as older workers are willing to work in positions different from their peak careers for appropriately lower wages commensurate with reduced responsibilities and lower productivity, employers will consider them a good bargain. Furthermore, mandatory retirement is increasingly meaningless as early retirement becomes more widely practiced.

Sex discrimination in employment is another matter. It will be more difficult to eliminate, for the Equal Employment Opportunity Law has no teeth. The law only encourages employers to endeavor not to discriminate against women in various facets of employment management—hiring, training, assignment, promotion, retirement, and the like. The fact that national efforts against sex discrimination are still at this stage in the mid-1990s merely indicates that values change slowly and that there is no guarantee that economic growth always brings about changes in values in favor of gender equality.[40] However, the ongoing decline in the fertility rate implies that the women's reproductive "duties" are weakening and that women will have more time for employment outside the households. At the same time, women's level of education is rising all the time, and technological progress increasingly favors highly educated workers. A high degree of gender equality is long overdue in Japan. That it has not been attained even at the close of the twentieth century probably will be remembered as a mystery of Japan that defies the usual correlation between economic development and social progress.

Conclusion

At present, Japan is in turmoil, to say the least. One era is over, and another era is beginning. It is amazing that so many indicators for all sectors of Japanese polity, society, and economy converge to testify to one era's end. Past policies, rules, and practices have broken down, and something has to be done about them. Some people only want them repaired. Repair may produce a restoration of the status quo ante or a minimal renovation within the existing structure. Others wish for a clean break with the past and a new beginning. Amazingly, it is the LDP's Prime Minister Hashimoto who espouses this radical wish most ardently. He envisages a totally new design of the government and economy by 2001.

Prosaic inferences from well-known socioeconomic fundamentals would turn up no great surprises. Japanese society is aging rapidly with implications for increased social security burden and reduced savings. Domestic capital formation is also slowing down, and a sustainable economic growth for the mature economy of Japan may be about 3 percent or less in the long run.

Savings still would continue to be larger than domestic capital formation, the difference being exported and invested in foreign assets or production. Restructuring, deregulation, and reengineering heighten resource mobility inside Japan and between it and the rest of the world. As more Japanese investment takes place in other countries, more foreign investment will come into Japan, helping Japan take on a more internationalized appearance. Increased foreign presence implies increased foreign practices in production, marketing, management, employment relations, and the like. At the same time, deregulation will encourage Japanese firms and workers to move away from "uniquely" Japanese practices toward winning strategies, whether domestic or foreign in origin. Japan finally would become a "normal" country, looking and acting very much like any other industrialized country.

Deregulation at the national policy level and restructuring/reengineering at the industry and firm levels are consciously pursued by Japanese politicians, administrators, and businessmen in the context of a closer integration of the world economy. Major Japanese companies—those that are regular members of the "horizontal" *keiretsu*—have been increasingly multinationalized. The top-tier suppliers in their "vertical" *keiretsu* also have followed them into other countries. However, as measured by the proportion of production abroad or of headquarters personnel who are foreign, the Japanese multinationals still lag far behind American multinationals. In the aggregate, in the mid-1990s, Japan's stock of outward foreign direct investment was about half as much as that of the United States. Given Japan's high rate of savings, however, foreign direct investment by Japanese firms, already large and vying with British for the second position after the United States, will continue to grow unabated.

The growth of Japanese firms' international operations, coupled with Japan's becoming the largest donor nation of official development assistance to developing countries, once caused a widespread speculation of possible Japanese hegemony over the world. This speculation was based on a facile assumption that economic power would translate into political/military leadership. Japan's political, military, and diplomatic history after World War II shows that there is no such correlation: Japan, an economic power, still remains a political/military midget. Not only does Japan lack a vision of the world order, but it also depends almost totally on the United States in the perception of, and response to, problems of peace and security in East Asia. As China and other Asian nations outperform Japan in economic growth and outsmart it in diplomatic maneuvers, Japan is compelled to cling more tightly to the one major safeguard of its security, the U.S.-Japanese mutual security and cooperation regime.

Clearly, the rise of China is the most important constraint on Japan's role in Asia. In East Asia the primary line of international friction is between China and U.S.-Japanese alliance. The Asian policy of the post–Cold War United States regards China as a principal adversary, which puts Japan in a very awkward position. Although Japan agrees with the United States on implications of a strong China for peace and stability in East Asia, it professes neighborly trust in its bilateral relationship with China. China exploits Japan's dependence on the United States for military security as well as Japan's moral disadvantage stemming from the legacy of its aggression in China and the rest of Asia in the 1930s and 1940s. Despite the Japanese government's considerable official development assistance to China and Japanese companies' extensive investments there, Japan continues to be disadvantaged in international policy initiatives vis-à-vis China.[41]

The Southeast Asian countries, most of which are members of the Association of South East Asian Nations (ASEAN), also welcome Japanese money by trade, aid, and investment but have no enthusiasm for expanding their relationship with Japan beyond economic transactions. In his recent trip to Southeast Asia, Prime Minister Hashimoto proposed to elevate the ASEAN-Japanese relations to "a summit-level forum that would regularly discuss security as well as trade and investment."[42] The proposal was shrugged off. On the one hand, the ASEAN countries still retain suspicions of Japan that go back to World War II. On other hand, they fear antagonizing China by teaming up with Japan in an arrangement that looks like an "encirclement" of China.

Everywhere, then, China stands in the way of Japan. In addition, Japan has no real friend anywhere in Asia because of its own past misdeeds—misdeeds for which the nation, in the eyes of the Asian countries, has not sufficiently atoned. Indeed, it was not until August 1993 that a Japanese prime minister ever admitted that Japan committed aggression against Asia in World War II and made expressions of regrets close to apologies. But later the effects of the prime minister's contrition were greatly reduced by denials of any wrongs on the part of Japan by other ministers of state. More than half a century after the end of World War II, Japan still is struggling to come to terms with its own past with no signs of success in generating right attitudes that might induce other Asian nations to welcome it as a trustworthy friend. Given these internal and external constraints, the optimum role for Japan in Asia will continue to be that of a helping hand (a good number two) for the United States in the future development of U.S.-Asia relations largely according to a scenario drawn by the United States.

Notes

1. See Herman Kahn, *The Emerging Japanese Superstate: Challenge and Response* (New York: Hudson Institute, 1970); and Edwin O. Reischauer, *Beyond Vietnam: The United States and Asia* (New York: Alfred A. Knopf, 1967).

2. See: Koji Taira, "Compatibility of Human Resource Management, Industrial Relations, and Engineering Under Mass Production and Lean Production: An Exploration," *Applied Psychology: An International Review* 45, no. 2 (1996): 97–152; Ezra F. Vogel, *Comeback: Case by Case: Building the Resurgence of American Business* (New York: Simon and Schuster, 1985); and J. P. Womack, D. T. Jones, and D. Roos, *The Machine that Changed the World* (New York: Macmillan, 1990).

3. Ezra F. Vogel, *Japan as Number One: Lessons for America* (Cambridge, Mass.: Harvard University Press, 1979).

4. Vogel, *Comeback*.

5. Ezra F. Vogel, "Pax Nipponica?" *Foreign Affairs* (Spring 1986).

6. See: Francis Fukuyama, "The End of History?" *National Interest*, no. 16 (Summer 1989): 3–18; Paul Kennedy, *The Rise and Fall of the Great Powers* (Lexington, Mass.: Lexington Books, 1987); and C. P. Kindleberger, "International Public Goods Without International Government," *American Economic Review* 76 (March 1986): 1–13.

7. George Friedman and Meredith Lebard, *Coming War with Japan* (New York: St. Martin's Press, 1991).

8. Koji Taira, "Japan as Number Two: New Thoughts on the Hegemonic Theory of World Governance," in Tsuneo Akaha and Frank Langdon, eds., *Japan in the Posthegemonic World* (Boulder, Colo.: Lynne Rienner Publishers, 1993), 233–263.

9. See: W. J. Baumol, R. R. Nelson, and E. N. Wolff, *Convergence of Productivity* (New York: Oxford University Press, 1993); and United Nations Development Program, *Human Development Report 1996* (New York: United Nations, 1996).

10. World Bank, *World Development Report 1995* (New York: Oxford University Press, 1995).

11. United Nations Development Program, Human Development Report 1996.

12. C. Fred Bergsten and Marcus Noland, *Reconcilable Differences? United States-Japan Economic Conflict* (Washington, D.C.: Institute of International Economics, 1993).

13. Koji Taira, "Dialectics of Economic Growth, National Power, and Distributive Struggles, in Andrew Gordon, ed., *Postwar Japan as History* (Berkeley: University of California Press, 1993), 167–186.

14. *Wall Street Journal*, October 2, 1992.

15. NLI Research Institute, *NLI Research*, no. 90 (April 1996): 14.

16. Alan J. Auerbach and Lawrence J. Kotlikoff, *Macroeconomics* (Cincinnati: Southwestern College Publishing, 1995).

298 • Koji Taira

17. *Asahi shinbun,* January 21, 1997.
18. Keizai Koho Center, *Japan 1997: An International Comparison* (Tokyo: Japan Institute for Social and Economic Affairs, 1996), 14.
19. William S. Dietrich, *In the Shadow of the Rising Sun* (University Park, Penn.: Pennsylvania State University Press, 1991).
20. Bill Emmott, *The Sun Also Sets* (New York: Simon and Schuster, 1989).
21. Ministry of Labor, *Monthly Labour Statistics and Research Bulletin* (March 1997): 30.
22. U.S. Government, *Economic Report of the President* (Washington, D.C.: U.S. Government Printing Office, 1996), 245–246.
23. Richard Katz, "From Growth Superstar to Economic Laggard: The Role of Trade in Japan's Sagging Fortunes," Paper presented to the Japan Economic Seminar, Columbia University, East Asian Institute, February 15, 1997.
24. "The Third Opening," *The Economist,* March 9, 1996.
25. "Deregulation in Japan. Unwinding Red Tape," *The Economist,* April 12, 1997.
26. *Ashai shinbun,* April 9, 1997.
27. Takahiro Miyao, "A Proposal for Dismantling the Ministry of Fianance," *Japan Echo* 23 (Spring 1996).
28. See: Bernard Eccleston, *State and Society in Postwar Japan* (Cambridge, Mass.: Basil Blackwood, 1989); and Chalmers Johnson, *Japan's Public Policy Companies* (Washington, D.C.: American Enterprise Institute, 1978).
29. Economic Planning Agency (EPA), *Keizai Hakusho* (Economic White Paper) (Tokyo: Ministry of Finance Printing Office, 1997).
30. See: Keichi Miyashita and David Russell, *Keiretsu: Inside the Hidden Japanese Conglomerates* (New York: McGraw-Hill, 1996); and Mark Tilton, *Restrained Trade: Cartels in Japan's Basic Materials Industries* (Ithaca, N.Y.: Cornell University Press, 1996).
31. See: Chalmers Johnson, *MITI and the Japanese Miracle* (Stanford, Calif.: Stanford University Press, 1982); and Koji Taira and Teiichi Wada, "Business-Government Relations in Modern Japan," in Mark S. Mizruchi and Michale Schwartz, eds., *Intercorporate Relations* (New York: Cambridge University Press, 1987), ch. 9.
32. William G. Ouchi, *Theory Z* (Reading, Mass.: Addison-Wesley, 1981).
33. Tilton, *Restrained Trade.*
34. Bergsten and Noland, *Reconcilable Differences?*
35. Miyashita and Russell, *Keiretsu,* 81.
36. See: Bergsten and Noland, *Reconcilable Differences?;* Katz, "From Growth Superstar to Economic Laggard"; and Koji Taira, "Productivity Assessment: Japanese Perceptions and Practices," in John P. Campbell and Richard J. Campbell, *Productivity in Organizations* (San Francisco: Jossey-Bass, 1988), ch. 3.
37. See: Taira, "Compatibility of Human Resource Management"; and Womack et al., *Machine that Changed the World.*

38. Edward Lincoln, *Japan Facing Economic Maturity* (Washington, D.C.: The Brookings Institution, 1988).

39. Ronald Dore, *Flexible Rigidities: Industrial Policy and Structural Adjustment in the Japanese Economy 1970–80* (Stanford, Calif.: Stanford University Press, 1986).

40. United Nations Development Program, *Human Development Report 1996.*

41. Wolf Mendl, *Japan's Asian Policy* (New York: Routledge, 1995).

42. "Japan and Asia. Not So Fast," *The Economist,* January 18, 1997.

CHAPTER 14

Social Enterprises and Civil Democracy in Sweden: Developing a Participatory Welfare Society in the Twenty-First Century

Victor A. Pestoff, Baltic Sea University, Stockholm

T he Swedish economy has been subject to growing criticism for many years now, making it possible to speak of the crisis of the welfare state in Sweden. The origins of this crisis include ideological, political, financial, economic, and demographic factors. Given this crisis plus Sweden's recent membership in the European Union and probable membership in the European Monetary Union, we are led to ask whether the Swedish welfare state can survive and whether it is possible any longer to have a universal welfare state in a single country.

The evidence and arguments provided herein suggest that the answer to both these questions can be affirmative, if ways and means can be found in Sweden to develop organizational models for promoting greater worker participation in the production of social services and for promoting greater citizen participation in the production of the social services they demand. Only then will citizens have a viable stake in the survival of publicly financed welfare services and the development of a welfare society in the twenty-first century. Unless such a course is taken, the future of the universal welfare state is bleak and that of the Swedish welfare state even more dismal, as it faces the risk of collapsing due to a growing lack of legitimacy.

The Crisis of the Welfare State in Sweden

The first signs of the emerging crisis of the welfare state in Sweden were related to the demise of the Swedish model, based on strong unions and employer organizations that bargained not only about wages and working conditions but also about many other economic, political, and social problems.[1] However, the Swedish negotiated economy and politics of compromise was replaced by deregulation and the politics of confrontation in the 1980s.[2] Some scholars date the political breakdown of the old social pact between organized labor and capital in Sweden to the adoption of a proposal for wage-earner funds by the main blue-collar trade union central, Landsorganisationen. That interpretation provides a too simple and one-sided approach to such complicated developments. A critical role in the process was played by the unions' counterparts, organized business and the employer organizations.

Thus changes in the actions and policies of both organized labor and capital must be considered in any serious account of the demise of the Swedish model and the growing ideological crisis of the welfare state. Research into the employer organizations and Svenska arbetsgivareföreningen (SAF), in particular, provides a more well-rounded and nuanced picture of the mounting ideological challenge to the Swedish welfare state. Changes in SAF leadership, a response in part to political radicalization in the late 1960s and early 1970s and in part to the growing internationalization of the Swedish economy, led employers to take a more aggressive stance on many questions, not only in collective bargaining but also in many other areas of the Swedish economy, politics, and society.[3] Significantly, the chairman of SAF, Dr. Curt Nicolin, described the 1980 labor market conflict as "an investment for the future."[4] Perhaps SAF's new leaders saw the wage-earner funds as both a substantive and a symbolic issue, one that they could exploit to challenge the power of the unions and Social Democrats.

Beginning in the 1970s SAF more than doubled the rate of its membership dues, thereby building up enormous reserves.[5] By 1992 SAF's income exceeded that of employer organizations in France, Germany, Italy, Japan, and the United Kingdom combined.[6] Thus during the 1980s SAF could afford to spend more than twice as much on opinion formation each and every year as all the *Riksdags* parties taken together in an election year, or four times the annual budgets of all Swedish political parties in off-election years.[7] SAF's chief executive officer then announced a "secret agenda for the privatization of Sweden" at its congress in 1990, one where Sweden would be completely "privatized" by the turn of the century.[8] Given the limited state ownership of industry and manufacture in the post–World War II period but the extensive public provision of welfare services, it is clear that the privatization agenda was one of the main targets of SAF's extensive opinion formation campaigns.

Much of the political struggle in Sweden in the 1980s and 1990s over the future of the welfare state has taken the form of SAF campaigns designed to delegitimize the universal welfare state by calling into question its efficiency, fairness, and financing. Moreover, the growing concentration and internationalization of Swedish firms, together with Swedish membership in the European Union, provided fuel to their criticism of "too high wages, too high taxes, and too lavish welfare provisions." Many firms also operated in nearby countries with lower wages, taxes, and levels of welfare provision. A decentralized model of collective bargaining could weaken the position of labor, particularly at the national level. Thus the ideological crisis of the welfare state in Sweden had clear political origins and was closely related to the breakdown of the Swedish model, the negotiated economy, and the politics of compromise.

Another recent political challenge to the legitimacy of the welfare state stems from the growing "democratic deficit" in Sweden. This deficit is felt most acutely at the level of local government, after the municipal reforms in the 1970s that resulted in much larger local government units but also eliminated many nonprofessional and part-time politicians. More recently the growing use of market models for providing local services increases this democracy deficit. Public accountability is circumvented by the provision of publicly financed services by municipally owned limited companies. During the past decade an additional 9,000 nonprofessional or free-time politicians have been relieved of their responsibilities; decisions have been delegated to local bureaucrats; buy-sell models have taken over a growing part of public services and contracting-out to private for-profit suppliers has increased dramatically; municipal limited companies have restricted both public accountability and the possibilities of their employees informing the public about their operations. The excessively generous "golden parachutes" for directors of marketized public companies provided new fuel to the discussion, as did numerous scandals concerning financial license and/or sex involving the directors of municipal limited companies and/or municipal politicians.

In addition, numerous scandals involving national politicians also have contributed to a growing mistrust of politics and politicians in Sweden.[9] One of the most spectacular examples involved the first would-be female chair of the Social Democratic Party and thereby the assumed prime minister, Mona Sahlin. As a result of some credit card oversights she had to withdraw her candidacy, and the current prime minister, Göran Persson, was drafted as the sole candidate to succeed Ingvar Carlsson in 1996. All these developments have sharply eroded public confidence in politicians, civil servants, and the public sector. They also have contributed to an increasing democratic deficit in Swedish politics at the national, regional, and local levels.

The 1990s also brought high unemployment to Sweden. During most of the post-war period Sweden had near full employment, with only approximately 2 or 3 percent unemployment, one of the lowest in Europe. This figure was replaced in 1991 by one of the highest unemployment levels in Europe, at nearly 15 percent; and it persists at a high level. Both the Swedish model and its wage policy of solidarity plus the Swedish welfare state were built on an assumption of full employment.[10] Extensive long-term unemployment erodes both the financial and the social basis of a generous universal welfare state, and Sweden is no exception to the rule. A large increase in unemployment insurance expenses and a substantial loss of tax revenues due to unemployment are a heavy drain on public finances used for generous universal welfare services. The personal and social crisis caused by long-term unemployment also places a heavy burden on public finances, as citizens demand other services and forms of economic support to try to maintain their standard of living.

The growing public deficit at the beginning of the 1990s, due partly to rising unemployment insurance costs, has led the ruling nonsocialist coalition government to make dramatic cuts in public expenditure. The cuts were continued by the Social Democratic government, which was returned to power in 1994, notwithstanding its promise to improve the personal benefits of the welfare state for ordinary citizens. A tough austerity package, based on sharp reductions in the level of cash payments for various kinds of social insurance, was introduced. This resulted in a dramatic drop in the popularity of the Social Democrats in the polls; in the spring of 1997, they fell below 30 percent behind the Conservative Party, for the first time since the early 1930s. Here we see the interaction of the political and financial crises of the welfare state in Sweden, where the one aggravates the other.

Demographic changes in Sweden and most other European Union countries pose another urgent challenge to the welfare state. The growing ranks of pensioners who live longer and demand more social and medical services as they age and become frail have been called a "ticking financial bomb." The baby-boom generation of the 1940s poses a particular problem; as they approach retirement, the ratio of active persons on the labor market to those not active will decrease sharply. Reductions in public spending combined with increasing demand for services mean that citizens are beginning to look for other, often private, for-profit, solutions to their needs of today and tomorrow, including private health insurance to supplement that which is not covered by public insurance. Doing so further undermines the legitimacy of the universal welfare state based on tax financing.

Each of these five trends—ideological, political, financial, economic and demographic crisis—challenges the future of the welfare state as we know it in Sweden. Together they also reinforce each other, contributing to the urgency of finding new solutions to the crises and challenges facing the welfare state. They make finding alternative models for providing personal social services imperative. Political and financial constraints on the welfare state in Sweden in the final decade of the twentieth century have rapidly changed the relationship between the state and its citizens. Privatization, the freedom-of-choice revolution, brought about by radical reorientation of politics during the Bildt coalition government (1991–1994) and the austerity policy pursued by the subsequent Social Democratic governments (1994-) have already resulted in sweeping changes in the Swedish welfare state.

Alternative Solutions—Social Enterprises

Numerous solutions have been put forward for resolving the crisis of the welfare state at the turn of the century. By far the best known is the neoliberal recipe for drastically lower taxes and a minimal night-watchman state, combined with a dramatically increased reliance on market solutions to meet citizens' needs. I reject this proposal, however, since it solves many problems of the welfare state by introducing price mechanisms and pricing public services out of reach for many citizens, while retaining only a minimal safety net and charity that would cater mainly to the "deserving poor." This proposal would surely increase the legitimacy of publicly financed services in the eyes of the well-to-do and those with well-paying jobs; nevertheless, it would exclude the less well off, the unemployed, single-parent families, and so on, and further undermine the legitimacy of such a regime in their eyes.

Another way of resolving some of the challenges facing the welfare state and of eliminating the growing democratic deficit it faces calls for dramatically and radically changing the relationship between the state and its citizens through the development of a participative welfare society. One such proposal presented herein is for developing "civil democracy."[11] It is based primarily on augmenting collective voice and citizen participation in the production of publicly financed social services. It bears some resemblance to proposals for "associative democracy," but the latter appears to rely more heavily on increasing exit rather than voice.[12]

One of the main underpinnings of civil democracy is a realization that democracy is interactive in its nature, that is, in the relationship between the rulers and the ruled. A democracy that only permits its citizens to vote every second, third, fourth, or fifth year, and expects little or nothing else of them will cause the democratic spirit of its citizens to atrophy. Moreover, a democracy that attempts to meet most or all of the needs of its citizens without also expecting them to participate actively in the provision of public services, at least occasionally, turns its citizens into passive consumers of public services rather than active coproducers of the services they demand.

Democracy rests on a moral base, which grows when exercised but dwindles when left fallow for long periods. Unless Robert Putnam's concept of social capital is related to local civil democracy, participation in local decision making, and the like, it will also become, at best, a passive resource.[13] If the provision of personal social services and other local services belongs exclusively to the domain of professional civil servants, and if it does not directly involve and concern the citizens in their daily life, then their social capital will atrophy. They become merely the passive objects of a well-intended and well-organized universal welfare state that is decided on and run by professional bureaucrats. Paying taxes is not enough to keep solidarity, social capital, and civil democracy alive. In order for social capital to be turned into a resource available to many citizens in the economic, political, and social spheres, it must be exercised more often than in general elections.

Furthermore, in order for citizens to temper their demands and expectations, they must actively participate in real-world situations where they sometimes are forced to make hard choices. They may have to choose among child care service for one hour longer per day, higher parent fees, or an unacceptable deficit that threatens to close their parent co-op day care center; or they may have to decide whether to allocate new funds for trainers and sport facilities for girls or more for football and ice-hockey rinks for boys. It is from these everyday but sometimes tough choices that the moral resources are derived which are so necessary to nourish a thriving social capital and civil democracy. Without regular exercise and without active participation, the citizens, social capital, and civil democracy will not become an active resource for democracy and the welfare society.

A variety of alternative models for providing social services is being tried in various parts of the country. Contracting out to the third sector, purchaser-provider models, cooperative social services, volunteering, and third-party provision are but a few of the models now being tried in order to resolve the acute ideological and financial problems currently facing the Swedish welfare state. Privatization and contracting out have led to the growth of many new social enterprises that have become an important alternative to the public provision of such social services.

Taking day care services as an illustration, the number of "private" or nonmunicipal day care centers more than tripled between 1988 and 1994, going from 538 to 1,768 facilities, while the number of children attending them more than quadrupled during the same period, increasing from 8,500 to 39,100.[14] Nearly two-thirds of these "private" day care centers are parental or worker cooperatives or voluntary organizations.[15] Nonmunicipal day care now accounts for more than 10 percent of all children enrolled in day care facilities and includes more than one-fourth of the children in the nation's major urban areas. Social enterprises have also been established in other areas, such as elderly care, health care, and handicap care.[16]

Social enterprises are firms that try to fulfill several goals simultaneously, recognizing that no single goal can be maximized constantly but rather that several of them will be fulfilled or satisfied satisfactorily, at the same time. Social enterprises do not exist to maximize the return on capital or the revenues over expenses, rather they are willing to accept a lower but nevertheless satisfactory economic return on their efforts in order to combine the necessary economic goal with other important social goals, that can also be maximized or satisfied, thereby providing a more rewarding occupation to the employees, socially meaningful goals to the firm, and greater value creation for the consumers. This leads to a positive selection of the staff, where employees are not one-dimensional utility maximizers seeking the highest possible wages but rather wish to maximize several goals simultaneously, such as caregiving, satisfying financial rewards, a meaningful occupation, and stimulating and flexible of working conditions. It also leads to a positive selection by clients who want to play a more active role as coproducers of personal social services. Social enterprises can also facilitate and enhance the self-realization and professional development of their employees, improve the work environment, and promote the influence and empowerment of their clients/consumers on the services produced.

The main competitive advantage of social enterprises is that they generate trust between their staff and clients/consumers, since they clearly have more than one goal, including one or more social goals. By simultaneously trying to fulfill these diverse and multiple goals, while accepting a satisfactory rather than a maximal return on their capital, they are clearly indicating a policy of not exploiting the information asymmetries related to their services/products for their own personal and private benefit; in other words, they will not behave opportunistically vis-à-vis their clients. Thus, by operating on a policy that is clearly committed to a satisfactory return on revenue over expenses, while promoting social goals, they are thereby providing a minimal guarantee of trust to their clients/customers and to the local community in which they operate. Such trust could be greatly facilitated and enhanced by the development of an annual social audit and by the multistakeholder organizational form.[17]

Social enterprises can take the legal form of a nonprofit or ideal organization, a cooperative or economic association, and even a private firm. However, while the latter is normally the privileged and preferentially treated business form in national legislation in most European countries, nevertheless it can undermine the main competitive advantage of social enterprises in Sweden—that is, trust. It is important to study these new social enterprises and cooperative social services that involve citizens in the production of the social services they demand to explore their implications for renewing the relationship between the state and its citizens, and thereby also for transforming the public sector and welfare state into a welfare society in the twenty-first century, one based on active citizens.

Before presenting a brief summary of our findings concerning social enterprises, in Sweden, we will introduce a few of the main theoretical considerations of the project on Work Environment and Cooperative Social Services (WECSS) in Sweden. These theoretical concepts are necessary to understand the contribution of social enterprises to renewing the welfare state, to enriching work life, to improving the work environment, and to empowering citizens as coproducers. They specify the values associated with different types of social cooperatives, and the concepts of civil democracy and of citizens as coproducers. Some concepts are discussed at length regarding the proposed new participatory model for providing personal social welfare services, one based on continued public financing but cooperative self-management and citizens as coproducers. This model gains inspiration from the Scandinavian negotiated economy, which provides an alternative both to the neo-liberal and the planned economy models for organizing society.[18] The extensive materials gathered here about cooperative self-management and citizens as coproducers in Sweden permit us to test our ideas about the development a new participatory welfare society. We maintain that cooperative self-management and the innovation of citizens as coproducers can provide a vision worthy of transforming the universal welfare state into a voluntary and participatory welfare society in the twenty-first century.

Cooperatives, Nonprofit Organizations, and the Privatization of Personal Social Services

Various actors in complex organizations have different interests, and they also have different social relations with each other. The social relations in an organization are determined in part by whether one or another interest is the dominant actor. The dominance of one of these interests is also important for our discussion of the social dimension of cooperatives is the implication. If we assume that a dominant actor pursues its own interest, then variations in social relations have different implications for a firm's social dimension and also for society at large.

Private firms are noted for their contribution to efficiency in production and the allocation of resources. Their activities are geared towards maximizing returns on invested capital. Public bureaucracy and public enterprise are associated more often with equity than efficiency, and they also assure the availability of various goods and services to the general public, without extensive consideration to prices. Third-sector and cooperative organizations are often seen as an alternative, or at least a complement to both the public and private sectors. They are associated with innovation, advocacy, and the promotion of civic values.[19] Social enterprises have clear social goals and satisfice in the achievement of several of them.

The first major potential contribution of cooperative firms and social enterprises concerns the renewal and enrichment of working life associated with changes in providing welfare services. Each form of social enterprises, however, implies quite different work relations. There are three basic forms or models for providing cooperative or third-sector social services. The first form is the worker cooperative model, where all or most of the providers of a social service are also members of the service cooperative, but where the clients have a formal customer relation with the cooperative or providers. Here we can expect to find worker empowerment most clearly manifest. The second form is the consumer cooperative model, where the consumers own or run the cooperative and the staff are merely employees. Here consumers become coproducers, which is primarily associated with consumer empowerment. The third form is comprised of voluntary organizations, where the employees and clients share common social values related to the organization's purposes.

Thus, the three main potential contributions of cooperatives and third-sector organizations are the renewal and enrichment of working life, the empowerment of consumers or clients, and the enhancement of other social values and/or goal fulfillment in the public sector. Each of these contributions is more closely related to one type of cooperative or third-sector alternative than another, and all in turn are related to differences in the social relations within each of the cooperative or third-sector alternatives. It is important to keep these differences in mind when discussing the social dimension and comparing cooperatives with each other or with private firms or public bureaucracies. The provision of cooperative and third-sector social services is local and small scale in nature. These alternatives can provide the producers of social services, the consumers or clients of such services, and the resource-poor or risk groups who depend on such services with greater influence in their operation. This results in greater citizen control over the social services they demand and depend on, and it also promotes local grassroots democracy. Moreover, not only do greater employee influence and client empowerment result in greater involvement as producers and/or consumers of social services; normally they also result in better service quality.

Civil Democracy and Citizens' Involvement as Coproducers

R. Saltman and C. V. Otter argue that in the modern welfare state, democratic theory concerns opportunities for formal participation in three major aspects of modern life, but not a fourth.[20] They discuss participation in relation to political institutions through elections; social institutions, particularly social insurance and economic institutions through trade unions; and codetermination in working life. What they excluded, however, is formal participation in civil institutions, particularly residence-related human services such as health care, education, child care, and elderly care.[21] They continue to lament that large organizations will pursue their own internal objectives and self-interests rather than meeting diffuse consumer needs, unless, of course, public accountability or market-driven accountability are better developed.

While their discussion is enlightening, their alternative brand of empowerment goes exclusively through the market and the power attributed to exit, not through the third sector and the power of collective voice. In light of this, we argue that civil democracy could provide the grounds for a fourth wave or pillar of democracy. The concept of civil democracy is related to the idea of social capital. R. D. Putman's seminal book, *Making Democracy Work—Civil Traditions in Modern Italy* discusses the historical and contemporary importance of the third sector and its contribution to economic and social development.[22] One of the main concepts Putman works with is "social capital." He points out that success in overcoming the dilemma of collective action and the self-defeating opportunism of the prisoner's dilemma depends on the broader social context in which human interaction takes place. "Voluntary cooperation is easier in a community that has inherited a substantial stock of social capital, in the form of reciprocity and networks of civic engagement." Putnam proceeds to define social capital with reference to "features of social organization, such as trust, norms and networks, that can improve the efficiency of society by facilitating coordinated action. . . . Like other forms of capital, social capital is productive, making possible the achievement of certain ends that would not be attainable in its absence."[23]

Most forms of social capital, such as trust, are what A. O. Hirschman has called "moral resources"—resources whose supply increases rather than decreases with use, but that also become depleted if not used.[24] Moreover, social capital is ordinarily a public good and, like all public goods, it tends to be undervalued and undersupplied by private agents. This means that social capital, unlike other forms of capital, must be produced as a by-product of other social activities, in keeping with the theory of M. Olson.[25] The greater the level of trust within a community, the greater the likelihood of cooperation, whereas cooperation in turn breeds trust.[26]

Putnam notes that if horizontal networks of civic engagement help participants solve dilemmas of collective action, then the more horizontally structured an organization, the more it should foster institutional success in the broader community. Thus, membership in horizontally ordered groups, such as sports clubs, choirs, and cooperatives, should be positively associated with good government, while membership in hierarchically ordered organizations, such as the Mafia or the Catholic Church, should be negatively associated with good government.

Social engineering solutions to the problems now facing the Swedish welfare state, whether the type promoting étatist, hierarchical, and centralized solutions or the neoliberal type of tearing everything down and replacing it by market mechanisms, both miss the mark. Both étatist and neoliberal perspectives fail to understand the potential of the third sector to create social capital and trust by bringing citizens together in small horizontal groups to achieve the goals they decide on or produce the services they demand. The third sector, however, provides a possibility for breaking this ideological deadlock and for finding a common ground for proposing alternative solutions that fit neatly into neither the square nor the round holes proposed by étatists or neoliberals.

We maintain that the third sector and cooperative self-management of personal social services would provide a better and more durable base for creating institutions to facilitate the accumulation of social capital. Thus, the term "civil democracy" will be employed here to refer to *citizen empowerment* through cooperative self-management of personal social services, where the citizens become members in social enterprises and where they participate directly in the production of the local services they demand, thereby becoming coproducers of these services.

A Summary of Our Empirical Findings

As mentioned, cooperative day care has grown dramatically in recent decades in Sweden. More than half of all children under the age of seven are enrolled in child care services financed by public funds. More than one in eight of these children attend day care services contracted out to nonmunicipal providers, mostly to different types of cooperatives and voluntary organizations. In the major urban areas such as Stockholm, Gothenburg, and Malmö, more than one in four children attending day care services is enrolled in a cooperative facility.[27] The empirical part of the WECSS project comprises three different data sets from three different sources. Sixty cooperative day care centers were chosen in a quasi-random sample from six different parts of Sweden, and the managers were interviewed in the Organization Study. Two hundred fifty personnel questionnaires from the same day care centers were returned and analyzed in the Staff Study in terms of the Karasek/Theorell model of psychosocial work environment.[28] Almost 600 client questionnaires were collected and analyzed in the Parent Study. We will briefly summarize some of the major findings of the WECSS study and draw conclusions concerning enrichment of working life, empowerment of consumers as coproducers, and social enterprises and civil democracy as a vision for the welfare state in twenty-first century.

Enriching Work Environment:
Social Enterprises Provide Good Jobs

The analysis of the WECSS Staff Study findings follow R. Karasek and T. Theorell's model and provides extensive empirical material and is based on more than 200 questions.[29] We present the different profiles of these different types of social enterprises, followed by a retrospective comparison of the psychosocial work environment of the three different types of social enterprises with that of municipal day care services. Our Staff Study divided social enterprises parent cooperatives, voluntary organizations, and worker cooperatives. The worker cooperatives are consistently rated higher by the staff on most of the over 200 items employed in our study of psychosocial work environment. This should not be simply interpreted to mean that worker cooperatives provide a superior model for worker empowerment. Rather the worker cooperative model is based on organizational structures that facilitate group processes that positively promote the interest of workers/employees. Thus they help bridge the gap between employees' instrumental and expressive values.[30]

Greater worker influence may be achieved at the expense of parent involvement and engagement. Moreover, in one or two examples the manager of a worker cooperative was repeatedly criticized by one or more staff members for treating the cooperative and her fellow workers as if they were employees in a private firm. Voluntary organizations appear often to function like mixed or multistakeholder cooperatives, with the big difference that they have a common ideology or pedagogical perspective that unites the interests of various stakeholders. Parent cooperatives often demonstrate several clear signs of less-functional parent/staff relations, which detracts from the psychosocial work environment.

We also wanted to compare the psychosocial work environment of these three distinct types of social enterprises with that of municipal day care services, in order to explore the possibility of creating good jobs, renewing and enriching work life, and improving the psychosocial work environment in publicly financed day care services. We were able to employ a retrospective comparative method, since most of the personnel had worked previously in municipal day care services. Those with experience in both forms of day care services were asked to compare nearly 30 aspects of their present jobs in cooperative day care services with than found in municipal day care facilities. The overwhelming majority (80.8 percent–88.4 percent) of the staff had no previous personal experience with cooperatives before starting to work in cooperative day care. They chose to work with cooperative day care primarily because they found it meaningful, wanted more influence over their work, or appreciated the cooperative's specific pedagogical profile.

The overwhelming majority (68.3 percent–85.5 percent) of those with experience of both forms clearly preferred working for cooperative compared with municipal day care services. In almost all respects of work life, cooperatives were rated better or clearly better than municipal day care services by the staff of all three types of cooperative services. But the clearest improvement of work life was noted by the staff of worker cooperatives. The staff of all three types of cooperative day care showed a similar high level of engagement at the start of their employment in a cooperative. But more of the staff of worker cooperatives (43.3 percent) declared a current higher degree of engagement than the other two types of cooperative day care services, while more of the staff of parent cooperatives (37.9 percent) claimed a lower degree of current engagement today than at the start. Finally, given the chance to do it all over again, twice as many staff members in worker cooperatives (66.7 percent) as in parent cooperatives and voluntary organizations (33.3 percent) would definitely choose to work in a cooperative social enterprise. Only a tiny fraction of the staff at any of these three cooperative forms would, however, consider working in municipal day care services again.

Numerous comments to these questions illustrated both the positive as well as the negative side of work life in cooperative day care services. The overwhelming impression from these comments supports the picture provided by the collected data. Social enterprise day care services permit the staff much greater influence on their own work, much greater responsibility for and participation in decision making, greater contacts with parents, greater possibilities for improvements in their work environment, and greater work satisfaction than municipal day care services do. At the individual level, greater worker power and a more active promotion of other social values comprise the social capital necessary for healthy civic democracy, for renewing the public sector, and for developing the welfare state into a welfare society based on fully enfranchised citizens cable of becoming co-producers of the social services they demand. At the collective level, we find more engaged staff and better quality service.

Karasek and Theorell present their ideal of bad and good jobs. The latter sound very much like the cooperative social enterprises studied here, whereas the former sound like anything but. Thus, the authors characterize good jobs in the following ways:

1. *Skill discretion:* The job offers possibilities to make the maximum use of one's skills and provides opportunities to increase skills on the job.
2. *Autonomy:* Freedom from rigid worker-as-child factory discipline. Workers have influence over the selection of work routines and colleagues can participate in long-term planning.
3. *Psychological demands:* The job has routine demands mixed with a liberal element of new learning challenges.
4. *Social relations:* Social contacts are encouraged as a basis for new learning, and new contacts multiply the possibilities for self-realization through collaboration.
5. *Social rights:* There are democratic procedures at the workplace.
6. *Meaningfulness/customer/social feedback:* Workers gain direct feedback from customers, and workers and customers work together, customizing the product to meet the customers' needs.[31]

Based on Karasek and Theorell's criteria, social enterprises in Sweden provide good jobs. In addition to being psychologically demanding, they provide the workers with high decision latitude, high social support, and enduring interaction with the clients. These work-life attributes stand in sharp contrast with those found in the services provided by the large hierarchical bureaucratic organizations often associated with public sector services in Sweden, including municipal day care services. In this sense the social enterprise model cannot only help to transform social services jobs into active, participative, and interactive jobs. The social enterprise model also can help to enrich employee work life and transform the welfare state into a welfare society. One of the quickest and most direct ways of enriching work life, redesigning work, and promoting human resource management in the social service sector in Sweden thus, is to decentralize the provision of social services and to let social enterprises produce them.

We also noted that the women employed in worker cooperative day care services were more positive about these organizational changes than were their colleagues in parent cooperatives, which primarily promote other values, such as greater parental influence and greater parental participation in the daily life of their child(ren).[32] There are clearly two sides to the coin of organizational change, depending on which model of change is employed. Group interests and group conflicts therefore are not completely resolved by greater participation of a single group in social enterprise decision making. Greater worker participation does empower the workers but does not necessarily promote client interest. Similarly, greater consumer participation does empower clients but does not necessarily promote worker interest.

These last observations, in turn, suggest the limits of institutionalizing the interests of a single group in social enterprise decision-making structures. Organizational changes in social enterprises may indeed improve the work environment but nevertheless result in some trade-offs between the interests of workers and clients. Organizational change relying on multistakeholder models could provide the supporting structures necessary for promoting the interests of more than a single stakeholder. Multistakeholder cooperatives recognize the legitimate interest of several groups contributing to the success of a social enterprise and provide for the representation of their interests in the decision making of the internal institutions.[33]

In this context, voluntary organizations appear, to provide an alternative to both the worker and parent cooperatives. Often staff evaluated them more positively in terms of improving the work environment than were parent cooperatives; but parents of enrolled children also rated them more positively in terms of parent influence than were worker cooperatives. Voluntary organizations appear to be rudimentary form of multistakeholder organizations that are able to combine the interests of both groups in the pursuit of a common pedagogical program. Whether this is possible for other types of social services remains to be seen. More formal multistakeholder institutions in other areas may provide the necessary basis for facilitating the trade-off between different and sometimes conflicting interests of various groups that contribute to the success of a social enterprise.

Civil Democracy and Empowerment of Citizens as Coproducers

S. Wikström discusses how the changing patterns of interaction between firms and their customers open new possibilities of doing business.[34] Such changes are based on a much closer relationship between producers and consumers than that traditionally found in industrial society, a relationship in which consumers increasingly assume the role of coproducers. Customers are no longer seen as passive receivers of goods and services; rather they are perceived as active and knowledgeable participants in a common process, a joint venture on the marketplace. The company's role is no longer limited to supporting customers by providing goods or services. Rather the company designs systems of activities within which customers can create their own value.

The firm thereby complements the knowledge and resources already possessed by its customers, as was normally the case in the preindustrial period. From this interaction and cooperation in time and space, a value emerges that is the result of the cooperation. Coproduction implies a clear shift in perspective from the traditional producer and customer perspective. It is motivated in part by the perceived degree of uncertainty in the exchange between the company and its customers and the potential benefit accruing to them from eliminating such uncertainty.[35] The interactive way of working generates different types of values than those created by the logic of mass production.

Coproduction is a multifaceted phenomenon comprising several different aspects. It includes differing means of consumer participation in production, differing stages for consumer participation in the production process and varying degrees of consumer influence on that process. Our research pays greatest attention to the influence of final consumers, in particular that stemming from their membership in social enterprises for personal social services. For our purposes we want to specify the values associated with greater consumer involvement and coproduction of personal social services, in particular the specific value added for parents of children in various types of cooperative day care services in Sweden.

We are interested in exploring an extension and adaptation of the concept of coproduction to the area of personal social services and cooperative providers of such services. Our data collection included 580 questionnaires from parents to children in 60 cooperative day care centers throughout Sweden. All three different forms of cooperatives—parent cooperatives, voluntary organizations, and worker cooperatives—were included. Both parent cooperatives and voluntary organizations normally have a work obligation associated with membership, while worker cooperatives generally lack this feature, as parents cannot become members. The parents of both of the first two types of cooperatives express similar attitudes regarding the positive aspects of the work obligation: It facilitates their participation and gives them a feeling of belonging and valuable insights; in other words, it enables their integration into the organization and running of the day care services. These two groups attribute less weight to gaining influence through the work obligation.

The integrative aspects, already noted for the work obligation, were also rated highly by parents holding elective or honorary offices. Many more parents held such positions in parent cooperatives than voluntary organizations, while very few parents were able to hold such positions in worker cooperatives, and there only in advisory bodies. In contrast to attitudes about the work obligation, parent attitudes about their work on the board emphasized first and foremost the political aspect of holding an elective office—increased parental influence. Due to the higher rate of holding elective and honorary offices in parent cooperatives than in voluntary organizations, more parents have influence in the former than the latter type of cooperative day care services.

Turning to reasons for choosing a particular form of cooperative day care services we noted a clear profile for each type of day care service. Influence, wanting to participate more in the daily life of their child(ren), and closeness to home provide a profile for parents with children in parent cooperatives. Special pedagogics and a desire to influence and to participate more in the daily life of their child(ren) clearly dominate the motives of parents with children in voluntary organizations. For both these sets of parents, the choice of day care form was motivated more in terms of expressive values and less in instrumental terms. Closeness to home, a recommendation by relatives or friends, and the lack of other alternatives were the main motives of parents with children in worker cooperatives. Thus parents with children in worker cooperatives expressed more instrumental attitudes.

However, after parents had chosen which type of day care service to use, the advantages they experienced in all three types of cooperative day care services left more room for instrumental values. Parents in the cooperative day care services listed an enjoyable atmosphere, an engaged staff, and a possibility of influence among the four main advantages; participating in the child's daily life and pedagogics are still important for parents of parent cooperatives and voluntary organizations providing day care services. The disadvantages associated with each type of day care service are also typical for each organizational profile. Most or many parents in all three types of cooperative day care services stated that there was no disadvantage. However, while not minding the work obligation per se, parents in both parent cooperatives and voluntary organizations nevertheless were critical about the additional time required by the cooperative form and were also concerned with the difficulty of combining their roles as parents and employers. Parents with children in worker cooperatives named few specific disadvantages.

Parents strongly appreciated the willingness of the staff to discuss their suggestions for changes and improvements, and parents in all three types of cooperatives expressed a similar level of satisfaction with the running and administration of the day care service. However, given the clearly articulated instrumental attitude of parents with children in worker cooperatives, compared with the more expressive attitude of parents with children in parent cooperatives and voluntary organizations, it is unclear whether the latter parents would be as satisfied with the level of influence and participation offered to parents in worker cooperatives. We are suggesting that no single type of cooperative nor organizational formula can meet the needs and requirements of *all* parents for day care services. Rather a greater welfare mix and welfare pluralism requires a greater diversity of forms for providing personal social services to meet the various needs of different groups of citizens.

Many parents previously had a child(ren) in municipal day care services; these parents clearly felt that staff in the cooperatives were more open. Parents also strongly feel that cooperative day care services, regardless of type, were better than municipal services. Finally, given a free choice, they categorically stated a preference for the cooperative form, regardless of the type of cooperative.

Wikström argues that coproduction is motivated by the degree of uncertainty in the exchange between the producer and consumer of goods and services and the potential benefit to the participants from eliminating such uncertainty.[36] Social enterprises and cooperative social services with clear social goals and nonprofit motives help to generate trust between producers and consumers of such services by minimizing or eliminating opportunistic behavior. In the case of child care, some types of cooperative social services eliminate uncertainty by promoting parental participation as coproducers—by the work obligation combined with democratic procedures and parents holding honorary offices. Some types of cooperative day care centers create benefits related to parental values. In particular, the values of parent influence, participation in the daily life of their child(ren), special pedagogics, and feelings of belonging are important to the parents of children in parent cooperative and voluntary organizations. Coproduction eliminates the uncertainty related to interaction between producers and consumers of such services since it involves parents in the production, and their participation is the best guarantee of quality, according to some parents. Coproduction both enables the parents and empowers them in fulfilling their own values related to the institutional care of their children.

It is not as easy to promote the same goals in worker cooperatives or in municipal or private day care services, but the former nevertheless do promote parents' instrumental values. It can be argued that parent cooperatives and voluntary organizations day care services are unique in promoting the creation of the values related to co-production. Without the existence of this form of day care for children and without the participation and involvement of parents in the production of the cooperative day care services such values would not be achieved for these parents. Thus, these special forms of day care service have created value for the parents by engaging them as co-producers. If such alternatives no longer existed or were curtailed for political or financial reasons, the possibilities of coproduction would not enrich the lives and values of these parent and their children. None of the values associated with co-production are available in services provided by worker cooperatives or municipal or private day care services, as such services do not promote parent participation and coproduction. Thus, coproduction promotes unique values for large groups of parents. It thereby enriches publicly financed personal social services and contributes to the renewal the welfare state by turning it into a more participatory welfare society.

Social Enterprises and Civil Democracy— a Vision for the Twenty-first Century?

The distinctive social values promoted by cooperative day care services should be observable in other areas, such as chronic long-term health care; elderly care, both domestic and institutional; handicap care, both domestic and institutional; education; and the like. In recent years cooperatives have developed in all such areas in Sweden and in other European countries. These developments need to be studied closer in order to understand their unique contributions to the enrichment of work life, to the improvement of the psychosocial work environment, to developing good jobs, to the empowerment of citizens as coproducers, and to promoting civil democracy. There is no reason to believe that such benefits are restricted to day care services or to Sweden. Rather, we expect that many of the beneficial aspects of social enterprise and cooperative social services noted here will also be found in other areas and other countries. They probably take somewhat different expressions, due to variations in the organizational and legal constraints in various European societies and structural differences between various sectors of personal social service provision. Moreover, the interaction between the producers and consumers of these social services will also vary with differences in these organizational, legal, and sectoral constraints. The nature of this relationship is important for the development of good jobs and for empowering citizens as coproducers.

However, we expect that social enterprises and cooperative social services can help to renew the public sector by contracting out to the third sector and to develop a new type of welfare state by providing greater room for citizen participation as users and producers of social services. Thus society will be turned into a participatory welfare society. Social enterprises and cooperative social services can also help to enrich work life by promoting cooperative self-management; to improve the work environment by providing the staff with greater control, social support, and enduring interactions with clients; to empower citizens as coproducers by promoting cooperative self-management; to promote greater staff engagement, higher service quality, and often at a lower cost; and, finally, to develop civil democracy.

We also feel that comparisons of Swedish social enterprises and cooperative social services with those found in other parts of Europe, and perhaps also with those found in Japan and elsewhere serve a purpose. This is particularly true for countries such as Italy, Spain, and France, where social enterprises have grown rapidly in recent decades; but also in Germany and the Netherlands, where established voluntary organizations have traditionally played a more important, prominent, and active role in providing personal social services; as well as our Nordic neighbors, Denmark, Finland, and Norway. In all these countries, it seems worthwhile to compare social enterprises and cooperative social services with those found in Sweden, in particular their ability to promote the social values associated with these cooperative social services. But in order to do so we must strive to break the simple black/white, left/right ideological domination of the public vs. private perspective of providing social services. We need to recognize the contribution of social enterprises and cooperative social services for the unique social values they promote. We must stop trying to reduce the third sector, social enterprises, and cooperative social services to the lowest possible public or private denominator, and we must stop trying to perceive their contribution in simple economic terms that can be measured or aggregated solely by financial data.

The main reason for recognizing social enterprises and cooperative social services in their own right are, of course, the enrichment of work life, the improvement of the psychosocial work environment, the development of good jobs, the empowerment of citizens as coproducers, and the promotion of civil democracy. People who do not value such social goals will, of course, not be attracted by social enterprises and cooperative social services. Others might argue that the same social goals could be promoted by public services or private firms, but we strongly disagree with them. We hope this chapter has helped to place these important social values on the agenda of social science researchers in Sweden and elsewhere, and perhaps made a contribution to the public debate about the future of the welfare state, the renewal of the public sector, and the transformation of the welfare state into a new participatory welfare society. If the social values promoted by social enterprises and cooperative social services gain broader recognition in Swedish social science research and in the public debate, they may comprise a vision for the twenty-first century.

If not, they will remain an unappreciated relic of a past welfare state that collapsed from within due to the declining support by citizens who lost faith in the state's ability to provide the services they wanted at the quality they expected and at a price they were willing to pay. If the welfare state cannot be rejuvenated from within by expanding room for citizen participation and by promoting social enterprises, cooperative social services, and civil democracy, then it too may soon become a historical relic of the past. No social institution can survive without the support of its citizens, without renewing its legitimacy in the younger generations who are replacing those who built today's social institutions. To earn and retain the support of the younger generations, the welfare state must grow and develop to fit the needs and values of today's population rather than merely reflecting those of yesterday's.

We must try to determine whether the Swedish welfare state can overcome the crises it faces and whether the universal welfare state can survive in any country. The rapid and unexpected collapse of communism in Central and Eastern Europe is perhaps an omen. Moreover, the minimal safety net promoted there by the International Monetary Fund and World Bank for the "deserving poor," to replace the previous enterprise welfare state, bears witness to what certain groups would like to substitute in place of the universal welfare state.

Unless alternatives are actively developed for rejuvenating the welfare state from within, for providing more room for citizen participation as coproducers, and for developing it into a welfare society, the welfare state also faces a real risk of losing legitimacy and ultimately of collapsing under its own weight. In military strategy, the best defense is to go to attack, to take the offensive. It is often said that business strategy is fashioned on military strategy. Perhaps it is time for those who support the universal social values that underpin the welfare state to ask whether there might not be something to learn from business. An uncompromising defense of existing welfare state institutions in all the details that contributed to their original popularity and legitimacy might only speed the ultimate collapse of the existing institutions.

The evidence presented herein from the Work Environment and Cooperative Social Services Study suggests that some positive alternatives could contribute to the transition of Sweden from a welfare state into a welfare society. The one presented here is based on a clear strategy for promoting greater worker participation in the production of social services, in particular by worker cooperatives, and for promoting greater citizen participation in production of the social services they demand, in particular by empowering them as coproducers. This strategy give these groups a vital stake in the survival of publicly financed welfare services and a vision for developing the Swedish welfare state into a welfare society in the twenty-first century.

Without a vision for rejuvenating and developing the welfare state, without the development of a new participatory welfare society, without greater worker participation in the production of social services, and without the development of civil democracy, today's universal welfare state faces a serious risk of collapsing. In addition to the current crises of the welfare state and a growing resistance to increasing taxes, growing possibilities for capital to avoid high-tax countries, and the rapid internationalization of the Swedish economy will erode support for the universal welfare state. Internationalization of business not only facilitates social dumping, but the isomorphic tendencies promoted by global competition and multinational companies often result in the outright rejection of the universal values of the welfare state. The massive "rollback" campaigns of organized business can be met only by an invigorating vision for the rejuvenation of the welfare state and its development into a welfare society in the twenty-first century. It is hoped that this chapter will make a small contribution to that vision.

Notes

1. P. Thullberg and K. Östberg, *Den svenska modellen* [The Swedish model] (Stockholm: Raben & Sjögrens förlag, 1995).

2. V. Pestoff, "Joint Regulation, Meso-Games and Political Exchange in Swedish Industrial Relations," in B. Marin, ed., *Governance & Generalized Exchange. Self-Organizing Policy Networks in Action* (Boulder, Colo.: Westview, 1990): 315–346.

3. See the following works by V. Pestoff: "Towards New Swedish Model," in J. Huasner and B. Jessop, eds., *Institutional Frameworks of Market Economies— Scandinavian and Eastern European Perspectives* (Avebury, U.K.: Aldershot & Brookfield); reprinted in *Journal of Area Studies: Trade Unionism and Industrial Relations in Europe in the 1990s*, no. 5 (1994): 102–119; "Employer Organizations: Their Changing Structures and Strategies in Nine OECD Countries," in *Changing Structures and Strategies of the Employers' and Employees' Organizations* (Helsinki: Proceedings from the IIRA 4th European Regional Congress).

4. It was the largest labor market conflict in Swedish history, mainly in the form of an employer lockout, and thus SAF's largest lockout ever. A. Kjellberg, "Sweden: Restoring the Model?" in A. Ferner and R. Hyman, eds., *Changing Industrial Relations in Europe* (Oxford: Blackwell Publishers, 1998).

5. V. Pestoff, "Organisationernas medverkan och förhandlingar I svensk konsumentpolitik (Organizational participation and negotiations in Swedish consumer policy), in K. Nielsen and O.K. Pedersen, eds., *Forhandlingsökonomi I Norden* [The negotiated economy in the Nordic countries] (Copenhagen: DJÖF, 1989); reprinted in *Tidskrift för rättssociologi* (Journal of Legal Sociology) 6, nos. 3/4 (1989): 150–203.

6. Pestoff, "Employer Organizations."

7. See the following works by Pestoff: "Towards a New Swedish Model"; and "Employer Organizations."

8. V. Pestoff, "Towards a New Swedish Model," in J. Hausner, B. Jessop, and K. Nielson, eds., *Institutional Frameworks of Market Economies—Scandinavian and Eastern European Perspectives* (Avebury: Aldershot & Brookfield, 1993), 133–168; and "Trade Unionism and Industrial Relations in Europe in the 1990s," *Journal of Area Studies* no. 5: 102–119.

9. One prominent ongoing scandal involves Mr. S. Marjasin, former chairman of the Municipal Workers Union and former governor of the County of Örebrö. Recently he was forced to resign from the latter position due to indiscretions with the county governor's Representation Fund. He systematically cut his sales slips into three parts and eliminated the middle part with the list of items purchased, but retained those with the name of the store and the total sum of purchases, now referred to jokingly as "innovative accounting." He also charged both lunch or dinner guests for the costs of meals as well as his representation account for the same meal.

10. See works by: J. Stephens, "The Scandinavian Welfare States: Achievements, Crisis and Prospects," in G. Esping-Andersen, ed., *Welfare States in Transition: National Adaptations in Global Economies* (Thousand Oaks, Calif.: Sage Publications, 1996); and Y. Stryjan, "Personalkooperative—bättre än sitt rykte?" [Worker co-ops—Better than their reputation?] in *Förädring och*

förmuelse [Change and renewal] (Stockholm: Föreningen Kooperativa Studier, 1997).

11. V. Pestoff, *Social Enterprises and Civil Democracy in Sweden: Enriching Work Environment and Empowering Citizens as Co-Producer* (Stockholm: School of Business, 1996).

12. P. Hirsh, *Associative Democracy. New Forms of Economic and Social Governance* (Oxford: Blackwell and Polity Press, 1994).

13. R. D. Putnam, *Making Democracy Work—Civil Traditions in Modern Italy* (Princeton, N.J.: Princeton University Press, 1993).

14. See the following works by V. Pestoff: "Reforming Social Services in Postcommunist Europe: Shifts in the Welfare Mix and Mesolevel Institutional Change," in J. Campbell and O. K. Pedersen, *Legacies of Change: Transformations of Postcommunist European Economies* (Hawthorne, N.Y.: A. de Gruyter, 1996), 177–203; and Y. Stryjan, "Kooperativa dagis—de första åren [Cooperative day care—the first years], in *Kooperative and Välfärd* [Cooperatives and welfare] (Stockholm: Föreningen Kooperativa Studier, 1995).

15. V. Pestoff, "Reforming Social Services in Postcommunist Europe," 177–203.

16. I. Wahlgren, *Vem tröstar Ruth? En studie av alternativa driftsformer I hemtjänsten* [Who comforts Ruth? A study of alternative providers of home help services for the elderly] (Stockholm: School of Business, 1996).

17. Pestoff, *Social Enterprises and Civil Democracy.*

18. K. Nielsen and O. K. Pederson, eds., *Forhandlingsökonomi I Norden* [The negotiated economy in the Nordic countries] (Copenhagen: DJÖF, 1989); Pestoff, "Organisationernas medverkan och förhandlingar"; and "Towards a New Swedish Model."

19. R. Kramer, *Voluntary Agencies in the Welfare State* (Berkeley: University of California Press, 1981).

20. R. Saltman and C. V. Otter, *Planned Markets and Public Competition: Strategic Reform in Northern European Health Systems* (Philadelphia: Open University Press, 1992).

21. Ibid., 99.

22. Putnam, *Making Democracy Work.*

23. Ibid., 167.

24. A. O. Hirschman, *Exit, Voice and Loyalty: Responses to Decline in the Performance of Firms, Organizations and States* (Cambridge, Mass.: Harvard University Press, 1970).

25. M. Olson, *The Logic of Collective Action* (Cambridge, Mass.: Harvard University Press, 1965, 1970).

26. Putnam, *Making Democracy Work,* 169–171.

27. Pestoff, *Social Enterprises and Civil Democracy.*

28. R. Karasek and T. Theorell, *Healthy Work: Stress, Productivity, and the Reconstruction of Working Life* (New York: Basic Books, 1990).

29. Ibid.

30. A. O. Hirschman, *Shifting Involvements—Private Interests and Political Action* (Princeton, N.J.: Princeton University Press, 1982).
31. Karasek and Theorell, *Healthy Work,* 316–317.
32. V. Pestoff, "Social Reforms in Central and Eastern Europe," *Emergo, Journal of Transforming Economies and Societies,* vol. 5, no. 1 (1998): 15–42.
33. Pestoff, "Reforming Social Services" and *Beyond the Market and State: Social Enterprises and Civil Democracy in a Welfare Society* (Aldershot, 1998).
34. S. Wikström, "Value Creation by Company-Consumer Interaction," *Journal of Marketing Management* 12 (1996): 359–374.
35. Ibid., 363.
36. Ibid.

CHAPTER 15

Healing the Economy the Humanistic Way

Mark A. Lutz, University of Maine

Introduction

ntering a new millennium seems to go hand in hand with some pseudoapocalyptic expectations, the feeling that something drastically new and, it is hoped, much better is just around the corner. It's the time to leave the old and traditional behind in favor of something new and exciting. Something like this may also pertain to the unknown numbers of disillusioned economists appalled with the way their discipline has been going in the last five or six decades. Tired of the standard fare dished up by the mainstream theorists and the policymakers, many yearn for a breakthrough, for a brand-new perspective, or "paradigm," that would come to the rescue of the troubled world. Such wishful thinking may have been encouraged further by the recent and sudden demise of the Marxian perspective, which, for better or worse, has left a great vacuum among the critics of neoclassical economics.

It is the contention of this chapter that, almost from the beginning, there has been another perspective, born out of a set of social convulsions very similar to those we observe today. It was fathered by the Swiss J. C. L. Sismondi in the early decades of the nineteenth century and, thanks to the work of subsequent brothers in spirit such as J. A. Hobson and E. F. Schumacher, is still providing a critical alternative in economic thought, with much to offer in the decades—or perhaps even centuries—to come. For simplicity we label this alternative perspective the *humanistic view* in economics, an approach that moves a concern with human well-being to center stage.

Since it has been described in great detail elsewhere,[1] I will abstain from reviewing the humanistic view here and rest content with the more modest objective of considering the contemporary problems in a light similar to Sismondi's some 200 years ago. More specifically, I will consider some of today's challenging problems by means of a framework that allows us to approach the present situation in a Sismondian manner: to describe the new forces making for social change, to take note of the social problems that it creates, to diagnose those ills, and, finally, to seek some remedies meant to ameliorate socioeconomic life. As I will show, the problems and the remedial strategies have not really changed that much; as the French would say, "Plus ça change, plus c'est la même chose." Let us start by going back in history to the years following the Napoleonic wars.

Early Nineteenth-Century Economics: The Voice of Sismondi

Sismondi, one of the great scholars from Geneva, Switzerland, started out as an ardent admirer and follower of Adam Smith, but the events of the second decade of the nineteenth century, as well as repeated visits to England, soon taught him to reevaluate matters. At the time, France was in the midst of a transformation: Production based on small workshops and skilled artisans gave way to a new industrial system based on machine production and the factory system. In agriculture, meanwhile, technology encouraged also the trend of consolidating small peasant farmers into much larger units; scores of independent family farmers were turned into agricultural day laborers. At the same time the more developed countries in Europe were suffering from something new: recurrent industrial business cycles, or "slumps," which tended to bear down especially hard on already vulnerable segments of the population. In short, the world described by Adam Smith some 40 years earlier looked very different now, a circumstance that did not prevent leading economists of the day from continuing to support the prevailing wisdom consisting of laissez-faire, ever-increasing division of labor and rapid accumulation of a nation's capital stock. Meanwhile hungry workers, barred by law from associating in trade unions, sought refuge in activism for political reforms, while hoards of unemployed roamed the streets of industrial cities in search of bread and work.

It was a period of almost continuous worker unrest culminating sporadically in violent outbursts.[2]

The social malaise of those days was rooted in three interrelated new developments: inequality, poverty, and insecurity. Society had gone through some sort of transformation, dividing itself into a new class of masters and owners facing increasing numbers of "proletarians" (a designation Sisimondi resurrected from the Romans). Under the auspices of free enterprise, the social elites now took aim at profits and accumulation instead of the well-being of the community and its constituents. This situation led to the making of a new underclass of impoverished workers totally dependent on their employers for work and forced to live day by day in a precarious state of insecurity that was likely to worsen with each downturn of the business cycle.

To Sismondi, the historian and humanitarian economist raised in the tradition of Adam Smith, the new and cruel suffering of factory workers seemed so strongly to contradict the optimistic picture his master had painted three decades earlier that he experienced some sort of Gestalt switch: "Suddenly, [the new facts] seemed to fall into place, to clarify each other, because of the new development I gave to my theory; . . . all that had heretofore remained obscure in this science, became clear, and my assumptions gave me solutions to difficulties I had never dreamed before."[3] Sismondi thereafter put forward the first macroeconomic explanation of the social troubles. He pictured an economy suffering simultaneously from overproduction and underconsumption with both being rooted in a growing inequality of income distribution benefiting the profits of the few and hurting the wages of the masses. The basic problem was that competitive cost and wage reduction tended to replace high-income consumers with low-income consumers, with the result that the system had a propensity to create excess capacity, or glutted markets.

Sismondi emphasized the asymmetric bargaining power between the two classes: "necessity weighs daily on the workman [who] must work that he may live, [while the capitalist] may wait and live for a time without employing workmen."[4] Moreover, he deplored the competitive struggle to undersell one's rivals by minimizing wage costs through a relentless introduction of new machinery that was bound to aggravate matters further.[5]

Nevertheless, Sismondi never claimed that the ensuing crisis and disequilibrium would last forever but readily granted that, after some prolonged and painful adjustment process, the macroeconomy would eventually regain macroeconomic equilibrium. But he criticized the economists of his day, especially David Ricardo, for ignoring the time and human suffering it takes as the economy moves from one equilibrium state in search of another. The chief villain, according to Sismondi, was the economists' predilection "to throw themselves into abstractions which make us lose from view entirely the human being," and he warned his contemporaries to beware "of this equilibrium theory that reestablishes itself by its own accord [and which pretends] that it does not matter on which side of a scale one puts or takes a weight because the other will quickly adjust itself." In the real world lacking perfect mobility of both labor and capital, the human costs of market adjustments seemed too significant and too prolonged to ignore. To him, political economy was a moral science, not a mathematical science; and he felt it wrong to be guided only by numbers without considering also human needs and suffering.[6]

In the process of coming down hard on abstraction (even voicing that "every abstraction is always a deception"), Sismondi illustrated his basic concern by questioning the simplistic analysis underpinning the case for free international trade as practiced by the economists in their fight against the British Corn Laws. He drew attention to the fact that Eastern European wheat imports were produced by serf cultivation costing essentially nothing to its sellers and thereby threatening far more than merely the high-cost cultivators in England but agriculture as a whole, and asked: "What will happen to the hands no longer needed in that trade? What will be the cost to the manufacturing classes to maintain them and their families? What will manufacturers lose from the suspension of consumption by a whole class of English workers who make up close to one-half of the nation? What will become of English honor if the Russian czar, every time he should want some concession from England, can starve her by closing the Baltic ports?"[7]

Thus there are two essential elements that to Sismondi were responsible for the social convulsions of those days: First, the new separation of work from ownership caused by the competitive disadvantage and decline of the small farmer and the artisan. That in turn caused an increasing vulnerability of aggregate demand failure and the concomitant (man-made) insecurity and poverty with which the masses had to contend. Second was the unfortunate fact that the prevailing wisdom of the economics establishment upheld a static and abstract equilibrium theory, which acted more like a social sedative than a social science. By insisting that aggregate demand failure, on grounds of abstract logic, could not possibly be reason for the manifest problems of the poor,[8] economists paralyzed effective remedial action and instead recommended that we entrust ourselves to the benefice of the invisible hand operating in the competitive laissez-faire market system.[9]

Given those two causes, Sismondi proposed remedial action aimed at reuniting ownership and work, in the form of measures that would "bring together anew the interests of those who cooperate in production instead of setting them in opposition," and recommended that the legislator encourage a new situation where the worker "after a probationary period would come to possess a right of ownership in the business to which he gives his sweat," more specifically suggesting a 50/50 profit sharing between capital and labor.[10] Moreover, the government should intervene to make the employer, whether capitalist or landlord, legally responsible to maintain workers during a period of dead season, illness, or old age rather than merely shift those costs to the public at large, including their peasant and small-business competitors. Why should the latter have to subsidize the former?[11] Under such a proposal, there would be more of a level playing field; it would prevent that "everyone advances the interests of his group against the common interest, and [no longer would it be forgotten] that he will have to provide in his turn, through private charities, by his contributions to the hospitals, or though the poor rates, for the support of the wretches he labors to create."[12] With schemes such as these, enlisting the government as protector of the poor, Sismondi sought to remedy the harm done by the triumph of the factory and wage system and reintegrate private interests with the common good.

Economics, too, had to be drastically reoriented and carried "forward to new ground." Sismondi proposed a new political economy that would abstain from theorizing based on abstract assumptions and focus more on human welfare than on national wealth. With its insistence on Say's Law, its faith in rapidly self-adjusting markets, and its focus on abstract wealth, political economy could neither understand nor prevent the calamities that afflict so many citizens. Unlike the natural sciences, the observer here is called upon to recognize unjust suffering that comes from socially created institutions victimizing the poor and powerless. For Sismondi, a new political economy striving for human well-being ought to be concerned that the benefits of wealth get so diffused that everyone's basic material needs can be met. In all of this, Sismondi looked forward to a possibly quite remote time, "when the combined thoughts of economists will be able to recommend to sovereign authority a change in the system of laws."[13] Today, in spite of the prevailing orthodoxy having paid little attention to what he had to say, he is credited as the precursor of social legislation in France and is said to have anticipated much of the Keynesian revolution that took place almost 100 years after he died.

Late-Twentieth-Century Economics: A Humanistic Perspective

Today we are once again under the spell of some sort of economic transformation driven to a significant extent by the fall of communism opening the entire world to the play of free-market forces under the guise of globalization: the integration of trade, finance, and information creating a global market and culture. As collateral effects we also have been witnessing a wave of corporate-type privatization and commercialization inundating the globe. Once again, as it was 190 years ago, the transformation is to a large extent supported and encouraged by the now global teachings of economists who never tire of reminding the public of the great merits of free enterprise, free international trade, and free capital movements.

The Current Malaise

Unlike the painful times of the early nineteenth century, today's socioeconomic malaise is something we are all too well familiar with and can relate to personally. Lester Thurow, in his new book, *The Future of Capitalism,* devotes an entire chapter on making a comprehensive sketch, or "map," of the present situation.[14] There he paints a well-documented and rather grim picture composed of the growing inequality of income and wealth, the ongoing fall in real wages, the new and heavy unemployment in Europe, the growth of economic insecurity induced by the new phenomenon of corporate "downsizing," the emergence of a new "lumpen proletariat" manifest by the phenomenon of homelessness, and the disintegration of the family undermined by economic forces. Accepting his analysis and the data he marshals to support it, it appears redundant to cover the same ground here, except to mention some brand-new developments: the dismantling of the welfare state, the growing movement to tie up the future fortunes of social security with the performance of the stock market, and the mounting environmental threat looming over us, particularly the alarming depletion of the atmospheric ozone layer.

The socioeconomic turmoil confronting us today resembles in many of its manifestations in the world of Sismondi; yet in the Northern Hemisphere it cannot be attributed to the forces of industrialization but rather to the consequences of the current *deindustrialization* of the economy. Moreover, Sismondi's main concern was with the trouble and causes of *cyclical* instability, while today we are confronted with a phenomenon that appears to be structural in nature. Nevertheless, in both cases the ultimate villain turns out to be unbridled and dysfunctional competition driven by the imperative to cut costs in order to defend or augment the incomes of capital owners.

Diagnosing the Problem

In the mid-1980s humanistic economists such as John Culbertson from the University of Wisconsin started to predict a steady decline in the living standards of the West due to forces of unregulated international competition.[15] He had a strong influence on others, especially Herman Daly, who was about to take a position at the World Bank. Daly since has been vigorously attacking both unregulated international competition and modern trade theory.[16] In this chapter I would like to honor John Culbertson's pioneering insight by continuing in his tradition of focusing on international competition as the root of the problem. Since economists, misunderstanding the nature of trade, have been counterproductive in actively discouraging policymakers from apprehending, confronting, and solving the problem, I first have to demonstrate the fatal blind spot hindering trade theory. As in Sismondi's time, the origin of the problem is rooted in the clinging to a highly abstract theory based on unrealistic assumptions. More specifically, the economist, in looking at the "four horsemen" of today's workplace in the United States (global competition, technology, downsizing, and the growth of a contingent workforce) through the glasses of international trade theory, particularly the lens of comparative advantage, sees a distorted and false picture in which global competition can do no wrong, and technology takes the blame instead. Let us briefly discuss the deeply problematic aspect bedeviling contemporary international economic theory.

The notion of comparative advantage as driving trade between nations dates back to Sismondi's time when Ricardo first articulated the idea, but *only* in the context of zero capital mobility across international borders. To Ricardo, the concept of comparative advantage was applicable since capitalists in his day were observed to have a natural disinclination to entrust their capital to foreign hands and laws.[17] One of the cofounders of the newer version of trade theory had reservations too, cautioning that every argument about the gains from international trade is subject to very strong qualification. He emphasized that such argument "is based on a *far-reaching* abstraction, namely that trade will not affect the supply of productive factors."[18] But economists soon made it a habit to stick with the far-reaching (better, far-fetched) abstraction of simply assuming zero factor mobility between nations and then to look at the world that way. Every country has its own endowment of labor and capital, the relative proportion of each determining comparative advantage. More recently, perhaps to sidestep the mounting realization that our actual world is no longer one of fixed national endowments of labor and capital, there has been a shift: Instead of labor *and capital,* trade economists now talk in terms of a nation's relative endowment of skilled labor on one hand and unskilled labor on the other. With international migration still at relatively low levels, this move attempts to render Ohlin's "far-reaching abstraction" a little more palatable.

Armed with this novel concept, economists believe that trade, by enhancing efficiency and national income through international specialization, can do a lot of good but never any harm. One of the crown jewels of this doctrine is the theoretical finding that a country, let us say China, can be blessed with a situation where it could produce *every* good cheaper than any other country, and, still, it will be in its interest to specialize only in producing and exporting certain goods, while importing the rest from abroad. In such a textbook world there is simply not much to fear when it comes to low-wage competition from the South. Logically, a country *must* always have its share of industries where it enjoys a comparative advantage, regardless how high its factor costs might be. Neither is there any way by which trade could negatively affect productivity, real earnings, and growth. Trade in the textbook world is indeed a mutually beneficial game allowing countries to cooperate together rather than compete with each other.[19] It should come as no surprise that economists applying this theory will find that the current malaise must be due to lack of productivity growth, rigid labor markets, and technology. The one exception is the persistent rise in income inequality, but even in the latter case technology, not factor price equalization due to trade, generally is fingered as the main culprit.[20]

The problem is that comparative advantage ceases to be relevant even when put in the context of two types of domestic labor, because skills, understood as embodied knowledge, are no longer internationally immobile. With the new information technology, not only unskilled but also many highly skilled jobs can be, and are, being moved abroad.[21] These are brand-new changes, and much of them are the result of two basic developments, the first being the fact that the new technologies allow knowledge to be "disembodied," codified, and "reembodied" somewhere else. All that is needed is software, a modem, and a phone connection. The second development relates to Asia rapidly catching up in terms of technology. South Korea's expenditures on research and development (measured as a percentage of gross domestic product [GDP]) are now about as high as in the United States and much higher than in Germany or Britain. Taiwan outspends Canada and Italy and is now the world's second largest producer of notebook computers.[22] Furthermore, both China and countries of the former Soviet Union feature a highly educated labor force willing to work at a fraction of the cost of an American with the same educational credentials. There may also be trouble brewing for U.S. professionals who already witness their skills moved around the globe by U.S. corporations importing every year more than 100,000 qualified foreigners for temporary training by working alongside Americans and subsequently assigning them to overseas plants to practice what they learned.[23] The only skilled occupations that can be expected to successfully resist being shifted where labor is the cheapest are those where physical contact is an essential element, as in many domains of the service sector. Here again, as with capital mobility, it is the transnational corporation that lubricates the wheels by serving as "global knowledge brokers." Without multinational firms, we might still live in a world resembling that of comparative advantage based on a country's relative endowment of skills, but it is no longer the world we live in. As a result, international trade behaves according to the principle of *absolute* advantage. Unless this basic fact is recognized, we cannot be expected to explain the contemporary malaise.

Under absolute advantage production shifts where it is most profitable, where at world prices the costs are the lowest. As one theoretical study put it somewhat extremely: "a country can theoretically be 'undersold all round' and end up with zero employment and output. Technical progress or wage reductions elsewhere can cause the emigration of industries *with no mechanism to ensure their replacement*."[24] Of course, lowest cost is not to be measured by labor compensation alone, but the productivity of that labor needs to be considered as well. No doubt a country such as India with wage levels being a fraction of those in the United States suffers also from very low average productivity levels.[25] The mere fact that India imports some manufactured goods from the United States is already sufficient evidence that its labor costs per unit in those particular sectors may be significantly higher than in this country. But at the same time, there is no a priori reason why it cannot be imagined that in a world where capital, technology, and skills are mobile, India may in time find itself in a situation in which even those goods can be produced cheaper at home, at least as long as there is a surplus of labor.

It is my contention that just as in Sismondi's time, when economists wrapped up in the static logic of Say's Law could not understand and appreciate the character of the cyclical convulsions hitting economies periodically, so is it now with comparative advantage and deindustrialization, low wage growth, and insecurity. As many textbooks in trade theory make clear, the comparative advantage doctrine is based on a whole set of assumptions beyond the "far-reaching abstraction" already have mentioned. They include perfect factor mobility in the home market, full employment, and balanced trade.[26]

One common characteristic of any abstract theory is that it deliberately overlooks institutional content. Trade theory is no different. It is based on the view of a competitive labor market where wages are dictated by productivity. Every exchange is voluntary and therefore can be assumed to be beneficial. No considerations of power and dependency affect wage bargaining. Similarly, due to the full-employment assumption, laid-off workers made redundant by technological change find work quickly in another industry. As in Sismondi's time, the market is said to be self-adjusting, allowing a new equilibrium to be reestablished quickly. Not surprisingly, the actual human costs of being dislocated by trade are generally overlooked when economists attempt to demonstrate the increased efficiency of free trade.

One important implication of ignoring institutions pertains to the issue of labor standards. In contrast to standard economic theory, wages in a Third World country (or anywhere else for that matter) may not always increase with productivity gains. Only if they did so could we forget about the institutional context of the labor market and such matters as the need for a "social charter" in trade agreements such as the North American Free Trade Agreement (NAFTA) or the General Agreement on Tariffs and Trade (GATT). In the real world, however, such variables as minimum wages, collective bargaining, trade union strength, and social legislation do affect both wage levels and productivity, and as a result they also codetermine unit labor costs. Therefore, it is easy to visualize a country with an oppressive labor relations system that outlaws unions, lacks social security, and suppresses wage growth being able to keep wages from rising as fast as productivity does, with the result that the country becomes more inviting to multinational corporations. It's a beggarthy-neighbor strategy that tends to "harmonize" labor standards all over the world downward. Here we have dysfunctional competition where the "good guys" (in this case the socially responsible enterprises) finish last. This kind of realistic expectation permits economist James Stanford to conclude: "it is not 'cheap foreign labor' that workers need fear, instead it is the impact of repressive labor market institutions on the relationship between wages and productivity that poses the challenge," and he illustrates the problem with Mexico during the 1980s.[27] Mexico is not alone. In manufacturing, wages as a percentage of value added have been falling consistently in most countries, including the United States. Table 15.1 demonstrates the general tendency of labor's share of income generated in industry to shrink slowly.[28]

In the absence of any better data, we have plenty of reasons to suspect that in a global economy with major players such as China, India, and Russia, the dual phenomena of absolute advantage competition combined with competitive pressures to lower labor standards will not create a world that holds a lot of promise for working families either here or abroad. The fact that economists, imprisoned by trade theory and its abstract assumptions, are unable to see any problem does little to lighten the gloomy prospect.

Table 15.1   Total Earnings as Percent of Value Added in Manufacturing,
1970–1992

	1970	1990	1992
USA	47	36	35
Canada	53	46	47
UK	50	42	44
Germany	46	41	41*
Ireland	49	27	26
Japan	32	33	35
India	46	43	38
Indonesia	26	20	19
Thailand	26	16	12*
Chile	19	17	18
Mexico	44	20	22*
Malaysia	28	27	27
South Korea	25	28	26

*Figures are for 1991 and in the case of Germany pertain to borders prior to reunification.

The upshot of all these real-world developments seems to both empower corporations and disempower society. Clearly, the credible threat to move operations abroad has led to the weakening of bargaining power of labor.[29] Workers, both unskilled and skilled, have been under mounting pressure to negotiate their wages with utmost moderation, which would explain the stagnation in the growth of labor compensation in the United States.[30] The new pressures in the global economy, specifically the requirement of being large, have also led to a new wave of megamergers and acquisitions making scores of employees suddenly redundant.[31] Job security is rapidly evaporating and becoming a daily concern for many employees.[32] Growing corporate power combined with the pressure to cut costs in labor compensation has led to a sizable contingent of the workforce primarily in the nonunion sector, such as commercial banking. Meanwhile, corporate profits and stock markets have been soaring in most places, making for an increasingly polarized social economy that, as in Sismondi's time, may be becoming more and more vulnerable to a weakening of consumption demand in a world of rapidly growing supply capacity. The resulting macroeconomic fragility needs to be controlled more and more by spending hundreds of billions of dollars on corporate advertising and by the buildup of consumer debt.

Footloose corporations have also weakened the state by diminishing its power to tax, and with it, its ability to secure an adequate financing of the welfare state.[33] The resulting cuts in the safety net further increase job insecurity, thereby setting the stage for an ever-pervasive "jungle fighter" mentality where citizens can no longer afford to care for anyone except themselves.[34] In short, globalization creates a "new man" that may be very similar to the kind of individual assumed by economic theory: instrumentally rational, self-interested, calculating, and incapable of recognizing intrinsic value or dignity in others or in nature. More than likely, it will also pave the way for even more materialism and commercialism—not at all the fulfillment of a humanistic dream.

Another casualty of corporate power in the world of absolute advantage in international commerce is the global environment and with it the future generations of the world. As with labor standards, trade exerts a competitively driven downward pressure on environmental protection. Again, it is the threat of shifting production abroad where standards tend to be much more lax that induces governments to go easy on enforcement of existing regulations and be reluctant to pass new regulations. Things are made worse by the new World Trade Organization (WTO), which tends to see national standards protecting the environment as projectionist devices in disguise and therefore subject to challenge by trading partners.[35]

Last but not least, unregulated global trade tends to favor corporate agribusiness at the expense of small farmers, something that is not without consequences for the less-developed countries. It speeds up the flow of people from the countryside to the already overcrowded and polluted big cities as well as increasing the pressures to emigrate.[36]

In conclusion, the issue today seems to be no longer North vs. South but rather, as in Sismondi's day, labor vs. capital. The villain is dysfunctional competition pushing labor and environmental standards down to the lowest common denominator or, more specifically, to levels of the countries that have no standards at all. The logic of globalization appears to point to massive, global-scale human and environmental degradation in both industrialized and industrializing countries. This somber diagnosis is certainly in line with common sense and quite readily accepted by the layman. One has to be an academic economist trained in comparative advantage theory to see things differently and more optimistically. As Alan Ehrenhalt recently joked about economists' persistent denial of any harm done by trade, to him they continue to hold on to the maxim that the idea of blaming trade "might be fine in practice, but it does not work in theory."[37] Nothing so far seems able to change this mind-set; at this stage, we can only hope that academic economists too will soon face competition from the international marketplace.[38] Meanwhile, the kind of diagnosis offered here will be either ignored or shrugged off as not *real* economics but opinionated and uneducated journalism instead. Sismondi already had experienced much of the same fate when arguing against Say's Law and laissez-faire. Happily, truth is not a matter of social convention and has a way of asserting itself sooner or later.

The Medicine

Remedial action from the orthodox point of view hardly seems necessary. The market, if allowed to function freely, will react fast enough to the new technologically driven changes in labor demand and so reestablish a new equilibrium where the temporarily displaced will find new work in those industries that are more skill intensive. All state action might possibly accomplish is to lend a helping hand by encouraging retraining for the relatively unskilled and by trying to provide more and better education for all. Education will improve productivity and wages.[39] Another recommendation emanating from the standard view would be to increase reliance on global specialization and trade, fueling GDP growth and a rising standard of living. Without going into details here, all these remedies seem as questionable as the diagnosis that leads to their recommendation. We may note the following problems with such medicine: First, the displaced workers are not likely to find jobs in the export industries, since under absolute advantage foreign competition erodes many fronts. Second, more education does not take place in a global vacuum. Instead, every country is trying to do the same, and countries such as China and the former republics of the Soviet Union already have a highly educated labor force poised to be called to the global trading floor. Finally, and assuming it can be accomplished, higher growth rates are unlikely to be sustainable from an ecological viewpoint that stresses the logic of a limited carrying capacity of the Earth.[40] Time will tell just how well the neoclassical remedies will work and at what costs. Meanwhile, I will outline some of the remedial measures that would be consistent with a humanistic approach to healing the economy.

Humanistically speaking, we need *three reforms:* the reform of our political institutions, the reform of our economic institutions and, finally, the reform of economic science. The first type of reform is not a topic of this chapter; I mention it here because in a political democracy, it is a prerequisite for confronting the globalizing strategies of the multinational firms. Such reform must deal with taking money out of politics and returning government to the people through such measures as stringent campaign finance reform and restrictions of corporate lobbying. We need such a step to assure that government will be in the name of the people rather than according to the will of the wealthier tiers of society that represent corporate interests. Quite probably, such a first step presupposes some new political climate, perhaps the kind of populism that can reasonably be expected to emerge if the current socioeconomic malaise continues or gets worse. Similarly, effective attempts will have to be made to pry the media from corporate control, allowing thereby the political policy debates to be framed by an intelligent common sense and motivated by a concern for every citizen's need for human dignity and self-respect.[41] Regardless of how radical all this may sound, without prior change of the political context, much of the talk about redesigning the economy is not likely to change the way business is done.

The second reform pertains to the economy. As in Sismondi's time, much of the contemporary socioeconomic trouble has its roots in the divorce of work and ownership. Such a separation made for a much more fragile balance between consumption and production, something that preoccupied Sismondi. Today it creates the increasing gap between labor incomes and total value added that has been observed. More and more of the revenue goes to profits, capital, and stockholders, less and less stays with the workers. How to stop it? Sismondi had pointed to profit sharing and co-ownership; for him it was the way to harmonize the interests of labor and capital. With both feet firmly planted on the ground, Sismondi had little sympathy with the idealistic notions of communal cooperatives advertised by some of his Utopian contemporaries.[42] Neither could he anticipate the new ways of rewriting ownership and work.

Thanks to the Mondragon Cooperative Corporation (MCC) we now have a new *cooperative solution,* a model that allows an essentially cooperative firm to become as large as a regular corporation as well as to avoid the pitfalls of Yugoslav-style social ownership. Mondragon, one of Spain's leading industrial firms, has today more than 20,000 worker members who share in profits and can decide where to invest their capital.[43] By standing prevailing institutional practices on their head, labor hires capital and alone is the residual claimant. In this way all productivity gains would ultimately find their way into higher pay of worker members. Moreover, in order to cope with the competitiveness of large multinational corporations like their European competitors (Electrolux, Boesch, etc.), MCC has started to set up offshore plants in such places as Morocco, Egypt, Malaysia, China, and Mexico. As for now, it is their stated goal to convert those enterprises eventually to full-fledged cooperatives associated with MCC but also enjoying the right to become independent and autonomous forms, should their workforce so decide. For the interim, there is a plan to introduce progressively Sismondi-type profit sharing.[44] Should the MCC follow through on those intentions, there would be an effective mechanism to spread profit sharing and cooperatives to the low-wage countries, making it possible that even under the principle of absolute advantage the national interests of both North *and* South would be served. Labor standards in the industrializing countries would no longer be under pressure to be beaten down toward the lowest possible common denominator. In essence, we would have an ideal humanistic solution to some of the core problems of globalization we face today.

As explained elsewhere, the American equivalent to a Mondragon-type cooperative is the legal institution of Employee Stock Ownership Plans (ESOPs) allowing workers to buy the firm on borrowed finance with the acquired assets serving as collateral for the loan.[45] Such leveraged buyouts make it quite possible to convert even very large firms, such as United Airlines, into worker ownership. And regardless of whether we have a world of Mondragons or a world of ESOPs, technological progress and more capital-intensive production techniques would benefit labor as well as capital. Furthermore, the greater *diffusion* of national wealth and unearned incomes would minimize any tendency toward underconsumption or aggregate demand deficiency, the point that had been so crucial to Sismondi.[46] At least on theoretical grounds, we could expect a global economy that would tend to operate more smoothly and equitably than what we have today.

Add to this the fact that an economy with cooperatives instead of corporations would also encourage more moral and social restraint in the maximization of profits. This would be expected since cooperatives, by their very nature, are deeply linked to their communities, making them very hesitant to shut down local plants in order to produce cheaper abroad. Also, the absence of stock markets and shareholder pressure will allow cooperatives to better integrate community values into their decision making. So, for example, cooperatives *can* trade off extra profits for more social responsibility whenever circumstances demand, while management of the absentee-owned corporation, especially in the United States, is under formidable pressure to be concerned primarily with shareholder "value," or maximum quarterly dividends.

Short of the radical restructuring contemplated here, other policy measures also would help diffuse the current malaise and promote a healing of the economy, at least in the industrialized countries. Let me briefly mention some.

First, there is Culbertson's 1988 proposal of managed trade.[47] The United States, by means of a newly established and quasi-independent

Foreign Trade Agency, would plan and administer a policy of assuring mutually *balanced* trade with low-wage countries. This is a proposal of balancing imports with the prevailing level of exports by means of auctioning off import licenses.[48]

Second, a social clause on labor rights needs to be built into trade agreements. One way to do this is to overcome the resistance of low-wage countries by developing regional trade blocs that would admit newcomers only if they agree to play by such rules.

Third, and here again we follow Sismondi's principles of reform, the owners of multinational corporations have to be given financial disincentives that will prevent them from reaping extra profits by shifting costs to the public. One way to do this is to establish tax policies that would discourage the hiring of contingent workers with no benefits. Such a move may be facilitated by shifting taxes from labor (the payroll tax) to capital, especially a new tax on corporate wealth or its financial assets. Similarly, a tax could be levied that rises with the relative proportion of employment abroad, thereby making it more profitable to hire domestic workers. There could also be some tax relief for the hiring and training of low-skilled employees in the United States. Ideally, such tax policies could be implemented at the supranational level.

Fourth, public policy has to reflect more the basic humanistic concern that the striving for global growth may endanger the planet and future generations everywhere. Deprivation and poverty at home and abroad will demand increasingly some scheme of redistributing incomes. In other words, when dealing with the less-developed countries in Latin America and Africa, there has to be a new realization that helping them through targeted foreign aid is preferable to tolerating immigration motivated by economic reasons. So, for example, the revenue from Culbertson's import auction may be rebated to the country in question as long as it demonstrates progress in sharing productivity gains with its workforce and shows respect for internationally relevant environmental standards. Debt relief may be another commendable move, especially for those strangled African countries that often are compelled by material circumstances to neglect environmental imperatives in order to afford payments on the debt. In short, the ultimate goal of economics may no longer be overcoming scarcity by means of relentless global growth but using the alternative approach of moderating extreme human privation by means of steady-state, environmentally sustainable economies in the North transferring resources rather than jobs to the South.

This point brings us to the last of the three reforms: Sismondi's basic concern that economic science has to change, be brought forward to new ground. The public invests in its arts and sciences expecting to get some benefits in terms of cultural enrichment and sound policy recommendations. The common interest is not saved by a value-free, highly abstract and positivistic approach grounded in counterfactual assumptions and mathematics. Do we really need a "mathematical politics" informed by two-centuries-old "Whig" values? The humanistic answer is simple and clear: Reality has to be put first, elegant theory only second. We need to heed Sismondi's call for a normative economics that respects human dignity and is sensitive to human suffering and unmet basic human needs. In other words, we need an economics that does not, in the name of natural science, shy away from ethical considerations. Sismondi offered a more social economics centered on human well-being. Today we need it more than ever when dealing with the current predicament of a laissez-faire global economy. Sadly, international economic theory has become increasingly ideological, centered on the dogmatic economic teachings of comparative advantage. It is capitalist, intellectualized ideology that is likely to keep the world enchained for many more years to come. And if it ever should lose its grip on humanity, in all likelihood it won't be as a result of academic argument. As Sismondi observed 160 years ago:

> writing makes little impression when it attacks a dominant system. Facts are more obstinate and more rebellious. They do not manifest themselves less from its being supposed that they can be refuted without being heard, as if they were only writings; they often increase from having been neglected, and then they fall with their whole weight on the most skillfully constructed theory, crushing and overthrowing it at the very moment when its author was congratulating himself on having victoriously refuted all his adversaries.[49]

Conclusion

Our descendants may remember the 1990s as the historic moment when socialism as an ideology collapsed. But the next decade or two may also become known as the time when capitalist ideology was on trial. If there is a great transformation of society in the twenty-first century, it may very well be guided by a new economics, an economics that does not mistake theory for reality, that does not abstract from history and social institutions and human needs. The so-called harsh reality of global competition is a man-made artifact. We do have a choice of whether to adjust human well-being to the imperative of international markets or to regulate global competition in order to preserve humanity. In pursuing the latter case, we honor Sismondi and his followers in proposing to heal the world along humanistic lines.

Notes

1. Mark A. Lutz, *Economics for the Common Good* (London: Routledge, 1999).
2. C. R. Fay, *Life and Labour in the Nineteenth Century* (New York: Greenwood Press, 1969; originally published 1920), part 1.
3. J. C. L. Simonde de Sismondi, *New Principles of Political Economy*, 2d ed. (New Brunswick, N.J.: Transaction Publishers, 1991).
4. Ibid., 285.
5. According to Sismondi, ibid., 299: "Surely no one will maintain that it can be advantageous to substitute a machine for a man, if this man cannot find work elsewhere," or "that it is not better to have a population composed of citizens than of steam engines, even though the cotton cloth of the first should be a little dearer than that of the second.
6. Ibid., 487, 232.
7. Ibid., 459, 204–205.
8. It was not until John Maynard Keynes that this logic was seen as faulty. Sismondi's early attack on Say's Law in *dynamic* terms now is generally considered to have been valid. See Thomas Sowell, *Say's Law: An Historical Analysis* (Princeton, N.J.: Princeton University Press, 1972).
9. See Rajani Kanth, *Political Economy and Laissez-Faire* (Totowa, N.J.: Rowman and Littlefield, 1986).
10. Sismondi, *New Principles of Political Economy*, 573.
11. In ibid., 579, Sismondi asks: "Is the wage subsidy the parish gives to the workers [of the rich] not as unjust as if the same parish were charged to furnish oats to their horses?"
12. Similarly, in the case of technological unemployment, a factory owner who would fire part of his workforce in order to replace them by machines would soon discover that such a move was not in his interest "if all the people who worked find no other means of working again, and he were bound to support them at the hospital while he stoked the boilers." Ibid., 583.
13. Ibid., 636.
14. Lester Thurow, *The Future of Capitalism* (New York: Viking Penguin, 1996).
15. John Culbertson, *International Trade and the Future of the West* (Madison, Wisc.: 21st Century Press, 1984).
16. Herman E. Daly and John Cobb, *For the Common Good* (Boston: Beacon Press, 1989), chap. 11. In private communication, Herman Daly told me that it was his coauthor, John Cobb, a philosopher, who first brought Culbertson's book to his attention and only after prolonged discussions was able to persuade him, the economist, of the irrelevance of comparative advantage theory. It cer-

tainly goes to show that interdisciplinary coauthorship can be a most fruitful approach to economic problems.

17. David Ricardo, *Principles of Political Economy and Taxation*, Sraffa ed. (Cambridge: Cambridge University Press, 1951; originally published 1826).

18. Bertil Ohlin, "The Theory of Trade," in Harry Flam and M. June Flanders, eds., *Heckscher-Ohlin Trade Theory* (Cambridge, Mass.: MIT Press, 1991; originally published 1924), 76–214; quoted on 164, emphasis added.

19. Because of this trade theory, protagonist Krugman rails against anybody who talks about countries competing against each other as "pop international economists." Paul Krugman, *Pop Internationalism* (Cambridge, Mass.: MIT Press, 1996). The list of offenders also includes his colleague at MIT, Lester Thurow; readers may want to consult a recent feature story in the *New York Times* comparing the two economists: Louis Uchitelle, "Like Oil and Water: A Tale of Two Economists," *New York Times*, February 16, 1997, sect. F1, 10.

20. Adrian Wood recently has challenged that type finding as strongly underestimating the effect trade has had. According to his analysis, about three-quarters of the 20 percent drop in the demand for unskilled workers during the last two decades can be attributed to manufacturing imports from the South. He points to the timing, magnitude, and cross-country variation of the relative deterioration of unskilled earnings. See Wood, *North-South Trade, Employment and Inequality: Changing Fortunes in a Skill-Driven World*, IDS Development Studies Series (Oxford: Clarendon Press, 1994), 17. His new findings must have been unsettling for many economists; witness, for example, how the (strongly pro free trade) magazine *The Economist* quite adroitly referred to his results as "something nasty in the woodshed" (October 1, 1994, 16). Nevertheless, Wood's study is still accepting the theoretical framework of comparative advantage; he merely modifies some of the empirical findings based on that theory.

21. There is plenty of anecdotal evidence today of this new phenomenon. The *Wall Street Journal* abounds with front-page stories about skilled work being shifted to Irish and Indian engineers, Boeing having passenger jets being developed in China, the German giant Hoechst shifting the bulk of its genetic research to the lower-wage United States. Swissair has been outsourcing its accounting to India. Intel and Hewlett-Packard are relying increasingly on bargain-priced Malaysians, while in Moscow we are told that "almost every programmer worth his salt works for a Western company." *The Economist* tells us that "more than 100 of America's top 500 firms buy software services from India, where programmers are typically paid less than a quarter of the American rate." Moreover, outsourcing now also stretches to processing hospital records, credit reports, insurance claims, and virtually all production of television cartoons being done abroad. *The Economist*, September 28, 1996, 32; and February 22, 1997, 75.

22. *The Economist*, September 28, 1996, 35.

23. *Wall Street Journal,* March 17, 1993, A1.

24. Anthony Brewer, "Trade with Fixed Real Wages and Mobile Capital," *Journal of International Trade* 18 (1985): 177–186; quoted on 180, emphasis added.

25. Stephen S. Golub, "Comparative Advantage and Absolute Advantage in the Asia-Pacific Region," Federal Reserve Bank of San Francisco, Working Paper 9, 1995.

26. Culbertson, *International Trade,* chap. 6; Robert E. Prasch, "Reassessing the Theory of Comparative Advantage," *Review of Political Economy* 8, no. 1 (1996): 37–55. These counterfactual assumptions also are embodied in most of the models with which economists assess prospective impacts of changing trade regimes. See James Stanford, "Continental Economic Integration: Modling the Impact of Labor," *Annals of the American Academy* (March 1993): 92–111. A classic illustration is the ill-fated predictions that economists derived from their models with respect to NAFTA. Instead of the advertised 170,000 new U.S. jobs by 1995, the country has lost hundreds of thousands. Neither can the peso devaluation be blamed. In fact, Jeffrey Faux, one of the leaders of the anti-NAFTA efforts, said in 1993: "Mexico is going to have a crisis . . . with or without NAFTA. The Peso is overvalued, and real estate and financial markets are going through a speculative excess. These bubbles will burst as soon as the NAFTA issue is resolved. Jeff Faux, "No to NAFTA," *Dissent* (Summer 1993): 309–315. Moreover, the devaluation coincided with the peasant uprising in Chiapas, a revolt aimed, to a significant level, at NAFTA.

27. James Stanford, "North American Economic Integration and the International Regulation of Labor Standards," in Bruno Stein, ed., *Contemporary Issues in Labor and Employment Law* (Boston: Little, Brown, 1994), 3–46; quoted on 18.

28. The newer report no longer contains this table. The idea for featuring these figures comes from reading William G. Grieder, *One World, Ready or Not (The Mania of Global Capitalism)* (New York: Simon and Schuster, 1997), a brilliant work that covers similar ground. Quite obviously, it could not have been written by an economist.

29. Thomas Palley, "Capital Mobility and the Threat to American Prosperity," *Challenge* (November-December 1994): 31–39.

30. A classic example is the Xerox case where employees accepted pay cuts averaging 30 percent in exchange for job security. See Thea Lee and Robert Scott, "Third World Growth," *Harvard Business Review* (November-December 1994): 18.

31. See, for example, the story in the *Wall Street Journal* of February 26, 1997, A1, which blames "above all, a globalizing economy in which companies often find they must become big to compete, either by acquiring or by being acquired."

32. Alan Greenspan cited a recent poll showing that 46 percent of employees at major companies were frequently fearful of being laid off in 1996. During the

early days of the 1990 recession, the corresponding figure had been only 25 percent. *Wall Street Journal,* February 26, 1977, A4.

33. Robert E. Prasch, "Free Trade and the Future of the Welfare State," *Global Justice* 1997.

34. The hypothesis that insecurity affects moral character has long been a central tenet of a humanistic economics. See Mark A. Lutz and Kenneth Lux, *Humanistic Economics: The New Challenge* (New York: Bootstrap Publishing, 1998): 124–125. It is also a primary implication derived from personality theory. See Abraham Maslow, *Motivation and Personality,* 2d ed. (New York: Harper & Row, 1970), chap. 4.

35. Lori Wallach, "Hidden Dangers of GATT and NAFTA," in Ralph Nader et al., eds., *The Case Against "Free Trade": GATT, NAFTA, and the Globalization of Corporate Power* (San Francisco: Earth Island Press, 1993), 23–64.

36. In Mexico, for example, the government, in accordance with the recent trade pacts, abolished price supports to farmers growing basic grains and has been phasing out credit programs and state agencies that provided distribution systems for agricultural products. Another trade-related reform was the altering of Mexico's constitutional provision establishing eijdos (communally held farmland) that, with the passing of NAFTA, may now be privately bought and sold. In terms of Mexican rural life, the anticipated flood of cheap imports of U.S. grains has been slowed down by the drastic peso devaluation; otherwise the damage done by free trade would in all likelihood be shockingly manifest.

37. Ehrenhalt, "Keepers of the Dismal Faith," *New York Times,* February 23, 1997.

38. A lot of routine, such as compiling relevant data sets or updating past research with new data, can easily be imagined to be carried out in the Philippines or India. In today's electronic age with the Internet, there is no obvious reason why a researcher with U.S. residence has any kind of significant advantage in terms of data collection and processing, especially the way most economic research is conducted today. To the extent that economic research is financed by corporations, the growing temptation to shift those skills abroad is very easy to imagine. Finally, teaching too is not invulnerable to being conveyed either live by cable or through videocassettes. Cash-strapped colleges may be tempted to get "a bigger bang for their bucks" by subscribing to a foreign service.

39. For a discussion of the inherent problems undermining the success of such strategy, see Thurow, *Future of Capitalism,* chap. 14.

40. Herman E. Daly, *Beyond Growth: The Economics of Sustainable Development* (Boston: Beacon Press, 1996); Paul Ehrlich, *The Population Explosion* (London: Hutchinson, 1990).

41. For a tightly argued humanistic treatise in political philosophy along these lines, see Alan Gewirth, *The Community of Rights* (Chicago: University of Chicago Press, 1996).

42. Sismondi, *New Principles of Political Economy,* 584–585.

43. Lutz, "Mondragon Cooperative Complex."

44. A recent visit by the author to MCC's Mexican plant in Guadalajara indicated little progress in this respect.

45. See, for example, David Ellerman, *The Democratic Worker-Owned Firm: A Model for East and West* (Boston: Unwin Hyman, 1990). In order to duplicate some of the essential features of a cooperative. ESOPs have to be structured "democratic," meaning that the employee-owners can instruct the trustees how to make the decisions. To date, only a small number of democratic ESOPs are functioning.

46. Already in 1815 he had written: "The diffusion of wealth, still more than its accumulation, truly constitutes national prosperity, because it keeps up the kind of consumption most favorable for national re-production." Sismondi, *Political Economy.*

47. John Culbertson, *The Trade Threat and U.S. Trade Policy* (Madison, Wis.: 21st Century Press, 1989).

48. Needless to say, consumer prices will be higher under this proposal, but what benefit are lower prices for the unemployed?

49. J. C. L. Sismondi, *Political Economy and the Philosophy of Government* (originally published in 1847) (New York: Augustus M. Kelley, 1996).

CHAPTER 16

The Quest for Universal Capitalism in the United States

Kenneth B. Taylor, Villanova University

The vision of the liberal society in America was forged in the intellectual crucible between the English and French revolutions. The American Revolution was based on liberal ideals and produced a call for release from commercial exploitation and political freedom. However, in the whirlwind of explosive global economic growth in the last decade of the twentieth century, a critical portion of the founding ideals have been lost amid a cacophonous, materialistic culture. This chapter follows the trail of thoughts advocating some form of Universal Capitalism from the eighteenth century to the present in America. It then briefly examines relevant socioeconomic forces shaping the early twenty-first century and reflects upon the prospects for serious movement toward a more democratic economy.

Before we begin the journey into the next century, it is worth taking a few moments to listen to what those who have envisioned America becoming a nation embodying economic democracy had to say; for in their vision runs a deep truth and a great hope.

The deep truth is that all humans live on Earth together and have a common destiny. Whatever that collective destiny may be, no individual will arrive there alone. Only within the context of community can we become whatever it is we will become as humans. In more recent times, Martin Luther King, Jr., reflected this truth when he spoke these words: "In a real sense all life is interrelated. All persons are caught in an inescapable network of mutuality, tied in a single garment of destiny. Whatever affects one directly affects all indirectly. I can never be what I ought to be until you are what you ought to be, and you can never be what you ought to be until I am what I ought to be. This is the interrelated structure of reality."[1]

The Past

The rallying cry of the French revolutionists, "Liberty, Equality, Fraternity," embodied the great hope. In simple terms that hope was that we throw off the chains of the past and find a way to live free and peacefully while fairly sharing the abundance of our Earth. Thomas Paine, the great American patriot, stated in "Common Sense" that "We have it in our power to begin the world over again. A situation similar to the present hath not appeared since the days of Noah until now. The birthday of a new world is at hand. . . ."[2] His sense of the opportunity to define liberal society within the American context was echoed in the writings of the founding fathers.

Among them, Thomas Jefferson was comprehensive in the particulars of this vision. From the vantage point of the late eighteenth century, Jefferson conceived the ideal society being an agrarian economy in which everyone owned sufficient land to be a voter. In those days land was the principal means for accumulating wealth and acquiring the right to vote. Jefferson's ideal society embodied widespread distribution of income-generating property and therefore political representation. Democracy to him meant "the absence of hereditary or arbitrary class distinctions or privileges relating to the common people." Jefferson's dream for America spanned the concepts of both political and economic democracy. In his mind the two were one and inseparable. He and the other founding fathers built the framework to support this concept of democracy into the Constitution.

By the early nineteenth century the architecture for Universal Capitalism, supported by the Constitution, was established and seemed to be producing the elements of a comprehensively democratic society.

The French statesman Alexis de Tocqueville observed that the emergent America embodied the notion of "self-interest rightly understood." He noted that the powerful force of self-interest in the context of wide dispersion of power and ownership moderated socially destructive greed, leading people to cooperate and realize that their welfare is intertwined with that of others. In these early years of the republic, the pursuit of one's own fortune nurtured the fortune of society at large. In fairness to de Tocqueville, not all his remarks about the young republic were favorable. His statement "I know of no country indeed where the love of money has taken a stronger hold on the affection of men" may have been a harbinger of the eventual erosion of the primary principal of economic democracy.[3]

The young republic began the nineteenth century as an agrarian nation with a small but rapidly developing industrial base in the northeastern states. It would not be until what is often called the "second" industrial revolution of the 1870s that the central role of land, and the American farmer, in the mercantile drama of this nation would begin to diminish. It was in the context of the post–Civil War grab for western lands, the growing corporate concentration in the East, and the rise of the "money monopoly" that we begin to see a distinct climate of economic inequality emerging.

In this era there appeared the next advocate of Universal Capitalism in North America: Henry George. George's first significant work, *Our Land and Land Policy*, was published in 1871.[4] There he noted that the economic development of the western portion of the country was making a few individuals wealthy while the majority grew poorer. The reason for this, George surmised, was that land ownership was concentrated in the hands of a small group who used their ownership to extract most of the gains from regional development. His solution, further developed in his book *Progress and Poverty* (1879), was to abolish all taxes save one on land.[5] His 1879 book established George as a crusader against the poverty and economic injustice flowing from modern capitalism. He spent the rest of his life promoting a doctrine of social reform based on a single tax imposed on land. Essentially his argument was that everyone has an equal right to the use of land; that land increases in value because of community economic development; and that this increase in value belongs to the community rather than the landowner.

George argued that the prevailing definition of property rights permitted landowners to retain all increases in value spilling over from community economic development. He contended that this was irrational and contributed to social inequality. He supported the principle of private property but advocated a tax on land equivalent to the socially created value of land. George supported all other institutions of capitalism and advocated free trade. He simply denounced the social inequalities that flowed from the prevailing definition of property rights.

During the three decades preceding World War II, the policies advocated to promote Universal Capitalism became associated with socialism and communism. When Americans spoke out for greater economic justice, equality, and opportunity through systemic reforms, they were automatically branded as socialists. Unfortunately, the American vision of economic democracy, which preceded Karl Marx's *Das Kapital* by nearly 100 years, became buried under a surge of nationalism and distrust engendered by the Cold War.

The great depression of the 1930s, in conjunction with the spread of communism and socialism throughout Europe, fed social and political insecurity within the United States. There is little wonder that politicians throughout the free world seized on the public policy ideas of economist John Maynard Keynes. According to Keynes, the problem in capitalist countries was not systemic but rather due to insufficient aggregate demand brought on by flawed social psychology. Government spending was needed to bridge the gap between aggregate demand and supply, thereby creating full employment. No one need question the mechanism for the distribution of purchasing power or any other aspect of the existing capitalist system. Increasing the size and involvement of government was all that was needed to cure the temporary problem of economic depression.

Karl Marx was right on at least one point: The primary force driving increased economic inequality had shifted from land to capital as the industrial revolution unfolded. *The Capitalist Manifesto,* published in 1958 by Louis Kelso and Mortimer Adler, was the first unique work by a North American since Henry George advocating reform to enhance economic democracy within the capitalist context.[6] In their view, capitalism and democracy together create an approximation of the ideal classless society in which all people are citizens and all are capitalists. Given that labor is a diminishing factor of production relative to capital, economic democracy can be achieved only by increasing the number of individuals who participate in production and earn income through their ownership of capital. When the great bulk of additional wealth is produced by capital instruments, maintaining economic democracy requires that the largest possible number of households participate in production through the ownership of such instruments.

Kelso and Adler's solution is to broaden the ownership of existing enterprises through equity-sharing plans. They also advocate the termination of certain government policies that promote concentration of ownership and modification of the existing tax system to bring about wider capital ownership. Eight separate models for disseminating capital ownership are described in their book. Each covers a different realm of industrial capital ownership and is designed to reunite ownership and control through a system of investor preferences. One common element of the plans is preferential credit financing of the acquisition of capital interests by non-capital-owning households or households with below-average capital holdings. Households with very large holdings of capital would be given low investment preferences that might limit them to investment in fixed-income bonds. Capital acquisition under any of the proposed plans would amortize the acquisition costs out of the net earnings of the newly acquired capital.

One of the eight advocated programs was the Employee Stock Ownership Plan (ESOP). By the 1970s Louis Kelso focused his efforts on ESOP and its variants, which were designed to make workers shareholders in the companies that employed them. He abandoned his own Financed Capitalist Plan (FCP), a universal capital ownership concept, as unworkable since he came to regard it as a top-down, utopian vision. His post-1960s approach was to focus on smaller-scale opportunities, such as privatization of public property and legislation to support the creation of constituency trusts (i.e., ESOPs). Kelso argued in the media and Congress that capital ownership by the masses had never been tried and that it was the only thing that could keep the United States from joining most other nations in the slide toward state ownership of capital. Kelso's ideas were intriguing to Senator Russell Long (D, La.), the influential chairman of the Senate Finance Committee, who introduced ESOP legislation in Congress. Much of this legislation was enacted eventually, and it included attractive financial incentives, in the form of tax breaks, for corporations that established such plans. Since the 1970s, ESOPs have become widespread in the United States and, despite their notable shortcomings, have helped bring capital ownership to many who formerly were not capital owners.

Stuart Speiser, a New York lawyer and writer, was inspired by Louis Kelso yet disagreed with him on several key points. From the very beginning, Speiser was attracted to the grand vision of universal capital ownership, which he sought to build on Kelso's FCP. Speiser defined Universal Capitalism as a system that will give everyone a chance to be a capitalist, mainly by enabling people who have no savings to own corporate stock. He put to paper his vision of a Universal Stock Ownership Plan (USOP) in his 1977 book *A Piece of the Action.*[7] Speiser made a distillation of Adler and Kelso's theories and decided that social justice is the strongest underpinning of the Universal Capitalism concept. He went on to reject Kelso's Two-Factor Theory and concluded that Kelso's capital theory of value suffers from the same simplistic flaw as Marx's labor theory of value. The crux of the problem is that the ownership of capital under the current system is highly concentrated and that the associated institutions for the distribution of the social product exacerbate this overconcentration. What traditional economists have ignored is the possibility that capital ownership can be turned into a source of significant income for everyone through a USOP plan that would in turn enhance social justice and stability.

In subsequent work Speiser reformulated and retitled his plan Super-Stock.[8] By 1982 he had done the statistical groundwork missing from Kelso's work and incorporated feedback from a 1977 seminar held at the

Brookings Institution on the FCP model. Speiser now focused on formulating a simple structure of a USOP knowing full well that the details would be complex and controversial.

According to the SuperStock plan, legislation establishing the program would mandate the participation of the nation's 2,000 largest corporations. Once a firm is designated to participate, it will no longer finance its capital expansion plans through the current choices of common stock, preferred stock, debt, and retained earnings. When a firm needs money for capital expansion, it will obtain it through the USOP apparatus by issuing a new form of stock, which Speiser labeled SuperStock. The institution charged with the job of administering the USOP would be obligated to accept the newly issued SuperStock and to provide the participating firm with equivalent market value in checkable deposits. To finance any new SuperStock issue, the USOP administrators would issue new debt instruments in private capital markets.

To liquidate the debt that was floated to finance SuperStock shares, all corporate earnings would be required to be paid out as dividends. The only exception allowed would be a small pool of retained earning for daily operations and unforeseen contingencies. All SuperStock shares would be held in escrow until the dividends flowing in paid off the debt initially incurred. At this point, the paid-off SuperStock shares would be owned free and clear by the American citizens to whom they had been distributed.

Speiser's proposal is meant to distribute SuperStock shares to Americans who are not currently capitalists. Speiser suggested that the first recipients be all households with current net worth below $100,000. As an alternative, he suggested that a point system for eligibility be established. To prevent inequities and to spread risk, Speiser proposed that the USOP create a mutual fund or unit trust. Recipients then would receive a portfolio of mutual fund shares from the central USOP. Once the initial loans were paid off, future dividends would be passed through the trust to participating citizens. Holders of a SuperStock mutual fund would be entitled to a share of all income earned by the 2,000 largest corporations for the rest of their lives. As a final note, Speiser hoped that over time, a viable USOP would replace both America's social security and welfare programs. If successful, such a program would indeed redemocratize the U.S. economy.

The work of Kelso and Speiser drew the attention of the Council on International and Public Affairs (CIPA) during the 1970s and early 1980s. Based in New York, CIPA is a nonprofit organization dedicated to promoting economic justice throughout the world. In the mid-1980s, CIPA began to sponsor a series of essay competitions concerning USOPs. These competitions engendered a virtual flood of ideas concerning Universal Capitalism in general and USOPs in particular. While the essays are interesting in their details and in the light they shed on economic democracy in the United States, there is not sufficient room in this chapter to review the constructive insights gained from them. Interested readers are referred to a series of books published by CIPA in the subject.[9] The introduction to one of these volumes, entitled *Mainstreet Capitalism: Essays on Broadening Share Ownership in America and Britain,* points out that the plans developed for the essay competitions fall into one of three groups. The first group, or Type A plans, are based on redefining employment relationships and building bridges between ESOPs and a USOP. The second group, or Type B plans, focus on savings enhanced by tax relief, redefining the existing Individual Retirement Account/Keogh mechanism so that participants receive extra incentives to purchase stock. The third group, or Type C plans, open ownership to all citizens regardless of their employment status or net wealth. These Type C plans include innovative variations of the SuperStock theme.

After the final essay competition in this series, it became clear that eight potential reservoirs exist within American capitalism that could be modified to provide sources of expanded capital ownership. These are:

1. Capital additions of major companies, as featured in the Kitty Hawk model of USOP . . .
2. A National Mutual Fund would use money borrowed from the Federal Reserve to make stock and bond purchases from private industry, stimulating the economy and increasing productivity. Profits would be paid to the general public (every adult citizen) as dividends. . . .
3. Corporate profits . . .
4. Privatization: government-owned assets and services that could be owned and operated privately.
5. The credit power of major companies, as used now in leveraged buyouts.
6. Consumer payments to public utilities . . .
7. Extension of the USOP principle beyond shares of corporate stock to other assets such as public lands, natural resources, privately owned real estate, and art objects.
8. Stock contributed by successful companies as patronage dividends, or for public relations/patriotic purposes in their own enlightened self-interest. . . ."[10]

The space available does not permit detailed discussion of other post–World War II plans for universal capital ownership, such as John Perry's

"National Dividend Plan," the Sabre Foundation's "Capital Formation Plan," James Meade's "Labor-Capital Partnership" and "Social Dividend" concepts, and James Albus's "National Mutual Fund" concept (although it is cited in the potential reservoirs just outlined).[11] Each offers a unique idea and intriguing insights yet represents little more than a variation of the themes already discussed. The basic conclusion of the students of Universal Capitalism is that the existing definition of property rights and institutions for the distribution of income and wealth need to be altered in some incentive-compatible manner in order to achieve true economic democracy.[12]

Also omitted from this review has been the debate over a top-down vs. bottom-up approach to achieving Universal Capitalism. Louis Kelso had advocated ESOPs, a narrowly targeted bottom-up approach, during the 1960s and 1970s and eventually won support in Congress for legislation institutionalizing this program. Jon Wisman's 1984 winning CIPA essay had suggested another bottom-up approach to Universal Capitalism centered on the worker self-management model. George Burress's 1988 winning CIPA essay stressed that a bottom-up approach based on voluntarism had the greatest probability of acceptance. While applauding the ESOP and similar concepts, many supporters of Universal Capitalism worry that bottom-up approaches run the risk of benefiting only a small, select segment of Americans who are fortunate enough to hold long-term jobs with successful companies.

In any event, introduction or expansion of most bottom-up approaches would require some minimal amount of supportive government legislation. The issue is, in part, the nature and extent of associated legislation and government involvement. More important is the issue of timing. The existing socioeconomic environment during the final decade of the twentieth century is decidedly negative for inaugurating any form of Universal Capitalism.

The Present

The post–World War II era has seen a number of promising innovations on the microeconomic level. These include not only ESOPs but also a modest expansion of the cooperative movement, incorporation of Japanese practices in American business, pay-for-performance plans centered on equity, self-managed teams, and the spread of various types of individual retirement accounts. All these incentive schemes and business innovations have boosted economic democracy while many have helped to broaden participation in equity ownership in America to 43 percent of the adult population.[13]

These structural adjustments within the American economy promote economic democracy and are all well and good for the people directly involved. Still, they do not help the majority of Americans to become more vested in our capitalist system. They broaden the participation in ownership of capital beyond the traditional circle yet still leave a people deeply divided. In other words, they do little to promote Universal Capitalism.

An important question for the early twenty-first century is what will happen with the 57 percent of voting Americans who are not participating in equity ownership, the approximately 107 million adults over 18 years of age in 1997? To form a realistic answer to this question demands a discussion of the economic state of this group with some forecast on how this state is likely to change during the next 25 years. In what follows readers must keep in mind that these individuals represent a potential voting bloc in future elections.

It is by now a well-known fact that between 1973 and 1995 real gross domestic product (GDP) rose 36 percent while real hourly wages of nonsupervisory workers declined 14 percent.[14] Nonsupervisory workers constitute the vast majority of the 107 million adult Americans just referred to. What is unique about this fact is that it marks the first time in American history when real per-capita GDP and real wages for the majority of Americans moved in opposite directions. What, then, explains this seeming contradiction?

Part of the answer is that during the 1980s, all of the earning gains went to the top 20 percent of the workforce. Even among the top 20 percent there was uneven distribution of increased earnings; an astounding 64 percent went into the pockets of the top 1 percent of earners. Between 1968 and 1988 inequality began to accelerate and structurally change. During this period not only did inequality accelerate between social groups, it rose within groups as well. Between- and within-group income inequality rose for every industrial, occupational, educational, demographic, and geographic group.[15] Economist Lester Thurow summed up these developments by saying: "As the data on falling wages indicates, the unskilled in the first world are on their way to becoming marginalized."[16] Despite an apparent slowdown in these trends in the mid-1990s, the overall increase in inequality is not likely to reverse for some time.

Reasons for this increase in inequality and structural change in income distribution are somewhat unclear and hotly debated. A brief presentation of some of the main elements of the debate will help set the stage for a discussion of the prospects for advancing Universal Capitalism in the United States during the early twenty-first century. It also will support the assertion made earlier that the trend toward increasing inequality is not likely to reverse in the foreseeable future. While scholars argue over the extent to which each of these factors contribute to the phenomena just described, all agree that each plays some significant role.

The first factor concerns the skill set brought by the majority of immigrants to the United States over the past 20 years. Unlike past waves of immigrations to this country, the current one has a high representation of unskilled workers.[17] This influx has put downward pressure on wages received by most American citizens with no more than a high school education. This factor alone would not, in itself, cause a decline in real wages if it had been accompanied by a proportionate, or more than proportionate, increase in the demand for unskilled workers. Unfortunately, this did not happen.

The rise in the demand for unskilled workers in the United States over the last quarter of the century has been muted by two other developments. First is the phenomenon described as globalization: the inexorable global transformation, which has affected every aspect of American economic life. Although it began to accelerate during the 1960s, the past decade alone has witnessed global trade increasing at double the rate of GDP growth while foreign direct investment has grown three times as fast. Since the fall of the Berlin Wall in 1989, more nations than ever have opened their economies to international trade and finance. Immense sums of money swiftly cross borders at the stroke of a computer key. Daily foreign-exchange trading in global capital markets has steadily risen to the equivalent of U.S. $1.3 trillion and continues to rise.

Globalization has been accompanied by a restructuring of production, with American corporations increasingly shifting, or threatening to shift, production to those countries with relatively cheap unskilled or semiskilled labor. Rapid transformation of information technologies and transportation has augmented this restructuring by creating an economic climate where many goods and services can be produced anywhere on Earth.

Recent studies have suggested that approximately 20 percent of this rise in income inequality can be explained by globalization.[18] Some economists argue that international trade is an even more important cause of increasing income inequality in the United States than the studies indicate. Dani Rodrik, a Harvard economist, argues in his recently published book that economists are missing important facts.[19] Specifically, he argues that globalization makes it easier than it has been supposed for business to shift production elsewhere in the world and, in the process, replace expensive American workers with cheaper foreign workers. Current economic thinking underestimates the potential and assumed consequences of the dramatic structural changes in the American/global economic systems. Furthermore, even the threat to shift production abroad becomes a powerful deterrent to wage and nonwage benefit increases, weakens trade unions, and increases job insecurity. Economic models currently ignore this last fact.

However one looks at the impact of international trade, it can be said conclusively that restructuring of American production since 1970 has dampened the increase in domestic demand for unskilled labor. Furthermore, this feature of our changing economy has contributed to the increase in income inequality and will not change under current conditions.

While these last few paragraphs help to delineate the primary reasons for falling real wages for those without a college education, it does not explain the growing gap between skilled and unskilled workers. In 1979 the average American male college graduate earned 49 percent more than a high school graduate; by 1993 the gap had widened to 89 percent.[20] The rise in the real income earned by college graduates as a group is the final factor to introduce in explaining rising income inequality.

The United States, driven by the imperatives of the information age, has become a producer of intangible products (finance, communications, the media, and services in general). Transformation of the economic landscape has been driven largely by the changing structure and hence needs of capitalism. Mounting economic pressures have forced firms to develop and adopt new technologies. Growing profits in a low-inflation environment demands driving costs down in whatever manner possible. The new information technology (IT) ultimately drives communication and transaction costs down while driving productivity and profits up. Those who develop the skills to use IT gain a strategic advantage within dynamic free markets.

The distinguishing features of IT are its pervasiveness and its rate of deployment. IT is applicable across all sectors of the economy and impacts every function of an enterprise. Not only has IT transformed existing production and distribution, it also has spawned vast new markets of its own.

While electricity, an equally pervasive technology, took 46 years to spread to 25 percent of American households, the personal computer took 15 years while cellular phones took 13 years.[21] IT's pervasiveness and rapid adoption rate has added turbulence to labor markets. Specifically, it has caused a rapid increase in demand for those people with the skills to manage the diverse aspects of IT. Despite a constant increase in those with college and technical school educations over the past quarter century, the rate of increase in demand for these individuals has exceeded the growing supply. Consequently, these individuals have experienced rising real wages. In addition, many of these fortunate individuals also have been ushered into the inner sanctum of capitalism through 401k and stock option plans.

Many pundits have argued that IT is unlike previous technologies and will destroy more jobs than it creates. They go on to state that even if IT creates more jobs than it destroys, they will mostly be low paying with few fringe benefits. This issue could be important to the prospects for Universal Capitalism becoming a reality in the twenty-first century, yet its resolution is not crucial. The fact remain that the majority of Americans have experienced, and are likely to continue experiencing, declining real income for the foreseeable future due to the forces already discussed. Their economic circumstances and shrinking opportunities will increasingly stand in stark contrast to those who ride the technological wave of IT into the new century.

Some would argue that another factor contributing to growing inequality is the government's retreat from social programs. This researcher suspects that this development, dating back to 1980, is more an effect of other systemic changes in society not discussed in this chapter. However, what is quite clear is that during the final two decades of this century, the federal government has exacerbated the rise in economic inequality at least through tax changes. These changes began in the early 1980s and range from the Investment Tax Credit provisions of the Kemp-Roth tax bill to the reduction in capital gains tax on homes and equities in the tax bill of 1997.

Why have those Americans who have been left in the wake of the powerful emergence of "brainpower" industries not found a collective voice in Washington? One would expect these people to have exercised their democratic rights and demand remedial political action: more progressive income taxes, expansion of social programs and trade sanctions. Despite nearly 30 years of falling purchasing power, they have not. This conundrum is both complex and poorly understood. Still, some brief discussion is in order; for until these people find their collective voice, Universal Capitalism will remain no more than a dream.

First, the end of communism has ushered in an era in which capitalism has no viable ideological competition. Some have called this the "end of history." One positive feature of the Cold War was that it caused some Americans to reflect critically on the economic system in which they lived. In the tension of that era, Americans, and their representatives in Washington, paid serious attention to accusations of systemic political and economic injustice. The fear of a "drift toward socialism" motivated government to write new laws and institute innovative programs to lessen social and economic inequality. While economic inequality rises, a growing number of Americans appear to have a waning concern for their fellow man and society at large.

Second, popular culture distracts and confuses Americans through distorting perceptions of social issues and existing social institutions. If religion was the "opium of the masses" in the nineteenth century, the electronic media is the "opium of the masses" in the late twentieth century. Without a drama of epoch proportions on the world stage to attract their attention, most Americans turn their heads to their television or computer screens.

Like the rise in economic inequality, the manner in which television is becoming the defining factor in the formation of individual and familial values is well researched and documented. The amount of free time the average American spends in front of a television and the percentage of Americans watching television have grown to unprecedented levels. Along with the growing sophistication of advertising and television programing, TV has become a powerful, permeating cultural force. Not since the reigning days of the Roman Catholic church in Europe has there been an equally pervasive power in Western society shaping human culture and values. Unfortunately, what sells is visual appeal, base emotions, and instant gratification. The profit-maximizing electronic media glorify individual consumption and teach the viewer that what one believes to be true is often more important than what is true. There are no overt or covert political agendas in this; the media and its sponsors just want to make money. Like the blessing and absolution given the European aristocracy by the church during the Middle Ages, the electronic media blesses and absolves modern capitalism and its principal agents.

The Future

The electronic media will maintain their commercial grip as long as there is peace and prosperity. What will awaken the slumbering giant, the "silent majority" of Americans experiencing declining real income, will be protracted military conflict, a serious macroeconomic disturbance, or a mass cry for help when existing trends create a critical mass of relative impoverishment. The long, virtually uninterrupted economic expansion that began in 1982 has made jobs plentiful and given most workers confidence that the rising economic tide eventually will lift their boat. Relatively easy credit has permitted many who have experienced declining real wages to borrow against future earnings in order to fulfill the "American Dream" today. Of the potential wake-up calls, the most likely is pronounced economic contraction. I make no attempt here to predict when or how this will happen, only that such an event likely will occur within the next 25 years. When it happens, Washington politicians will be pulled from the grip of special interest groups and held accountable to the mandate of American political democracy. Special interests rule Capital Hill during good times; the people rule in bad times.

Therefore, it seems clear we are between two eras of "big government." The term "big government" is not meant to imply a growth in the *size* of government as a proportion of GDP. Despite appearances, public spending in the United States has remained at roughly 33 percent of GDP over the past quarter century. This percentage is not anticipated to change significantly over the next 25 years. What has, in fact, occurred since 1980 is a restructuring of the roles of the federal, state, and local levels of government in such a way as to push functional responsibility down the hierarchy. The prediction being made here is for a reversal of this trend with responsibility moving back up the hierarchy. I expect that the federal government will become increasingly involved in controlling and directing the private sector and in redistributing income and wealth through legislative initiatives.

There is no arguing the facts that gross inefficiencies in government have occurred in the past and that the structure of many social programs may not have adequately reduced the social problems they were intended to address. A fear of a return to "big government" assumes that we are unable to learn from our past mistakes. This fear contradicts the established human propensity to learn from experience.

Robert Kuttner argues in *Everything for Sale* that free-market economics have serious limitations in the social realm.[22] Relying more and more on markets leaves an increasing portion of the poor without health care, housing, or food. In the Libertarian extreme, one finds vast numbers of people with marginal social costs exceeding their marginal social benefits: In theory they should and will perish. Projecting current socioeconomic trends takes us to such an inhumane extreme. This cannot and will happen within a democracy. Kuttner further argues that markets do not always produce the ideal outcomes predicted by economic theories. He shows that from scientific research, to electric power, to city ambulance services, government outperforms markets. Finally, he states that the excesses of today's unleashed market forces are as bad as the worst from the days of big government. Socioeconomic cycles tend to swing to excess before reversing course. The current cycle may be longer than usual due to globalization and a domestic economy powered by IT. Yet the cycle inevitably will turn.

The extent and nature of a resurging federal government depends on the particulars of U.S. national economic problems and the state of the global economy at the time the federal government is called upon to intervene. While it is impossible to say much about the specifics of future changes in government's role and structure, they will be shaped by several easily identified forces. To understand we must recall what has been said about global-ization and technological change and add a few more facts.

First, changes in technology, transportation, and communications are creating an interconnected global web of markets that support efficient pro-duction and distribution almost anywhere on Earth. The potentially disrup-tive consequences of this have not been realized in the United States: A disconnect is developing between the goals and objectives of corporations that think "globally" and those of a democratic government that think "na-tionally." If the people call for, and politicians enact, higher tariffs, quotas, legal restraints on free enterprise, a more progressive tax system, and in-creased social spending, there is nothing to stop corporations with opera-tions in the United States from just moving to a more profit-friendly nation elsewhere in the world.

The rise of brainpower industries makes this scenario more problematic for those industries without natural predetermined homes. Brainpower, un-like capital, cannot be owned and is as mobile as the individual. Being geo-graphically free makes these industries, and the people who power them, the most sensitive to the economic environment in which they are located.

A recent article in the *Wall Street Journal* put it this way: "The glass-tower people are highly skilled knowledge workers in sleek office buildings. They are worldly in the literal sense of the word, part of a global communications web. Cosmopolitan, they may have more in common with their counter-parts in Germany and Japan than with their fellow Americans who work the assembly line across town."[23]

In the book cited earlier by Dr. Dani Rodrik, he argues that globalization makes it increasingly difficult for the federal government to provide social insurance. Ultimately, the more mobile capital and brainpower workers be-come, the harder it becomes to collect sufficient tax revenue to moderate the effects of freer trade and to finance social spending. Electronic commerce has the potential to further weaken the power of the government to tax Americans for it makes it easier for people to flee a nation financially. Some brainpower firms may be able to evade taxes altogether by moving their busi-ness into cyberspace.

In an era of rising government intervention, some politicians may call for an introduction of controls on the outflow of capital. But as Lester Thurow has said, "with both the technologies and the financial institutions to move money using a personal computer, it is difficult to imagine the enforcement of capital controls. Laws could be passed but they would not be enforceable."[24]

If the economic contraction that the United States eventually faces is global, so that all major trading nations face a similar set of problems, we will likely see a global increase in government involvement in the private sector. In such an environment the growth of government is likely to be swift and analogous among countries in the Organization for Economic Cooperation and Development (OECD). Facing a similar set of demands by citizens, OECD governments will be enabled to legislate remedial programs, raise taxes, and establish protectionistic policies. When all OECD governments are taking steps to deal with the same economic problems, each will have little to fear from either capital flight or an outflow of business operations.

If the economic problems are unique to the United States, a resurging federal government could cause a massive outflow of international capital and brainpower industries in search of friendlier economic environments. These circumstances would lead to a slow, fitful, and unbalanced growth in government within the context of a festering domestic economic crisis. Critical under either scenario, or anything in between, will be the way in which big government reemerges.

An expansion of traditional social programs would mandate an increase in taxes. The federal borrowing binge since 1980 will limit additional debt issuance as an avenue for financing social program growth for a considerable portion of the early twenty-first century. Raising taxes would only worsen any domestic crisis by reducing consumption and investment while speeding the departure of international capital and brainpower workers. Raising interest rates through restrictive monetary policy may keep international capital in domestic markets yet it would worsen domestic economic problems. How then could the U.S. government reengineer itself to meet the mounting demands of its people for social reform while attracting foreign capital to domestic financial markets?

Universal Capitalism programs, such as the USOP, have been shown to be incentive-compatible with existing capitalist institutions. Establishing a USOP would reconstruct the institutions that define the distribution of income and wealth but do so in a gradual, nonconfiscatory manner. Debt issued in conjunction with a USOP is self-liquidating since it is tied directly to corporate earnings. A USOP has the potential to replace existing social welfare programs, creating an alternative that not only provides an economic "safety net" for participants but also spreads capital ownership to all citizens. Expanding the vested interests in corporate America has a strong potential to boost productivity through ownership and a renewed sense of pride in being an American. Participation in an ESOP has been found to increase the productivity of workers by an average of 10 percent. There is every reason to suspect that participation in a USOP will have a positive impact upon productivity as well. Furthermore, a USOP is deeply patriotic since it calls upon the principles of economic democracy inscribed in the Declaration of Independence, Bill of Rights, and Constitution.

Students of USOPs have developed strategies for extending the concept in such a way that stakeholder groups retain a relatively greater equity interest in the corporation with which they are associated.[25] These ideas in no way diminish a USOP as a vehicle for promoting Universal Capitalism. In fact, these expansions on the USOP theme make the concept compatible with the evolving body of thought on humanistic economics and stakeholder capitalism.

All of this makes a USOP the perfect centerpiece in a restructuring of government in any of the aforementioned climates that may emerge during the early twenty-first century in the United States. The federal government, hemmed in by outstanding debt and not wanting to increase taxes, will find the institution of Universal Capitalism a cost-effective way to meet the people's rising demands for action. A USOP covers operating expenses out of corporate earnings and thus does not require tax revenues. In fact, a strong argument can be made that a carefully crafted USOP eventually will shrink government expenses, permitting a reduction in taxes. Corporations are likely to accept the concept, for participation is voluntary and provides incentives that can enhance profitability of those firms involved. International capital and brainpower industries are likely to think twice about leaving, because the concept holds the promise of creating systemwide productivity gains, does not increase taxes, and incorporates provisions to expand entrepreneurship.

During the 1940s, Karl Polyanyi argued that the two world wars and the intervening depression marked the end of nineteenth-century capitalism. The social mechanisms established in the aftermath of the Keynesian revolution had created a "safety net" to protect citizens from the potential brutality of market forces. The countervailing power of unions, new social programs, and the multilateral agreements put in place at Bretton Woods created a system of economic checks and balances within which Western nations could reconstruct and Western workers could flourish.

Between 1973, when blue-collar real wages peaked, and 1980, when the first serious postwar attack on the role of the federal government began, the tide of the Keynesian era turned. Trade unions continue to weaken, the "safety net" is being dismantled or redefined, and the remaining institutions of the Bretton Woods Agreement are increasingly dwarfed by the international financial market juggernaut.

I cannot speculate on what events will mark the end of twentieth-century capitalism. Whatever they may be and whenever they may happen, current trends strongly suggest that they will occur early in the twenty-first century. Political democracy, which believes in "one man, one vote," stands in stark contrast to the beliefs of capitalism. Under capitalism, each person is free to act within legal limits to accumulate as many economic votes (dollars) as possible. The dynamics of this process, given existing institutions, create stark inequalities in economic opportunities and power. Twentieth-century politicians finessed this systemic, ideological contradiction by grafting the social welfare state onto capitalism and democracy. This experiment was declared a failure in the United States and by the early 1980s was replaced rapidly by a more robust form of capitalism. The next attempt to resolve this ideological contradiction may very well be a series of social experiments centered on the concept of Universal Capitalism.

The United States has been fortunate to experience a confluence of historical events that created relatively widespread economic equality, opportunity, and affluence for the better part of 200 years. As this chapter has shown, it is questionable whether we can expect a continuation of such good fortune in the twenty-first century. Statistical evidence suggests that the economic tides have taken a major, negative turn for the majority of Americans.

Economic systems tend toward inertia and it is only when a crisis develops that real institutional change occurs. It is during times of crisis that the national leadership searches for new alternatives and those adopted depend on ideas previously introduced in the public domain.

Currently the irresistible forces of the information revolution and global competition seem to be changing the nature of economic progress in such a way that a narrower segment of the population benefits directly. Until the unfolding dilemmas are understood in the proper context of eroding economic democracy, the vision of Universal Capitalism will remain unfulfilled. Given the enshrined institutional matrix surrounding American political democracy in the context of mounting economic inequality, hope remains that we will return to the encompassing vision of democracy upon which this country was founded. To quote Thomas Paine once more: "Time makes more converts than reason."[26]

Notes

1. Martin King, *Strength to Love* (New York: Harper & Row, 1963), p. 73.
2. Thomas Paine, "Common Sense," in M. Foot and I. Kramnick, eds., *The Thomas Paine Reader* (New York: Viking Penguin, 1987), 65.
3. Alexis de Tocqueville, *Democracy in America*, vol. 1, pt. 1, chap. 3, 1835, V. P. Mayer and Max Lerner, eds., George Lawrence, tr., (New York: Harper and Row, 1966).

4. Henry George, *Our Land and Land Policy,* (New York: Doubleday and Mc-Clure, 1902; originally published 1871).

5. Henry George, *Progress and Poverty* (Canaan, N.H.: Phoenix Publishers, 1979; originally published 1879).

6. Louis Kelso and Mortimer Adler, *The Capitalist Manifesto* (New York: Random House, 1958).

7. Stuart Speiser, *A Piece of the Action* (New York: Van Nostrand Reinhold, 1977).

8. Stuart Speiser, *SuperStock* (New York: Everest Publishers, 1982).

9. Stuart Speiser, *Mainstreet Capitalism: Essays on Broadening Share Ownership in America and Britain* (New York: New Horizons Press, 1988).

10. Stuart Speiser, *Equitable Capitalism: Promoting Economic Opportunity Through Broader Capital Ownership* (New York: The Apex Press, 1991), 4–5.

11. John H. Perry, Jr., *The National Dividend* (New York: Ivan Obolensky, Inc., 1964); and James Meade, *Efficiency, Equality, and the Ownership of Property* (London: George Allen Unwin, 1964).

12. NASDAQ Stock Market Survey, *New York Daily News,* February 24, 1997.

13. See the following: *Economic Report of the President* (Washington, D.C.: U. S. Government Printing Office, 1995), 276, 311, 326. Council of Economic Indicators (Washington, D.C.: U.S. GPO, August 1995), 2, 15; Daniel Feenberg and James Poterba, *Income Inequality and the Incomes of the Very High Income Taxpayers,* NBER Working Paper 4229, (December 1992): 31; Claudia Goldin and Robert Margo, "The Great Compression: The Wage Structure of the United States at Mid-Century," Quarterly Journal of Economics (QJE) (February 1994): 4.

14. See the following: Robert Frank and Philip Cook, *The Winner-Take-All Society* (New York: Free Press, 1994); U.S. Bureau of the Census, *Current Population Reports, Consumer Income, 1992,* Series P-60 (Washington, D.C.: U.S. Government Printing Office, 1993); and Sheldon Danziger and Peter Gottschaulk, eds., *Uneven Tides* (New York: Russell Sage Foundation, 1993), 7.

15. Lester Thurow, *The Future of Capitalism* (New York: William Morrow & Company, 1996), 77.

16. Steven Holmes, "A Surge in Immigration Surprises Experts and Intensifies a Debate," *New York Times,* August 30, 1995, 1.

17. Bernard Wysocki, "The Big Trade Debate Heating up Again," *Wall Street Journal,* March 24, 1997, A1.

18. Dani Rodik, *Has Globalisation Gone Too Far?* (Washington, D.C.: Institute for International Economics, 1997).

19. "The Hitchhiker's Guide to Cybernomics," *The Economist,* September 28, 1996, 24.

20. G. Christian Hill, "Technology (A Special Report): No Place Like Home— Bringing It Home," *Wall Street Journal,* October 28, 1992.

21. Robert Kuttner, *Everything for Sale* (New York: Alfred A. Knopf, 1997).

22. Dennis Farney, "The American Civilization—Turning Point," *Wall Street Journal,* October 28, 1992; "Even U.S. Politics Are Being Reshaped by a Global Economy," *The American Civilization,* October 28, 1992, A1.

23. Thurow, *Future of Capitalism,* 129.
24. Ken Taylor, "The American Trust: Creating Full Employment Opportunity," in Speiser, ed. *Equitable Capitalism,* 9–24.
25. These and other positive features of the concept can be found in: Stuart Speiser, *The USOP Handbook* (New York: The Council on International and Public Affairs, 1986).
26. Paine, "Common Sense," in M. Foot and I. Kramnick, eds., *The Thomas Paine Reader* (New York: Viking Penguin, 1987), 65.

CHAPTER 17

A Community-Oriented Economy

Severyn T. Bruyn, Boston College

Introduction

The strength and solidarity of local communities declined with the rise of industrialization and urbanization in the eighteenth and nineteenth centuries. At present, some communities may be destroyed completely with the rise of global markets; the power of self-determination for people in local communities erodes with expanding market forces. Because corporations centralize their control in big cities to compete more effectively with one another, small communities and city neighborhoods then have fewer local firms where resident owners can be responsive to personal needs. Localities are served mainly by subsidiaries and franchises of big companies under the command of absentee executives.[1]

Corporations have little choice in a competitive and unregulated global market but to use their economic and political power to externalize their costs onto the community. The dynamics of competition favor the cost externalization process as they pit workers and communities against one another in a destructive race to the bottom. By competing for jobs that corporations offer, workers and communities are compelled to deplete real wealth to make corporations more profitable.[2]

Absentee executives, out of touch with local needs and the community's ability to sustain itself, decide whether to transfer local offices, move retail outlets, or shut down factories on the basis of demands in national and global markets. Whether local economies can sustain themselves becomes determined by managers making decisions in distant cities. If communities contract and suffer economically, local crime and delinquency grow. As a reflection of this trend, some city planners have given up designing self-reliant neighborhoods and self-sufficient communities. They argue that the ideal of community control and local self-reliance is a hopeless utopia, that the extended megalopolis and the world market is the "future." There is seldom any vision of community in public planning, only a response to a system of global markets and a vast network of metropoli.[3]

But there do exist healthy, constructive responses by people to the centralizing trends of business and government. This chapter is about local groups, localizing power and authority, and building civil society. Corporations too are finding that their centralizing trends cause problems in their own command bureaucracy, and in their own self-interest, some corporations are reversing the trend and localizing their operations. We look at how some corporations are decentralizing operations to become more accountable to people in localities. We review these trends in conjunction with the cooperative movement that keeps growing quietly in the capitalist setting.

A new mix of cooperation and competition is emerging in capitalism. It follows that research models should be devised to tell us more about how a globalizing economy can decentralize in the midst of centralizing forces. Public policies could be formulated to support the movement of a global economy toward becoming accountable and profitable, and bringing back power to people in local communities.

Civic Movements around the World

Civil-society analysts see democratic associations being forged in a third sector, separate from both big government and big corporations. A civil economy grows from the inside out, they say, like the Big Bang, from particles, to atoms, to molecules, to cells, moving upward and outward, not mainly from the outside in, and not so much by top-down decisions of big governments and corporations, although that is part of the story. This inside-out (and "down-up") development is happening around the world; some early signs occured where people in organizations reacted against oppressive states.

For example, the destruction of a centralized system happened dramatically in the Solidarity movement in Poland, in the Velvet Revolution in Czechoslovakia, and with the African National Congress. It happened also in the democratization of Argentina and Chile—all movements forged from below, toppling regimes that appeared to have absolute power over people.

Associative democracy is the philosophy underlying a community-oriented economy. This civil-society concept is not libertarianism, because authority rests in a socially mediated market. Associative democracy evolves through local movements with the transfer of power from big government to civic groups and big corporations to local organizations that become self-governing.[4]

The Logic of These Movements: Associative Democracy

Civil society is evolving through local associations—local political organizations, social clubs, nonprofit corporations, community development corporations, civic-minded religious associations, and small businesses. There is an emergent ecology of associations where people make decisions by personal agreement, consensus, and one-person vote, more than by command bureaucracy, or by the power of money, or by voting on the stock market. It is a decentralized system, a cooperative commonwealth—a dream vision of civil society evolving in the midst of the centralized forces in the government and global markets. Civic-oriented movements are happening around the world. Civic movements build a different society within and beyond conventional markets and states.

In December 1993 representatives from dozens of countries announced the formation of a new international association called Civicus. Its mission is to help worldwide civic movements "cultivate volunteerism and community service." Civicus organized to aid the development of the "third sector." The first executive director, Miklos Marschall, saw the growth of nongovernmental organization (NGOs) as a new "civil society."[5]

Local Civic Movements in the Third Sector

The movements to be enumerated point to a third sector emerging between business and government. NGOs are part of this worldwide movement, generally called the third sector because conventional business is excluded. Civil society happens when people in associations go beyond sheer competition as the defining value of the economy, to emphasize cooperation and self-reliance.

A civic movement took place in a suburb of Karachi, Pakistan, where the Orangi Pilot Project enlisted the voluntary help of 28,000 families to construct 430,000 feet of underground sewers and built more than 28,000 latrines for local residents. A civic movement happened in India where the Self-Employed Women's Association, a trade union of poor women in

Ahmedabad, provides free legal services for women, child care services, and training courses in carpentry, plumbing, bamboo work, and midwifery. A movement occurred in Nepal, where grass-roots NGOs, working with local populations, built sixty-two dams at one-fourth the cost of comparable construction done by the government.

In Sri Lanka, the Sarvodaya Sharanadana Movement lists 7,700 on its staff working in more than 8,000 villages, helping local populations mobilize resources and create self-sufficient communities. A movement is visible in Malaysia, where the Consumers Association of Penang works with rural communities, helping them secure governmental assistance and protecting them from exploitative development schemes. In Senegal the Committee to Fight for the End of Hunger has 20,000 members helping farmers promote food crops rather than exports. A civic movement is evident in the Philippines, where PAMALAKAYA, an NGO representing 50,000 fishermen, lobbied to preserve communal fish ponds and provides ongoing training and education for its members.

The Chiapas people in Mexico struggled for greater local autonomy, economic fairness and equity, and political rights within their communities. Gustavo Esteva, a Mexican political analyst, calls the Chiapas rebellion the "first revolution of the twenty-first century." Unlike earlier rebellions, in which local citizens called upon their fellow Mexicans to take up arms against the state, in this case citizens joined with one another to liberate local spaces from outside colonization.

David Korten sees these protest movements as responses to the specter of an era "when corporations will rule the world." Dai Qing protested a proposed dam that would displace 1.2 million people, flood 100,000 hectares of fertile agriculture land, inundate a "magnificent stretch of canyons," and destroy the habitat's endangered species.[6]

Indigenous people are at the forefront of these social movements. In Ecuador, for example, they have organized to reclaim their lands, protect the rain forests from foreign oil companies, and block a government agricultural modernization program that would drive them off their farms. In Peru they have formed a 300,000-member alliance to initiate projects that combine environmental and indigenous land objectives. National Indian organizations from Peru, Bolivia, Ecuador, Brazil, and Colombia have formed an international alliance representing over 1 million people to press for Indian land rights.

New models of civic organization are developing in these movements. The women of Kenya's Greenbelt movement have established a cooperative that created 1,500 nurseries and planted over 10 million trees. The fisherfolk of Kerala State in India have organized cooperatives to protect their coastal fisheries resources. Japanese women have organized their own *(Seikatsu)* cooperatives with suppliers to assure safe and healthful products and require that they treat workers and nature properly. In hundreds of communities in Canada, Argentina, Australia, New Zealand, the United States, and elsewhere, people are creating their own community currencies, named variously LETs, green, or time dollars—to free themselves from colonization by the global financial system, to revitalize their communities, and build economic self-reliance.[7]

We can think of the new forms of nongovernmental organizations in developing countries as *social markets*. People who are very poor create a market of microenterprises, such as cooperative taxis for public transport or intervillage food trading networks. These networks are shaped as much by the social (personal exchange) as by economic change. In addition, people in this third sector promote businesses to finance their own sectoral expansion but remain in charge, with the nonprofit sector in charge of the profit sector. Today there are more than 35,000 voluntary associations in "developing" nations.[8]

The same associative trends can be seen in "developed" nations. England has more than 350,000 voluntary organizations; France has more than 43,000; and Germany is "growing" a third sector at a faster rate that its business or its government sector: Between 1970 and 1987, the nonprofit sector grew by more than 5 percent. In the late 1980s there were more than 300,000 voluntary organizations in Germany. In Italy during the 1970s, the voluntary sector was largely centered around the Catholic church, but in the past two decades nonreligious volunteer associations and groups have been taking an increasingly important role in local communities; more than 15.4 percent of the adult population in Italy volunteer their time to activities in the third sector.

Today in Japan the third sector has grown so dramatically that thousands of nonprofit organizations attend to the cultural, social, and economic needs of the populace. Some 23,000 charitable organizations, called *koeki hojin*, operate in Japan. In addition, there are 12,000 social welfare organizations, known as *shakaifukushi hojin*, which administer day care centers, services for the elderly, maternal and child health services, and women's protective services.[9]

The popular terms "social market" and "social economy" refer to a system of exchange characterized by its human interdependence. The terms generally refer to third-sector activity, but capitalist corporations and associations are beginning to reflect a similar consciousness of interdependence with stockholders.[10]

Decentralized Corporations: Sustaining the Community

A change is taking place within the ranks of capitalism itself. While pressure grows from grassroots organizations to decentralize and for local authority, actions of some trade associations and big corporations are proceeding in a similar direction. Trade associations are writing codes of conduct for their industries; setting health norms, safety rules, and environmental standards; and establishing self-monitoring procedures. Trade associations, being nonprofits, are thus functioning, in part, like other nongovernmental organizations, even though they still retain the function of self-interested lobbying activities.

Some big corporations are decentralizing their command systems and encouraging stakeholders to accept more authority in policymaking. Civil-society proponents have reason to be suspicious of top-level corporate changes favoring decentralization; a business corporation is still a command system. Nevertheless, these corporate policies, mostly ignored by third-sector analysts, run parallel in principle to that ideal for localizing authority through grassroots organizations.

When Bell Atlantic merged with TeleCommunications Inc. (TCI) and announced a $33 billion merger, the media focused on its huge size, but the purpose of the merger in the minds of executives was to position the new organization to better serve localities and individuals. The coming together of Bell Atlantic and TCI was intended to enable people to communicate through new systems of communication. IBM had conversations with Time Warner about collaborating on advanced digital cable-TV technology, and with TeleCommunications about developing a two-way information system. Chief executive officers (CEOs) argued that the potential for giving more power to local voices is within the realm of possibility. AT&T is scheduled to invest $3.8 billion for a stake in McCaw Cellular Communications, America's biggest cellular telephone operator, which suggests the possibility of wireless systems and putting AT&T back in the local telephone business. Decentralization is the declared intent, resulting from a mix of factors: the ineffectiveness of big command systems, the miles of executives seeking higher profits, and perhaps the power of civil society as an idea of growing influence in the field of business.

This new "combine" of telecommunications firms is worldwide. Digital Equipment Corp. (DEC) increased its share in Italy's Ing. C. Olivetti & Co. BCE Inc., a Canadian telecommunications firm situated in a small home market, announced a major alliance with Cable and Wireless PLC, a leading British telecommunications company, which, in turn, paid $4.3 billion for a 20 percent stake in MCI Communications Corp., the U.S. long-distance carrier. Merging continues as a new era in telecommunications approaches.

No one can fully predict how fiber optics, cellular phones, computers, pagers, and new computer software will combine to centralize or decentralize authority, but we hope that these mergers will be in the direction of humane, decentralized communications.

The key issue in these changes is whether the formal authority of these merging firms really can become local as well as global. Local corporations, such as community land trusts, community development corporations, and customer-owned banks, are capable of contracting with global corporations, thereby keeping these big "centralized mergers" accountable through the third-sector link. At this time social contracts between community corporations and global corporations are not widely practiced, and community corporations only dot the landscape of a much more complex global civil market; but the trend is there, and it can grow. Another trend is for corporations to decentralize their authority and build a new management culture.

A growing trend is for CEOs in leading-edge corporations to surrender formal authority to managers of lower divisions. CEOs are now reorganizing their companies into profit centers, encouraging competition and cooperation among centers. Centers are encouraged to build markets and alliances inside and outside the firm and to substitute their own inspiration for the old administrative fiat and direct command authority. Hewlett-Packard's corporate policy, for example, is for its executives to guide by persuasive leadership rather than by demand; at MCI, in an effort to preserve the autonomy of operating managers, executives stimulate creative argument between top and lower managers. Johnson & Johnson encourages coalitions of business subsidiaries by creating separate companies with their own boards of directors, hoping to provide a measure of local control and ownership.

The logic of this decentralizing movement in management is to advance greater self-direction by lower managers and local self-reliance. What could happen in the future based on this logic is illustrated in one telecommunications company, the *Milwaukee Journal*. At first the *Journal* sought to develop a centralized command system, but then it reversed its direction and created a decentralized association of locally managed subsidiaries, giving more local power to their employees in distant cities.

Model 1—The Milwaukee Journal

The *Milwaukee Journal* is an employee-owned company in the state of Wisconsin with over 2,000 employees. In the 1940s the original owner gave the employees ownership shares in the company, and the company subsequently grew in size and productivity, eventually buying subsidiary firms in allied markets. Company headquarters in Milwaukee had a community council of employee representatives (organized by departments) to offer advice to management appointed by the employee-elected board of directors. But when the *Journal* began buying new companies, management did not practice the same mode of democracy in these subsidiary firms. As they bought out independent firms in different parts of the country, the firms were made part of the command system of management in Milwaukee headquarters.

When employees in the *Journal's* subsidiaries learned about the democratic practices in Milwaukee, they complained to the board of directors. The issue was whether to extend the democratic ideas across the country to the *Journal's* extended business system.

The board discussed whether the subsidiary employees should remain under the command of the Milwaukee firm, or whether local subsidiary employees should have the option to buy shares and be given representation on the Milwaukee board of directors. The board decided that subsidiary employees should be given the right to buy into the ownership, to buy shares in the main company.

Today the Milwaukee company takes these geographically distant employees seriously in its management policies. When deciding whether to shut down or transfer work in subsidiaries overseas, it must consult with representatives of these subsidiaries on the top board. The result is a greater concern and interest in maintaining local relations in this growing firm.[11]

The *Milwaukee Journal's* system of worker ownership is not typical, yet it is not the only example. Other corporations are finding this decentralizing pattern to be more effective for their administrative operations. For example, United Parcel Services (UPS), an employee-owned company, has created UPSNET, which will keep track of the 1 million packages picked up and delivered by the company each day. More than 50,000 UPS trucks are linked to UPSNET via mobile telephones; many are automatically and continually located via Global Positioning Systems satellites. Federal Express Corp. also built its own radio network to keep track of the millions of packages that pass through its hub. Customers can call a central number and within seconds a dispatcher can tell them exactly where their package is and when they can expect delivery. These decentralizing systems have developed because of new technology.[12]

Model 2: Ularco in Mondragon

Ulgor was a Mondragon, Spain, firm of 2,000 workers. Although its board of directors was employee-elected, management had a strong command bureaucracy over workers. At one point dissident workers under this strict command system went on strike. The employee-elected board was embarrassed by a strike among its own workers who had elected them. After some deliberation the board crafted a federation of companies and restructured their departments and divisions into autonomous companies, each with its own corporate boards. A new corporate structure emerged called Ularco. Ularco became a federation of company subsidiaries, each of which had employee representation on separate boards.

The new Ularco organization included a higher board to represent all the autonomous companies (former departments in the one company), whose powers were restricted to administrative matters, such as uniform bookkeeping and marketing products for the autonomous firms. The overarching board of this Ularco federation had no power to intervene in local management or local systems of work. By centralizing their accounting and marketing operations, however, the federation kept its corporate community and the necessary uniformity in accounting, as well as their sales power in European markets. Simultaneously, job autonomy and self direction in local work systems was preserved.[13]

Theoretically, the transformation of command bureaucracies into democratic federations of companies reduces the likelihood that local communities will be destroyed.

Top officers no longer can make arbitrary, uninformed decisions from a distance when representatives of local companies serve on the board of directors. There is a greater balance of power between management and local employees in a structure of autonomous companies.[14]

It is important to remember that the principle of decentralizing authority is not a panacea: All principles of development have their limits. Decentralized institutions and local communities can develop problems of their own. We are interested in that kind of sharing power in which a *positive synergy* develops between centralization and decentralization, enhancing the possibility of local and global corporations working together for the common good. Successful examples suggest that CEOs can reverse the decline of communities by making their corporations more effective and profitable in a localized system of management.

The next cases describe corporations that might have gone vertical and global but went horizontal and local to create an environmentally protected community. In the first example, local companies' unusable waste products became the raw materials and organic feedstocks for other local companies to create an ecologically oriented community.

Model 3: An Ecological Community in Denmark

The Danish town of Kalundbourg is about 80 miles west of Copenhagen. Kalundbourg is a model of what is called industrial symbiosis, involving a coal-fired electric power-generating plant, an oil refinery, a biotechnology product plant, a plasterboard factory, a sulfuric acid producer, cement producers, a local heating company, and local agricultural and horticultural interests. Asnaes, the electricity-generating plant, supplies processed steam to the oil refinery and a pharmaceutical plant.

These local industries in Kalundborg have made innovative cost-benefit moves that factored in an ecological social responsibility component. Gyproc, the plasterboard producer, buys surplus gas from the refinery, reducing its need to burn coal. The refinery removes excess sulfur from the gas to make it cleaner burning; the removed sulfur is sold to the sulfuric acid plant. Asnaes has desulfurized its smoke, using a process that yields calcium sulfate as a side product, which is sold as industrial gypsum to Gyproc. In addition, fly ash from the desulfurazation process is used for cement making and road building.

Asnaes uses it surplus heat to warm to its own salt-water fish farm, which produces 200 tons of trout and turbot a year for the French market. Local farmers use sludge from the fish farm as fertilizer. Novo Nordisk, which runs the pharmaceutical plant, also provides hundreds of thousands of tons of nutritious sludge that local farmers then use as a liquid fertilizer. Previously the sludge has been disposed of as waste; then Novo Nordisk began adding chalk lime and heating it to neutralize remaining microorganisms.

None of the initiatives taken by companies in this community was required by law; each exchange was negotiated independently between the firms themselves. Collectively these companies represent a synthesis of social and economic values; they created a network of local market interdependencies that helps to sustain community life. This special example is an ideal that can be imitated by other locales interested in building a civil economy.

If the development of civil society involves a creative synthesis of values in the cultures of government, business, and voluntary organizations, and for decentralization in all three sectors, then a good example of such a convergence is illustrated by Sweden's innovative Natural Step. Natural Step is a national movement building consensus around environmental sustainability. Some 10,000 government officials are active in 16 specialized networks developing and carrying out action programs to achieve objectives that include: 100 percent recycling of metals, eliminating the release of compounds that do not break down naturally in the environment, maintaining biological diversity, and reducing energy use to levels of sustainability. Forty-nine local governments, members of the Swedish Farmers Federation, and 22 large Swedish companies are working to align themselves with these objectives.

The next examples are American ones, concerning energy conservation. In a typical American community, because 70 to 80 cents of every dollar spent on energy immediately leaves the local economy,[15] finding ways to reduce these costs has become essential. When local businesses, governments, schools, and households cut energy expenses, they have more disposable dollars to spend on other priorities. The money saved from reduced energy bills circulates in the community economy, strengthening its economic base.

Model 4: Sustainable Energy in Local Economies

- Osage, Iowa (pop. 3,500), started an energy-efficiency program in 1974 through its public utility, which resulted in keeping an additional $1 million a year in the local economy. This program, relying on simple tools such as caulk guns, duct tape, insulation, light bulbs, and education, created an annual community economic stimulus equal to $1,000 per household.
- Ellensburg, Washington (pop. 12.000), started energy-efficiency programs in 1989 that resulted in an additional $6.84 million in industrial output. This saving was enough to support many more jobs per year.
- San Jose, California, established an energy management program in the early 1980s. Residents, businesses, and agencies cut more than $5.5 million from annual energy bills and saved enough energy each year to power 7,600 homes. San Jose predicts its sustainable energy programs will produce a countywide $33 million increase in wages and salaries and a net employment gain of 1,753 job years over a ten-year period.
- Davis, California (pop. 40,000), is a university town; more than half of its population consists of students, faculty, or staff at the Davis campus of the University of California. When the city council refused to construct bike lanes, Davis faculty members got themselves elected to the council and worked with others to construct more than 28 miles of bike paths. Today in Davis there are more than 28,000 bicycles, which make up an important part of the transportation system. In addition, the council helped to organize the Energy Conservation Project, which took account of the unique local climate. An energy conservation code was devised that led to the restructuring of buildings to better utilize solar energy.[16]

These examples are related to what sociologist James Coleman and other social scientists call social capital. Social capital is a "sharing and trust" among people in organizations that becomes related to productivity; in these cases social capital has developed through cooperative structures created by the nonprofit and business sectors.[17]

In other cases, social capital is developed through codes of conduct constructed by employees and executives in individual corporations for the common good as well as in their own interests. Take the following case as an example.

Model 5: Code of Conduct in a Chemical Corporation

Scott-Bader is a plastic resin manufacturing company in Wallaston, England, employing over 500 people. It is a worker-owned firm, civic-oriented, decentralized, productive, profitable, self-accountable, self-regulated, and democratic. It calls itself a Commonwealth, and membership is open to all employees after a probationary period of one year. Each member of the Commonwealth has one vote. The main legislative body is the General Meeting, which meets quarterly. The following principles are exerpted from its corporate code.

Code of Practice for Members
A. We recognize that we are first a working community and that it is our basic attitude to our work and to our fellow workers that give life and meaning to the Commonwealth.
B. We have agreed that as a community our work involves four tasks, economic, technical, social and political, neglect of any one of which will in the long term diminish the Commonwealth . . .
. . .
E. We recognize that since management by consent rather than coercion is an appropriate style for the Company, a corresponding effort to accept responsibility is required from all . . .
. . .
G. We are agreed that in the event of a downturn in trade we will share all remaining work rather than expect any of our fellow members to be deprived of employment, even if this reduction in earnings by all . . .
. . .
J. We recognize that we have a responsibility to the society in which we live and believe that where we have some special talent or interest we should offer this to a wider community . . .
K. We are agreed that . . . our social responsibility extends to:

1. Limiting the products of our labour to those beneficial to the community, in particular, excluding any products for the specific purpose of manufacturing weapons of war.
2. Reducing any harmful effort of our work on the natural environment by rigorously avoiding the negligent discharge of pollutants.
3. Questioning constantly whether any of our activities are unnecessarily wasteful of the earth's natural resources[18]

A firm such as Scott Bader expresses principles of democracy as well as profit making. Employees build mutual trust and cooperation along with the usual values of the market: competition and profit making. Put another way, capitalism in these cases is changing itself slowly by integrating stakeholders into its administration, building social capital.

The following are some interesting examples of companies cooperating with customer-stakeholders.

Model 6: Corporate-Client Participation

- Herman Miller sends its design teams to work at clients' offices to understand their furniture needs and produce prototypes to test on site, thereby speeding development time, reducing costs, and increasing client satisfaction. One manager said, "We bring customers in at the very beginning to become partners in design."
- Black & Decker assigned a design team to work with 50 typical "do-it-yourself" homeowners around their homes, workshops, and on shopping trips to learn what they wanted in tools. This fresh understanding produced an award-winning product line, Quantum, with interchangeable power sources, new safety features, free maintenance checkups, and a toll-free hot line for advice.
- Honda videotaped customers testing new cars and had line workers call 4,700 Honda owners to get their criticisms and suggestions. The results were used to make thousands of changes over the past few years that made Honda the top-selling auto in the United States.
- Westinghouse has developed such a close working relationship with the public utilities it serves that some managers exchange business plans and engage in joint reviews of each other's operations. "We work with the utilities in partnership arrangements to share our responsibilities," said a Westinghouse program manager.
- Baxter Laboratories provide on-site inventory management of medical supplies for hospitals, sharing in both losses and gains. "This goes beyond

loyalty," said a Baxter executive. "We share a common P&L. You both make money by keeping costs down."
- General Electric (GE) forms cross-company teams of its own employees and those of its clients to handle tough technical problems, even sending teams to training programs together. "Working as a single entity enhanced communications," said a GE vice president.[19]

These examples represent tiny pieces of change in a larger giant picture puzzle of the business economy. Has the business system altered fundamentally? No. But business leaders are beginning to see that it makes sense to work with stakeholders, even "logical" to meet with them regularly. If managers really want to serve their customers better, why not have them (or their representatives) on corporate boards?

When Louis Gestner replaced John Akers as CEO of IBM in 1993 and was exploring ways to revitalize the corporation, a prominent analyst advised the following: "If Gerstner is sincere, he should create a new board made up of IBM customers, suppliers, partners, employees . . . a new kind of IBM that couldn't help but be more responsible because the people in charge represent the company's future . . . and clearly signal that business as usual is dead at IBM.[20]

The principles of profitability and accountability are showing signs of connecting synergistically in corporate life. The principles of cooperation and competition are converging. Cooperation has had a bad name in capitalism, suggesting collusion and corporate illegalities, but it is being reconsidered as an important aspect of business. Companies making the synergy happen are beginning to resemble a cooperative movement, although most CEOs would not connect these changes to the cooperative movement, which always has been perceived as being part of the third sector, fundamentally different from capitalism. But can it now be seen, in principle, as linking with changes in capitalism and the conventional market?

The Cooperative Movement in the Capitalist System

I would argue that the "cooperative movement" has been part of capitalism for more than a century; I believe that it is evolving in the same way capitalism emerged from feudalism, taking centuries to bloom as a complete system. Today cooperatives are increasingly visible, acquiring a momentum within competitive markets, even though their self-characterizations are very different from the "competitive sector."

The following statement was adopted at the 1995 General Assembly of the International Cooperative Alliance (ICA) held in Manchester, England, on the occasion of the Alliance's Centenary. "Cooperatives are based on the values of self-help, self-responsibility, democracy, equality, equity, and solidarity. In the tradition of their founders, cooperative members believe in the ethical values of honesty, openness, social responsibility, and caring for others."

Let us examine model cases in the cooperative movement in the third sector.

Co-op Model 1: The Seikatsu Consumer Cooperative Club

The Seikatsu Consumer Cooperative Club was founded in Tokyo for families to buy pure milk at affordable prices. Beginning in 1965, this Cooperative Club evolved into an activist network so that by 1992 Seikatsu, with 225,000 families, had $700 million in total sales that included 161 related worker collectives with 4,200 worker owners. The club relies on a group structure based on the *han,* an association of eight to ten neighbors who facilitate local decision making. Its aim to sustain a society of communities emphasizing cooperation. Seikatsu evolved from being a network of buying clubs with the work done by members, to offering goods and services to the public. It began to organize worker co-ops, managed on a one-person, one-vote basis. Members generated most capital for the co-ops, with some assistance from Seikatsu.[21]

Co-op Model 2: Co-op Atlantic

Co-op Atlantic is a cooperative system serving Canada's Atlantic provinces: Labrador, Newfoundland, New Brunswick, Nova Scotia, and Prince Edward Island. It was founded in 1927; today it serves the needs of its owners, 161 retail, producer, agricultural, housing, and fishing cooperatives, and a co-op newspaper. It wholesales groceries, hardware, petroleum, dry goods, and livestock supplies; provides assistance with management training; and operates Atlantic People Housing Ltd., a subsidiary that manages and constructs co-op housing. In 1993 Co-op Atlantic wholesale sales to member co-ops exceeded $440 million. Membership includes over 168,000 families of primary producers and consumers representing more than 500,000 people. Member co-ops have over 5,000 workers and over $300 million in assets. Co-op food stores now account for 19 percent of all food sales in Atlantic Canada. Efforts are under way to expand into other business and production areas. Each co-op is self-governing and democratic in operation.[22]

According to the National Cooperative Business Association, there are 47,000 cooperatives in the United States that generate more than $100 billion in annual economic activity. All told, as many as 100 million Americans—40 percent of the population—are directly served by some type of cooperative endeavor.

It should be noted that there are both producer co-ops and consumer co-ops. In both the United States and Great Britain, the consumer co-op movement developed more co-ops than the producer co-op movement, but wholesale co-ops and agricultural co-ops also emerged. In Great Britain, retail (consumer) co-ops bought shares in wholesale co-ops, which then purchased goods from producers. Consumer co-ops were given voting rights in wholesale co-ops according to the number of purchases they made.

Of course, producer co-ops and consumer co-ops have different goals. Producer co-ops, where *workers* acquire rights to company ownership, seek the highest prices possible; consumer co-ops, where customers acquire rights to ownership, seek the lowest possible prices. Nevertheless, in some countries co-op markets are organized in a relative balance of power. Producer and consumer cooperatives seek different outcomes but can work together because they are equally powerful, as in the Swiss diary industry.

Co-op Model 3: Swiss Diary Products

Swiss milk producers are organized into more than 4,000 local cooperatives, 13 regional associations of cooperatives, and the Central Association of Swiss Milk Producers, a confederation of associations representing all milk producers and, hence, a large share of all Swiss farmers. In addition to milk production, the local cooperatives and the regional associations are active in milk processing. The local cooperatives normally own the buildings and machinery of about 1,500 village dairies, about 80 percent of which are independent cheese-makers, often family enterprises employing only a few people. About 20 percent are run by the cooperatives themselves.

Milk processes are organized into 6 business associations divided into 2 large groups. One consists of cheese manufacturers, with more than 1,000 members in all, organized into a complex system of 3 interlocking associations, 2 of which represent independent cheese-makers. The other group, with about 10 to 20 member firms, consists of industrialized dairies. Because of its wide and dispersed memberships, the cheese manufacturer's association is divided into many regional subgroups and employs a full-time professional staff. Both the cheese manufacturers and the industrial dairies are democratically organized.

The Central Association of Swiss Milk Producers and an Association of Milk Buyers jointly regulate the general conditions of purchase between buyers and sellers of raw milk. Regional and local associations of milk producers and milk buyers negotiate contracts that regulate both prices and various services. This matching between supply and demand takes place through democratic associations outside government. The two main retailers, MIGROS and COOP, represent the consumers directly; together they have 39 percent of the market. In other cases, producer-consumer co-ops successfully "self-regulate" product quality, safety, and level of output without government controls.[23]

The cooperative movement exists quietly in the background of capitalism in South America, North America, Japan, India, and Africa. Its norms and structures show signs of mixing with the competitive market, a movement that may help us construct an image of how civil markets will emerge in the twenty-first century.

Research to Support Community-Based Economies

The seemingly opposite principles in the culture of the market economy, such as cooperation vs. competition and profitability vs. accountability, are now converging.

The convergence is visible in such widely different movements as grassroots protests, the decentralization of megacorporations, and the cooperative movement, but it is the simultaneity of development here that is impressive and should become part of the international research.

The three sectors of the economy—government, business, and nonprofits/grass-roots organizations—are forging both civil principles that guide the direction of capital and associations in these different sectors and high-minded principles for their members. These principles, some of which are enumerated below, deserve to be the subjects of careful study.

Associations should:

- Provide regular opportunities for opinions to be formed intelligently among members.
- Connect the thinking of each member to the larger good as well as to the organization itself.
- Respect the civil rights of people in localities in organizational decisions.
- Look for what is self-actualizing for individual members as well as what is useful to the organization.
- Protect the integrity of people and cultivate their personal well-being in decision making.

- Promote activities that encourage a higher purpose for members, engaging their own humanity in corporate work.
- Avoid strict dogma in decision making.
- Provide equal access to information for members of the association.
- Offer fair petition for redress of injustices.
- Encourage the participation of constituencies in the government of an association.[24]

These civil principles, evolving both in grass-roots organizations and socially innovative businesses, can be studied like ideal types. Associations and businesses can be tested: To what extent are these attributes present or absent? This kind of research could help establish guidelines for understanding a civil economy.

Since I am defining a "civil economy" as a system of self-governing firms and markets that work for the common good, rooted in cooperation among competitors, then another area for research would be conflict resolution modes that are evolving within a system of countervailing powers. In the cooperative movement, for example, new methods of conflict resolution were created to mediate between competing (power-balanced) producers and consumers. In the Swiss diary market, the distributive associations became an important middle negotiator; since producer associations wish to sell at high prices and consumer associations wish to buy at low prices, wholesale associations helped facilitate a negotiated price.[25] Mondragon followed a different model for conflict resolution between producers vs. consumers, based on stakeholder representation: retail stores have stakeholders (customers, employees, and producers) on the board of directors, schools include teachers on their top boards, and housing co-ops include employees, along with residents, on boards. Such stakeholder representation needs further study.

Comparative research could be done across national boundaries. The Seikatsu system, the Mondragon system, the Atlantic Co-op system, and the Swiss dairy system of markets are global experiments in civil society. People in these cases resolve problems based on the principle of subsidiarity, with minimum government interference.

In the U.S. examples, a movement toward a new system of civil governance for American corporations is clearly evident, but research is needed on the kind of culture that supports it. The new "culture" for corporate governance remains to be understood in the context of the U.S. economy. Robert Monks, president of Institutional Shareholder Partners in Washington, D.C., sees the need for cultural studies on corporate governance. "No set of laws can ensure an adequate system of corporate governance," he contends, "without supporting culture and institutional structure. The informed and active involvement of owners is essential."[26]

Research can help bridge the cultures and language of different sectors of the economy. "Systems of social accountability" and "civil governance" are unfamiliar terms to many CEOs in the United States, yet CEOs are actively engaged in cultivating them. CEOs would look with disfavor at the cooperative movement (retail stores typically do not include customer representatives on their boards), yet the number of employee-owned/managed firms is growing in the United States and they eventually could become producer cooperatives. Top managers quietly are moving in the direction of the civil principles represented in the cooperative movement.

In sum, these examples tell us how economies become decentralized and localized in a capitalist economy. The ecology of exchange relationships created at Kalundborg, Denmark, illustrates how competing companies maximized economic returns at local levels and strengthened community life. Other cases tell us how the market works to reduce government costs and how decentralized corporations enable local community life to become stronger.

We need studies on the degree to which localities are strengthened by a synthesis of social and economic factors created when companies make profits while empowering local communities. Our examples suggest how profits and nonprofits, competitive markets and cooperative markets, can intermingle in the next century.

Formerly, the profit corporation set economic goals as primary and social goals as secondary, while the nonprofit corporation set social goals as primary and economic goals as secondary; today these two types of corporation are not so far apart.

Profit and nonprofit corporations both make an income to survive, and profit margins can be similar. The salaries of executives in big nonprofits can exceed those of profit-making corporations. The cases presented suggest that "intersects" are happening: When profits become more socially oriented, and nonprofits emphasize economic goals, the differences between the two types diminish. Business has been developing a stronger commitment to customers and communities while nonprofits (NGOs in the third sector), learning from the profit sector have been seeking to make a better income and establish efficiency standards. Nonprofit and for-profit corporations have become interwoven in "partnerships" to solve social problems and make mutual investments.

The new connections and convergences between the profit-nonprofit sectors are phenomenal, changing the marketplace, and requiring research.

Businesses contribute to the capital formation of nonprofits, such as universities and NGOs, and influence policies. Religious institutions and businesses have joined forces to eliminate slum neighborhoods, through housing construction by business and training programs by churches to educate new homeowners. The two sectors are moving closer as their social and economic goals become synthesized in daily practice. The partnership between profits and nonprofits is synthesizing financial and human values in ways that could create a more community-oriented economy.

Notes

1. The sociological literature on the loss of community life in the United States is extensive Some examples are Arthur Vidich and Joseph Bensman, *Small Town in Mass Society* (Garden City, N.Y.: Doubleday, 1958); Maurice Stein, *The Eclipse of Community* (Princeton, N.J.: Princeton University Press, 1960); and Roland Warren, ed., *Perspectives on the American Community* (Skokie, Ill.: Rand McNally, 1973). For studies on the role of the automobile in destroying community life, see Jane Holtz Kay, *Asphalt Nation* (New York: Crown, 1997; Moshe Safdie with Wendy Kohn, *The City after the Automobile* (New York: Basic Books, 1997).

2. Corporations play a positive and negative role in community development. We refer here to the negative side because we are looking for solutions. On the negative side, corporations deplete community and natural capital. They move production to places where they can pay less than a living wage, and they use the threat of moving jobs to break up labor unions and bargain down wages. They deplete community capital when they hire young women in places like the Mexican *maquiladoras* under conditions that lead to their physical burnout after three or four years. Once eyesight problems, allergies, kidney problems, and repetitive stress injuries deplete their efficiency, the women are replaced with a fresh supply of younger women. Corporations deplete the earth's natural capital through local strip mining, depleting forests, fisheries, and mineral deposits, dumping wastes, and aggressively marketing toxic chemicals. Globalization is part of the reason for civic movements reviving and continuing. For more on the negative side, see: Samuel Bowles and Herbert Gintis, *Democracy and Capitalism: Property, Community, and the Contradictions of Modern Thought* (New York: Basic Books, 1986). For more on the positive side, see William E. Halal, *The New Capitalism* (New York: John Wiley & Sons, 1986).

3. See Warren, ed., *Perspectives on the American Community.*

4. Paul Hirst, *Associative Democracy: New Forms of Economic and Social Governance* (Amherst: University of Massachusetts Press, 1994); John Mathews, *Age of Democracy: The Politics of Post-Fordism* (Melbourne: Oxford University Press Australia, 1989).

5. "World Volunteerism Group Forms," *New York Times,* December 21, 1993, A12 Historians argue that NGOs were an effective force in toppling the authoritarian regimes in Eastern Europe and the Soviet Union, more than resistance groups steeped in political ideology and backed by paramilitary campaigns. Soviet historian Frederick Starr argues that the rapid growth of the third-sector activity placed enormous pressure on the already weakened party apparatus. The effervescence of NGOs of all types is the single most distinctive aspect of the revolution of 1989. Frederick Starr, "The Third Sector in the Second World," *World Development* 19, no. 1: 65.

6. David Korten, *When Corporations Rule the World* (Hartford, Conn: Kumarian Press, 1955), 295.

7. See articles in *YES!: A Journal of Positive Futures* (Spring, 1997); Thomas Greco, Jr., *New Money for Healthy Communities* (Tucson, Ariz.: Thomas Greco, 1994).

8. Julie Fischer, *The Road from Rio: Sustainable Development and the Non-Governmental Movements in the Third World* (Westport, Conn.: Praeger, 1993), 91.

9. Jeremy Rifkin, *The End of Work* (New York: GP. Putnam's Sons, 1995), 275–277. U.N. Secretary-General Boutros Boutros Ghali gives different figures. He says that "In France, 54,000 new associations have been established since 1987. In Italy, 40 percent of all associations have been set up within the last 15 years. This phenomenon is also occurring in developing countries. Within a short space of time, 10,000 NGOs have been established in Bangladesh, 21,000 in the Phillipines, and 27,000 in Chile. In Eastern Europe, since the fall of communism, non-governmental organizations have been playing an increasingly important role in people's lives." Boutros Boutros Ghali, "Foreword," in Thomas Weiss and Leon Gordenker, *NGOs, the UN, and Global Governance* (Boulder, Colo.: Lynne Rienner 1996), 7–8.

10. Bishan Singh, "A Social Economy: The Emerging Scenario for Change," in Tina Liamzon, ed., *Civil Society and Sustainable Livelihoods Workshop Report* (Rome: Society for International Development, 1994). In India, Tasmania, Canada, Thailand, France, Hungary, and elsewhere, people are joinging Dai Quing in saying no to dam projects that threaten their homes, livelihoods, and wild places. The women of India's Chipko movement are wrapping themselves around threatened trees to save them from loggers; Penan tribal people of Srawak, Malaysia, are blockading logging roads with their bodies; and the 1 million strong Future Forest Alliance is organizing protest demonstrations and media campaigns in Canada.

　　People are mobilizing to protect mangroves in the Ivory Coast, reef systems in Belize, and wildlife in Nambia. They are opposing toxic dumping in the United States and campaigning to protect Antarctic as natural preserve. Japanese citizens are pressuring Japanese logging companies to change their practices abroad. Germans are calling for an end to foreign aid that destroys primary forests. Indigenous pocket miners, farmers, and fisherfolk in the

Philippines are mobilizing to challenge the right of a few powerful mining corporations to destroy the livelihood of thousands of people.

11. This story is drawn from my conversation with personnel at the *Milwaukee Journal*. For details on company origins, see Will Conrad et al., *The Milwaukee Journal* (Madison: University of Wisconsin Press, 1964); "Partners in Ownership" is published by the Journal Company

12. The telecommunications revolution makes clear that efforts are underway to create a "network of networks" that will allow everyone to be connected with everyone else. This digital global web of networks makes it possible for anyone to communicate with anyone else on the planet in real time, altering the way people will do business in the future. With fiber optics, each light pulse represents 3.4 billion bits a second, the equivalent of 50,000 simultaneous phone calls on a single pair of fibers. Soon it will be possible to transmit 1 trillion bits per second, or about 70 million simultaneous conversations on a single pair of fibers These speeds and volumes are possible because the messages are digitized.

13. William Whyte and Kathleen King Whyte, *Making Mondragon* (Ithaca, N.Y.: ILR Press, 1991) The governing council of ULARCO originally consisted of three members from each member cooperative. The council is responsible to planning and coordination, for recommending annual and long-range plans for each co-op member, and for coordinating commercial policies. 60ff.

14. Osborne and Gaebler argue that *decentralizing institutions* have a number of advantages:

"First, [decentralized institutions] are far more flexible than centralized institutions; they can respond quickly to changing circumstances and customer's needs . . . Second, [they] are more effective than centralized institutions. . . . Frontline workers are closest to most problems and opportunities. . . . Third, [they] are far more innovative than centralized institutions. . . . Fourth, [they] generate a higher morale, more commitment, and greater productivity. David Osborne and Ted Gaebler, *Reinventing Government* (New York: A Plume Book, 1993), 252–253.

15. *The Jobs Connection: Energy Use and Local Economic Development* Cities and Counties Project, U.S. Department of Energy. National Reviewable Energy Lab, July 1994.

16. The first three cases in sustainable energy cases (Model 4) are drawn from Alice Hubbard and Clay Fong, *Community Energy Workbook* (Snowmass, Colo.: Rocky Mountain Institute, 1995), 3 The fourth case (Davis) is from David Morris, *Self Reliant Cities* (San Francisco: Sierra Club Books, 1982), 122–123.

17. James Coleman, *Foundations of Social Theory* (Cambridge, Mass.: Harvard University Press, 1990), 360–361. Political scientist Robert Putnam argues similiarly that civic organizations add social capital to the community, creating an order of mutual trust. See Robert Putnam, *Making Democracy Work* (Princeton, N.J.: Princeton University Press, 1993); "Bowling Alone: America's De-

clining Social Capital," *Journal of Democracy* 6 (1995): 65–78. I would say that Ularco's confederation of companies added social capital when it was designed to create an order of mutual confidence among employees. An organization creates "social capital" when it reduces the costs of labor strife and government regulations.

A civil economy develops from democratic associations and civic organizations promoting social capital with the principles of democracy, freedom, and justice. The problem in cultivating a civil economy is whether these values will mesh with profit making, efficiency, and productivity. A civil economy articulates this synthesizing process, creating a shared purpose for people working in firms and associations.

18. See the *Social Report*, Department of Sociology, Boston College, Chestnut Hill, Mass.: This preamble to their "social constitution" was formulated in 1974.

19. This summary is drawn from William E Halal, *The New Management: Democracy and Enterprise Are Transforming Organizations* (San Francisco: Berett-Koehler, 1996), 118. His sources were: "The Tough New Customer," *Fortune* (Autumn/Winter 1993). Rahul Jacob, "Why Some Customers Are More Equal Than Others," *Fortune*, September 19, 1994.

20. Michael Schrage, "To Reshape IBM, Gerstner Should Work from the Boardroom Down," *Washington Post*, April 2, 1993. This quotation was cited in ibid., 76.

21. The Japanese Consumers Cooperatives Union was founded in 1951. By 1990 it had 674 member organizations with 14.4 million members and sales equal to 2.5 percent of the total Japanese domestic retail trade. Forty-four percent of co-op sales were generated by *han*-based buying clubs as opposed to 56 percent from retail stores. "Seikatsu," *Grassroots Economic Organizing Newsletter* (March-April 1994): 1–8.

22. Co-op Atlantic became part of the larger Antigonish Movement, started by Moses Coady in 1928 David Bedford and Sidney Pobihushchy, "Towards a People's Economy: The Co-op Atlantic Experience," Interculture (Summer 1993). For historic origins, see Moses Coady, *Masters of Their Own DestiNew York: The Story of the Antigonish Movement of Adult Education Through Economic Cooperation.* (Antigonish, N.S.: Formac Publishing Co., 1967). For more sources and details on the Seikatsu and Atlantic models, see Roy Morrison, *Ecological Democracy* (Boston: South End Press, 1995).

23. In Switzerland, about 80 percent of Swiss cheese and almost 100 percent of hard cheese are manufactured in about 1,500 village dairies, often family enterprises employing only a few people The Swiss diary industry is organized into higher levels of association, local to national. For case studies on European cooperatives and trade associations, see Phillipe C. Schmitter, ed., *Private Interest Government* (Beverly Hills, Calif.: Sage, 1985).

24. The following list of principles of common rights and responsibilities, enumerated by the Commisssion on Global Governance, says that associations around the world support the right of people to:

A secure life; equitable treatment; an opportunity to earn a fair living and provide for their own welfare; the definition and preservation of their differences through peaceful means; participation in governance at all levels; free and fair petition for redress of gross injustices; equal access to information; and, equal access to the global commons At the same time, people share a responsibility to: contribute to the common good; consider the impact of their actions on the security and welfare of others; promote equity, including gender equity; protect the interests of future generations by pursuing sustainable development and safeguarding the global commons; preserve humanity's cultural and intellectual heritage; Be active participants in governance; and work to eliminate corruption.

25. Quoted from The Commission on Global Governance, "A Call to Action," Geneva, 1995, 10. I discuss this model in more detail in Severyn T. Bruyn, *The Social Economy* (New York: John Wiley and Sons, 1977), 182-183.

26. Robert Monks, "Growing Corporate Governance: From George III to George Bush," in Brenda Sutton, ed., *The Legitimate Corporation* (Cambridge, Mass.: Blackwell, 1993), 171.

CONCLUSION

On the Other Side of the Millennium: A Synthesis of Progressive Economic Thought

William E. Halal and Kenneth B. Taylor

With these diverse views in mind, let's review what has been learned. Our intent is to integrate the trends and models of various contributors into a coherent whole, a scenario that sketches out the likely shape of economies in the twenty-first century.

Trends of Economic Change

Table C.1 summarizes the key points made in the preceeding chapters so that we may gain a sound grasp of broad patterns in the data. By scanning across the rows of different authors, we can identify common concepts that appear in various chapters and also can see broader themes running through the book.

There are limits to what we can conclude, of course. These chapters do not comprise a scientifically selected sample of economic perspectives and they may not cover other topics of unexpected importance. Intensive analytical rigor does not seem possible, or even very useful, when attempting to forecast the future shape of economic systems that are in flux around the world.

Table C.1 Summary of Concepts

Chapter Number	Author	Forces/Trends	Institutional Concepts/Policies	Economic Concepts/Policies
1	Sternberg	Information revolution Culture of images Globalization Social movements Fundamentalism	Global corporations International management elite	New mercantilism A new interpretive economics
2	Dicken	Information revolution Globalization Effects of distance	Global corporations	Political economy in global order Role and importance of location
3	Halal	Information revolution Free enterprise Cooperation Knowledge and purpose	Internal markets Corporate community Intelligent infrastructures	Governments: Compete to attract global corporations
4	Scott	Information revolution Globalization Regionalization Externalities and transactions costs	Global corporations Synergies of location	Economic blocs Regional confederations
5	Etzioni	Breakdown in traditional values Knowledge society Human needs and response Consumerism	Redefinition of individual/household relationship with economy	Individual: voluntary simplicity Community: voluntary simplicity

(continues)

Table C.1 Summary of Concepts *(continued)*

Chapter Number	Author	Forces/Trends	Institutional Concepts/Policies	Economic Concepts/Policies
6	Thore	Technology Dynamic markets Accelerating change Product life cycles	Industry structure and effects of hypergrowth Corporate product-cycle management	Industrial development Disequilibrium
7	Miles et al.	Information revolution Decentralization	Corporate: restructuring around network/cellular organizational concepts	Efficiency, employee empowerment, and enhanced competitiveness
8	Ackoff	Decentralization	Corporate: restructuring using internal markets	Efficiency, employee empowerment, and enhanced competitiveness
9	Ekins	Globalization Environmental decay	Corporate: clean business accounting as a competitive advantage	Environmental taxes and regulations
10	Lehrer	Decentralization Global competition	Corporate: restructuring using internal markets (case study)	Efficiency, employee empowerment, and enhanced competitiveness
11	Angresano	Evolution of knowledge	Socioeconomic evolution: thoughts of Myrdal, Hayak and Schumpeter	New interdisciplinary paradigm
12	McIntyre	Transformation of former communist nations	Neoclassical policies in transition economies	Economic systems: a "third way"

(continues)

Table C.1 Summary of Concepts *(continued)*

Chapter Number	Author	Forces/Trends	Institutional Concepts/Policies	Economic Concepts/Policies
		Decentralization	Social disorder and reaction to change	
13	Taira	Privatization		
		Globalization		
		Globalization	Flexibility in Japanese corporate practices	Deregulation of markets and institutions
14	Pestoff	Japanese socioeconomic transformation		Lowering Japanese trade barriers
		Globalization	Social enterprise as corporate model to promote social welfare	Government: promote civil democracy
		Decline of welfare state		
15	Lutz	Effects of markets	Human-centered corporate policies and organization	Humanistic economics
		Consumerism		
		Corporate practices		
16	Taylor	Conflict between political democracy and capitalism	Corporate participation in USOP	Universal capitalism
		Growing inequality	Spreading equity ownership	
17	Bruyn	Decline of welfare state	Third sector: role of social enterprises	Stakeholder capitalism
				Civil society

Despite these obstacles, we think this chapter can offer a rough approximation of leading economic thought. The contributors represent a broad spectrum of views from prominent scholars working at major universities around the globe, and their topics have been carefully selected to cover the full range of interest today. Thus we feel confident in claiming that the following conclusions portray a plausible outline of how economic systems are most likely to evolve over the next decade or two.

The Information Revolution and Globalization

Looking over the first column in the table, the most striking conclusion is that almost all scholars accept the defining role now being played by the information revolution and globalization, each of which is characterized by multiple subtrends. Indeed, from Sternberg, to Dicken, to Halal, to Scott, to Thore, the consensus is so widely held that there is little to debate. The revolutionary power of information technology (IT) and the forces of globalization amount to a de facto background of the future economic world that is now taken for granted. Attention today is concentrated on understanding how these two supertrends will play out in detail.

These two trends are closely related. The revolution in IT is largely responsible for the way markets are spreading rapidly around the world, deepening and becoming more integrated. Further, forecasts for the future growth of IT suggest that both trends are simply beginning their major ascent upward. The bulk of IT now is being used in the developed world, but, as developing nations such as China leap into modernity, the market for telecommunications services is expected to grow from its current level of roughly 1 billion people to about 4 billion people. Worldwide spending on IT is estimated to reach $1 trillion per year by 2001 alone. Even now daily calls to prayer in Saudi Arabia begin: "God is great. Please turn off all pagers and cellular phones."[1]

Traditionally, most information traffic has been carried by state monopolies. But that is also changing as the privatization of telecommunications companies and competition across borders becomes the norm. In 1997, 60 nations signed an agreement opening up their telecom markets to global competition, which is expected to unleash such a tidal wave of efficiency that prices are likely to fall by half or more.[2]

As this wave of global information networks continues to unite the workings of individual economies through electronic capital flows, exchanges of knowledge, labor movements, cross-border trade, and other activities, the world should operate increasingly as a more integrated economic system.

This does not mean that the world economy will become unified, structured, and managed according to similar policies. Obviously, national differences will long remain: Dicken and Scott are convinced that the twenty-first century world will be forged by social, economic, and political processes in which location matters. However, the world will behave as a single system in that actions of one nation will affect others more keenly, producing a global economy that interacts as a whole.

Further, dysfunctional mismatches among economies will come under increasing competitive pressure, thereby tending to alter the present design of the global economic system to a more efficient, unified whole. If economic blocs are advantageous for a group of nations, for instance, why would this same logic not extend eventually to include all nations? Our first conclusion, therefore, is as follows:

> *Conclusion 1:* Economies of the twenty-first century are likely to be integrated by sophisticated information networks into some type of unified global system.

The Flowering of Enterprise

The unprecedented level of technical complexity and cultural diversity within this global order is the relentlessly spreading free markets, enterprise, and democracy throughout economic systems. Once again, this trend is so well accepted that almost all of our contributors assume that twenty-first century economies will be fiercely competitive. The most notable examples include the affirmation of free markets in the postcommunist nations of Russia, Eastern Europe, and China. Meanwhile, there is a continued deregulation of capitalist economies in the United States, Britain, Western Europe, and Japan. And as we will note a bit later, the same trend can be seen in the introduction of free-market forces *within large corporations.*

The power of this trend to economic freedom is explained by James Angresano in chapter 11, which reminds us that some economists, notably Hayek, long have argued that the complexity of industrial societies cannot be managed by command-and-control systems. Hierarchical control simply is unable to process the overwhelming flow of detailed information generated by the differing needs, choices, and innovative ideas of millions of people. The problem of managing this vast complexity is becoming ever more acute in an information age where knowledge is purposely intended to grow exponentially.

A dramatic instance of the move to freedom can be seen in the plans of the U.S. Federal Aviation Administration (FAA) to replace the current system of controlling aircraft through air corridors. With the rapid growth of traffic clogging the system, the FAA is testing a new system called "free flight" that allows aircraft almost total freedom to fly wherever they choose. A new form of "self-control" is provided by Global Positioning Systems, which gives pilots precise information on their location, and by an automatic safety system, which warns when aircraft approach one another. The system has been shown to permit large increases in traffic, avoid delays, and reduce costs, while improving safety. An FAA official claimed, "It's the most successful program [we've] put forward."[3]

We submit that complex technological and institutional systems of this type are becoming common, which in turn makes the need for the self-organizing features of markets and democracy almost inevitable. Thus, our second major conclusion is:

Conclusion 2: Twenty-first-century economies are likely to become even more deregulated to the point where market systems may approach that textbook ideal of perfect competition: large numbers of competing players, good economic information, and freedom to enter and exit markets.

Containing the Forces of Creative Destruction

While these two conclusions clearly point to a more integrated global economy composed of myriad competing enterprises, the challenge of governing this enormously complex, turbulent, and socially disruptive world is not at all clear. Angresano reminds us that Gunnar Myrdal and Joseph Schumpeter were deeply concerned about these inevitable consequences of creative destruction. The dramatic economics crisis that leveled Asia in 1998 seems to echo their concerns.

The list of such problems described by our contributors is long. In chapter 1 Ernest Sternberg is concerned about the growth of an endless number of social movements each pursuing its own agenda, a retreat into fundamentalism, and the power of sophisticated digital media permeating popular culture to alter perceptions and human minds on a massive scale. In chapter 6 Sten A. Thore expects today's hectic pace of innovation to accelerate as the IT juggernaut intensifies thereby driving competition, markets, and change to a degree of disequilibrium that defies traditional analysis. Paul Ekins and Halal note that a huge increase in global consumption looms ahead, which cannot conceivably be handled within the present techno-economic system, and so some major transformation in unavoidable. Victor Pestoff and Severyn T. Bruyn are deeply concerned that these competitive pressures are eroding the social supports of the welfare state, leaving the unfortunate with shrinking alternatives. And in chapter 15, Mark A. Lutz condemns harsh employment practices, such as downsizing, which led to greater economic insecurity and disrupted careers and families.

In chapter 12 Robert J. McIntyre tells a tale of market logic gone rampant in former communist countries. The problem is that capitalism is not compatible with the cultural heritage and social institutions of these nations. Recent polls confirm the widely held fear that a majority of people are still suffering because reforms have mainly enriched the "neo-robber barons" of a new capitalist ruling class. Only 10 percent of Russians in 1996 thought their country was moving in the right direction. Blair Rubble, director of The Kennan Institute for Advanced Russian Studies, concluded that, "Such conflicts point to the heart of Russia's present conundrum: An ideological center is missing, something that gives meaning to the new Russian state."[4]

All in all, these chapters rightly paint a grim picture of epochal stress as the revolutionary forces of IT, globalization, and free markets disrupt the social order. Some contributors do point to hopeful solutions. Amitai Etzioni's data indicate that many people are reacting to rising affluence and increasing economic stress by voluntarily simplifying their lives to focus on family and community. And Halal observes that knowledge-based economies behave differently in that cooperation has become efficient. But these voices of optimism are the exception, leaving confusion and doubt about the hopes for forging economic systems that can contain all this disorder through some new form of civil society.

This seems a universal dilemma in an age when *all* economic systems are in upheaval. Lester Thurow sounded an eerily similar concern about the American system of capitalism. With no guiding ideology other than avarice, Thurow notes, capitalism's very strength of efficiency could become the system's undoing because it contributes to growing economic imbalances. Missing is a set of common goals and values that citizen's can rally around.[5]

A third conclusion can be drawn from this analysis:

Conclusion 3: The creative destruction caused by today's transition to a knowledge-based global economy will continue to create social disorder until new ideologies are defined for economic systems of the twenty-first century.

We now turn to a synthesis of parts II and III, which we hope may offer grounds for a more optimistic future.

Emerging Models of the Firm

The concepts in this part of the book polarize around two central themes taking place in global corporations that appear opposed to one another but may, in fact, be complementary. The first theme can be seen as the micro-economic equivalent of the rush noted above toward markets and enterprise that is more apparent at macroeconomic levels. Driven by the same imperative of managing exploding complexity, large corporations seem to be making a similar transition to what Halal, Ackoff, and Lehrer call "internal markets" and "internal enterprise."

Just as nations are dismantling command-and-control economies for free markets, corporations are dismantling their traditional hierarchies to encourage entrepreneurial behavior. Thore stresses that this more dynamic form of management is essential to cope with hypercompetition and short product development cycles. Sternberg observes the same trend, and Lehrer offers the Lufthansa case to demonstrate this concept in practice. Miles, et al. describe a related but slightly different version of entrepreneurial firms by focusing on how individual units, or "cells," form rapidly changing alliances. Collectively, these concepts describe the self-organizing movement of entre-preneurial units that more closely resemble a living organism than the hier-archical pyramids of the industrial past.

The second major theme is described by Lutz as a move toward "human-centered business," by Pestoff as "social enterprise," and by Taylor as "universal capitalism." Bruyn sees in all this the seeds of a more civil society based on "cooperative enterprise." Common to all these concepts is the recognition that the modern corporation is increasingly regarded as far more than property owned by shareholders to realize profits. Companies must carry out this economic role, of course, but they also must serve the interests of various stakeholders: primarily employees, customers, local communities, and associated suppliers and dealers.

We think the significance of this theme is profound because it logically leads to a dramatic redefinition of the role of the firm, and, by implication, the purpose and character of free-market economic systems. Halal calls the model that seems likely to emerge as "corporate community," in recognition of the fact that modern business must form cooperative working relationships with all of its constituencies in order to gain their support. The new economic era is replacing capital with knowledge as the critical factor of production, and knowledge is unique in that it *increases* when shared. That explains why cooperation has become one of the most powerful forces in business today.[6] This is most clearly visible in the explosive growth of strategic alliances, but it also is occurring in the realization that corporations must now empower their employees, gain the trust of their clients, and so on with all stakeholders.

Note that this view differs from the older notion of social responsibility because it is not simply a question of doing good but a more powerful form of business intended to enlist the support of these groups to improve economic performance. In short, corporate community is a competitive advantage. In chapter 9 Ekins notes that today progressive chief executive officers (CEOs) often advocate environmental protection because it can reduce operating costs and gain customers.

Considering the long history of harsh behavior that is synonymous with capitalism, we realize this is a bold claim that is not likely to be accepted readily. But we think the evidence summarized in these chapters makes a compelling case, although it may take a decade or so until this trend becomes apparent and widely practiced. Even now, astute observers of American business note that the harsh practices of downsizing, poor working conditions, and low employee pay seem to have run their course, and a more enlightened view is appearing that recognizes this view is essential. James Miller, a former CEO, observed, "I think the pendulum is starting to swing toward more humane bosses."[7]

Thus, our analysis of part II concludes that the global corporation of the twenty-first century is likely to become a far more dynamic, entrepreneurial system that more closely resembles an internal market economy rather than a hierarchy. Yet it is also likely to move beyond a sole concern for profit to integrate the interests of its employees, clients, the public, and associated partners into a tightly knit but frequently changing microeconomic system that is more productive as well as socially responsive. This can be stated in the following conclusion:

> *Conclusion 4:* Corporations in the twenty-first century are likely to be structured as internal enterprise systems to manage complexity, and they also will unify their various constituencies into sociopolitical alliances that increase economic value.

Because the firm is the basis for economic behavior, this conclusion has powerful implications for resolving the ideological crisis all economic systems are facing.

Economic Policy in the Twenty-First Century

We are now prepared to address the challenge noted at the beginning of this chapter: How can policymakers reconcile the need for free markets with the need for a civil society?

The views of our contributors suggest that no well-recognized solution is in sight but that national policy must come to grips with this formidable dilemma. In chapter 13 Koji Taira provides a vivid account of how the Japanese are wrestling with this challenge. Globalization in the context of protected domestic markets and inflexible economic institutions led to the current crisis. Now Japanese policymakers in government and business are struggling to deregulate their economic system while simultaneously preserving the harmony among various parties that is traditional in much of the East. The lack of clear movement indicates the formidable challenge posed by this problem.

Europe is caught in roughly the same clash of opposing interests. Even though the 1997 and 1998 elections replaced right-wing leaders with left-wing leaders in France, Britain, and Germany, there has been no return to socialist policies because of this vital recognition that the era of big government is over. McIntyre sees a backlash brewing in Russia that will lead the state to reassert control over domestic markets and fledgling development processes. We think these examples illustrate that the traditional concepts of left and right are increasingly meaningless in the face of a mounting urgency to resolve the pressing demands for both free enterprise and civil order.

In the interim, we can see in the thoughts of our authors how various nations are muddling through with incremental plans that move in the general direction of a solution. Angresano offers the work of another great economist to guide us in this direction: Myrdal's philosophy of economic development along a socially responsible path that serves all interests. Sternberg sees nations developing a "new mercantilism" that attempts to steer economic activity, and Scott focuses on the formation of economic blocs that strengthen entire regions. Ekins favors taxes and regulations to minimize social costs of pollution. McIntyre's account of the disastrous effects of shock therapy in Russia suggests that a "third way" is feasible to solve the economic problems of such nations. Taylor advocates a national policy that extends the advantages of stock ownership to all stakeholders and citizens, and Bruyn sees merit in forming a civil society through cooperative enterprises.

This brief review shows no definitive answer, but some broader themes may suggest the general directions in which economic policy may evolve. As noted before, the first significant development is that a resolution of this clash between enterprise and society is occurring at the level of the firm. If it is true that the role of corporations will expand to include social interests out of sheer competitive advantage, much of the conflict now facing governments would be greatly relieved. Government policy then could focus on creating a supportive economic infrastructure and providing leadership.

Second, the IT juggernaut is likely to continue its course, altering products, firms, markets, and lives in this general direction. Scholars have noted that information empowers consumers by offering more knowledgeable choices, it gives employees increased status and rights as they become more valuable sources of innovation in a knowledge-based economy, and so on. And if progressive firms do realize advantages by cultivating social alliances more intense competition should drive this broader role of the firm throughout economies.

Finally, today's assumptions about the values and philosophy guiding economic behavior may undergo a major paradigm shift in the early years of the new millennium. Today's raging interest in knowledge-based economics is likely to mature and fade, as has happened in all other technological epochs. Insightful scholars think the next phase in economic development will focus on cultivating higher values, worthy social purposes, and other transcendent concerns.[8] This is certainly a highly controversial assertion, but that is true of all paradigm shifts. The editors suggest that signs of this impending transition is growing, as witnessed by the surge of interest in values and even spirituality during the 1990s. Many corporate executives today will go so far as to claim that a spiritual philosophy permeates their entire approach to business.[9]

These three developments lead to our final conclusion:

Conclusion 5: Over the longer term of 10 to 50 years, twenty-first century economies are likely to develop new ideological foundations that incorporate varying degrees of both free-market behavior and social cohesion within the context of some higher purpose, values, and meaning.

On the Other Side of the Millennium

These five conclusions are tentative, obviously, especially the last one, which is admittedly based on a large amount of informed speculation. It is also true that economic fate is not inscribed in history, as Sternberg reminds us, but the outcome of several simultaneous forces pulling in different directions. We also make no claims that twenty-first century economies will be free of the perennial problems people have always struggled to overcome: pockets of poverty, social inequities, class differences, market failures, and so on.

However, we do think that the wealth of knowledge represented by the chapters in this volume offers a reliable guide to the approximate shape of economic systems in the first half of twenty-first century. The relentless march of information technology can be expected to wire economies together into a fairly coherent global system in which free markets and entrepreneurial behavior reign. Although the forces of creative destruction may produce serious social disorder over the next several years, there are signs that new systems of political economy may emerge in a decade or so that represent hybrids of free markets and civil society. Foremost among these developments is the rise of a new theory of the firm for knowledge-based economies that combines the advantages of both free enterprise and economic cooperation.

In fact, Halal contends that this development would mean that free-market economies may no longer accurately be thought of as "capitalism," although they will be even more free and more entrepreneurial. With the critical factor of production moving from capital to knowledge, economic systems on the other side of the millennium could be thought of more usefully using such terms as "democratic enterprise" or "human enterprise."

If the information revolution is in fact a true economic revolution that compares in significance with the industrial revolution, it seems reasonable to conclude that the outcome will prove to be a dramatically different society. The evidence assembled here suggests that the economic order of the twenty-first century will synthesize the power of free markets and social community into a more broadly conceived philosophy of economics.

Notes

1. Jim Hoagland "All Globalization is Local," *Washington Post,* August 28, 1997.
2. William E. Halal, *The Infinite Resource* (San Francisco: Jossey-Bass, 1998).
3. "New Freedom in the Sky," *Newsweek* August 25, 1997.
4. Quoted in *Annual Report, 1995* (Kennan Institute)
5. Lester Thurow, *The Future of Capitalism* (New York: Morrow, 1996).
6. Halal, *Infinite Resource.*
7. Quoted in Sharon Walsh, "Captains Courteous," *Washington Post,* August 31, 1997.
8. Willis Harman, *Global Mind Change* (Indianapolis: Knowledge System, 1988).
9. William Halal, *The New Management* (San Francisco: Berrett-Koehler, 1997).

Index